RESTLESSNESS AND BELONGING

RESTLESSNESS AND BELONGING

Augustinian Wisdom for the Digital Empire

Autumn Alcott Ridenour

BAYLOR UNIVERSITY PRESS

Cover and book design by Elyxandra Encarnación
Cover art: Saint Augustine of Hippo with burning heart and believer, engraving
(paper), courtesy of the Rijksmuseum, Amsterdam, The Netherlands. Schelte
Adamsz Bolswert, print maker.

Library of Congress Cataloging-in-Publication Data

Names: Ridenour, Autumn Alcott author
   http://id.loc.gov/authorities/names/no2003115418
   http://id.loc.gov/rwo/agents/no2003115418
Title: Restlessness and belonging: Augustinian wisdom for the digital empire
   / Autumn Alcott Ridenour.
Description: Waco, Texas: Baylor University Press, [2025] | Includes
   bibliographical references and index. | Summary: "Evaluates the role and
   potential dangers of technology in contemporary society through an
   Augustinian theological-ethical lens"—Provided by publisher.
Identifiers: LCCN 2024055250 (print) | LCCN 2024055251 (ebook) |
   ISBN 9781481319744 hardcover | ISBN 9781481319775 adobe pdf |
   ISBN 9781481319768 epub
Subjects: LCSH: Augustine, of Hippo, Saint, 354–430
   http://id.loc.gov/rwo/agents/n80126290 | Technology—Religious
   aspects—Catholic Church
   http://id.loc.gov/authorities/subjects/sh2020004548 |
   Technology—Moral and ethical aspects http://id.loc.gov/authorities/
   subjects/sh85133162
Classification: LCC BX1795.T42 R53 2025 (print) | LCC BX1795.T42
   (ebook) | DDC 230/.2—dc23/eng/20250620
LC record available at https://lccn.loc.gov/2024055250
LC ebook record available at https://lccn.loc.gov/2024055251

To my students—past, present, and future—learning with
you is a privilege and gift. This book was inspired
and written for you.

To my family—a continual source of love, joyful responsibility,
and transformation. Together, when we look toward the
same end, we are changed.

To them, the truth would be literally nothing but the shadows of the images.

Plato, *Republic* 7.515

I spent an hour mulling over this set of characteristics that came pretty close to defining me as a person. Of course, that data cloud wasn't a true representation of reality—it had missed out much of the nuance that made me, me—but through a pattern picked out of my online data, the cookies had created an approximation, a shadow of me that was somehow recognizable.

Madhumita Murgia, *Code Dependent:*
Living in the Shadow of AI

For now we see in a mirror dimly, but then face to face.

1 Cor 13:12 (RSV)

Contents

Contents

Preface

With advancements in artificial intelligence and smart glasses by Apple and Meta, wearable technology promises to enhance our everyday vision.[1] Intimately connecting our digital habits with our line of sight offers a seamless transition for intersecting the virtual and real worlds. Altering our experience with handheld devices, wearable technology like these glasses further eliminates the space between virtual and embodied reality.

Yet simultaneous to these advancements lie other concerns in what David Brooks identifies as an "Epidemic of Blindness."[2] He draws on

---

[1]   See Mike Isaac, "Meta Unveils New Smart Glasses and Headsets in Pursuit of the Metaverse," *New York Times*, September 25, 2024, https://www.nytimes.com/2024/09/25/technology/meta-products-artificial-intelligence.html; Mark Gurman, "Apple Ponders Whether to Make Smart Glasses, Fitness Ring," Bloomberg, February 25, 2024, https://www.bloomberg.com/news/newsletters/2024-02-25/apple-ponders-making-new-wearables-ai-glasses-airpods-with-cameras-smart-ring-lt1kb7cd; Apple Vision Pro, accessed June 11, 2024, https://www.apple.com/apple-vision-pro/.

[2]   David Brooks, *How to Know a Person: The Art of Seeing Others Deeply and Being Deeply Seen* (Random House, 2023). The opening metaphor for spiritual blindness should be qualified given literature on the significance of disability and difference as individuals experiencing physical and mental disabilities bear the image of God and contribute to community and society through differing perspectives on the world. See also Brian R. Brock, *Wondrously Wounded: Theology, Disability, and the Body of Christ* (Baylor University Press, 2020); Martha C. Nussbaum, *Frontiers of Justice: Disability, Nationality, and Species Membership* (Harvard University Press, 2006). Also, the analogy used for blindness regards spiritual sight, an analogy used throughout the Hebrew and Christian Scriptures in the Old and New Testaments in which individuals are

research that social psychologists term a loneliness epidemic, saying, "We live in an environment in which political animosities, technological dehumanization, and social breakdown undermine connection, strain friendships, erase intimacy, and foster distrust. We're living in the middle of some sort of vast emotional, relational, and spiritual crisis. It is as if people across society have lost the ability to see and understand one another."[3] Despite these tech vision enhancements, we're somehow seeing past each other. Might it be that when training social media algorithms and new forms of AI to recognize images, we also reshape our own vision along with it?[4]

Max Fisher's *The Chaos Machine* offers a scathing diagnosis of social media and the tech titans who changed the world.[5] Reviewing how social media and big tech utilize psychological vulnerabilities catering to individual desire, he questions their true motive for engagement and ability to shape the world in its own image.[6] Likewise, questions now surround "A.G.I.-ism" as the new ideology embracing artificial general intelligence and its grandiose claims to "elevate humanity by increasing abundance," where "not using it to save the world seems immoral."[7] Despite its controversy, AI tech progresses at lightning pace.

It's an interesting moment. The race to build human innovation through AI comes on the cusp of research unmasking the problems posed by social media over the past two decades.[8] Yet social media outlets, along

---

severed from wisdom, an issue explored throughout this book. Those experiencing physical blindness can sometimes have greater spiritual sight or wisdom, as seen with the elder Simeon (Luke 2:30–31), who sees with keener spiritual vision in his old age even though he may have experienced diminished physical sight.

[3]   Brooks, *How to Know a Person*, 97–98.

[4]   Stephen Wolfram, *What Is ChatGPT Doing . . . and Why Does It Work?* (Wolfram Media, 2023), 15; Kenneth Wenger, *Is the Algorithm Plotting Against Us? A Layperson's Guide to the Concepts, Math, and Pitfalls of AI* (Working Fires Foundation, 2023), 77.

[5]   Max Fisher, *The Chaos Machine: The Inside Story of How Social Media Rewired Our Minds and Our World* (Back Bay, 2023).

[6]   Fisher, *Chaos Machine*, 104, 122–24.

[7]   Sam Altman, quoted in Evgeny Morozov, "The True Threat of Artificial Intelligence," *New York Times*, June 30, 2023, https://www.nytimes.com/2023/06/30/opinion/artificial-intelligence-danger.html; see also Evgeny Morozov, *To Save Everything Click Here: The Folly of Technological Solutionism* (PublicAffairs, 2014).

[8]   See Jonathan Haidt, *The Anxious Generation: How the Great Rewiring of Childhood Is Causing an Epidemic of Mental Illness* (Penguin Books, 2024); Cecilia Kang and Natasha Singer, "Meta Accused by States of Using Features to Lure Children

with their owners and influencers, continue to capture digital attention and political influence at alarming rates—despite the Surgeon General's warning of its harms to mental health.[9] These harms pose significant questions. What is the purpose of the social media apps that radically altered global communication beginning as early as 2004? Now, with generative artificial intelligence moving at "unbelievable speed," what does it mean to be human?[10]

According to Meta's (formerly Facebook) revamped mission statement, Mark Zuckerberg aimed to save the world.[11] Steeped in religious metaphor, the accompanying graphic to the *New Yorker* article "Facebook's Broken Vows" features a Holy Book with an "f" on the cover recognizable as Meta's omnipresent font. Citing the company's own statement, "To give people the power to build community and bring the world closer together," Jill Lepore says that "Facebook's mission amounts to the salvation of humanity."[12] While she quickly acknowledges the true purpose is to make money for investors, the article's religious indictment seems appropriate.

For those aware of the Jewish and Christian sacred texts, Meta's mission statement sounds vaguely reminiscent of another story in which the characters communicate in a single language while aiming to bring the

---

to Instagram and Facebook," *New York Times*, October 24, 2023, https://www.nytimes .com/2023/10/24/technology/states-lawsuit-children-instagram-facebook.html.

9   Lora Kelley, "The Endless Cycle of Social Media," *Atlantic*, July 7, 2023, https://www.theatlantic.com/newsletters/archive/2023/07/threads-meta-twitter -competitor-mark-zuckerberg/674655/; Ezra Kline, "Why Are Teens in Decline? Here's What the Evidence Says," *New York Times*, May 19, 2023, https://www .nytimes.com/2023/05/19/opinion/ezra-klein-podcast-jean-twenge.html; Matt Richtel, Catherine Pearson, and Michael Levenson, "Surgeon General Warns That Social Media May Harm Children and Adolescents," *New York Times*, May 23, 2023, https://www.nytimes.com/2023/05/23/health/surgeon-general -social-media-mental-health.html.

10   Adrienne LaFrance, "The Coming Humanist Renaissance: We Need a Cultural and Philosophical Movement to Meet the Rise of Artificial Superintelligence," *Atlantic*, June 5, 2023, https://www.theatlantic.com/magazine/archive/ 2023/07/generative-ai-human-culture-philosophy/674165/; see also David Brooks, "How America Got Mean," *Atlantic*, August 14, 2023, https://www.theatlantic.com/ magazine/archive/2023/09/us-culture-moral-education-formation/674765/.

11   Jill Lepore, "Facebook's Broken Vows: How the Company's Pledge to Bring the World Together Wound Up Pulling Us Apart," *New Yorker*, July 26, 2021, https:// www.newyorker.com/magazine/2021/08/02/facebooks-broken-vows.

12   Lepore, "Facebook's Broken Vows."

world together through the glory of human technology. Unfortunately, their innovative project ends in disorder, miscommunication, and chaos. Famously known as "The Tower of Babel" from Genesis 11, the name Babel becomes a word associated with confusion.[13]

When an acquaintance sent me an email request to become his "friend" on a new platform known as Facebook while I was working at Yale in 2007, I didn't think much of it. Providing access to friends and acquaintances from the past seemed relatively benign: family photographs, job and move announcements, cat memes, and more. When completing my graduate studies six years later in the greater Boston area, the social media scene had vastly changed. Entering the college classroom as a newly minted PhD, I was not entirely prepared for the changes this phenomenon brought to teaching. Learning became a different experience than what I had known. Even when they weren't physically visible, digital devices vied for my students' attention and intruded on my classroom. I competed for my students' attention in a whole new way. But it wasn't just pedagogy in terms of creative teaching and learning that required change—it was everything.

Relationships, politics, communication, marketing, and advertising—everything is now influenced by the world of social media, made increasingly accessible by the rise of the smartphone by 2012.[14] The world is literally at our fingertips; we are captured by enhanced algorithms. But does it fulfill Zuckerberg's mission to "build community and bring the world closer together"?[15] Do these handheld devices and the social networks that keep our attention in fact build such community and closeness? Or do they rewire the world with algorithmic vengeance?[16]

Psychologist Jean M. Twenge's 2017 book *iGen* cites data reflecting steep shifts in adolescent and student behavior in light of the near ubiquitous presence of smartphones coupled with social media. I felt like I

---

[13]   Social psychologist Jonathan Haidt wisely uses this metaphor for discussing the harms associated with social media and digital devices on his Substack, AfterBabel.com. The premises of this book parallel ideas in his work while also drawing more substantively from this scriptural narrative through the lens of St. Augustine and Jacques Ellul, among others.

[14]   Jean M. Twenge, *iGen: Why Today's Super-Connected Kids Are Growing Up Less Rebellious, More Tolerant, Less Happy—and Completely Unprepared for Adulthood* (Atria Books, 2017), 4.

[15]   Lepore, "Facebook's Broken Vows"; Fisher, *Chaos Machine*, 104–6, 122–25.

[16]   See Malcolm Gladwell, *Revenge of the Tipping Point: Overstories, Superspreaders, and the Rise of Social Engineering* (Little, Brown, 2024).

found the diagnosis to the problems plaguing my classroom. The more I read tech authors, the more I realized the attention economy was the new gold rush of venture capitalists, mining my students'—and everyone's for that matter—time and attention. MIT sociologist Sherry Turkle coined the phrase *Alone Together*, acknowledging that community and belonging were everywhere and nowhere at the same time.[17]

By the time of the COVID-19 global pandemic, nations and communities found themselves in a series of crises—health, racial injustice, politics, and communication. One standard approach during the pandemic's early stage was to safely socially distance using technology. While this practice did not come without critique, utilizing the internet, social media, and tech services for work and personal communication grew even more as part of the global common good. Perhaps technology functions as a kind of savior? Yet by the 2024 US presidential election, the power of tech companies was on full display as industry leaders sat in front of incoming political cabinet members at the 2025 inauguration.[18] Questions about power abound. So do concerns about our humanity and capacity to communicate. Ironically, perhaps, following the previous 2020 US presidential election, the Augustinian Institute hosted a webinar panel among Catholic and Protestant scholars entitled "Reading Augustine in a Time of Crisis."[19] The last question to the panel posed a new crisis: what does it mean to be human in this context? This book is an attempt to regain, at least in part, a sense of what it means to be human from an Augustinian lens and apply this to the world of social media and digital devices given the increasingly dehumanized ways we communicate.

Founded in 2004 as a college social network at Harvard, the relatively new startup company of Facebook grew exponentially with each passing year. As Lepore reported, after the recent college dropout, Zuckerberg, moved to California and set sail with venture capitalists, "Zuckerberg would end meetings by pumping his fist and shouting, 'Domination!'"[20] An interesting word choice for a company that

[17]   Sherry Turkle, *Alone Together* (Basic Books, 2011).
[18]   Michael Scherer and Ashley Parker, "The Tech Oligarchy Arrives," *Atlantic*, January 20, 2025, https://www.theatlantic.com/politics/archive/2025/01/tech-zuckerberg-trump-inauguration-oligarchy/681381/.
[19]   Joseph T. Kelley et al., "Reading Augustine in a Time of Crisis," webinar, New City Press, The Augustinian Institute, November 17, 2020, https://www.youtube.com/watch?v=IBtHKUCO_1M.
[20]   Lepore, "Facebook's Broken Vows."

professes a more positive and constructive desire to build connection in their explicit mission statement. The term shows up again when former and current employees critique OpenAI in its "reckless race for dominance," downplaying transparency and ethics in its sprint to build A.G.I. with increased market share.[21]

The term domination has many implications and roots, so do the promises of connection and belonging. As an ethicist steeped in the world of Augustinian thought, I began to see relatable themes in St. Augustine's context and theology, wondering about his relevance for our own world and the lives of my students. Confusion, chaos, and even domination were not strange ideas to Augustine. Living through the rise and fall of Rome (354–430 CE), Augustine was acutely aware of the power found in empire, including its promises, illusions, and outright lies.[22] Lies that masked destructive consequences by promising benefits for those seeking safety and security.[23]

Political interests fostered group belonging, and citizens could contribute to the glory of Rome while benefiting from its rewards and protection. The lies served a social function as Augustine himself was deeply familiar. Trained as a rhetorician, he acknowledged that his successful career came from his ability to persuade the masses using political rhetoric.[24] He was incredibly good at it. So good that he ended up working as the chief political speech writer for imperial Rome. Yet in his success, he questioned whether his speech was true speech and whether his success resulted in real happiness.[25] Somehow, he made it to the top of the food chain careerwise, yet his heart was still restless, and power seemed empty.

During his intellectual and spiritual journey through philosophy to theology, he listened to St. Ambrose, Bishop of Milan, to gain career tips for his own oratory skills.[26] Ambrose could really draw a crowd. Augustine

[21]   Kevin Roose, "OpenAI Insiders Warn of a 'Reckless' Race for Dominance," *New York Times*, June 4, 2024, https://www.nytimes.com/2024/06/04/technology/openai-culture-whistleblowers.html.

[22]   Serge Lancel, *St. Augustine* (SCM, 2002), 391–410.

[23]   Robert Dodaro, *Christ and the Just Society in the Thought of St. Augustine* (Cambridge University Press, 2004), 27–43; Paul R. Kolbet, *Augustine and the Cure of Souls: Revising a Classical Ideal* (University of Notre Dame Press, 2010), 66–67.

[24]   Dodaro, *Christ and the Just Society*, 27–43; Kolbet, *Augustine and the Cure of Souls*, 66–67.

[25]   Augustine, *Confessions*, trans. Henry Chadwick (Oxford University Press, 1991), 6.6, pp. 97–98.

[26]   Lancel, *St. Augustine*, 78–88.

found himself understanding the Christian Scriptures for the first time. He wondered whether Ambrose's appeal included not only persuasive words, but possibly true words.[27] Not long after, he found himself in a Milan garden, renouncing former sources of identity and acceptance for a new way of being and belonging in the world, one which brought about deeper fulfillment.[28]

I hope to take a close look at themes in Augustine's theology, seeking their intersection and relevance to the digital empire that we perhaps willfully, unexpectedly, or reluctantly now inhabit. Moving between past and present, we will consider how this might impact our approach to the technology that shapes the habits we cultivate—and whether such practices might require thoughtfulness and change. I want to think with Augustine, dialogue with him, and understand the concepts—and loves—that drove him so we too might have a vision for a different way of being, living, and communing with the world.[29] With this vision comes a different set of questions and commitments about agency and belonging.[30] Engaging ancient wisdom from Augustine, who also faced rapid cultural shifts within the Roman Empire, poses significant insight for our time if we have "eyes that see" (Matt 13:16).

Even while writing this volume, the epicenter of the tech empire continues to shift. Not only does social media persist, but new generative artificial intelligence such as OpenAI moves at rapid speed. Adrienne LaFrance writes "In Defense of Humanity" or why "we need a cultural and philosophical movement to meet the rise of artificial superintelligence."[31] She says, "The technocultural norms and habits that have seized

---

[27] Lancel, *St. Augustine*, 78–88.

[28] Augustine, *Confessions* 8.1.1, p. 133ff.

[29] The caveat to writing this book includes acknowledging that I do not agree with Augustine on every detail in his writing. I depart from him on a number of significant issues as one situated in the Protestant tradition inheriting many of Augustine's ideas through the Reformation. Also, this book is not an apology for every word in his work. Instead, this volume draws deeply from Augustine's understanding of humanity (theological anthropology) along with his prescient understanding of empire, power, security, belonging, and identity in its implications for human desire and action. My aim is not simply to take his writings and import them into our modern world. Instead, I want to think with Augustine and understand how his ideas might help us face the empire(s) of our time.

[30] See also Craig M. Gay, *Modern Technology and the Human Future: A Christian Appraisal* (IVP Academic, 2018), 13–14.

[31] LaFrance, "Coming Humanist Renaissance."

us during the triple revolution of the internet, smartphones, and the social web are themselves in need of a thorough correction. Too many people have allowed these technologies to simply wash over them. We would be wise to rectify the errors of the recent past, but also to anticipate—and proactively shape—what the far more radical technology now emerging will mean for our lives, and how it will come to remake our civilization."[32]

This volume seeks not only philosophical wisdom, but also theological and spiritual wisdom on questions of moral agency and belonging that push back on the many ways in which social media and digital technologies shape us. Less a how-to book, especially given the daunting shifts in technological advancement even as I type, instead the aim of this work involves casting spiritual vision.[33] "Where there is no vision, the people perish" (Prov 29:18 KJV). We need moral imagination informed by deeper theology, vision, and formation as digital users and designers more than ever.

In order to cast this vision, the chapters in this volume draw together Augustinian themes across his works. My approach is one where we think with Augustine as pilgrims on a journey through time. While simple and complex, we tread along switchbacks between the heights of God's expansive love and the challenge of navigating the ever-changing digital universe we inhabit. The overarching theme is one where restlessness drives us into communion with God and one another. Belonging to God, neighbor, and creation in interdependence unifies the fractured parts of our self despite our daily—if not momentary—temptation to unravel.

The first chapter awakens us to our tech reality and its impact on our emotional development and social belonging within the digital empire. Yet emptying nature of meaning, technology driven by individualism and individualization ends in nihilism and personalized devices that ironically leave us more isolated than ever. The second chapter identifies the digital empire as the new Babel in which communication descends into confusion. Seeking spectacle rather than wisdom devolves into disordered communication and disordered love. Confronting the source of knowledge and wisdom, along with the order of love, offers meaning and interpretation given that communication reflects a broader desire for communion. The third chapter explores "the book of nature" (doctrine of creation) as imaging God, conveying divine presence in its significance for identity, interdependence, and belonging. Encountering God and creation builds

32   LaFrance, "Coming Humanist Renaissance."
33   See also G. K. Chesterton, cited in Gay, *Modern Technology*, 13–14.

a sense of identity across time and memory in our desire for wholeness, communion, and eternity.

The fourth chapter considers the significance of facing one another through intentional presence and belonging as distinct images of God united through the incarnation and fellowship with Christ. Facing Christ and one another, we image the one whom we love in unity and diversity. Communion and embodied relationships are the space in which we practice intentional presence. The fifth chapter identifies our teleological orientation toward Sabbath that marks time with eternity as an identity received rather than achieved through profit, workism, or the tyranny of technological urgency. The sixth chapter returns to the technological empire and the significance of the kingdom of God. Drawing from Augustine and Jacques Ellul, we consider the importance of the incarnation for moral vision and virtue as we participate in the kingdom while inhabiting the digital empire with discernment.

Finally, I conclude with our desire for communion through belonging and the significance of transfiguration for fellowship with God and neighbor in fulfillment. Awaiting the fullness of knowing when we shall see face to face, we patiently live in love strengthened by hope. In this "epidemic of blindness" we need a stronger vision than digital glasses can give. Confronting the challenges of the digital empire, we must understand the journey of how we arrived here, where we are going, and how we might see and inhabit the world differently.

The journey of this specific project dates to 2014. By 2018 the research became my focus. Many colleagues and friends accompanied me on the journey to whom I owe thanks. Working at Merrimack College, a university founded by the Order of St. Augustine, I simultaneously stumbled on the need for this project while engaging the beauty of Augustinian ideas in its continued relevance for today's pilgrims. Teaching at Merrimack shaped me as much as my students. With Augustine, I learned to care about the issues that most impacted them and in doing so, realized the impact on all of us. Conversations with students and fellow faculty members encouraged the early stages of this project, particularly Joseph T. Kelley who dialogued about ways to interface Augustine with our digital environment. I am grateful for those years of community, engrained in my memory with continued impact on my approach to Augustine and the world we inhabit today.

I took these concerns with me to Gordon-Conwell Theological Seminary where I began teaching in 2021. Re-entering the fraught evangelical terrain with which I identified was buoyed by the thoughtful and determined commitment of GCTS faculty and students.[34] Their willingness to avoid reactionary tropes while seeking sincere faithfulness with integrity, compassion, creativity, and nuance inspired me. I'm thankful the school honored an early sabbatical request, which enabled me to continue writing.

Dave Nelson at Baylor University Press believed in the project early on and helped me see its continued relevance while grounding its focus. Conversations along the way were enriching, whether coffee with Andy Crouch, dialogue with John Swinton at the Conference on Medicine and Religion, or Jeffersonian Dinners hosted by Rosalind Picard, Nathan Barczi, and Mia Chung-Yee with the MIT Octet Collaborative. MIT faculty at these events reminded me of the best intent behind technological innovation and the need for interdisciplinary dialogue in ethics. My thinking also benefited from constructive challenges by Toni Alimi and Conor Kelly at the annual Society of Christian Ethics and the Evangelical Ethics working group led by Theo Boer and Jonathan Cahill. GCTS teaching and research assistants empowered this project throughout its stages, including Christian Schmitt, Noah Karger, Michael Haegeland, Sydney Hughes, Alan Tung, Peter Fiore, Oliver van Ruth, Fredric Schille, and Katherine DeVane Brown. Kara Miller and Chelsea Levis also provided important dialogue for the book's early stage and copyediting needs.

I'm also thankful to the faith communities that continually develop me, including the culture of discipleship and spiritual formation at GCTS as well as my own faith community of First Baptist Sudbury that sustains me in love. Love is born through service in the communities that shape us most. From this, my family supports and deepens my life on a regular basis. Together, they embody joy, laughter, and play, those restful Sabbath

---

[34] By the term "fraught," I reference unfortunate ways American evangelicalism has more recently been identified as a political or sociological movement, departing from ways that "speak and act consistent with the gospel" or demonstrate Jesus's cruciform way of life. Instead, appealing to what Kevin Vanhoozer describes as "a canonical-linguistic approach," the theology I aspire to includes "a christocentric focus, a canonical framework, and a catholic flavor. The aim of such theology is performative understanding and creative fidelity. Evangelical theology is a matter of 'joyful faith seeking creative understanding of the word and act of God'" (Kevin J. Vanhoozer, *The Drama of Doctrine: A Canonical Linguistic Approach to Christian Theology* [Westminster John Knox, 2005], 25–26).

relationships that shape me in love. We also bump into one another regularly, requiring us to develop habits of ongoing confession, forgiveness, and change. Life together is simply better with them. They embody glimpses of what I hope to write in some way. For Jay, John Charles, William, and Benjamin, I am eternally grateful.

1

The Digital Empire

INTRODUCTION

Even before COVID-19, in which the world largely went remote,[1] screens were everywhere. Digital displays filled common spaces, whether lounges, lobbies, elevators, gas pumps, or restaurants. And as the health, social, and communication crises prevalent during the pandemic highlight all that is *uncommon*, screens and social media remain *common* in their connection to each crisis. Faces bent toward phones appear normal, making it hard to remember a time before devices replaced human interaction.

Screens are part of our everyday life much like a wallet or even an appendage. How exactly did this happen? What are the ways that social media and digital devices tap into human vulnerability and impact intellectual, moral, and social development? Theologian Oliver O'Donovan describes the moral life as one in which we awaken to questions and responsibilities even before we're aware of the problems.[2] Can Augustinian ideas on human vulnerability and the relational requirements that forge identity and belonging bring clarity to this technological impact? What exactly is our tech reality and what are the ways in which it has changed our moral and social development, especially among adolescents

[1]   "Going remote" became the term for the digital pivot for many primary, secondary, and higher educational institutions during COVID-19 shutdowns around the globe in spring 2020.

[2]   Oliver O'Donovan, *Self, World, and Time*, vol. 1 of *Ethics as Theology* (Eerdmans, 2013), 4, 6–9.

and young adults? And what are the broader implications of the digital empire and the journey by which we arrived here?

AWAKENING TO THE TECH REALITY AND ITS IMPACT ON INTELLECTUAL, MORAL, AND SOCIAL DEVELOPMENT

Digital technology's expanded presence in our lives has changed our experience of the world and one another. Sherry Turkle's tech volumes entitled *Alone Together* (2011) and *Reclaiming Conversation: The Power of Talk in a Digital Age* (2015) are increasingly relevant. Turkle famously says, "We expect more from technology and less from each other."[3] But this digital expansion didn't occur overnight. In fact, these small screens stand in a long line of products aimed at purchasing our attention. In *The Attention Merchants* (2016), Tim Wu notes how newspapers, radio, television sets, computers, and handheld devices each entered our personal space in their respective era. Wu says, "By means of new technologies, advertising and its master, commerce, would enter what had been for millennia our attention's main sanctuary—the home."[4] Handheld screens were the next step. Digital smart devices entered not only the home, replacing the radio and TV, but they also further disrupted face-to-face interaction, escalated distraction, and began mediating interpersonal relationships. While the mission of social media is to connect individuals, the mediums are ironically adept at drawing us away from one another.

Though offered as a free service, someone is paying. When advertisers pay social media platforms, we become the product and our attention the "raw material."[5] Seeking our time, advertisers and social media algorithms have grown ever more cunning. Wu says, "Whatever our personal goals, the things we'd like to achieve, the goals of the attention merchants are generally at odds with ours."[6] Imbedded in our search are algorithms set to hook us according to our individual preferences.[7] Advertisers have long been purveyors of human desire, knowing *how* to entice consumers with

[3] Sherry Turkle, *Alone Together* (Basic Books, 2011), xii.

[4] Tim Wu, *The Attention Merchants: The Epic Scramble to Get Inside Our Heads* (Vintage Books, 2016), 84, 207.

[5] Wu, *Attention Merchants*; Shoshana Zuboff, *The Age of Surveillance Capitalism: The Fight for a Human Future at the New Frontier of Power* (Public Affairs, 2019), 96, 98–101; Adam Alter, *Irresistible: The Rise of Addictive Technology and the Business of Keeping Us Hooked* (Penguin Books, 2017); Tristan Harris, quoted in *The Social Dilemma*, dir. Jeff Orlowski (Exposure Labs, 2020), Netflix.

[6] Wu, *Attention Merchants*, 207.

[7] Wu, *Attention Merchants*, 258–59, 263–64.

promises of products that bring improved life. But with devices, the attention merchants monopolize the *when*, granting unlimited access to our attention in ways that behavioral psychologist Adam Alter appropriately describes with his title *Irresistible: The Rise of Addictive Technology and the Business of Keeping Us Hooked.*

Alter tracks ways that advertisers along with video game and social media designers utilize behavioral psychology to include goals, feedback, progress, escalation, cliffhangers, and social interactions.[8] Noting that tech innovators such as Steve Jobs prevented his children from using his own products, Alter quotes rapper Biggie Smalls, "Never get high on your own supply."[9] Such technologies come at a cost, not only to society, but also ourselves.

Recent social psychologists track the significance of these costs. Jean M. Twenge's book *iGen* follows Gen Z, born during the years 1995–2012, the first generation to grow up with smartphones. In her research on generational data Twenge tracks "large, abrupt shifts in teens' behavior and emotional states" around 2012, "exactly when the majority of Americans started to own cell phones that could access the Internet."[10] Twenge records patterns that include delaying adult behaviors associated with risk taking such as holding jobs, but also disinterest in reading for leisure, whether books or magazines.[11] Technological devices are a possible contributor to these patterns.[12] Her analysis acknowledges the decline in reading for pleasure correlates with a decline in reading comprehension scores on SAT exams. After interviewing and surveying over two hundred San Diego State freshmen and sophomores, she found most students avoid reading print for fun. Twenge says,

> Apparently, texting and posting to social media instead of reading books, magazines, and newspapers are not a boon for reading comprehension or academic writing. That might partially be due to

[8]   Alter, *Irresistible*.

[9]   Biggie Smalls, quoted in Alter, *Irresistible*, 1; see also Rose Horowitch, "The Elite College Students Who Can't Read Books," *Atlantic*, October 1, 2024, https://www.theatlantic.com/magazine/archive/2024/11/the-elite-college-students-who-cant-read-books/679945/.

[10]   Jean M. Twenge, *iGen: Why Today's Super-Connected Kids Are Growing Up Less Rebellious, More Tolerant, Less Happy—and Completely Unprepared for Adulthood* (Atria Books, 2017), 4.

[11]   Twenge, *iGen*, 61–62.

[12]   Twenge, *iGen*, 63.

the short attention span that new media seem to encourage. One study installed a program on college student's laptops that took a screenshot every five seconds. The researchers found that students switched between tasks every nineteen seconds on average. More than 75% of the students' computer windows were open less than one minute. This is a very different experience from sitting and reading a book for hours.[13]

With a decreased ability to focus on reading, students begin missing key ingredients for reading comprehension, such as locating the main idea or thesis presented by an author. The foundation for communication and understanding helps build the ability to exchange ideas in conversation.

Conversation is foundational for knowledge building and relational communication. Turkle has researched the interactions between students and technology over the course of her career. In *Reclaiming Conversation*, she describes an evening discussion with twenty-five young people involved in a Boston summer program in which the group converses while simultaneously participating in a group chat on WhatsApp. Turkle says, "Everyone is always elsewhere or just getting on their way. With everyone on the app, people switch rapidly between the talk in the room and the chat on their phones. At least half of the phone chat takes the form of images—cartoons, photos, and videos—many of which comment on the conversation in the room. As students see it, images connect them, equal to any text or any talk."[14] But such interruptions involve tradeoffs. The group started a conversation on the challenges of separating from friends and family while at college, but the talk was soon disrupted by scrolling.[15] The "elsewhere effect" often dilutes the substance of conversation while masking important social cues once available through nonverbal communication. Instead, focus is directed downward, away from one another.

This effect can lead to a negative impact on empathy and the ability to concentrate. Turkle continues, "Hyperconnected, we imagine ourselves more efficient, but we are deceived. Multitasking degrades our performance at everything we do . . . Frequent multitasking is associated with

---

[13] Twenge, *iGen*, 64; Sherry Turkle, *Reclaiming Conversation: The Power of Talk in a Digital Age* (Penguin Books, 2015).

[14] Turkle, *Reclaiming Conversation*, 35.

[15] Turkle, *Reclaiming Conversation*, 35.

depression, social anxiety, and trouble reading human emotions."[16] By disrupting our ability to connect with others through conversation and eye contact, the use of smartphones harm not only relationships but also our capacity to perform—the presumed goal of such technology.

Prevalent internet use not only divides our attention but also rewires the human brain in our capacity to think and relate.[17] Nicholas Carr says, "The Net delivers precisely the kind of sensory and cognitive stimuli—repetitive, intensive, interactive, addictive—that have been shown to result in strong and rapid alterations in brain circuits and functions. With the exception of alphabets and number systems, the Net may well be the single most powerful mind-altering technology that has ever come into general use."[18] Common arguments push back by suggesting that current changes are neutral or perhaps positive when compared to technological changes over time, such as print and book reading. Certainly, there are positive advancements with new technologies in their capabilities for speed and efficiency, connecting us across distance and time. At the same time, much is lost with new digital habits and the ways they are shaping our relational capacities and neural networks.

The cost of our captive attention to tech merchants is high for adolescents and young adults.[19] As a professor in higher education, I recognize the increased challenges students bring with them to the classroom from academic to mental health issues further exacerbated by disruption from in-person learning through COVID-19. While Twenge aims to provide some balance in her assessment with *iGen*, the sobering title for her article in the *Atlantic*, "Have Smartphones Destroyed a Generation?" indicates her fear that the group is "on the brink of a mental health crisis."[20] She

[16] Turkle, *Reclaiming Conversation*, 35.

[17] Jonathan Haidt, *The Anxious Generation: How the Great Rewiring of Childhood Is Causing an Epidemic of Mental Illness* (Penguin Books, 2024), 95–97, 113–15, 125–29.

[18] Nicholas Carr, *The Shallows: What the Internet Is Doing to Our Brains* (W. W. Norton, 2011), 116.

[19] Haidt, *Anxious Generation*, 125–29; Cecilia Kang and Natasha Singer, "Meta Accused by States of Using Features to Lure Children to Instagram and Facebook," *New York Times*, October 24, 2023, https://www.nytimes.com/2023/10/24/technology/states-lawsuit-children-instagram-facebook.html.

[20] Jean M. Twenge, "Have Smartphones Destroyed a Generation?" *Atlantic*, September 2017, https://www.theatlantic.com/magazine/archive/2017/09/has-the-smartphone-destroyed-a-generation/534198/. Twenge reiterates this position in Ezra Kline, "Why Are Teens in Decline? Here's What the Evidence Says," *New York*

explains, "The twin rise of smartphone and social media has caused an earthquake of a magnitude we've not seen in a very long time, if ever. There is compelling evidence that the devices we've placed in young people's hands are having profound effects on their lives—and making them seriously unhappy."[21] Twenge and Jonathan Haidt find a correlation—if not causation—between increased screen activities (described as social media use, texting, and browsing the web) and increased rates of unhappiness and depression.[22]

Many students experience insecurity, anxiety, and depression which social media only amplifies; "iGen'ers look so happy online, making goofy faces on Snapchat and smiling in their pictures on Instagram. But dig deeper, and reality is not so comforting. iGen is on the verge of the most severe mental health crisis for young people in decades. On the surface, though, everything is fine."[23] Twenge accounts for several reasons that might contribute to these insecurities, including reported FOMO (Fear of Missing Out), the need to maintain artifice and brand, and social media's ability to "steal sleep."[24]

Students suffer from sleep deprivation in astounding ways compared to previous generations.[25] New data reveals that students look at screens and stay awake for several more hours per night than medically recommended.[26] As one of my previous students once reported, "Yeah, we try to start homework around 10:30 p.m., but we suddenly look up from Netflix or social media and find it's 1:30 a.m. or later."[27] Repeatedly losing time not only impacts their cognitive work capacities, but also their sense of moral agency and self-control, which contributes to higher levels of depressive symptoms.[28]

With less sleep and more time on social media, it's not surprising that new behavioral patterns impact relational and academic performance.

Times, May 19, 2023, https://www.nytimes.com/2023/05/19/opinion/ezra-klein-podcast-jean-twenge.html. See also Haidt, *Anxious Generation.*

[21] Twenge, "Have Smartphones Destroyed a Generation?"
[22] See Kline, "Why Are Teens in Decline?"; Haidt, *Anxious Generation.*
[23] Twenge, *iGen,* 93.
[24] Haidt, *Anxious Generation,* 97–99, 113–16.
[25] Twenge, *iGen,* 93.
[26] Twenge, *iGen,* 93.
[27] "RTS 2800: Social Ethics: Christian Perspectives," course, Merrimack College, February 7, 2019, North Andover, MA.
[28] Twenge, *iGen,* 116.

With more time spent on social media, new habits emerge that impact self-perception through artifice and brand raising additional cause for concern in terms of social development and its impact on mental health. In the testimonials of teens and college students Twenge interviewed, students describe public posturing of happy emotions while tears roll down their face in private—an adolescent experience exacerbated by social media.[29]

Participation in the Digital Empire: Commodifying Self-Image as Brand

Zuckerberg implements the new rules implicit for human interaction: performative agency brings about self-branding as image and identity. Zuckerberg says, "Think about what people are doing on Facebook today. They're keeping up with their friends and family, but *they're also building an image and identity for themselves, which in a sense is their brand . . . It's almost a disadvantage if you're not on it.*"[30] A revelatory statement, participation became a new social pressure if not requirement. Not only does Zuckerberg encourage self-commodification through brand, but he also helps reinforce FOMO as the motivation for social belonging. Given the volume of Facebook's reach, Zuckerberg's ambition furthers the interests of his digital empire with the benevolent promise of belonging. Along with digital acceptance and social affirmation, Zuckerberg's branding involves negative implications for nonparticipants. Individuals without Facebook find themselves marginalized at their own peril.[31] Appealing to the basic desire for belonging and acceptance, he plays on fear of exclusion from authentic connections forged on the web.

---

[29]   Twenge, *iGen*, 25. Candice Odgers counterbalances Jean Twenge's and Jonathan Haidt's argument by challenging the moral panic around smartphones and the harm incurred. Instead, she challenges their research studies as correlational outcomes rather than causation, recognizing complexity when following mental health data alongside the significance of offline risk and family support. I don't deny complexity when following mental health trends, the significance of offline risks, and questions about familial support. Still, significant testimony and evidence reflects the ways social media shapes our thinking and affect, particularly given the Augustinian assumptions that we image or reflect our social influences and the appetites we habitually indulge. See also Candice Odgers, "The Panic over Smartphones Doesn't Help Teens," *Atlantic*, May 21, 2024, https://www.theatlantic.com/technology/archive/2024/05/candice-odgers-teens-smartphones/678433/.

[30]   Wu, *Attention Merchants*, 298.

[31]   Wu, *Attention Merchants*, 298.

Fear of exclusion taps into our basic desire for social belonging. It also reflects peer pressure and dynamics inherent to empire.[32] Wu says, "The credible claim of being a social necessity was, in retrospect, the most important thing that Facebook achieved."[33] And while Zuckerberg did not create the idea of self-branding, Facebook became a tool by which the new "Facebook generation" emerged as "products to be marketed, professionally and even socially. As celebrities had become, the ordinary individual was now more of a business proposition."[34] The face was one more commodity to observe online for self-promotion and branding. In this sense, the face was rapidly becoming a new form of currency, transforming individual image into products.

When image becomes associated with self-branding, communication becomes reduced to performance. While Facebook originally marketed itself as a place for authenticity and connection, this was misleading. Wu illustrates,

> Here was a place where friends always congratulated and celebrated; where couples did little but eat at nice restaurants, go on vacation, or announce engagements or newborns; and where children never cried or needed diaper changes or hit each other. On Facebook, all happy families were alike; the others may have each been unhappy in their own way, but they were not on Facebook. Of course, all human communication is slightly inauthentic, but in person or even on the telephone there are limits to our dissimulations. The sugar-cookie-cutter self-styling enabled by Facebook made America seem a Lake Wobegon online. In retrospect, the 1950s looked dark and angst-ridden by comparison.[35]

---

[32] Nicholas Rowe identifies the key ingredients to empire as expansion, exclusion, and exploitation (cited by Sean McDonough, "'Come Out of Her': Johannine Critique of Contemporary Empire [and a Challenge to the Church]," lecture, "Exegesis of Revelation" course, Gordon-Conwell Theological Seminary, April 28, 2023).

[33] Wu, *Attention Merchants*, 298.

[34] Wu, *Attention Merchants*, 298.

[35] Wu, *Attention Merchants*, 301–2. Newer social media platforms such as TikTok, BeReal, and more "realistic" approaches to Instagram challenge Wu's original analysis in their attempts to offer transparency and authenticity. Yet even with changes through these platforms, critics acknowledge superficial, performance-oriented communication persists. A 2023 debate considered the pros and cons of the United States's TikTok ban among US lawmakers and the American public. See also Natalie Proulx, "Should the United States Ban TikTok?" *New York Times,*

Wu makes an astute observation about authenticity and sharing. While posts are more diverse and perhaps honest since Facebook's inception, online communication still involves performance in comparison to non-recorded, offline conversation. While communication morphed with online platforms like Instagram, Snapchat, TikTok, and Tinder, among others, the commodity of face and image is the primary exchange.

Social Media, Image, and Performance

Thanks to changes with social media, there is increased virtual connection, equating self-identity with posts and pronouncements while reducing friendship to accumulated likes and emojis impacted by algorithms and data analytics. In the digital space, images of countless faces are a new form of currency and mediate actual human contact from real life dialogue. Typical communication skills of speak and response, give and take—core ingredients to interpersonal conversation—are now missing. Haidt contrasts real-world relationships that are "embodied, synchronous, one-to-one" or "one to several" involving a "high bar for entry and exits" with virtual relationships that are "disembodied, asynchronous, one-to-many" that "enter and exit with ease."[36]

At root, relationships involve vulnerability between speaker and respondent. Mutually shared conversation builds understanding and trust. The new terms of relating, however, have the opposite effect. Shifting vulnerability from in-person communication to a distant, disembodied virtual conversation involves image projection with low-commitment feedback. As LaFrance explains, "Tapping a 'Like' button is not friendship; it's a data point. And a conversation with an artificial intelligence is one-sided—an illusion of connection."[37] Identity and social affirmation are depersonalized if not dehumanized into what former Facebook vice president of operations, Chamath Palihapitiya, describes as shallow

---

April 3, 2023, https://www.nytimes.com/2023/04/03/learning/should-the-united-states-ban-tiktok.html; Sapna Maheshwari and Kalley Huang, "What's Hot on TikTok? Defending Its C.E.O.," *New York Times*, March 28, 2023, https://www.nytimes.com/2023/03/28/technology/tiktok-users-defend-app.html.

[36]   Haidt, *Anxious Generation*, 9–10.

[37]   Adrienne LaFrance, "The Coming Humanist Renaissance: We Need a Cultural and Philosophical Movement to Meet the Rise of Artificial Superintelligence," *Atlantic*, June 5, 2023, https://www.theatlantic.com/magazine/archive/2023/07/generative-ai-human-culture-philosophy/674165/.

dopamine surges requiring continual participation in a kind of negative feedback loop.[38]

No wonder we find young people facing a mental health crisis.[39] From a spiritual lens, mind and body are connected. Increased time inhabiting social media and digital spaces disconnects our minds and bodies from friendships involving in-person, give-and-take conversation that builds agency in the real world. As adolescents and college students developmentally forge their sense of agency, identity, and meaning, they are barraged with images—contrived projections—in which they compare themselves to others while sensing they fall short. A digital economy that encourages branding, performance-based, or evaluative standards leaves many individuals feeling vulnerable and fragile. How do these social media giants tap into human vulnerability?

TECH, HUMAN VULNERABILITY, AND THE COST OF OUR ATTENTION

We are all born into the "world around us" without choice.[40] We appear because of someone else's action, namely our biological parents and caregivers, as well as the social forces that shape us. The task of Christian ethics involves awakening to the social world around us as particular selves in time.[41] Engaging the theology and ethics of Augustine from a different time and culture offers tools for evaluating our current practices, particularly the ways social media and digital devices impact our moral lives and agency. Here I find significant connections between Augustine's theology and current psychology on misguided love.

Alter's eye-opening *Irresistible* tracks the short history of substance and behavioral addiction as it relates to the technology effectively vying for our attention. Alter states, "There isn't a bright line between addicts and the rest of us. We're all one product or experience away from developing

[38]   Chamath Palihapitiya in Jaron Lanier, *Ten Arguments for Deleting Your Social Media Accounts Right Now* (Picador, 2018), 9.

[39]   Greg Lukianoff and Jonathan Haidt, *The Coddling of the American Mind: How Good Intentions and Bad Ideas Are Setting Up a Generation for Failure* (Penguin Books, 2018); Twenge, *iGen.*

[40]   Adam Alter offers several categories describing the "world within us," "the world between us," and "the world around us" (Adam Alter, *Drunk Tank Pink: And Other Unexpected Forces That Shape How We Think, Feel, and Behave* [Penguin Books, 2013]).

[41]   O'Donovan, *Self, World, and Time,* 4, 6–9.

our own addictions."[42] With increased access to emerging technologies, he finds the capacity for behavioral addiction rising. He recognizes that emerging technologies hit "just the right neurological notes" and adds:

> Instagram, like so many other social media platforms, is bottomless. Facebook has an endless feed; Netflix automatically moves on to the next episode in a series; Tinder encourages users to keep swiping in search of a better option . . . According to Tristan Harris, a "design ethicist," the problem isn't that people lack willpower; it's that "there are a thousand people on the other side of the screen whose job it is to break down the self-regulation you have."[43]

Technology as the "world around us" seems ever more cunning in its power to shape our behaviors and wear down self-control through subtle appeal.[44]

Whether we recognize it or not, digital media shapes our perception of the world, luring us through finely tuned algorithms catering to individual preferences.[45] These algorithms appeal to our basic appetites and promote new forms of behavioral addiction. This addiction is by design; "If 35% of the people suffer from a disorder, then it's just a part of human nature."[46] He suggests it may be better to view behavioral addiction as a social issue rather than a medical issue alone.[47] Here Alter distinguishes between debilitating behavioral addictions and moderate ones—debilitating addictions affect fewer members of the population while moderate addictions are more common. He continues, "[Moderate behavioral addictions] make our lives less worthwhile, make us less effective at work and play, and diminish our interactions with other people. They inflict milder psychological traumas than severe addictions, but even milder traumas accumulate over time to degrade a person's well-being."[48]

---

[42]   Alter, *Irresistible*, 4.

[43]   Alter, *Irresistible*, 3.

[44]   Alter, *Drunk Tank Pink*; see also Nir Eyal, *Hooked: How to Form Habit-Forming Products* (Portfolio, 2014).

[45]   Eyal, *Hooked*, 1–6.

[46]   Alter, *Irresistible*, 23.

[47]   Alter, *Irresistible*, 24. Philosopher Kent Dunnington agrees. He describes addiction as habit, drawing together categories of disease and choice. Beyond medical attention alone, addiction involves philosophical, theological (spiritual), and sociocultural dynamics (Kent Dunnington, *Addiction and Virtue: Beyond the Models of Disease and Choice* [IVP Academic, 2011], 10–11, 99–123).

[48]   Alter, *Irresistible*, 24.

Acknowledging the rise of behavioral addiction, Alter adds that "40% of the population suffers from some form of Internet-based addiction, whether to email, gaming, or porn. Another found that 48% of its sample of U.S. university students were 'Internet addicts,' and another 40% were borderline or potential addicts."[49] If Alter's statistics are accurate and more of the population reports addiction tied to the internet, is it possible to acknowledge a growing social problem rather than individual issues with tech use?

Research also suggests broad internet addiction comes by way of corporate design. Digital media sites program content with algorithms intended to keep us hooked.[50] Targeting our attention, finely tuned algorithms exploit the vulnerability of human attention, shaping the social world that we inhabit. Awakening to our moral context involves identifying the problem and recognizing how this social world shapes us.[51] One temptation is to negate the problems of technology given its positive benefits, but this attitude cloaks our addiction by highlighting technology's strengths while downplaying its power over our lives.[52] Alter suggests, "Just as cocaine charmed . . . today we're enamored of technology," warning against a sense of moral superiority in our ability to cite technology's benefits without offering a humble—if not harrowing—analysis of its weaknesses.[53]

Such an account reiterates the importance in identifying technology's use or abuse as a social issue. Broadening our understanding of behavioral addiction allows us to raise further questions about human vulnerability and weaknesses—issues that also interest Augustinian theology. Citing breakthrough science, Alter finds human nature predisposed to addiction rather than targeting specific individuals. Indeed, he concludes that "perhaps, under the right circumstances, we could all become addicts."[54] Turning the focus from individual to society exposes questions about human nature in our created goodness and capacity for harm, deceit, and even

---

[49] Alter, *Irresistible*, 25–26; see also Nicholas Kardaras, *Glow Kids: How Screen Addiction Is Hijacking Our Kids—and How to Break the Trance* (St. Martin's Griffin, 2016).

[50] Eyal, *Hooked*; Alter, *Irresistible*.

[51] O'Donovan, *Self, World, and Time*, 4, 6–9.

[52] Alter, *Irresistible*, 38–39; see also Kardaras, *Glow Kids*.

[53] Alter, *Irresistible*, 39.

[54] Alter, *Irresistible*, 53; Kardaras, *Glow Kids*.

self-destruction.[55] This conclusion that behavioral addiction is impacted by social circumstances as much as genetic predisposal places significant weight on environmental factors.

But Alter and behavioral psychologists find pleasure alone doesn't drive addiction. Instead, addiction rises from a combination of pleasure and its ability to meet some psychological need. Alter adds, "The missing ingredient is the situation that surrounds that rise in dopamine. The substance or behavior itself isn't addictive until we learn to use it as a salve for our psychological troubles."[56] Pleasure combined with comfort causes individuals to seek out repeated behaviors. Repeated behaviors turn into habits. Addictive patterns emerge when habits impact overall quality of life. Given technology's ability to target neurological pleasure, the uptick in tech addictions seems plausible given that researchers estimate "tens of millions of people in the developed world today [exhibit] one or more behavioral addiction."[57] Addiction feeds on human vulnerability and deep-seated desire.

At one point, Alter even describes addiction as "misguided love."[58] He distinguishes between liking (a form of pleasure) and wanting (a form of desire) in which the latter pursues short term pleasure at the expense of long-term well-being. The intensity of such desire can result in addiction. He says, "There was a big difference between liking a drug and wanting a drug. Addiction is about more than just liking. Addicts aren't people who happened to like the drugs they are taking—they are people who wanted those drugs very badly . . . [and] wanting is much harder to defeat than liking."[59] With substance addiction, such as drug abuse, individuals can want something without liking it; want becomes craving. Alter says, "The same is true of behaviors: even as you come to loathe Facebook or Instagram for consuming too much of your time, you continue to want updates . . . misguided love, and falling in love with the wrong person is a classic case of wanting without liking."[60]

Misguided desire aimed at the wrong substance, behavior, person, or social affirmation derived from digital platforms offers short-term relief.

[55]   Alter, *Irresistible*, 57.
[56]   Alter, *Irresistible*, 73.
[57]   Alter, *Irresistible*, 73.
[58]   Alter, *Irresistible*, 75.
[59]   Alter, *Irresistible*, 87.
[60]   Alter, *Irresistible*, 87–88.

But short-term relief can bring about long-term consequences that shape us in ways we recognize and misrecognize—especially during our adolescent years when many of our core habits are formed.[61] Yet as bleak as it sounds, addiction is not hopeless given neuroplasticity and the malleability of the human brain.[62] While retraining our appetites and habits takes work, part of the key involves understanding desire and misguided love and its influence on us.

Augustine was also deeply aware of misguided love. His theology centers on a concept of ordered and disordered love. Searching for truth, meaning, and eternity, Augustine finds we often substitute ultimate fulfilment with temporary, short-term sources of satisfaction. The problem is that fulfilling our fundamental restlessness with short-term solutions leaves us hungry for more. Reflecting on happiness in the *Confessions*, Augustine describes the difference—and possible similarity—between the experience of the joyous beggar who finds temporary happiness through drunkenness on the streets of Milan as opposed to the temporary satisfaction Augustine found in performing political speeches for the glory of Rome.[63]

Recognizing the temporary nature of both activities, Augustine suggests the beggar was happier given the worries that accompanied Augustine's political performance, leaving him frequently anxious and fearful.[64] The reward of the beggar's performance resulted in wine while the reward of Augustine's contrived political performance resulted in social capital. Augustine's success immediately "flew away," leaving him with a sense of futility.[65] The short-term effects of fulfilling pleasure for both the beggar and Augustine resulted in a perpetual desire for more. He concludes that the source of a person's happiness matters, distinguishing between temporary and eternal loves. Misguided love seeks short-term fulfilment while long-term satisfaction comes from an eternal source.

Later, Augustine describes the conflict of desire in his description of a divided will. Longing for ultimate freedom, he says, "I sighed after such freedom, but was bound not by an iron imposed by anyone else but by the iron of my own choice. The enemy had a grip on my will and so made a

---

61   Haidt, *Anxious Generation*, 227, 230.

62   Carr, *Shallows*, 21–34.

63   Augustine, *Confessions*, trans. Henry Chadwick (Oxford University Press, 1991), 6.7.10–11, pp. 98–99.

64   Augustine, *Confessions* 6.7.10–11, pp. 98–99.

65   Augustine, *Confessions* 6.7.10–11, pp. 98–99.

chain for me to hold me a prisoner. The consequence of a distorted will is passion. By servitude to passion, habit is formed, and habit to which there is no resistance becomes necessity."[66] For Augustine, bad habits are hard to break. Indulging certain passions—or indulging them in the wrong way—creates unhealthy habits that are vulnerable to becoming necessity. Misguided love or attachment is a perennial problem for all of us, feeding on human vulnerability. Any created good can become a problem when we seek after it as our source of ultimate meaning, happiness, or belonging. Temporary by nature, such goods were never intended to bear such weight. By placing too weighty a hope in a created good—any lower good—we become vulnerable to that object's power over us. Our modern reach for technology to pacify social needs makes us vulnerable to habits that emerge as new necessities.

Subtly appealing to our psychological needs, Turkle discusses the power technologies hold over us by catering to human vulnerability. Despite increased data that devices distract students from learning, texting and social media persist in the classroom. Turkle recounts a former student, saying, "You just *want* to see who *wants* you. And once you are in that 'circuit of apps,' you *want* to stay with them."[67] Tech devices and social media's ability to connect humans with others harnesses a powerful force. The pull of "wanting" is difficult. The tug of human desire for social approval and the anticipation of who might communicate is hard to ignore, even when it knowingly goes against the individual's best interest.

Social psychologist's analysis of behavioral addiction as misguided love sounds like Augustine in his description of the weight of human desire and disordered love.[68] Writing centuries ahead of us, Augustine was keenly aware of human desire and its vulnerabilities, capacity for deceit, and misguided goals. For Augustine, to be human is to love. The critical question will be not only what or whom we love, but also how we love.

Augustine was deeply reflective, writing about the interior life throughout his famous *Confessions*. Often described as an autobiographical work, Augustine's *Confessions* is more like a memoir interpreting his past, present, and future in light of philosophy, theology, and prayer. Augustine outlines his own sense of longing through countless examples, such as his analysis of the happy beggar and his own false motivations for success

---

66 Augustine, *Confessions* 8.5.10, p. 140.
67 Turkle, *Reclaiming Conversation*, 215 (emphasis added).
68 Turkle, *Reclaiming Conversation*; Alter, *Irresistible*.

through political speech writing. He opens *Confessions* with the oft-quoted line, "You have made us for yourself, and our heart is restless until it rests in you."[69] What unfolds following this line is Augustine's account of his own restless search while interpreting human longing as ultimately deep-seated desire (or want) for God.[70] Love is what defines human creatures: the question will be what is loved and how love works. In *You Are What You Love*, James K. A. Smith offers three insights to Augustine's opening statement on the restless heart. First, he says, "it recognizes that human beings are made by and for the Creator . . . to be truly and fully human, we need to 'find' ourselves in relationship to the One who made us and for whom we are made."[71] This initial statement reflects a core theological idea that humans are creatures. To be a creature implies the existence of a Creator. It also implies the prior existence of a relationship that identifies us as social beings. Learning what it means to be human includes relating to others or belonging to others, particularly, a divine Other.

Second, the statement is "dynamic" given it recognizes we are creatures with drives and purposes moving us toward particular goals. Smith continues, "To be human is to be on the move, pursuing something, after something. We are not just static containers for ideas, we are dynamic creatures directed toward some end."[72] Intentionality and purpose are part of what makes us human. The American legal system assumes intentionality and purpose are what makes humans distinctive in how motives are analyzed to determine moral and legal accountability. Intentionality is assumed as a part of basic human agency and behavior that elicits responsibility.

Third, Smith quotes the Gospel of John, "We love because he first loved us."[73] Humans love by default. Created in love, our end goal ultimately resides in love. Attaching to others through love is a creaturely quality much like breathing. The question is what we love. To find our end in something other than God proves to be a weak substitute for our ultimate purpose.

Augustine exposes the power of technology's grip in his most quoted statement on restlessness. We were made for belonging—we are restless

[69] Augustine, *Confessions* 1.1, p. 3.

[70] Dunnington also acknowledges social contributors to addiction. In a culture that lacks transcendence, individuals develop habits replacing worship with some temporal object (Dunnington, *Addiction and Virtue*, 10–12, 141–94).

[71] James K. A. Smith, *You Are What You Love* (Brazos, 2016), 8.

[72] Smith, *You Are What You Love*, 8.

[73] Smith, *You Are What You Love*, 10.

until we find it. Every attempt to find belonging in something created or temporal will leave us restless for more. In this sense, Augustine's maxim acknowledges the significance of our social identity and our capacity for addiction through attachment. Perhaps this might be why technology holds an increased influence on our culture. We want to be wanted. We want to belong. Social media and digital forces are alluring, but also addictive with their fleeting nature and algorithmic design appealing to our basic appetites. From an Augustinian lens, social media offers cheap imitations for belonging through shallow "likes" rather than an abiding sense of approval and presence.

Also embedded in Augustine's search is the desire to know himself. But for Augustine, knowing himself is deeply tied to his social existence, which includes knowing God and neighbor. Not long after opening his famous *Confessions* with an acknowledgment of restlessness, he breaks into praise and wonder of God as Creator. Here Augustine demonstrates that he understands himself by encountering difference. Just like growing infants and toddlers learn about their own identity by encountering difference in the world (be it parent or sibling), spiritual identity is forged through encountering difference with the divine. To see more deeply in the face of the divine is to know oneself more clearly. Belonging involves knowing and being known more intimately without the medium of device, one cultivated through an inner life of listening and quiet—quiet that makes space for divine presence and recognition.

Turkle voices a similar concern when describing the role of solitude and alterity for developing empathy. Lacking solitude given the constant presence of digital devices, she increasingly finds individual capacity for empathy in short supply. Solitude is important for individual identity, but it's also a necessary ingredient for relating to others well. Solitude helps to cultivate self-awareness, and self-awareness is necessary for understanding the distinctive other. This opens the pathway for empathy in which we can now imagine ourselves in another's shoes by seeing both our commonality and distinctiveness.[74] In a similar line of thought, Augustine also finds self-awareness necessary. Throughout the *Confessions*, he demonstrates his deep sense of self-awareness that leads him to encounter others through his fundamental relatedness to God as a creature. Understanding ourselves as creatures, we become open not only to empathy but also compassion in the shared vulnerability that composes the human condition.

---

[74] Turkle, *Reclaiming Conversation*, 46–50.

Interaction through give-and-take is where individuals develop the ability to see the world through another's eyes, composing key ingredients for empathy and relational health. The important role of alterity or difference is critical—encountering others in their complexity and situation in life.[75] Digital filters amplify egocentric vision since we now encounter information and consume the world through corporate algorithms fixed to individual preferences that feed individualization.[76] From this perspective, the world relates to us rather than our relating to the world. Considering the significance of alterity, or the ability to relate to others, Turkle further explains,

> The psychoanalyst Heinz Kohut described barriers to alterity, writing about fragile people—he calls them narcissistic personalities—who are characterized not by love of self but by a damaged sense of self. They try to shore themselves up by turning other people into what Kohut calls *selfobjects*. In the role of selfobject, another person is experienced as part of one's self, thus in perfect tune with a fragile inner state. The selfobject is cast in the role of what one needs, but in these relationships, disappointments inevitably follow.[77]

Narcissism is not simply love of self but evidence of a fragile self. Lacking the ability to relate to others results in using the other as object.

In *The Road to Character*, David Brooks describes an increase in narcissism in our culture for the past fifty years. Writing on the shift from the Greatest Generation as the "Little Me" culture to Millennials and Generation Z as the "Big Me" culture, Brooks explains, "Psychologists have a thing called the narcissism test . . . The median narcissism score has risen 30 percent in the last two decades. Ninety-three percent of young people score higher than the middle score just twenty years ago."[78] With the rise of technology, social media, and the phenomenon known as the selfie, posting in the form of social branding only amplifies the issue further.

Instagram, even more than Facebook, captures the social branding trend. Though created in 2010, by 2012 Instagram had 30 million users. Facebook purchased the site in 2012 for $1 billion, and by 2015, it had

---

75   Turkle, *Alone Together*, 55.

76   Zuboff, *Age of Surveillance Capitalism*, 31–37.

77   Turkle, *Alone Together*, 55.

78   Jean M. Twenge and W. Keith Campbell, *The Narcissism Epidemic* (Simon & Schuster, 2009), 13, cited in David Brooks, *The Road to Character* (Random House, 2015), 7.

over 400 million users, exceeding Twitter (now X)[79] only later to be succeeded by TikTok.[80] Wu attributes the early success of Instagram to several factors, including its use of attractive filters, its primary mode through image (with optional message), its increased use of the smartphone's full functionality (both camera and internet), and its increased market for "aspiring celebrities."[81] He says, "Instagram thus occupied the territory on which Zuckerberg had originally positioned Facebook: the place to be. And the real-time fix of 'likes' and comments would become for untold numbers an addictive form of self-affirmation."[82]

With the rise of Instagram came the rise of the term "selfie," entering the Oxford Dictionary as the "Word of the Year in 2013."[83] Directing attention toward oneself authorized self-attention as an "accepted form of currency."[84] Outsourcing self-affirmation to countless others, the new way of relating to the world through social media evolved into an ironic boomerang in which you now reach out to others to simultaneously affirm and receive status in an online world.

Describing the need for recognition and its redefinition through social media, Wu explains, "This is the essential problem with the preening self-unbound by social media, and the democratization of fame. By presenting us with example upon example, it legitimates self-aggrandizement as an objective for ever more of us. By encouraging anyone to capture the attention of others with the spectacle of oneself—in some cases, even to the point of earning a living by it—it warps our understanding of our own existence and its relation to others."[85] In Wu's analysis, online relationships have become a form of mutual self-projection and affirmation. From this trajectory, the self is formed through media declarations, likes, and corporate algorithms rather than a malleable self shaped by conversation and the healthy reciprocity Turkle describes as necessary for empathy and mutuality forged through vulnerability.

---

[79]   Wu, *Attention Merchants*, 311–17.

[80]   Chris Stokel-Walker, "How TikTok Beat Instagram: Instagram Is Becoming as Uncool as Facebook—and It Has Only Itself to Blame," *Business Insider*, February 2, 2023, https://www.businessinsider.com/why-instagram-cant-compete-tiktok-videos-algorithm-influencers-engagement-2023-2.

[81]   Wu, *Attention Merchants*, 311.

[82]   Wu, *Attention Merchants*, 312.

[83]   Wu, *Attention Merchants*, 312.

[84]   Wu, *Attention Merchants*, 312.

[85]   Wu, *Attention Merchants*, 315.

Augustine's order of love, in contrast, poses differentiation as the necessary ingredient for proper self-assessment. One must love something or someone radically different from oneself to discover identity and belonging through divine recognition. Augustine will argue that in order to truly love oneself, one must love the ultimate, eternal end in God as well as neighbor. To love well involves the virtue of humility. Knowing and loving begins with awareness of one's creatureliness, foibles, and flaws. It wasn't until Augustine recognized his fragility and sin through the spiritual practice of confession and repentance that he felt whole. Recognizing his weakness through vulnerability gave him the space to open to the divine, neighbor, and world. By opening himself to the divine, he knew himself more fully.

This greater sense of fullness also enriches his relationships. Alypius journeys with him from Manichaean philosophy to Christian theology and eventual conversion.[86] His mother, Monica, communes with him through a sense of eternal presence in a beatific vision at Ostia.[87] He engages in both intellectual and spiritual conversation with his friends in *The Cassiciacum Dialogues* shortly following his conversion.[88] These relationships were even present with him near his death as witnessed by Possidius, who hung Scripture on the walls at which Augustine might gaze in his final hours of life.[89]

But more than these rich friendships, Augustine consistently reflects deep intimacy with his Creator. In fact, his famous *Confessions* is written as a prayer in which the reader is invited into his conversation with God. Upon the death of his own mother, he describes how he tried to hold back the tears. It wasn't until hours later when he was alone, in the presence of God, that he let out his tears and found comfort. Thus his prayers and cries to God become his consolation, evidence of an active sense of communion with his Creator. It was this kind of vulnerability—creature before Creator, child before Father—that forged his identity.

Keenly aware of his sense of fragmentation and brokenness, Augustine reflects on his own self-identity as a journey and his communion on that journey through fellowship or union with God. Explaining his desire as fragmented, Augustine accounts for the One who apprehends, gathers,

86   Serge Lancel, *St. Augustine* (SCM, 1999), 46–48.
87   Augustine, *Confessions* 9.10.23–24, p. 171; Lancel, *St. Augustine*, 116–17.
88   Lancel, *St. Augustine*, 99–109.
89   Lancel, *St. Augustine*, 475.

and unifies him.[90] He writes, "But now 'my years pass in groans' (Ps 30:11) and you, Lord, are my consolation. You are my eternal Father, but I am scattered in times whose order I do not understand. The storms of incoherent events tear to pieces my thoughts, the inmost entrails of my soul, until that day when, purified and molten by the fire of your love, I flow together to merge into you."[91]

For Augustine, to be loved and found by God was to find his very self.[92] His being was made for completion or participation in the Divine, the creature-Creator relation. At the heart of this intimacy is vulnerability and openness rather than self-protection. However, such vulnerability and transcendence play a role not just for one's identity through intimate relationship with God, but also in terms of interpersonal relationships, communication, and its implications for political or social empire.

AUGUSTINIAN EMPIRE AND *LIBIDO DOMINANDI*
On Vulnerability, Control, and Empire

Augustine's famous *City of God* is more than a political treatise. This volume is a lengthy consideration of theology, philosophy, and moral motivation. Rather than assert a political theory of state, Augustine offers a theology of history and eschatology in which individuals and social arrangements compose two cities most defined by love. The love in these cities pertains to their ultimate allegiance and destiny. Offering his overarching thesis in *City of God* book 14, Augustine says, "Two loves have built two cities. Love of self, even to the point of contempt for God, made the earthly city, and love of God, even to the point of contempt for self, made the heavenly city."[93] Throughout the thousand-page treatise, Augustine deconstructs false happiness found in Roman philosophy, religion, and empire, while reconstructing happiness grounded in Christ through eternal faith, hope, and love.

Responding to critiques of Christians following the Visigoth attack on the Roman Empire in 410, Augustine questions the good found in the empire's expanse when people face "disasters of war and the spilling of blood . . .

[90]   Augustine, *Confessions* 11.39, p. 244.
[91]   Augustine, *Confessions* 11.39, p. 244.
[92]   To this day, the symbol of the Order of St. Augustine in the Roman Catholic Church is a heart aflame with love.
[93]   Augustine, *The City of God*, abridged study edition, trans. William Babcock, notes by Boniface Ramsey, abridgment by Joseph T. Kelley (New City Press, 2018), 14.28, p. 310.

always living under the dark shadow of fear and in the lust for blood."[94] Augustine compares the Empire to fragile glass. The shadow of fear hangs over the Empire just as glass is vulnerable to shattering. His critical lens challenges the security found in empire, noting its perennial ambivalence in its capacity for temporary benefits—though at great expense. In book 19, he notes the good when political structures provide temporal peace. But unlike classical political theories' emphasis on the good of the state when organized around reason, order, and virtue in the work of Plato, Aristotle, or Seneca, Augustine's more realist account recognizes empire—and the state along with it—as subject to both sin and grace.[95]

R. A. Markus considers Augustine's perspective on the *saeculum*, or secular space and time, as the theater of sin and grace. Describing time as the "vehicle of sin and tragedy as well as the medium for redemption," Markus finds the *saeculum* as commingled space in which good and evil reside.[96] The ambivalence of time marks all human activities, including social arrangements such as empire. Markus illustrates, "The Empire—as all actual societies of men—hovers between the 'earthly' and the 'heavenly' cities, or, more precisely, it exists in the region where the two cities overlap. Its achievement is radically infected with the ambiguity of all human achievement."[97] Here empire serves an intermediary role, meeting temporal or "limited" needs as opposed to ultimate goals relating to human destiny.[98]

In Augustine's schema, order is preferable to chaos but turns sour when "misused for ends other than justice and . . . tranquility."[99] Unfortunately, this is commonly the case. Empire might begin with a beneficial motive desiring peace, but quickly becomes sinister given our proclivity for sin. In *City of God* book 19, Augustine describes ways the earthly city benefits members of the heavenly city through temporal peace. Peace provides temporary freedom from material harm. Yet Augustine questions the limits of peace. Redefining a republic, Augustine finds no true justice exists

---

[94]   Augustine, *City of God* 4.3, p. 70.

[95]   R. A. Markus, *Saeculum: History and Society in the Theology of St. Augustine* (Cambridge University Press, 1970); Eric Gregory, *Politics and the Order of Love: An Augustinian Ethic of Democratic Citizenship* (University of Chicago Press, 2008).

[96]   Markus, *Saeculum*, 98.

[97]   Markus, *Saeculum*, 98.

[98]   Markus, *Saeculum*, 98.

[99]   Charles Mathewes, "An Augustinian Look at Empire," *Theology Today* 63, no. 3 (2006): 298.

in societies that fall short of justice toward God.[100] Instead of defining a republic based on justice, he defines one based on love.[101] The better the loves, the better the republic. The worse the loves, the worse the republic. But even this ambiguous role of empire is tinged with fear, power, and possible coercion given the reality of sin.

Augustine's understanding of original sin, developed in response to the Pelagian controversy, includes an early account of social or structural sin. He finds the more people involved in a household, republic, region, or empire, the greater opportunity for sin and thus, greater opportunity for evil.[102] Not unlike social media, the greater the network, the more opportunity for negatively wielding power with confusion and control. He even says more friends bring on more heartache. Empire in its broad social arrangements moves down in the hierarchy of ordered loves and too easily demonstrates disordered love and injustice. Augustine even compares empires to large gangs of robbers and suggests the conquests of Alexander the Great might be likened to pirates aided by governing power.[103] Thus, while social arrangements are necessary parts of temporal living, Augustine prefers smaller arrangements that might hold its leaders as well as members more accountable. Fewer people make for fewer disagreements and lawsuits.[104]

The ambivalence of empire is also tied to Augustine's description of sin as the *libido dominandi*, translated as the "lust to dominate" or the "dominating lust." All human behavior is tempted with sin as the lust for domination like the fall of Adam and Eve.[105] Even in their first sin,

---

[100]   Augustine finds the republic differs from Scipio's description as a commonwealth built on justice (*City of God* 3.21, pp. 38–41).

[101]   Augustine, *City of God* 19.2, pp. 443–45.

[102]   Augustine, *City of God* 19.7, pp. 426–27.

[103]   Augustine, *City of God* 4.4, p. 71. Too often empire includes what historian Nicholas Rowe calls "expansion, exclusivity, and exploitation"—factors present for Rome and for today (McDonough, "'Come Out of Her'"). Conquering small communities for broader protection, the Roman empire was rife with these characteristics in its military and economic expansion.

[104]   Augustine, *City of God* 19.5–6, p. 425.

[105]   Augustine offers both a literal and allegorical account of the creation/fall narratives in Scripture (*On Genesis: A Refutation of the Manichees*, in *On Genesis*, ed. John E. Rotelle, trans. Edmund Hill, The Works of Saint Augustine: A Translation for the 21st Century, part 1, vol. 13 [New City Press, 2002]). Distinguishing between dominance and domination is also important when considering the Genesis narrative. The context and meaning of dominion never assumed ownership, but

Adam and Eve demonstrate self-assertion above the divine prohibition against eating fruit from the tree of the knowledge of good and evil. In the desire to be like God, or perhaps God on their own terms, they displace the foundation of their identity. Rather than rest in their status as God's image bearers, they now "play God," using their creative powers in unjust or idolatrous ways.[106] Through sin, Augustine says Adam and Eve attempt self-creation, loving self and one's glory at the expense of God. The city of earth might be viewed as this lust for power.

City of God book 14 describes the fundamental difference between the two cities and two loves. The city of earth rooted in prideful self-assertion grasps at God in self-exaltation. In this way its members become less god-like through pleasure in themselves. Augustine says, "But they would have been better able to be like gods if they had clung to the true and supreme principle in obedience, instead of taking themselves as their own principle in pride. For created goods are not gods by virtue of any truth of their own but by virtue of *participation* in the true God."[107] Through dependence and participation, identity is found.[108] Belonging to the Creator, creatures best enact their creaturely identity. But when they forget this belonging, they lose their sense of core identity.

Humility, however, results in the opposite effect. By recognizing the Creator, one receives creaturely limits and identity rather than grasping for identity. Recognizing limits and the God in whose image one's made "lifts the heart up."[109] The pattern set forth in Adam and Eve follows in

---

stewardship, trust, and care. The difference in dominion from Gen 1:28, in which creatures subdue the earth as caregivers under God's authority, should include creation care. The lust to dominate or *libido dominandi* reflects a sinful struggle after the fall (Gen 3) in the human temptation to "play God" or act as God over creation and others. See Andy Crouch's distinction between creative power used in helpful ways as opposed to power used in harmful ways. The language of "trustee" or care for land and institutions reflects thoughtful responsibility associated with the creation mandate as opposed to domination (Andy Crouch, *Playing God: Redeeming the Gift of Power* [IVP, 2013], 207–20).

[106] Crouch, *Playing God*, 66–67; see also idem, *The Life We're Looking For: Reclaiming Relationship in a Technological World* (Convergent, 2022), 23–25.

[107] Augustine, *City of God* 14.13, p. 301 (emphasis added).

[108] Brian Rosner describes creatures as made in the image of God, known by God, and renewed in Christ. He considers the motif "child of God" as primary across Scripture. For a more comprehensive discussion of biblical and theological interpretations of identity see Brian Rosner, *Known by God: A Biblical Theology of Personal Identity* (Zondervan, 2017), 39.

[109] Augustine, *City of God* 14.13, p. 300.

the subsequent lives of ancient characters, parsing out differences between pride and humility, whether Cain and Abel, the conception of Ishmael and Isaac, or Romulus and Remus.[110] Conflict occurs when pursuing the flesh above the spirit or domination above creaturely limits. The cities of earth and heaven differ based on domination or humility found in service.

Domination as pride impacts the foundation of civilization. Augustine cites Cain as responsible for founding a city through self-exaltation.[111] Abel, however, remains a pilgrim, receiving a city or kingdom from on high.[112] Contrasting domination with humility, pride with service, involves both personal and social consequences. Pride is central to building the Tower of Babel and the Babylonian Empire. Both represent the city of earth in its self-sought security. The city of heaven, however, represents recipients of grace through humility and sacrifice. Together, the two cities commingle throughout time awaiting their eschatological distinction. Those driven by pride and domination participate in the earthly empire at the same time as those driven by humility and love anticipate the kingdom or city of God.

However, Augustine does not equate the city of earth to the world and the city of heaven to the church.[113] In fact, Augustine is deeply realistic that all individuals and institutions, including the church through time, are subject to domination and pride. One of the key tenets shaping his theology includes humility found in the invisible church rather than the visible church, requiring ongoing repentance and faith. Even followers of Christ can play God and problematically utilize power—whether consciously or subconsciously.[114]

110 Augustine, *City of God* 15.2–5, pp. 316–19.
111 Augustine, *City of God* 15.1–2, pp. 314–15.
112 Augustine, *City of God* 15.1–2, pp. 314–15.
113 Augustine, *City of God* 19; Tarcisius J. Van Bavel, "Church," in *Augustine Through the Ages*, ed. Allan D. Fitzgerald (Eerdmans, 1999), 172–73.
114 Augustine describes a troublesome case where even a Christian judge might unintentionally condemn an innocent victim as a criminal in a realist world riddled by sin. This doesn't condone condemning innocent victims. In fact, elsewhere Augustine says it's better for an unjust person to go free than an innocent person to be condemned. This might be one of the lower points in Augustine's writing. While he acknowledges realist challenges as "miserable necessities" in this passage, in other places he requires moral accountability. Given his caveat that it's better for an unjust person to go free, he acknowledges that one should err on caution when offering judicial condemnation (*City of God* 19.6, p. 425; *Confessions* 4.1–2, pp. 52–53).

The city, society, and world involve difficult choices and sometimes result in war. Yet even just wars—if pursued for legitimate reasons—should be circumscribed and never pursued without grief.[115] The goal of a just war is peace. Peace benefits the earthly and heavenly city alike. Here he is consistent about the ambivalent work of political empire and the good found in contributing to the city's welfare. Citing both 1 Timothy 2:2 and Jeremiah 29, he exhorts Christ's followers to live a quiet life while seeking the good of Babylon.[116]

In this sense, empire is more a theological than political concept that can best be described as "worldliness." Worldliness is our attempt to live apart from God on our own terms through power and control, escalating to political heights and consequences as seen through the Babylonian empire in Isaiah and Revelation as well as the Tower of Babel.[117] Empire becomes more sinister when corroborating with what Charles Mathewes calls "'the powers of this world' . . . that attempt to make the world self-governing, separate from God . . . For Christians, then, to think about life in this world after the fall is to think, directly or not, about empire, and to think about empire is to think about worldliness."[118] Worldliness is our perennial drive for security apart from God.

Fearing Death as Not Belonging

Augustinian priest Robert Dodaro offers a fascinating interpretation on the *City of God* as a treatise responding to fear of death.[119] In fact, Dodaro says the varying philosophies and heroes exalted by Rome are attempts to deny or control that which is uncontrollable. In doing so, one denies human vulnerability. Forgetting their Creator and their identity as creatures, individuals and society mask their vulnerability and mortality through the *libido dominandi*.[120] Instead, most pursuits in society—be they economic, political, social or even entertainment—are forms of distraction from death.

---

[115] Augustine, *City of God* 19.7, pp. 426–27.

[116] Augustine, *City of God* 19.26, pp. 452–53.

[117] Charles Mathewes, *Republic of Grace* (Eerdmans, 2010), 40–41.

[118] Mathewes, *Republic of Grace*, 40–41.

[119] Robert Dodaro, *Christ and the Just Society in the Thought of St. Augustine* (Cambridge University Press, 2004); see also Ernest Becker, *The Denial of Death* (Free Press, 1973).

[120] Charles Mathewes, "Lecture 6: The Price of Empire (Books 2–3)," in *Books That Matter: The City of God* (The Great Courses, The Teaching Company, 2016), 110.

Dodaro says, "Masking fear of death is the concluding theme of Book I. Augustine suggests that the Roman elite indulge in various forms of luxury (*luxuria*) accompanied by a variety of illicit pleasures (*uoluptates*) to distract them from the inevitability of death."[121] Rome acted as protector and provider of interests, masking vulnerability to death. Rome also strategically ignored its enemy, Carthage, to ensure political motivation against future external threat. The accumulation of power and wealth functioned as tools to assuage insecurity. In one of Dodaro's most insightful passages, he says,

> Fear of death expresses itself as the fear of a loss of status and comfort which has been typical of Rome since the decline of the republic. Empire is thus a murky, ambivalent symbol in Augustine's thought. To a limited extent, he interprets it as a sign of at least temporary divine favor. In the long run, however, the cost in resources and human suffering of maintaining and expanding the Empire reveals an underlying, ever-increasing social anxiety about annihilation. In effect, the overdependence upon military force characteristic of empire institutionalizes and internalizes the visible, permanent security threat . . . Thus, a vicious circle links the threat of annihilation with an ever-growing political and military response to foreign threats, disseminating anxiety throughout the Empire . . .[122]

Thus, "empire" for Augustine symbolizes an ambiguous state in which individuals benefit, but at the cost of empire's expansion into their lives. Fear of death accompanies such expansion given its vulnerability to defeat from outside enemies. Yet after gaining power, one feels fragile or insecure at the prospect of losing such power. Fueled by vulnerability and anxiety, power begins to dominate. In order to distract Roman participants from their vulnerability to death, Rome institutes forms of entertainment as seen in the gladiatorial games to bemuse spectators while redirecting their gaze from the insecurity found in their mortality.

Augustine's understanding of empire relates to today's digital empire in multiform ways. Empire becomes much like Chamath Palihapitiya's concept of a negative feedback loop with social media. Power works best by gaining more. Social media's initial allure involved its power to connect real time relationships across time and space. But its influence grew in

---

[121] Dodaro, *Christ and the Just Society*, 41.
[122] Dodaro, *Christ and the Just Society*, 42.

its ability to connect not only real time relationships, but also strangers and eventually corporate interest through carefully calculated algorithms based on preferential cookies drawing our attention. The algorithmic cookies contain great power ranging from the ability to influence our next connection made through suggested "friends," economic purchase, or political persuasion. Andy Crouch recognizes this as the extravagant promise of all idols: hooking us with their allure, they promise "You shall not surely die" in their endless cycle and availability. Likewise, they promise "You shall be like God," in their ability to hide our insecurities through perceived feelings of control.[123]

For Augustine, the *libido dominandi* and its proclivity to be like God functions at both the individual and social (political) level.[124] Following sin in the garden of Eden, creaturely amnesia manifests in self-deception (ignorance) and self-reliance (weakness) that results in grasping onto temporal goods for the glory of self or glory of Rome through pride.[125] Mathewes calls this self-indulgence a fantasy driven by anxiety, reinforcing the idea that domination is tied to happiness.[126] Ultimately, Augustine finds these false hopes for happiness end up bankrupt through "restless" or "endless" attempts to masquerade our vulnerability and its accompanied fear through pride and self-protection.

At first blush, technology seems unrelatable. Yet, according to Ernest Becker, fear of death drives human activity.[127] In a modern world devoid of transcendence, "that fear of insignificance in the face of nonexistence must be dealt with in some way."[128] While related to repressed "fear of death," social media certainly plays on fear—in this case, fear of not belonging.[129] FOMO is tied to social anxiety and desire for belonging. Zuckerberg knows exactly how to use this fear through his own form of domination.

In this sense, Augustine's use of empire or social organization as an ambivalent murky symbol that temporarily brings benefits while requiring more from its adherents than originally agreed seems fitting. Empire feeds on fear in our longing for security and happiness. Knowing our keen

123 Crouch, *Playing God*, 64.
124 Augustine, *City of God* 14.33, p. 310.
125 Dodaro, *Christ and the Just Society*, 29.
126 Mathewes, *Books That Matter: The City of God*, 114.
127 Becker, *Denial of Death*, xvii.
128 Timothy Keller, *On Death* (Penguin Books, 2020), 15.
129 Becker, *Denial of Death*, xvii; Keller, *On Death*, 14–15.

desire to relate to others, technology and social media designers offer benefits of belonging and connectedness, while subtly wanting more through algorithms. Digital technology promises efficiency, connectedness, and time while demanding more from us than ever imagined.

THE DEVELOPMENT OF TECHNOLOGICAL EMPIRE

Jacques Ellul, the City, and Technology

Perhaps no other contemporary theologian better critiques the role of technology and its false promise as empire than Jacques Ellul. In *The Meaning of the City*, Ellul builds on Augustinian themes, emphasizing the tension found in the city as counter-creation or those creative projects tainted by sin in ways that assert themselves over God.[130] Describing the origins of the city, Ellul says Cain seeks his own security apart from God following separation from God's presence through sin.[131] He compounds the problem by seeking his own legacy or home apart from his prescribed position as wanderer. Like Augustine before him, Ellul finds self-assertion central to Enoch, Cain's city, that anticipates Nimrod and later the Babylonian empire's power, war, and conquest.[132] Ellul likens Nimrod's city to Babel, asserting its own name—or dominion—over the Creator. Rather than follow the creation mandate through filling the earth and spreading out power, Babel concentrates power, constructing its own identity that results in confusion and misunderstanding.[133] The creation mandate, on the other hand, disperses power in an ordered way while Babel concentrates power in a disordered way.

The story of Babel precedes Babylon, which becomes the city representing the hub of civilization through business, industry, and innovative technology: its tower is marked by restlessness and commodification.[134] Participating in the French resistance movement and post–World War II France, Ellul critiques modern cities, whether Paris, Venice, or New York, through this Babylonian interpretation and its "inhuman road" aimed at endless building.[135] As in the book of Revelation, the city of Tyre and

---

[130] Jacques Ellul, *The Meaning of the City*, trans. Dennis Pardee (Wipf and Stock, 2003); see also Sean McDonough, *Creation and New Creation: Understanding God's Creation Project* (Hendrickson, 2017).

[131] Ellul, *Meaning of the City*.

[132] Ellul, *Meaning of the City*, 1–13.

[133] Ellul, *Meaning of the City*, 18.

[134] Ellul, *Meaning of the City*, 21.

[135] Ellul, *Meaning of the City*, 22.

Babylon are critiqued for love of money. Through love of money or mammon, the city asserts its own sovereignty and reason for existence.[136] Shutting out God, its inhabitants use creation for luxury, demonstrating that "everything is for sale, including the bodies and souls of men."[137] Humanity is lost in a land of false gods and images to be consumed.[138]

Not only is humanity lost to images and false gods, but also the crowd. The individual is reduced to nothing but a "crowd in the city." He says,

> He is never separate, never physically alone, never one, face to face with himself. In the city we find the strange phenomenon of man separated from himself and others by a sheet of glass, invisible yet present, unbreakable, impassable. Never alone yet deserted. One man in a crowd, this is the constant situation of all of us. A crowd is not just a number of people gathered in one place, a material phenomenon observable by counting the people in the crowd. It is also a psychological, sociological, and spiritual situation which we today usually refer to as a mass.[139]

The mass reflects a kind of group think or social *geist* present in the city. Physically connected, there is "no silent zone" but "perpetual noise" without room for solitude, reflection, or stillness.[140]

Without time or space for contemplation on the spiritual meaning of life, the city's connected networks, like technology, become all-consuming.[141] Restless, he finds the crowd "always seeking . . . knowing that something is missing, but not knowing what. It has a terrible undefined sense of something's being absent, and desperately wants that presence."[142] Through relentless absence, the activity of the city aims at presence or completion, though one devoid of spiritual satisfaction. Instead, human creativity, blended with the prince and powers of this world, takes on a life of its own that consumes its users.

Much like the ambivalent description of Augustine's empire asserting power against powerlessness, the city—and technology along with

---

136   Ellul, *Meaning of the City*, 51–52.
137   Ellul, *Meaning of the City*, 55.
138   Ellul, *Meaning of the City*, 58, 150–51.
139   Ellul, *Meaning of the City*, 125.
140   Ellul, *Meaning of the City*, 125.
141   Haidt's research confirms increased time with virtual relationships correlates with an increased sense of spiritual poverty (Haidt, *Anxious Generation*, 199–202).
142   Ellul, *Meaning of the City*, 127.

it—promises freedom but demands everything. Ellul explains, "The city tries to substitute liberty, that is, the possibility for man to do what he wants when he wants . . . But this liberty is a farce. The city must, in order to stay alive, have its night shifts, the accumulation of a proletariat, alcohol, prostitution, an iron schedule of work hours."[143] All freedoms come with a cost. In their best moments, they require work and in their darkest moments, exploitation. The city is more than a simplistic tool, but "an almost indistinguishable mixture of spiritual power and man's work."[144] The city represents human creation merged with problematic counter-creation in the form of technique or the totalitarian use of technology. Through the illusive promise of efficiency and ease, we achieve godlike status through our own counter-creation, that in turn negatively devours us.

The Rise of the Digital Empire and Machine-Based Culture

Several recent authors offer historiographical accounts for what I call the rise of the digital empire and machine-based culture. Craig M. Gay offers one of the most insightful overviews on the history of modern technology in the west, arguing tech is anything but neutral in the way it shapes us. Moving from a tools-based culture building on what we naturally use in an embodied sense (hammer, shovel) to a contrivance culture whereby natural forces work with nature (windmill, waterwheel), we now find ourselves in a machine-based culture. Drawing upon vast amounts of scientific knowledge and practice that act on nature, a machine-based culture bends nature to our will through mechanistic laws in the form of control.[145] Gay details how we arrived here by way of theology, philosophy, the scientific revolution, and capitalistic business practices contributing to the modern turn from the medieval worldview.

Drawing on the work of Martin Heidegger, he describes the difference in posture toward "nature made present" as opposed to "standing reserve."[146]

---

[143] Ellul, *Meaning of the City*, 152.

[144] Ellul, *Meaning of the City*, 169.

[145] Craig M. Gay, *Modern Technology and the Human Future: A Christian Appraisal* (IVP Academic, 2018), 28. For a similar historiographical account see Albert Borgmann, *Technology and the Character of Contemporary Life: A Philosophical Inquiry* (University of Chicago Press, 1984).

[146] See Martin Heidegger, "The Question Concerning Technology," in *The Question Concerning Technology and Other Essays*, trans. William Lovitt (Harper & Row, 1977), 3–35, cited in Gay, *Modern Technology*, 118, n. 53, 119. For more on Heidegger see Ashley Moyse, *The Art of Living for a Technological Age: Toward a Humanizing Performance* (Fortress, 2021), 24–34.

The first views nature as given in its own internal integrity while the second views nature as opportunity for future use. Contrasting the contrivance approach that works with nature, the machine-oriented approach enables the unlocking of "forces previously hidden within nature," but also involves a "violent kind of making . . . that is both restless and relentless. It discloses a relation to nature that seeks to regulate and to secure but that can never arrive at regulation or security."[147] Restlessness ensues.

While the Industrial Revolution capitalized on natural resources over nature, the technocratic revolution capitalized on human resources.[148] Now the digital revolution capitalizes on social resources (networks, i.e., "friendships") over connection. Gay attributes these social changes to machine living, in particular automatic machine technology that "enables enormous power and control."[149] He continues, "With its unremitting emphases upon efficiency, continuous motion, predictability and prearranged effects, standardized measurements, interchangeable parts, and so forth, modern machine technology seems to have produced a world that is often artificial and occasionally even strangely alien to human feeling."[150] Perceiving the world primarily as machine for instrumental purposes parallels the master/slave relation, a relation that dehumanizes the master as much as the slave.[151]

Gay recognizes dehumanizing effects take place through a variety of machines, whether the mechanical clock described by non-Westerners as "gods on their wrists" or the contemporary "gods in the palms of our hands."[152] Smartphones and social media—along with devices such as GPS (global positioning systems)—place individuals at the center of interpretation and location.[153] More than individualism (asserting individual choice), individualization ensues in which "the self is all we have."[154] Lacking shared meaning, increased individualization commodifies nature and relationships. Increased power over relationships through social media results in

[147] Gay, *Modern Technology*, 118–19.
[148] Zuboff, *Age of Surveillance Capitalism*, xv.
[149] Gay, *Modern Technology*, 28–30.
[150] Gay, *Modern Technology*, 30.
[151] Gay, *Modern Technology*, 30.
[152] Gay, *Modern Technology*, 31.
[153] See Graham Lee, *Human Being: Reclaim 12 Vital Skills We're Losing to Technology* (Michael O'Mara, 2023), 18–22.
[154] Zuboff, *Age of Surveillance Capitalism*, 31–37.

dehumanization, viewing faces as commodities to swipe, friendships as numbers to accumulate, and self-reflection as tweets to post.

We arrived in this milieu through a series of theological and philosophical shifts. Canadian political writer George Grant cites ways in which theological reasoning, particularly the Protestant Reformation and its emphasis on the will, contributed to the technological empire's development in the West or North Atlantic region. Grant, like Ellul, acknowledges the ways in which Western technical achievement shaped civilization: "It molds us in what we are, not only at the heart of our animality in the propagation and continuance of our species, but in our actions and thoughts and imaginings . . . its pursuit has become our dominant activity and that dominance fashions both the public and private realms."[155] Technology is a power that shapes us—whether we recognize it or not.

Emptying Nature and Its Ends: Individualism, Nihilism, and the Social Media Empire

Significant shifts in theology as well as philosophy contributed to the tech ethos over time. Grant reflects on the sobering role of Protestant theology in technology's development, particularly in the Dutch and English Calvinist traditions and their influence through the Puritans in North America. Reformed theology's emphasis on revelation rather than medieval teleological doctrines associated with natural theology impacted early understandings of nature and its purpose. The Protestant turn departs from prior Thomistic and medieval foci on metaphysical causality and unity in nature.[156] Emphasizing God's freedom, William of Occam's nominalism prioritizes divine and human agency over nature, removing intrinsic purposes (formal and final causes) from the material world.[157] What remains are instrumental or efficient causes acting directly on nature. Over time, the focus on divine agency shifts to human agency as central. Merging this with Baconian science comes the desire to relieve and

---

[155] George Grant, "In Defence of North America," in *Technology and Empire* (Anansi Press, 1969; 2018), 5; see also Moyse, *Art of Living*, 11, 34–37.

[156] Grant, "In Defence of North America," 10–11. Significant shifts occur with Dun Scotus's focus on the will and William of Occam's emphasis on divine freedom in action rather than appeal to natural law. See Charles Taylor, *A Secular Age* (Belknap Press, 2007), 97–98.

[157] Taylor, *A Secular Age*, 97–98; Jeffrey P. Bishop, *The Anticipatory Corpse* (University of Notre Dame Press, 2011), 19–21.

improve the material world without specified ends from within nature.[158] Disenchanted, nature loses its meaning. Nature is no longer discovered or received as gift but is now meaningless matter to be harnessed, mastered, and sold.[159]

Changing views on nature hold significant impact. While theological motives initiated this shift, Charles Taylor notes changes from a "normative order, in which God has revealed himself through signs and symbols" to an order in which "we inhabit it as agents of instrumental reason, working the system effectively in order to bring about God's purposes."[160] The first demonstrates a posture of reception and response while the latter emphasizes a posture of actor and activity. These two views can work against each other when viewed in isolation.

The first view seeks signs and symbols in the natural world for meaning associated with the Aristotelian cosmos of Aquinas, Pseudo-Dionysius, and Augustine. The second view disenchants nature at both the popular and scientific level. Rather than view nature as mystery or ordered cosmos, nature becomes a system of interactive parts to be acted upon more like "a machine."[161] While Protestant theology emphasized the freedom and sovereignty of God to act on nature, emphasizing revelation alone, Baconian science and new forms of humanism, with its roots in the Renaissance and Enlightenment, redefined human agency in terms of reason and its capacity to improve nature through progress.[162]

Protestant theology initiated the turn to divine agency and freedom over nature while enlightened philosophy and science emphasized human agency over nature. Over time, nature became subject to greater usefulness through specialization—as seen through scientific specialization and

---

[158] Taylor, *A Secular Age*, 97–98; see also Allen Verhey, *Nature and Altering It* (Eerdmans, 2010), 22–26.

[159] Michael Sandel argues for viewing children—and perhaps nature—as gifts "open to the unbidden" rather than created or willed (Michael J. Sandel, "The Case Against Perfection," *Atlantic*, April 2004, https://www.theatlantic.com/magazine/archive/2004/04/the-case-against-perfection/302927/). See also Gay, *Modern Technology*.

[160] Taylor, *A Secular Age*, 98.

[161] Taylor, *A Secular Age*, 98.

[162] Taylor, *A Secular Age*, 98. Taylor reiterates disenchanted nature in its modern mechanistic turn from the ancient and medieval world in *Cosmic Connections: Poetry in the Age of Disenchantment* (Belknap Press, 2024), 45–47. In this volume he describes Romantic poets in their appeal to transcendence in nature as opposed to modern scientism that instrumentalizes nature, removing its moral meaning.

the varying fields of modern medicine—rather than contemplated for its harmonious contribution to the overarching cosmos or whole.[163] An emphasis on freedom and agency combined with industrial capitalism contributed to a sense of purpose extrinsic to nature. Without intrinsic purpose to the world, nature remains open to mechanistic improvement through science, medicine, and technology aided at times by theology.[164]

No longer seeking the end and goals of nature, theology in North America becomes more associated with practice rather than contemplation.[165] Nature becomes easily subject to utilitarian use rather than something to behold. Losing a sense of enchantment, nature is devoid of revelation or wisdom.[166] In a theological environment combining John Locke's liberal democratic emphasis on individual freedom and the steam engine of the Industrial Revolution, worldly asceticism became "ever more worldly and less ascetic"—gradually dissolving the Protestant vision initiated by the Puritans in the Massachusetts Bay Colony.[167]

Individualistic ethics involving reason and control over passions loosen. Control over sex and sloth persist (for a season) while

> the passions of greed and mastery were emancipated from traditional Christian restraints. [Max] Weber was brilliantly right to place [Ben] Franklin near the centre of his account of English-speaking Protestantism . . . It takes one quite outside the traditionally contemplative roots of European science, into the world of Edison and

---

[163] I am not entirely eschewing the gains made from modern medicine and specialization through varying fields. However, specialization can miss the holistic picture when focusing on specific parts such as normalizing young bodies in medical education and focusing on cure-based practice. See Louise Aronson, *Elderhood: Redefining Aging, Transforming Medicine, Reimagining Life* (Bloomsbury, 2019); Tia Powell, *Dementia Reimagined: Building a Life of Joy and Dignity from Beginning to End* (Avery, 2019).

[164] Grant, "In Defence of North America," 10–11, 13. See Taylor's descriptive development of civility over carnival through Calvinist social reforms, Stoic-influenced theology through Justus Lipsius, rationalistic approaches to natural law (whether Hugo Grotius or John Locke), and an emphasis on mind over matter influenced by Rene Descartes among others (Taylor, *A Secular Age*, 105–45).

[165] Grant, "In Defence of North America," 13.

[166] See Autumn Alcott Ridenour, "Re-enchanting Nature and Medicine," *Christian Bioethics* 25, no. 3 (2019): 283–98. In this article I argue nature is revelatory, conveying wisdom (citing physician Sherwin Nuland, *Wisdom of the Body* [Random House, 1997], xixx–xx).

[167] Grant, "In Defence of North America," 13ff.

research grants. In 1968 Billy Graham at the Republican Convention could in full confidence use [Ben] Franklin in his thanksgiving for what the Christian God had done for America.[168]

Protestant theology's emphasis on individual choice in salvation along with an emphasis on practice and activity became central.[169] Focusing on

[168]   Grant, "In Defence of North America," 12. This statement is qualified in that, technically, Benjamin Franklin was a deist rather than professing Christian. Still, Grant's point is well taken given the pragmatism in American Protestant evangelicalism that emphasizes praxis over contemplation. I also qualify Grant's argument as one who sees benefits and losses within twentieth-century evangelicalism. I regularly enter Gordon-Conwell Theological Seminary's South Hamilton, MA, campus by "Billy Graham Way," so his impact and the various emphases of evangelicalism are not lost on me. Graham also recognized the ambivalence of technology's possibility and limits while also making use of tech in his own ministry. See Billy Graham, "Technology, Faith, and Human Shortcomings," TED Talk, February 1998, https://www.ted.com/talks/billy_graham_on_technology_and_faith. Part of the challenge with twentieth-century evangelicalism resides in the simplicity of its gospel message and its ability to reach large numbers, particularly through technological means, coupled with the losses incurred through reductionistic tendencies and easy accommodation to individualism, consumer culture, and political persuasion. Its simplicity is also vulnerable to instrumentalist views of salvation when pursued without significant transformation, commitment, discipleship, and communal responsibility.

[169]   I recognize individual choice in salvation and practice as central themes in the Second Great Awakening and twentieth-century American Protestant evangelicalism. See Billy Graham, How to Become a Christian (Good News, 2016), 1–6. While individual choice is significant for accountability and agency in Christian formation, emphasis on different theological themes related to Jonathan Edwards and the First Great Awakening helps curtail American individualism (somewhat) in its emphasis on divine sovereignty as well as the beauty of nature pointing to theological realities. See chapter 3, where I explore the importance of Edwards's Protestant theology as a helpful corrective against instrumental views of nature only in its holistic glory and opportunity for contemplation/reflection. See Jonathan Edwards, "Heaven Is a World of Love," in The Works of Jonathan Edwards, vol. 8, Ethical Writings, ed. Paul Ramsey (Yale University Press, 1989), 366–97; idem, "Images or Shadows of the Divine," in Selected Writings of Jonathan Edwards, 2nd ed., ed. Harold P. Simonson (Waveland Press, 2004), 161–62, 167–68. That said, I also offer a caveat that Edwards was by no means a perfect saint, given he also reflected the bias and social sin of his day by owning at least two slaves during his lifetime. His son, Jonathan Edwards Jr., later critiqued this practice. George Marsden also notes Edwards's ambivalence in his willingness to own slaves while recognizing theological problems with the overarching African slave trade (George M. Marsden, Jonathan Edwards: A Life [Yale University Press, 2003], 255–58).

practice, the new world departed from nature's teleological goals associated with mystery and discovery, opening the way for more instrumental and mechanistic views of nature that welcomed industrialism into its dominion and economic mastery.[170]

However, Grant does not confine the technocratic empire to the democratic West alone. He also recognizes Eastern socialist and communist cultures demonstrating control over nature through technology and science. Like Ellul, he finds civilization in both the West and East vulnerable to technological rule and annihilation given the proliferation of weapons for mass war and technological bureaucracy, whether through private means or state control.[171] "Both sail down the same river in different boats"—the river of technological empire.[172] Interestingly, today's political scene is not entirely different given the role of mass media, social media, propaganda, and polarization at work in different geopolitical contexts. Whether Russia, China, Brazil, Myanmar, Brexit in Britain, or the 2016, 2020, and 2024 US presidential elections, each have been impacted by the technological empire even if there remain significant differences in overall political freedoms. Tech provides a new means of fueling power with words—even weaponizing political speech. Nearly everyone is impacted by the rule of technological means.

More specifically, the technological empire's presence in the West hinges on the absence of philosophical and religious meaning, here called contemplation.[173] Without contemplative values from nature, philosophy, or religious ethics, industrial society is vulnerable to nihilism.[174] Without external or objective ethics, the combination of individual freedom and industry tends toward technocratic rule. Science and technology serve human purposes—beyond good and evil, to play on the title of Fredric Nietzsche—apart from derived ends inscribed in nature. Grant critiques Western culture as subject to the dominant technocratic milieu, leaving the meaning of nature open and the community enslaved to individual freedom writ large thanks to market demands. Shoshana Zuboff calls this "instrumentarian," in which the Other, Big Data, observes individuals to influence—if not control—in human decision-making.[175] Nature is not

---

[170]   Grant, "In Defence of North America," 7.

[171]   Grant, "In Defence of North America," 18–22.

[172]   Grant, "In Defence of North America," 18–22.

[173]   Grant, "In Defence of North America," 18–22.

[174]   Grant, "In Defence of North America," 26.

[175]   Zuboff, *Age of Surveillance Capitalism*, 376ff., fig. 4, and 396–97.

simply instrumental. We are. Humans now supply the resources for profit and corporate benefit. Without God, transcendence, or contemplation, nihilism leaves a vacuum for a new "techno-ontology," in which technology defines the value and worth of human reality.[176]

Whereas Taylor's *A Secular Age* concludes in describing "the immanent frame" by which Western culture broadly shifts from belief in God to a pluralist perspective largely dominated by unbelief in the transcendent, he also cites "a number of ways in which our modern culture is restless at the barriers of the human sphere . . . far from settling in to a comfortable unbelief."[177] Instead, Taylor finds the present milieu fractured given the range of meanings now pursued in the wake of expressive individualism in which individuals pursue their sense of inner destiny.[178] Consumer culture is one more variant that operates in the "immanent frame," offering short-term happiness that caters to individual desire apart from transcendent reference.

Taylor and Grant offer sober accounts on the ways in which theology contributed to our current fragmentation through the Protestant Reformation's emphasis on Scripture alone, freedom, and modern liberalism's focus on reason and autonomy. Making way for what Taylor calls "excarnation," he describes "the steady disembodying of spiritual life, so that it is less and less carried in deeply meaningful bodily forms and lies more and more 'in the head.'"[179] Protestant theology in its departure from contemplation beholding the mystery and beauty of nature or the sacraments can err on more rationalistic forms of excarnation that deemphasize the incarnation.[180]

Here Protestant theology and practice is subject to critique for the ways in which it contributes to our sense of alienation from our embodied selves in nature and community.[181] Instead, confusion ensues from

[176]   See Moyse, *Art of Living*, 34.
[177]   Taylor, *A Secular Age*, 726–27.
[178]   Taylor, *A Secular Age*, 727.
[179]   Taylor, *A Secular Age*, 771.
[180]   Turning to Ivan Illich, Taylor critiques the way in which institutional Christianity can become the bureaucratic hardening of the church that misses love as its primary motivation, while institutional medicine can alienate the patient through scientific progress rather than attentive presence. When institutionalized or domesticated in problematic ways, "corrupted Christianity gives rise to the modern" just like the demands of bureaucratic paperwork can overlook the bedside need for presence in medicine (Taylor, *A Secular Age*, 740).
[181]   I'm comfortable critiquing and challenging Reformed Protestant theology and evangelicalism as one situated within the movement. As a participant, it's

theology's individualistic focus that is inadvertently shaped by market pressures. In this way, Christian theology participates in advancing the technological empire through its implicit desire to improve nature alongside industry. Denuding nature allows for utilitarian approaches driven by individualism and market demands to take over, resulting in nihilistic impulses that deny transcendence and accountability for our technological actions. Like Augustinian pride, we benevolently play God in our attempts to control nature through digital devices resulting in social isolation and technological medicine warding off death and disease.[182] But in pursuing ease, comfort, and control, the technological empire promises benefits while also posing confusion and harm.[183]

According to Crouch, this is technology's false promise.[184] Blurring the line between magic and science, technology offers benefits but also drawbacks. Flipping the script between person and machine, or user and thing, results in individuals becoming "used things." Citing 2 Peter 2:9, Augustine acknowledges that people become slaves to whatever masters them.[185] Technology—along with economics, politics, medicine, and philosophical ideologies—becomes *chthonic* or "lordless powers" that bear down on us when we act as creatures alienated from the Creator of such capacities.[186] Stripped of their origin and purpose, our human capacities for great good become disordered and in turn, bear down on us. Changing us into its servants, the flip side of our creative technological powers appear like *The Sorcerer's Apprentice* personified in Disney's

---

important to evaluate trends in the past, questioning cultural (at times syncretistic) assumptions while seeking faithful interpretation of Scripture and wisdom for present and future practice.

[182]   Through the benevolent aims of healing and the efficient means of controlling our surrounding environment, technological creation often compounds harm. See Raymond Downing, *Death and Life in America*, 2nd ed. (Cascade, 2021); L. S. Dugdale, *The Lost Art of Dying* (HarperOne, 2020).

[183]   Downing, *Death and Life in America*; Dugdale, *Lost Art of Dying*.

[184]   Crouch, *Life We're Looking For*, 61.

[185]   Augustine, *City of God*, trans. Henry Bettenson (Penguin Books, 1984), 139; Augustine, *City of God* (trans. Babcock), p. 71. Shoshana Zuboff notes the oldest political questions, saying, "Home or exile? Lord or subject? Master or slave? These are eternal themes of knowledge, authority, and power that can never be settled for all time. There is no end of history; each generation must assert its will and imagination as new threats require us to retry the case in every age" (Zuboff, *Age of Surveillance Capitalism*, 3).

[186]   Karl Barth, *The Christian Life: Church Dogmatics* IV/4, *Lecture Fragments*, trans. Geoffrey W. Bromiley (Eerdmans, 1981), 213–20.

Fantasia where the magic of dancing brooms and cookware turn on the main character, Mickey Mouse.[187] While illustrative, the fable's moral holds essential truths: creation (in this case, technology) bears the weight of controlling its creator(s).[188] The lust to dominate now becomes the dominating lust over its owner. Habit becomes necessity.[189] Restlessness, unending.

Former Google design ethicist and cofounder of Center for Humane Technology, Tristan Harris, agrees: "Any sufficiently advanced technology is indistinguishable from magic."[190] The problem with magic, however, is that it overpromises through the power of illusion or, what Augustine might call, deception.[191] Overpromising and underdelivering, we find ourselves in a matrix of the technological empire. Through its demands on our time and attention, tech exploits human vulnerability, whether through data mining, algorithmic nudges, or its more troubling form involving fake news, deepfakes, or large language models (including ChatGPT) when imitating human voice or image without accountability or limits.[192] Karl Barth's description of chthonic powers preceding the new digital empire sounds hauntingly relevant:

> In simplifying and easing his life, they also complicate it and make it more difficult. They take away his little anxieties but create new and bigger ones. They seem to promise him courage and a greater zest for life, but increased worry about life is the fulfilment of their promise. Like the spiritual forces, but in a way that is felt more directly, the chthonic powers, which for a change draw downward instead of up, serve in and of themselves to bind the man who has broken free from God, to put him under obligation, to tyrannize him, to lead

---

[187] Crouch, *Life We're Looking For*, 62; Paul Dukas, dir., "The Sorcerer's Apprentice," in *Fantasia* (Walt Disney Productions, 1940).

[188] Barth, *Christian Life*, 220; Crouch, *Life We're Looking For*, 62–63.

[189] Augustine, *Confessions*, p. 140.

[190] Harris, quoted in Orlowski, *Social Dilemma*. Harris also acknowledges the vulnerability and social anxiety exploited through social media, saying, "We're training and conditioning a whole new generation of people that when we are uncomfortable or lonely or uncertain or afraid we have a digital pacifier for ourselves that is kind of atrophying our own ability to deal with that."

[191] Harris, quoted in Orlowski, *Social Dilemma*.

[192] Mustafa Suleyman and Michael Bhaskar, *The Coming Wave: Technology, Power, and the 21st Century's Greatest Dilemma* (Crown, 2024), 61–78, 107–16.

him where he does not want to go, to rob him of his freedom under the pretext and appearance of granting every kind of freedom.[193]

In exchange for freedom, the *chthonic* or created power binds him. The empire gives while taking away.

Social media and digital devices serve as the new chthonic powers that incur distractions through temporary benefits and shallow dopamine surges. Bringing short-term satisfaction and long-term deprivation, the tech empire shapes our personal, relational, and sociopolitical health. Our time watching advertisements yields large returns for these companies—the most profitable in the history of humanity.[194] The ambivalence of the new digital empire and its cost to our lives continues to unfold. The extent to which the new empire influences and even controls us will be further explored in the next chapter, as we question the role of its limits and the need for wisdom.

[193] Barth, *Christian Life*, 228–29. In utilizing the theology of Karl Barth, I offer a caveat given his problematic affair with his assistant and mistress, Charlotte von Kirschbaum. I do not condone this relationship but recognize the challenge in citing human authors in their intentional and unintentional choices involving sin and moral harm. See Christiane Tietz, *Karl Barth: A Life in Conflict* (Oxford University Press, 2023).

[194] Zuboff, *Age of Surveillance Capitalism*.

2
Knowledge Without Wisdom?

DIGITAL TECHNOLOGY AS THE NEW BABEL

In the April 2022 *Atlantic* story "Why the Last 10 Years of American Life Have Been Uniquely Stupid," social psychologist Jonathan Haidt compares social media to the famous Tower of Babel. Recognizing the challenges incurred through the "like" and "share" buttons designed for social media platforms like Twitter (now X), Facebook, and Instagram, Haidt delineates the rise and fall of Babel's tower. What began as congenial public updates about one's social life became emotionally driven content that dissolved into anger and intensified political polarization, threatening democracy.[1] Communication and the desire to connect somehow ended in confusion and moral crisis over the course of a decade. Haidt continues, "But Babel is not a story about tribalism; it's a story about the fragmentation of everything. It's about the shattering of all that had seemed solid, the scattering of people who had been a community."[2]

---

[1]   Jonathan Haidt, "Why the Last 10 Years of American Life Have Been Uniquely Stupid," *Atlantic*, April 11, 2022, https://www.theatlantic.com/magazine/archive/2022/05/social-media-democracy-trust-babel/629369/; see also Paul Lewis, "'Our Minds Can Be Hijacked': The Tech Insiders Who Fear a Smartphone Dystopia," *Guardian*, October 6, 2017, https://www.theguardian.com/technology/2017/oct/05/smartphone-addiction-silicon-valley-dystopia.

[2]   Haidt, "Why the Last 10 Years." I also qualify the implication that life in the United States prior to social media involved strong community ties without room for critique. The advent of social media allowed for public pressure among

But how did this shattering take place and why? Haidt offers helpful analysis, drawing from social and moral psychology that critiques the ways algorithms feed on emotionally charged information that spreads across the internet instantaneously like wildfire, sparking outrage and negative social dynamics.[3] Through outrage, togetherness and community splinters into fragmentation and separation. The term *Babel* is apt for linguistic and social considerations, but also moral and theological reasons. Saint Augustine was aware of these same dynamics. An astute observer of moral behavior—psychologically and theologically—one might diagnose his entire anthropology as one moving from unity to disunity or togetherness to separateness while longing for wholeness and belonging. Whether picking up his *Confessions*, *City of God*, or commentaries *On Genesis*, Augustine describes the theological fragmentation at work in the individual and society. Yet alongside this sense of fragmentation remains his longing for wisdom—not simply knowledge—in his search for truth that coincides with his search for identity and belonging. Augustine's fundamental restlessness drove his desire to know and understand not only information but also its meaning.

Perhaps most telling in Haidt's diagnosis is his description of Zuckerberg's plan to "rewire the way people spread and consume information."[4] In his 2012 plans to make Facebook public, Zuckerberg wrote a letter to his investors "giving them 'the power to share' [that] would help them . . . 'once again transform many of our core institutions and industries.'"[5] With the power to share came many questions, most notably concerning the purpose of sharing. In other words, the power to share what? Or the power to share about whom? To whom? Zuckerberg lacked a

---

dissenting voices challenging the status quo, particularly related to issues of sexual abuse, racial injustice (invoking the #MeToo and #BLM movements), and the faith-oriented Jude 3 Project. As Andy Crouch acknowledges, all institutions need change, particularly when harboring injustice. While institutions are gifts, they are often broken with sin. Change is necessary not only to survive but also thrive (Andy Crouch, *Playing God: Redeeming the Gift of Power* [IVP, 2013], 169–220). That said, the increased acerbic tone involving deconstructive dialogue without constructive appeal followed by the cacophony of voices that surfaced during the 2016, 2020, and 2024 US presidential elections, in addition to information exchange during the COVID-19 pandemic, reflect disarray in politics and communication that continues to unravel through heightened political polarization.

3   See Jas 3:6–12.
4   Haidt, "Why the Last 10 Years."
5   Haidt, "Why the Last 10 Years."

clear predicate or object to his verb, leaving interpretation for "sharing" exposed to the masses. And in so doing, his goal to rewire the way people spread and consume information results not only in Haidt's dismal psychological diagnosis, but also Babel's hairline fracture: a moral and engineering fracture small enough to topple the greatest of towers built on human ingenuity in its ability for everyone to build a name—or image—for oneself.

COMMUNICATION AND CONFUSION

Haidt is not the first contemporary author concerned with the problem of technology and the pitfalls of communicating through mass media. Jacques Ellul critiqued modern society as one captive to technique, which he defines as "nothing more than means and the ensemble of means . . . in the reality of modern life, *the means, it would seem, are more important than the ends.*"[6] Differentiating between intrinsic and instrumental purposes, Ellul recognizes the modern era privileges efficiency or the instrumental means to accomplish some project rather than the project itself. "The means" become primary as opposed to the purpose or goal associated with a particular action.[7]

Virtual engagement reflects how we often digitize and instrumentalize nature. Instead of riding bikes in the real world or learning a new physical skill, we watch YouTube videos telling us how to pursue these activities.[8] Activities posted in the digital realm are no longer pursued simply for their own sake, but for the purpose of being watched—or for the purpose of generating money. In an economy based on attention and instrumental exchange, productivity and performance become supreme. Hence the race to create ever more content and YouTube shorts. Garnering our time and attention exposes more users to advertisers. Instead of pursuing goods for intrinsic value, we pursue them for instrumental purposes.

[6] Jacques Ellul, *The Technological Society*, trans. John Wilkinson (Knopf, 1964), 19 (emphasis added).
[7] Jeffrey Bishop critiques medicine from a similar perspective. Lacking metaphysical premodern causes, such as Aristotle's formal and final causes, modern medicine and society rely on efficient and material causes (Jeffrey P. Bishop, *The Anticipatory Corpse* [University of Notre Dame Press, 2011]).
[8] Haidt distinguishes between play-based childhood and phone-based childhood. The latter involves less physical risk and activity while allowing for more online activity (Jonathan Haidt, *The Anxious Generation: How the Great Rewiring of Childhood Is Causing an Epidemic of Mental Illness* [Penguin Books, 2024], 49–110, 180–87, 214–15).

Mediating the world through mass technology, human agents lose a sense of the original goals implicit in the natural world. This could be mass food production (such as the chemicals involved in baking bread) or mass communication in which information spreads to a large group without context, purpose, nuance, individuality, reciprocity, or response.[9] Such communication remains vulnerable to mass control or propaganda through a kind of group think, herd mentality, or its opposite, the descent into triviality.[10]

Communications and media theorist Neil Postman issues a similar warning through his prophetic works *Technopoly* and *Amusing Ourselves to Death*. Writing in the 1980s and '90s, Postman opens with the provocative quote from his mentor Marshall McLuhan saying, "The medium is the message."[11] Offering a sobering diagnosis on the state of mass communication, Postman recognizes how technology and digital media changes "the structure of our interests: the things we think about. They alter the character of our symbols: the things we think with. And they alter the nature of our community: the arena in which thoughts develop."[12] Technology controls the medium by which we communicate and therefore the content as well. Like Ellul explored, technology is concerned with the "means" rather than the "end." Flipping the ends for the means, the "medium is the message."[13] With its control over the ways we communicate, information shared through new technologies alters the meaning of our communication.

Numerous technological examples alter the way we encounter the world, whether it be the mechanical clock, printing press, or telescope.[14] Outlining the change from a medieval tools-based culture in which tools serve natural purposes or end goals, Postman's *Technopoly* describes how technology "attacks" culture, changing the symbolic world of "tradition, social mores, myth, politics, ritual, and religion."[15] His overarching

---

9   Haidt, *Anxious Generation*, 21–22, 327, 332–34; Jacques Ellul, *Propaganda: The Formation of Men's Attitudes*, trans. Konrad Kellen and Jean Lerner (Knopf, 1968), 6–8.

10   Ellul, *Propaganda*, 6–8.

11   Neil Postman, *Technopoly: The Surrender of Culture to Technology* (Vintage Books, 1993), 14.

12   Postman, *Technopoly*, 9, 20.

13   Postman repeats Marshall McLuhan's phrase "The medium is the message," in Postman, *Technopoly*, 13–14.

14   Postman, *Technopoly*, 28.

15   Postman, *Technopoly*, 28.

historiography parallels Ellul, Craig Gay, and Charles Taylor's argument in *A Secular Age*, whereby modernity replaces the medieval world, pursuing autonomy and power (control) over nature through science, mechanization (specialization/compartmentalization), and organization (bureaucracy).[16] Technopoly occurs when technique becomes dominant, and new technologies compete for mainstream worldviews with the power "to change everything."[17] Wisdom is no longer derived or discovered but created as part of a system of practice.[18] Technopoly occurs when technology becomes the primary mode and meaning of knowledge.

The advent of the telegraph serves as a key example of technopoly in which communication occurs without context.[19] Communication suddenly traveled faster than railway speed (35 mph). Traversing time and space with the speed of electricity removed information from its source location. Without context shaped by the human limits of time and space, information takes on new meaning and statements become vulnerable to misinterpretation. A few words or phrases could now traverse a continent with little to no surrounding narrative.[20] Postman illustrates,

> In the United States, the telegraph erased state lines, collapsed regions, and, by wrapping the continent in an information grid, created the possibility of a unified nation-state. But more than this, telegraphy created the idea of context-free information—that is, the idea that the value of information need not be tied to any function it

---

[16] Ellul, *Technological Society*; Postman, *Technopoly*, 37, 83–87; see also Charles Taylor, *A Secular Age* (Belknap Press, 2007); Allen Verhey, *Nature and Altering It* (Eerdmans, 2010), 22–33.

[17] Postman, *Technopoly*, 16, 18; see also "techno-ontology" in Ashley Moyse, *The Art of Living for a Technological Age: Toward a Humanizing Performance* (Fortress, 2021), 39–42.

[18] Postman says technopoly formally occurs following Frederick W. Taylor's creation of the scientific management system akin to Henry Ford's conveyor belt. The scientific management system makes all life more efficient—whether applied to the railroad, armed forces, legal profession, home, church, or education (Postman, *Technopoly*, 51).

[19] Postman, *Technopoly*, 67–68.

[20] Postman opens *Technopoly* by discussing the disagreement between Thamus and Plato over the invention of writing. Plato finds the written word problematic in its separation from the oral tradition and its reliance on memory or wisdom. Plato fears the reliance on recollection over wisdom in which individuals lose the ability to "think for themselves" while relying on others for wisdom rather than the philosopher king (Postman, *Technopoly*, 3–5).

might serve in social and political decision-making and action. The telegraph made information into a commodity, a "thing," that could be bought and sold irrespective of its uses or meaning.[21]

As commodity or thing, information is now bought and sold, changing the nature of communication in its purpose and ability to create shared interest around a common good.

Postman expands his description in *Amusing Ourselves to Death*. The news of the day—a kind of telegraphic information spread—becomes fragmented conversation and descends into irrelevance, impotence, and incoherence.[22] Individuals consume waves of information from around the globe often with little ability to change or make a difference. The ability to change or make a difference has become heightened with the advent of social media, where posting in the virtual world could directly impact political movements in real time.[23] Communication popularly spreads in ways that

[21]   Postman, *Technopoly*, 67–68.
[22]   Neil Postman, *Amusing Ourselves to Death* (Penguin Books, 1985), 65, 113.
[23]   Interestingly, social media changed experiences of low "information-action" ratio given that individuals can now spread news on the internet for a specific cause or social justice movement. Political movements such as the 2011 Arab Spring, the 2014 ALS Ice Bucket Challenge, and more recently the Black Lives Matter movement following the deaths of Black Americans, including the deaths of George Floyd, Ahmaud Arbery, and Breonna Taylor, raised broader public consciousness. Shared information on social media significantly impacted public opinion and to some degree social change. These movements influenced public awareness while also attracting detractors on issues of criminal justice and economic practices involving redlining. See Bryan Stevenson, *Just Mercy: A Story of Justice and Redemption* (OneWorld, 2015); William J. Stuntz, *The Collapse of American Criminal Justice* (Belknap Press, 2013); and Matthew T. Martens, *Reforming Criminal Justice: A Christian Proposal* (Crossway, 2023). Alternatively, the 2023–24 spread of information leading to campus protests regarding the conflict in Gaza between Israel and Hamas involved confusion and university upheaval in the midst of a complex global challenge, with little opportunity for constructive conversation, dialogue, and nuance. In the latter case, action spread quickly while information continued to unfold in the United States and around the globe. See Isabelle Taft, Alex Lemonides, Lazaro Gamio, and Anna Betts, "Campus Protests Led to More Than 3100 Arrests, but Many Charges Have Been Dropped," *New York Times*, July 21, 2024, https://www.nytimes.com/2024/07/21/us/campus-protests-arrests.html; see also Saif Hasnat and Mujib Mashal, "At Least 70 Dead as Bangladesh Protests Grow; Curfew Is Reinstated," *New York Times*, August 4, 2024, https://www.nytimes.com/2024/08/04/world/asia/bangladesh-protests-curfew.html.

are "sensational, fragmented, and impersonal."[24] Knowledge spreads in vast quantities, leading to a broad array of responses from action to paralysis.

The spread of rapid information can lead to impulsive response on the one hand or to apathy on the other.[25] In 2020 the word "doomscrolling" entered the English dictionary tied to the inundation of negative news and information spread following COVID-19.[26] Interpretation is subjective and expertise democratized to anyone regardless of age, understanding, or depth on a given topic. Scrolling the internet, we are left with information overload much like a bloated gut following an unhealthy meal. But these symptoms often manifest through emotions—some positive, but often negative, whether apathy, anger, disdain, irritation, or sadness. Emotions are contagious, and we often reflect the mood shared whether in conversation or online.[27] Fatigued, we lack the moral tools to interpret words and arguments with wisdom.

Postman identifies an additional primal drive within this bleary schema: pursuing desire and pleasure for its own sake. Aldous Huxley's *Brave New World* envisions a dystopian technopoly that devolves into "a trivial culture," captive to the "feelies."[28] The rise of therapeutic self-help culture and expressive individualism in its preference for autonomy over communal obligation allows the digital culture to spread triviality and vice at high volume. Pursuing pleasure for its own sake equates entertainment and distraction with the good life.

Comparing Huxley to George Orwell's *1984*, Postman concludes, "In short, Orwell feared that what we hate will ruin us. Huxley feared that what we love will ruin us."[29] Perhaps there is a little of both: Huxley in our susceptibility to pleasure and Orwell in our susceptibility to power.[30]

[24] Postman, *Amusing Ourselves to Death.*
[25] See Max Fisher, *The Chaos Machine: The Inside Story of How Social Media Rewired Our Minds and Our World* (Back Bay, 2023).
[26] 1A, "Slow Your Scroll: Fighting the Urge to Doomscroll," NPR, April 27, 2021, https://www.npr.org/2021/04/26/990894563/slow-your-scroll-fighting-the-urge-to -doomscroll.
[27] Catching feelings or emotions reminds me of Plato's passage on music in its power to impact our mood. See Plato, *Republic*, trans. G. M. A. Grube (Hackett, 1992), 3.398–403, pp. 74–79. The same might be said of the digital content we imbibe. See also Haidt, *Anxious Generation*, 162.
[28] Postman, *Amusing Ourselves to Death*, 139–41, 163.
[29] Postman, *Amusing Ourselves to Death*, 139–41, 163.
[30] Postman, *Amusing Ourselves to Death*, ix, 110–13, 136–40. Recognizing the power of emotion, Postman anticipated a culture centered around distraction

Similar to Augustine's overarching diagnosis on the power of love and its ability to strengthen or dissolve our individual and communal identities, Postman concludes his *Technopoly* appealing to the "loving resistance fighter" who seeks "a sense of coherence, purpose, meaning, and interconnectedness" in learning.[31] Rather than becoming slaves to mass information cloaked as knowledge, Postman urges loving resistance that questions the role of technology and its purpose in our lives. Like Augustine, Postman appeals to something transcendent to analyze current culture and the philosophical assumptions at work behind new tech and its impact on community. Augustine, longing for coherence, questions the meaning of words, context, and belonging as well as self-sought pleasure. We see this in his description of spectacle and the love of curiosity.

AUGUSTINE: CURIOSITY, SPECTACLE, AND DISORDERED LOVE

Trained as a rhetor, Augustine was familiar with the power of words and their connection to meaning. He also reflected on common human behavior, beginning with his own desire and its connection to curiosity or spectacle. Zena Hitz describes "The Love of Spectacle and Life at the Surfaces" in Augustine's theology.[32] She interprets Augustine's "curiosity" as disordered love of knowledge, using the translation "spectacle."[33] Building on multiple examples from the *Confessions*, Hitz highlights Augustine's friend Alypius in his love for Rome's gladiatorial or circus games. While initially resistant, Alypius accepts an invitation from his friends to attend the games, though promises to keep his eyes closed.

---

that is ironically susceptible to corporate interest in the West and government interest in the East. Shoshana Zuboff argues today's surveillance capitalism draws from "instrumentarian power" rather than "totalitarian power." Building on the work of behavioral scientist B. F. Skinner, Zuboff speaks of the "Other-One" or Big Data which observes human behavior. Suggesting human freedom as illusive, Skinner finds the "dominion of science" might influence or nudge human behavior in particular social directions. The new instrumentarian power developed by Silicon Valley sacrifices human freedom for knowledge that benefits corporate interest. Zuboff says, "Certainty replaces trust," whereby the "means of production" serve the "means of behavioral modification" (Shoshana Zuboff, *The Age of Surveillance Capitalism: The Fight for a Human Future at the New Frontier of Power* [Public Affairs, 2019], 351, 360–75).

[31] Postman, *Technopoly*, 186.

[32] Zena Hitz, *Lost in Thought: The Hidden Pleasures of an Intellectual Life* (Princeton University Press, 2020), 132ff.

[33] Hitz, *Lost in Thought*, 133.

But upon hearing the roar of the crowd, he opens them.[34] Augustine says, "As soon as he saw the blood, he at once drank in savagery and did not turn away. His eyes were riveted. He imbibed madness. Without any awareness of what was happening to him, he found delight in the murderous contest and was inebriated by bloodthirsty pleasure."[35] Alypius is lost to the emotions of the crowd.

Finding delight in lurid pleasure, Augustine reflects on this activity further in book 10 as "cupidity" in which "the lust of the eyes" (1 John 2:16) play a leading role among the senses.[36] He questions the purpose of curiosity in general. Seeing is the sense most related to knowledge. The term "see" can be applied metaphorically to phrases such as "See how that sounds, see what smells, see what tastes, see how hard that is."[37]

From here he distinguishes two kinds of knowing: The first form of knowing involves ordered curiosity with a specific end in mind. An example might involve pleasure, which pursues a specific object. However, the second form of curiosity seeks "what the experiences are like . . . out of a lust for experimenting and knowing."[38] The latter curiosity is more exploitative, "gamifying" an object or experience that is curious for its own end. Rather than seek to understand or build relationships with a differing person, place, or experience, disordered curiosity involves knowing for the sake of knowing or experience for the sake of experience. This kind of knowledge is stunted as opposed to knowing in relation to some object or end—whether an original or final goal such as truth, goodness, or beauty.

In this way, curiosity functions much like Ellul's description of technique as "means" or instrumental purposes pursued without meaning. Without a clear object, purpose, or end goal, the pursuit of sensory experience alone results in "vain inquisitiveness," an appetite for "knowing."[39] Citing examples of a mangled corpse, public shows (Roman theater or violent gladiatorial games), lizards and spiders catching their prey, or dogs chasing rabbits, Augustine reflects on such distractions as a "mass of empty thoughts" that can "rush in and cut short an aspiration of the

---

[34] Augustine, *Confessions*, trans. Henry Chadwick (Oxford University Press, 1991), 6.7.13, pp. 99–100.

[35] Augustine, *Confessions* 6.7.13, p. 101.

[36] Augustine, *Confessions* 10.35.54, p. 211.

[37] Augustine, *Confessions* 10.35.54, p. 211.

[38] Augustine, *Confessions* 10.35.54, p. 211.

[39] Augustine, *Confessions* 10.35.54, p. 211.

deepest importance."[40] The problem is when these empty thoughts become habit and one seeks knowledge in experience or thrill alone.[41]

Hitz offers contemporary examples of Augustine's sense of curiosity as disordered knowledge. Citing the internet as a "Cesspool for love of spectacle," she describes it as "the bottomless temple of lurid fascination, always inviting us to 'See what happens NEXT!'"[42] Recognizing infinite information available at our fingertips, video reels and newsfeeds remain endless, urging users to descend into a rabbit hole of semi-related or tangential information based on internet algorithms. Voyeuristically scrolling serves not only as escape and distraction, but also instrumental use of others' experiences. Staring into a screen, individuals dream of a different life than the one they're living.[43]

Hitz also describes ways in which social media platforms like Twitter (now X) prefer falsehood or deception over truth, circulating negative emotional content in higher quantities than post-"corrective" statements.[44] Treading in the shallow cesspool of information, she likens spectacle to "life at the surfaces," in which the opportunities are rife for disordered love of knowledge. Spectacle also involves the fantasy of superiority that "know-it-alls" feel when accumulating facts—whether academic or populist consumers.[45] The internet offers the illusion of knowledge through information consumption but offers little by way of interpretation, sounding much like Postman's critique and desire for coherence through the "loving resistance fighter."[46] Likewise, spectacle is closely connected to Augustine's theme on the order of love expounded throughout his various works.

ORDERED AND DISORDERED LOVE

To read Augustine is to find the heart of his theology: love. Humans are creatures fundamentally motivated by desire. This love orients us toward our final telos. James K. A. Smith says our desires "propel us in that direction—like the magnetic power of the pole working on the existential needle of our hearts. You are what you love because you live toward what

---

40   Augustine, *Confessions* 10.35.57, p. 213.
41   Augustine, *Confessions* 10.35.57, p. 212.
42   Hitz, *Lost in Thought*, 135.
43   Wendell Berry, *The Memory of Old Jack* (Counterpoint, 1974).
44   Hitz, *Lost in Thought*, 135.
45   Hitz, *Lost in Thought*, 137.
46   Postman, *Technopoly*, 183–90.

you want."[47] We move and act on what we believe about ourselves—and what we most desire.

This personifies the primary thesis driving Augustine's famous *City of God*: "Two loves have built two cities. Love of self, even to the point of contempt for God, made the earthly city; and love of God, even to the point of contempt for self, made the heavenly city."[48] For Augustine, we are primarily defined by what—or whom—we most love. This is the "restless" drive or desire propelling his philosophical and spiritual journey in the *Confessions* and political theory in the *City of God* in addition to his various works from sermons, commentaries on Scripture, and philosophical treatises.

But it is Augustine's description in *On Christian Teaching* that sets forth his order of love in detail. In the opening book, Augustine describes what is known as his *uti et frui*, his categories entitled "use and enjoy." Offering a metaphor for the journey of life, Augustine says, "There are some things that are to be enjoyed, some which are to be used, and some whose function is both to enjoy and use. Those which are to be enjoyed make us happy; those which are to be used assist us and give us a boost, so to speak, as we press on towards our happiness."[49]

Enjoyment in its delineated meaning is associated with happiness or the final goal as the good life. Use involves everything that relates back to this purpose. He further explains the significance of enjoyment in the following way: "To enjoy something is to hold fast to it in love for its own sake. To use something is to apply whatever it may be to the purpose of obtaining what you love—if indeed it is something that ought to be loved."[50] In other words, Augustine's Latin term *frui*, translated as "enjoy(-ment)," relates to an ultimate end, also known as the final purpose, *telos*, or destination.

Returning to the journey metaphor, Augustine reminds his readers that they are pilgrims on a path toward their eternal, heavenly home. In this life they experience temporary goods for use in relation to what they enjoy

[47]   James K. A. Smith, *You Are What You Love* (Brazos, 2016), 12–13.

[48]   Augustine, *The City of God*, abridged study edition, trans. William Babcock, notes by Boniface Ramsey, abridgment by Joseph T. Kelley (New City Press, 2018), 14.28, p. 310.

[49]   Augustine, *On Christian Teaching*, trans. R. P. H. Green (Oxford University Press, 1997), 1.2.4, p. 9.

[50]   Augustine, *On Christian Teaching* 1.2.4, p. 9.

as their final, eternal good in God. Maintaining these distinctions is significant. Only an eternal good, the Trinity itself, can be enjoyed. All other things are subsidiary goods in relation to this original and final good.

Augustine further delineates what these many things involve, including things that are like us, our neighbor, as well as ourselves. In this way he builds on the command to love God and neighbor as oneself. He does not stop there, however. He continues and includes love for the created and material world.[51] Paralleling his description of the goodness in creation in his commentaries *On Genesis* and the *Confessions*, Augustine acknowledges the entire cosmos or created world as originally good. The world is good because God made it, recognizing the Creator as its original source. With an original source in God, the created world was intended for good purposes or ends.

This core idea will be significant for Augustine's description of evil as privation when he departs from the Manicheans and their dualistic approach to the cosmos (spirit vs. material).[52] Longing to understand why he does bad things or pursues evil, the quest in Augustine's own life journey as told through the *Confessions* is a deep look at his own interior life and motives. For Augustine, all created things are good insofar as they derive from the original source of their goodness, the Creator, and live in relation to this source.[53] They are referential goods given their created status. Insofar as created goods depart from this origin and end goal do we find them subject to abuse or misuse. Created objects relate to a beginning and end with means tied to their end goals. When the means are separated from the end, they lose their meaning; incoherence and fragmentation follow.

Created things should relate as means to the greatest good or purpose in the Creator God. While this may sound like instrumental reasoning to modern ears, the reasoning only makes sense when fundamentally aligned with intrinsic meaning in the natural world. While the distinction between natural and supernatural ends are later formalized in the theology of St. Thomas Aquinas, Augustine does not separate these categories, suggesting all things and virtue relate to the ultimate, eternal good in God.[54]

---

[51] Augustine, *On Christian Teaching* 1.28.

[52] Augustine, *Confessions* 4–5.

[53] Augustine, *On Christian Teaching*, 1.29.30, pp. 22–23.

[54] Augustine, *The Morals of the Catholic Church*, in *Basic Writings of St. Augustine*, vol. 1, ed. Whitney J. Oates (Random House, 1948), chs. 15, pp. 331–32; 18,

Things have value insofar as they exist in a created universe. God's good intention for creation supplies meaning and value to all things. Instrumental purposes are not to be separated from intrinsic purposes entirely, thus cheapening or altering the meaning of created goods. Michael Sandel's *What Money Can't Buy* offers a broad critique of social goods, whether sex, reproduction, or even reading for pleasure when these practices become coopted by instrumental or monetary exchange.[55] Instead, original and final goals coincide together in unity. While predating Aquinas, Augustine anticipates what is called formal and final causes through his initial description on use and enjoyment that relates to final ends. In this schema, created goods are best understood in relation to their final purpose. Formal and final causes (primary causes) unify efficient and material causes (as secondary, creaturely agents), bringing together instrumental and intrinsic value in coherence.[56]

If the philosophical categories seem illusive, consider a literary example. Twentieth-century writer C. S. Lewis offers one of the best contemporary allegories for Augustine's ordered and disordered loves in his short work *The Great Divorce*.[57] Set in the imagined afterlife, the story opens with the narrator waking up in a grey town in which houses are separated by great distance through time and space. When the narrator eventually

pp. 335–36. Modern scholarship debates Augustine's understanding of the neighbor or other humans as part of those objects to be "used" in loving God. This description sounds troubling in a post-Kantian world in which persons are to be treated as ends and not means only. In his own words, Augustine says that humans can enjoy one another and God together. As eternal beings, they have the capacity to share in this eternal love in ways that other creatures do not. Conor Kelly acknowledges ways that contemporary scholars contextualize Augustine, offering "a slightly more expansive interpretation" of Augustine's theology. On sharing in God with the neighbor, Kelly cites Sarah Stewart-Kroeker, saying, "When this doctrine is combined with the incarnation, it becomes possible to talk of enjoying a range of finite goods in which God's presence is mediated sacramentally." With Kroeker, Kelly also affirms that no finite good may serve as one's ultimate love so as to prevent idolatry (Conor Kelly, *The Fullness of Free Time: A Theological Account of Leisure and Recreation in the Moral Life* [Georgetown University Press, 2020], 16, 19).

[55] Michael J. Sandel, *What Money Can't Buy: The Moral Limits of Markets* (Farrar, Straus and Giroux, 2012).

[56] Thomas Aquinas, *Summa Theologica*, trans. Fathers of the English Dominican Province (Ave Maria, 1948).

[57] I'm grateful for Paul R. Kolbet's suggestion I read C. S. Lewis's *The Great Divorce* alongside Augustine's *On Christian Teaching* while taking his Augustine seminar course at Boston College during the fall semester 2008.

gathers with other individuals at a bus stop, the crowd bickers and argues at length over seemingly trivial nonsense—as if arguing for the sake of arguing.[58] From there, Lewis's narrator and his fellow companions ascend to what's described as a solid world filled with light. Illuminated next to the light, he realizes that he and his companions are mere shadows, ghost-like apparitions diminished in form and substance. In this new setting, each ghost encounters solid people that were former relationships with the ghosts during their earthly life.

It's here that Lewis portrays the heart of Augustine's order of love. Each solid person's conversation with their ghost, a former coworker, friendship, or family member, involves an appeal to reorient their loves. A painter encounters a peer who reminds him why he first started painting: for the love and enjoyment of beauty over production. A professor reminds his colleague why he first started writing: for the pursuit of truth over publication and fame. A woman encounters a friend, reminding her she married for love rather than controlling her husband through reform. A man is reminded why his lust falls short of a greater desire found in communion. In their journey toward an eternal home, each ghost is confronted with their sense of disordered loves and how they've sought the means as their happiness or final goal as opposed to the appropriate end. Exchanging means for ends, their life and existence become dim reflections (ghosts) of what they were originally intended to be (enspirited bodies) and even more so what they might become as re-created, solid, or transfigured selves.

In this way, Lewis, along with Augustine, portrays an anthropology by which creatures are most themselves when aligned with their original design and final purpose. To quote another early church father, Irenaeus: "The glory of God is the human fully alive."[59] When creatures align with their creaturely origins and goals, they are most happy or fulfilled. When they depart, loving the self first, they diminish and become miserable in spirit and attitude.

For Augustine, this is the key to understanding ourselves. He says in the opening line of the *Confessions*, "You have made us for yourself, and our heart is restless until it rests in you."[60] We are restless, desirous

---

58   C. S. Lewis, *The Great Divorce* (Touchstone, 1996), 20.

59   Irenaeus, *Against the Heresies: Books 4 and 5*, trans. Scott D. Moringiello and John J. Dillion, Ancient Christian Writers 72 (Paulist, 2024), 4.20, pp. 5–7; SC 100, pp. 640–42, 644–48.

60   Augustine, *Confessions* 1.1, p. 3.

creatures made for an eternal end and completion in God alone. Every lower good that we place our gaze upon—or faith, hope, and love in—falls short of this ultimate good. But they do not only fall short in Augustine's description of evil as privation. Disordered loves have a power or weight to undo these original ends. As seen through Lewis's *Great Divorce*, the creatures diminish in their essence and existence when depicted as ghosts. On the contrary, the solid creatures are fully alive in the presence of their Creator in heaven. Removed from their life source or meaning, the ghostly loves are deprived of the fullness for which they were originally intended. As Lewis says in *Mere Christianity*, "Evil is only ever spoiled goodness."[61] Privation or evil is an undoing of our creaturely origins and ends through disordered love.

Looking back at his own life, Augustine considers the motives and love leading him through his early life. Analyzing why he participated in particular behaviors, whether pursuing sexual encounters for lust, stealing pears for its thrill, or building his career as a Roman orator for success, he finds each experience falls short because it lacks relationship to the ultimate good in God, and thus, meaning and understanding. As Lewis says, it's not that our desires are "too strong, but too weak."[62] Seeking rest in lower goods leaves the individual dissatisfied and longing for more. But reorienting our loves through repentance and faith frees the will to love God and creation more deeply. Negative habits that become necessary (or addictive) need reform through renewed direction at higher ends. Becoming what we love, we unite with the thing or being we most love.

But this is easier said than done. Augustine is deeply aware of the human proclivity for self-deception and weakness. In fact, his anthropology is concerned with the dual temptation of ignorance and weakness from original sin. Delineating fallen anthropology in *On Free Choice of the Will*, *City of God*, *On Genesis*, and *Confessions*, Augustine acknowledges that creatures fell from a state of grace in which they were once "ensouled bodies" who were "able not to sin," *posse non peccare*.[63] But in losing their original union with God through choosing their own good

[61]   C. S. Lewis, *Mere Christianity*, in *The Complete C. S. Lewis Signature Classics* (HarperOne, 2002), 45.
[62]   C. S. Lewis, *The Weight of Glory and Other Addresses* (1949; HarperOne, 2001), 26.
[63]   Augustine, *The Literal Meaning of Genesis*, in *On Genesis*, ed. John E. Rotelle, trans. Edmund Hill, The Works of Saint Augustine: A Translation for the 21st Century, part 1, vol. 13 (New City Press, 2002), 6.25, p. 321; Augustine, *The*

apart from the Creator's purpose, i.e., sin, creatures lose the sense of "unchangeable truth" or wisdom once accessed through the Tree of Life in the garden.[64] They now act in ways that display confusion regarding their end goals, deceiving themselves in ignorance or weakness in their inability to act on what they know to be good.[65] Thus ignorance and weakness become a twofold challenge. Deceiving themselves becomes a disordered way of knowing, and lying becomes a disordered way of communicating.

In *Augustine on Evil*, G. R. Evans says,

> Augustine was in no doubt that here was an important aspect of the problem of evil, epistemologically speaking. A lie has all the properties he had learned to associate with evil, and which he had described in the *Confessions*. As good is opposed to evil, or light to darkness, so a lie is opposed to truth. There can be no compromise between them . . . a lie may appear to be true, but it will always have a hidden sense which is quite the opposite . . . indeed it may have some appearance of truth or it will not achieve its purpose, which is to deceive, for deceptiveness is of the essence of a lie.[66]

Lies work best when filled with partial truths. Deceptive, they divert, turn, or twist the end and the means, often intending some form of good but lacking its full meaning.

A large part of Augustine's search in the *Confessions* stems from his dissatisfaction with his own behavior and choices that left him restless. A persistent theme involves the way in which his training as a professional orator for imperial Rome afforded him great power and opportunity, yet little solace or meaning. He recognized the power in his persuasive use of words while questioning whether they were true words. As a professional rhetorician and teacher, he describes his life as one of "being seduced and seducing, being deceived and deceiving (2 Tim 3:13) in a variety of desires."[67] Claiming his work involved "smoke" and "the tricks of rhetoric,"

Augustine Catechism: The Enchiridion on Faith, Hope, and Love, trans. Bruce Harbert (New City Press, 1999), 28.104, p. 120.

[64]   Augustine, *Literal Meaning of Genesis*, pp. 320–21.

[65]   Joseph T. Kelley, ed., *Saint Augustine of Hippo: Selections from Confessions and Other Essential Writings* (Skylight Paths, 2010), 38.

[66]   G. R. Evans, *Augustine on Evil* (Cambridge University Press, 1982), 65.

[67]   Augustine, *Confessions* 4.1, p. 52.

he advises students not to use words against an innocent person, but that sometimes "they might save the life of a guilty person."[68]

For Augustine, lies always involve knotty issues—an entanglement of sorts.[69] Still, creatures long for truth but compromise when loving a lower good as the ultimate end. He says,

> Their love for truth takes the form that they love something else and want this object of their love to be the truth; and because they do not wish to be deceived, they do not wish to be persuaded that they are mistaken. And so they hate the truth for the sake of the object which they love instead of the truth. They love truth for the light it sheds but hate it when it shows them up as being wrong (John 3:20; 5:35). Because they do not wish to be deceived but wish to deceive, they love truth when it shows itself to them but hate it when its evidence goes against them.[70]

We are self-deceived in so many ways, longing for truth when applying it to others and not ourselves. Too often we prefer some created object of love in exchange for the truth.[71]

Looking back on his youth, Augustine considers his lustful desire. He boasted about participating in more sexual exploits than he committed. He found himself lying to seek his peers' approval. Likewise, stealing pears involved thrill-seeking with his friends. Transgressing the law was fun because they could get away with it. Still, he acknowledges he wouldn't have committed the crime alone. He stole *because he was with his friends*—and friendship is one of the highest goods in the order of love. Friendship is such a high good that when ordered rightly, things go very well and when ordered wrongly, things descend into serious problems. In his desire for friendship and social approval, he portrays what Hitz describes as a weak desire for communion.[72]

Finally, Augustine reflects on the anxiety he experiences when giving public speeches. This too is impacted by his desire for approval from his broader social circle. He participates in certain forms of disordered love

---

68 Augustine, *Confessions* 4.4, p. 53.
69 Evans, *Augustine on Evil*, 65.
70 Augustine, *Confessions* 10.23.33, pp. 199–200.
71 See Rom 1:25.
72 Hitz, *Lost in Thought*, 143.

to the point of lying about his actions for societal or group approval.[73] Hitz sees how enjoying spectacle—or the trivial for its own sake—escalates among groups. Contrasting spectacle and disordered curiosity, Hitz explains, "While the love of learning is exercised by Ambrose alone in his study, engrossed in reading, the love of spectacle seems always to be enmeshed in a crowd."[74]

The focus on crowd aligns well with Ellul and Haidt's critique on the spread of misinformation across social media in its power to erode public trust. As Immanuel Kant's *Groundwork for the Metaphysics of Morals* considers, lying only works against a backdrop of truth.[75] Like the categorical imperative, moral maxims should consider whether they can be universalized.[76] Lying is an example of an immoral action that doesn't fit this criterion. Lies don't work when they become our primary mode of communication. Yet the contemporary digital empire finds us in a milieu of lies. Public trust is at an all-time low in democratic societies.[77] What happens when trust erodes and confusion—if not chaos—ensues.

Social media algorithms often incite confusion through rapid information spread, sounding like Chicken Little as they remind us on a daily basis that "the sky is falling!"[78] Digital "like" and "share" buttons increase the amount of anger and high emotional content distributed across these mediums. Haidt says, "This new game encouraged dishonesty and mob dynamics: Users were guided not just by their true preferences but by their past experiences of reward and punishment, and their prediction of how others would react to each new action. One of the engineers at Twitter who had worked on the 'Retweet' button . . . watched Twitter mobs forming through the use of the new tool, [and]

[73]   In fact, he says he made a career of lying and decides to forgo his career in rhetoric upon his conversion. Recognizing common deception in his art, he formally departs from his "post as a salesman of words in the markets of rhetoric" following his conversion (Augustine, *Confessions* 9.2.2, p. 155).

[74]   Hitz, *Lost in Thought*, 140.

[75]   Immanuel Kant, *Groundwork for the Metaphysics of Morals*, trans. Arnulf Zweig, in *Justice: A Reader*, ed. Michael J. Sandel (Oxford University Press, 2007).

[76]   Kant, *Groundwork for the Metaphysics of Morals*, 176–77.

[77]   Haidt, "Why the Last 10 Years"; see also Richard C. Paddock, "Myanmar Executes Four Pro-Democracy Activists, Defying Foreign Leaders," *New York Times*, July 25, 2022, https://www.nytimes.com/2022/07/25/world/asia/myanmar -executions.html.

[78]   See *Chicken Little*, dir. Mark Dindal (Disney, 2005).

thought to himself, 'We might have just handed a 4-year-old a loaded weapon.'"[79]

Virtual-reality designer Jaron Lanier agrees that deception sits at the center of social media.[80] Imbedded within every conversation or interaction are third party interests, or algorithms, that seek to profit from online posts and exchanges.[81] Describing social media as "behavior modification empires," Lanier says, "Welcome to the cage that goes everywhere with you."[82] Questioning how social media and its algorithmic schemes challenge free will, he explains, "It's just not right to call direct manipulation of people advertising. Advertisers used to have a limited chance to make a pitch . . . Now everyone who is on social media is getting individualized, continuously adjusted stimuli, without a break so long as they use their smartphones. What might once have been called advertising must now be understood as continuous behavior modification on a titanic scale."[83] These influences can occur in terms of corporate or political interest.

Analogous to handing a four-year-old a loaded weapon, information and misinformation spread at lightning speed through the click of a "share" or "retweet" button. Social media encourages impulse rather than reflection associated with wisdom, feeding on reactionary responses and tapping into evolutionary biology's emphasis on survival in a way that works against the developments we have made through language and the rule of law.[84] Reacting from impulse displays a lack of the societal gains from civil discourse and civic virtue. Max Fisher says, "It makes you forget your internal moral senses and refer to the group's. And it makes inflicting harm on the target of the outrage feel necessary—even intensely pleasurable. Brain scans find that, when subjects harm someone they believe is a moral wrongdoer, their dopamine-reward centers activate."[85] On social media, individuals are more likely to respond with impulsive anger than

---

[79]   Haidt, "Why the Last 10 Years." For more on mob sharing see Fisher, *Chaos Machine*, 96–97.

[80]   Jaron Lanier, quoted in *The Social Dilemma*, dir. Jeff Orlowski (Exposure Labs, 2020), Netflix.

[81]   Lanier, quoted in Orlowski, *Social Dilemma*.

[82]   Jaron Lanier, *Ten Arguments for Deleting Your Social Media Accounts Right Now* (Picador, 2018), 5, 8; see also Zuboff's "instrumentarian power" in *Age of Surveillance Capitalism*, 360–75.

[83]   Lanier, *Ten Arguments*, 6–7.

[84]   Fisher, *Chaos Machine*, 96.

[85]   Fisher, *Chaos Machine*, 97.

in face-to-face interactions where empathy, shame, and remorse more often come into play.[86]

Harnessing mass impulse and communication ties to Ellul's understanding of propaganda. Utilizing specific techniques, propaganda appeals to the individual as part of a group or collective identity through mass communication, appealing to what the individual has "in common with others, such as his motivations, his feelings, or his myths."[87] Ellul says, "These individuals are moved by the same motives, receive the same impulses and impressions, find themselves focused on the same centers of interest, experience the same feelings, have generally the same order of reactions and ideas, participate in the same myths . . . what we have here is really a psychological, if not a biological mass."[88]

Appealing to a sense of alienation and group belonging, propaganda stokes the same emotions and impulses among individuals, drawing them together toward the same interest or cause. Thus, propaganda appeals to a sense of group identity located within the crowd. Group-think easily spreads like Alypius's response at the gladiatorial games, in which he opens his eyes as "part of the crowd."[89] This group think involves commodification and impulse—commodification because information is separated from its origin and goal, and impulse because thoughtless action spreads content rapidly. With the click of a button through like, share, or retweet, information driven by impulse, impressions, and feelings spreads like wildfire irrespective of facts.[90] With increased impulse comes increased emotion and vice. Here social media works against the significant gains made through self-control in its capacity to self-regulate and make space for other virtues gained through evolutionary psychology.[91]

Living through World War II Germany, Karl Barth also describes propaganda as deception in his account of the lordless powers and their play on ideology. He reduces ideology to "isms," where a particular philosophy or school of thought becomes idealized as in "Hegelianism, Marxism,

---

[86]   Fisher, *Chaos Machine*, 97.
[87]   Ellul, *Propaganda*, 7.
[88]   Ellul, *Propaganda*, 8.
[89]   Hitz, *Lost in Thought*, 140.
[90]   Hitz, *Lost in Thought*, 135–36.
[91]   Justin Barrett and Pamela King, *Thriving with Stone Age Minds: Evolutionary Psychology, Christian Faith, and the Quest for Human Flourishing* (IVP, 2021), 102–10.

Stalinism, and so forth."[92] Ideologies also occur through "slogans or catchwords."[93] He says, "The slogan is not designed to teach, instruct, or convince the hearer or reader. It aims to exert a drum-roll influence on people by awakening associations, engendering ideas and the associated feelings, and issuing marching orders. *It does not initiate or permit any reflection or discussion*, but it hammers home an axiom that must precede and underlie any possible reflection and discussion."[94] Like Ellul, Barth understands slogans to function through their appeal to emotions that draw individuals together over a group theme that galvanizes but also rejects open dialogue, reflection, or discussion. Today, slogans are easily shared through #hashtags, tweets, and political phrases that associate individuals with groupthink, often reducing ideas to bullet points without nuance or dialogue.

As Haidt attests, these reductionistic ideas often create polarizing discourse where we see groups and political affiliations that emphasize difference rather than shared experiences and interests. Yet individuals are more than group identity. Influenced and shaped by our ancestors as well as our cultural identities, environment, friends, education, and socioeconomic status, individuals remain more than one group affiliation.[95] As creatures, we inhabit three-dimensional space—if not four dimensions given our capacity for spirituality—while social media risks reducing us to one or two dimensions at best. Listening to individual stories is important for diverse interpretation and understanding each neighbor in particularity.[96]

Finally, these ideologies involve formal propaganda—both implicit and explicit. Devolving into short slogans used through conversive combat, they "swing" at their opponents in full force. Recognizing "a mouth to speak great things is given not only to the beast of Revelation 13 but to most of his associates and especially to ideologies,"[97] they promote "their own excellence and usefulness," while emphasizing their opponents as "valueless and harmful."[98] Barth acknowledges the world has always

[92]   Karl Barth, *The Christian Life: Church Dogmatics IV/4, Lecture Fragments*, trans. Geoffrey W. Bromiley (Eerdmans, 1981), 226.

[93]   Barth, *Christian Life*, 226.

[94]   Barth, *Christian Life*, 226 (emphasis added).

[95]   David Brooks, *How to Know a Person: The Art of Seeing Others Deeply and Being Deeply Seen* (Random House, 2023), 234–36, 249.

[96]   Brooks, *How to Know a Person*.

[97]   Barth, *Christian Life*, 227.

[98]   Barth, *Christian Life*, 227.

been vulnerable to propaganda since the advent of newspapers and the printed press, but this takes on "a new speed and a new degree" with more sophisticated technologies.[99] Both society and the church are vulnerable to ideology given that we're "daily washed around by so much open and hidden propaganda."[100]

Often taking on political ends, Barth challenges the church to recognize such lordless, creative powers at work in the world and to resist them through transcendent and gospel critique in the prayer "Thy Kingdom come."[101] Augustine also challenges the church to recognize ways the city of God doesn't belong to the institutional church. Power as well as deception can work through any human institution, including the visible church.[102] In today's digital empire, its citizens are exposed to an array of reductionistic political aphorisms and blame-casting. To use the metaphor of Smith, we are regularly discipled through the liturgies of social media and information excess promoted by media outlets and political pundits. Seeing through the veil of these lordless, creative powers requires wisdom, a subject that Augustine writes about at length.

WISE WORDS: COMMUNICATION FOR THE SAKE OF COMMUNION

As a rhetorician, Augustine was profoundly aware of the power in words. His understanding of sin is impacted by disordered power, often stemming from insecurity known as *libido dominandi*—whether through lust, theatrics, politics, philosophy, or rhetorical persuasion. But along with Augustine's conversion of the intellect and will comes his rhetorical conversion. He says he made a career of lying and decides to formally depart from his "post as a salesman of words in the markets of rhetoric."[103] Instead, he shifts his goal to beautiful words addressing the soul.[104] Revising and

---

[99]   Barth, *Christian Life*, 227.
[100] Barth, *Christian Life*, 227.
[101] Barth, *Christian Life*, 233–4.
[102] Augustine, *City of God* 19.
[103] Augustine, *Confessions* 9.2.2, p. 155.
[104] Paul R. Kolbet, *Augustine and the Cure of Souls: Revising a Classical Ideal* (University of Notre Dame Press, 2010), 73. Assuming the role of priest and later bishop, Augustine uses his rhetorical training in new ways. But as Daniel Doyle says, "It must be remembered first of all that homilies are not 'speeches' in the strict sense, since they imply a dialogue between preacher and people made possible by the Holy Spirit. The hearer's attentive listening and active engagement are essential ingredients in the process" (Daniel E. Doyle, "Introduction to Augustine's Preaching," in

recontextualizing Christian philosophy, Augustine now uses words that bring wisdom and healing, pointing to Christ.

As described in *On Christian Teaching*, all signs point to "things." Words are signs that assign meaning to things. His work *De Magistro* (*The Teacher*), an intimate letter written to his son Adeodatus, considers the significance of words and the objects/things to which they point. Through dialogue and exploration, Augustine guides Adeodatus on how objects are known along with the meaning of words. Leading Adeodatus inward, Augustine says, "When he sees he learns not from words uttered but from the objects seen and his sense of sight . . . when the question concerns not things which are present to our senses but which once were . . . we speak of the images derived from them imprinted on the memory."[105]

Influenced by Neoplatonism, Augustine finds the locus of memory to be significant for knowledge and understanding that involves both reflection and contemplation. Teaching is, in some sense, a reminder or recognition, recalling universal truths partially known.[106] The real learning comes through contemplation from the inward Teacher.[107] Augustine says, "Our real Teacher is he who is so listened to, who is said to dwell in the inner man, namely Christ, that is, the unchangeable power and eternal wisdom of God. To this wisdom every rational soul gives heed, but to each is given only so much as he is able to receive . . ."[108] Wisdom is not merely truth, it is not an object or thing, but a Person or Subject who might be known. Wisdom is not simply achieved or created but discovered and received. Deeply personal, this wisdom encounters individuals in both exterior signs and interior ways.[109] Wisdom comes through reception, a kind of contemplation and reflection that not only sees but also knows and loves.

Wisdom also comes through shared understanding and relationships with others. David Brooks describes the power of truth seekers gazing together at the same subject of interest. Whether an embodied community

---

Augustine, *Essential Sermons*, classroom resource ed., ed. Doyle, The Works of Saint Augustine: A Translation for the 21st Century [New City Press, 2007], 14).

[105] Augustine, *The Teacher* (*De Magistro*), in *Augustine: Earlier Writings*, ed. and trans. J. H. S. Burleigh (Westminster John Knox, 2006), p. 96.

[106] Augustine, *The Teacher*, p. 95.

[107] Augustine, *The Teacher*, pp. 96–97.

[108] Augustine, *The Teacher*, p. 95.

[109] Augustine, *The Teacher*, p. 100; see also Kolbet, "Christ's Inner and Outer Rhetoric," in *Augustine and the Cure of Souls*, 106–17.

or classroom, he conveys the sacred experience found in sharing love and truth together. He says,

> A funny thing happens to people in a community of truth. When someone shares a thought and others receive it, then suddenly the same circuit is in two brains. When a whole classroom is consider-ing the thought, it's like the same circuit in twenty-five brains. Our minds are intermingling. The cognitive scientist Douglas Hofstadter calls these circuits loops. He argues that when we communicate, and loops are flowing through different brains, we are thinking as one shared organism, anticipating each other, finishing each other's sen-tences. "Empathy" is not a strong enough word to describe this inter-mingling. It is not one person, one body, one brain that marks this condition, Hofstadter argues, but the interpenetration of all minds in ceaseless conversation with each other.[110]

Augustine understood this same experience of seeking after truth, the sharing of one mind.[111] Following his conversion, Alypius stands nearby and joins him as they embark on a faith journey together.[112]

With his mother, son, and closest philosophical companions, Augus-tine retreats to Cassiciacum, a Roman estate in the foothills of the Alps, where they might explore theological truth together in a fellowship of shared mind, will, and love.[113] Similarly, the disciples walking on the road to Emmaus listen to the stories of Jesus. When breaking bread, at once their eyes are opened and together "they recognized him" (Luke 24:31). After Jesus disappears, the two men ask each other, "Were not our hearts burning within us while he was talking on the road, while he was opening the scriptures to us?" (Luke 24:32). For Augustine, to share in truth and love is to share in the mind of Christ—like his shared vision with Monica at Ostia—in which together, they share in the divine presence, beholding wisdom while remaining recognizable as embodied mother and son.[114]

Augustine found shared understanding and wisdom integral to teach-ing and pastoral ministry as well. He describes joy in teaching listeners something new when love motivates instruction, saying,

110 Brooks, *How to Know a Person*, 264.
111 Augustine, *Instructing Beginners in the Faith*, in *Morality and Christian Ascet-icism*, ed. Boniface Ramsey, trans. Raymond Canning, The Works of Saint Augustine: A Translation for the 21st Century, part 1, vol. 10 (New City Press, 2006), 12.17.
112 Serge Lancel, *St. Augustine* (SCM, 1999), 95–98.
113 Lancel, *St. Augustine*, 99–109.
114 Lancel, *St. Augustine*, 114–19, 371.

> We should endeavor to treat students with a brother's, a father's, and
> a mother's love; and, if we are united with them in heart, to us no less
> than to them will these things seem new. For so great is the power of
> a sympathetic disposition of mind, that as they are affected while we
> are speaking, and we are affected while they are learning, *we have our
> dwelling in each other.* Thus, at one and the same time, they as it were
> speak what they hear, and we in them learn after a certain fashion
> what we teach.[115]

Empathy and solidarity lead him to care for the fellow listener. Watching
another learn something new keeps teaching fresh while both speaker and
listener are changed. He is no longer orator conveying information alone,
but a fellow pilgrim with his listeners and students on the path of discovery.

Another way of thinking about Augustine's theology involves his
relentless pursuit of understanding in his relentless pursuit of truth. His
desire to integrate truth with self-knowledge might best be described as a
heart seeking wisdom. Persuading others through the power of words or
communication for its own sake was dissatisfying. Instead, he wanted to
know the meaning of words. This sends him on a long philosophical journey through Manichaeism, Neoplatonism, and eventually Christianity,
where he encounters his beloved mentor, Ambrose. Observing Ambrose's
integration of philosophy and Scripture through his learned technique,
Augustine found Christianity intellectually convincing, which left him
thirsting and hungering for more. Once he tastes wisdom through communion with divine truth, he continually hungers for rest and satisfaction
from this fundamental source.[116]

WISDOM AND KNOWLEDGE

In *De Trinitate* (*The Trinity*), Augustine approaches faith and understanding as two dialectical poles, each illuminating the other in his search to
better understand the eternal mystery of the Trinity.[117] Whether describing his life journey through the *Confessions* as his own relentless pursuit
of truth through better self-understanding or his attempts to wrestle with
various angles of the Trinity reflected in humanity, Augustine is committed to understanding meaning behind moral motivation and action, a
form of wisdom. This is the opposite of knowledge for the sake of experience alone or life at the surface. This commitment to moral reflection or

---

115   Augustine, *Instructing Beginners in the Faith* 1.1.
116   See Pss 19:10; 119/103; Jer 15:16.
117   Lancel, *St. Augustine*, 369.

contemplation, cultivating an interior life beyond the surface-level reality is significant for understanding what makes humans unique and with it brings deeper self-knowledge.

In *The Shallows: What the Internet Is Doing to Our Brains*, Nicholas Carr claims the pursuit of wisdom is what makes humans distinctive. It's also the characteristic that defines humans as different from new forms of technology, whether artificial intelligence or robots. Whereas AI and robotics function with computational knowledge, Carr finds the more we create and program devices, the more these devices program us—or the more we image our own creation.[118] Recognizing gains made through new technologies but also their attendant disadvantages, Carr says when "we 'externalize' problem solving and other cognitive chores to our computers, we reduce our brain's ability 'to build stable knowledge structures'— schemas in other words—that can later 'be applied in new situations.' A polemicist might put it more pointedly: The brighter the software, the dimmer the user."[119] Carr finds repeated frenzied internet use is harming our capacity for slow thinking and contemplation, which impacts our capacity for empathy and emotional depth.[120] He concludes by saying, "We are welcoming the frenziedness into our souls."[121]

As seen through Augustine's commentary on his youthful pursuit of sensory objects, whether stealing pears or acting on lust, he questions his own frenzied soul and the disorder in pleasure pursued apart from motives associated with divine intention behind created goods. His search causes him to see the futility in pursuing temporal goods as if they were ultimate. Likewise, Augustine's political theology throughout *City of God* deconstructs ways that Roman identity and philosophy fall short of supplying an ultimate end or happiness in this life. Instead, he takes away the illusion of security in sensory, material power such as the glory of Rome, virtue, or happiness found in temporal philosophies, including Stoicism that denies basic emotions.[122]

Instead, Augustine seeks wisdom and ultimate happiness in an eternal source, the triune God. Thus, in seeking to understand the Trinity, he

[118] See Sabrina Tavernise, host, "The Godfather of A.I. Has Some Regrets," *The Daily* (podcast), *New York Times*, June 1, 2023, https://www.nytimes.com/2023/05/30/podcasts/the-daily/chatgpt-hinton-ai.html.

[119] Nicholas Carr, *The Shallows: What the Internet Is Doing to Our Brains* (W. W. Norton, 2011), 216.

[120] Carr, *Shallows*, 221.

[121] Carr, *Shallows*, 222.

[122] Augustine, *City of God* 14.6–10, pp. 555–67.

reflects on the goal of understanding the highest pleasure and emotion. Augustinian biographer Serge Lancel says, "To understand God, totally comprehend him (*comprehendere*) was impossible; but to touch him with one's mind (*attingere*), however, slightly, was a great joy. God was 'incomprehensible,' but he was not 'unthinkable.' The effort made to think of him comprises the entire undertaking of *De Trinitate*, approached by a mind still burning to 'seek his face' (Ps. 105.4)."[123]

Seeking his face, as the gift in knowing God, Augustine pursues the "Word," *logos*, or "wisdom" from the Gospel of John.[124] Writing *The Trinity* over the course of fifteen years, from his youth to old age, Augustine recognizes wisdom pertains to all three persons of the Trinity—Father, Son, and Spirit—but also its special relationship to the "Word" or Son.[125] Describing the Son as the divine image and humans as God's image bearers, Augustine says,

> For we too are the image of God, though not the equal one like him; we are made by the Father through the Son, not born of the Father like that image; we are image because we are illuminated with light; that one is so because it is the light that illuminates, and therefore it provides a model for us without having a model itself. For it does not imitate another going before it to the Father, since it is never by the least hair's breadth separated from him, since it is the same thing as he is from whom it gets its being. But we pressing on imitate him who abides motionless; we follow him who stands still, and by walking in him we move toward him, because for us he became a road or way in time by his humility, while being for us an eternal abode by his divinity.[126]

The Word is the light that illuminates meaning for all creation. This Word is inseparable from the Father, but also enters time and human experience through humility by becoming a road, the path of wisdom, through his divinity.[127]

In this way Augustine is like the Platonists in his understanding that wisdom is eternal, unchanging, and timeless beyond sensory experience

---

[123] Lancel, *St. Augustine*, 371.

[124] Lancel, *St. Augustine*, 371.

[125] Lancel, *St. Augustine*, 367; Augustine, *The Trinity* (*De Trinitate*), ed. John E. Rotelle, trans. Edmund Hill, 2nd ed. (New City Press, 1991), 7.2.4–5, pp. 224–25.

[126] Augustine, *The Trinity* 7.2.5, p. 225.

[127] Jonathan Haidt notes that all wisdom traditions seek higher understanding and communion apart from the stagnant goals of social media (Haidt, *Anxious Generation*, 203–18).

alone. But he is unlike the Platonists in that the Word or wisdom enters time and space, the material world, through the incarnate Christ, becoming the road to Wisdom. The end becomes the means. Wisdom enters time. Because of human sin and our inability to participate in God, the "Word through which all things were made became flesh and dwelt among us (John 1:14) . . . becoming a partaker of our mortality he made us partakers of his divinity."[128] Augustine explains that our enlightenment—or we might say, our wisdom—is to participate in the Word, which is the light and life of men (John 1:4).[129] How does this wisdom, or enlightenment, take place? For Augustine, it will involve mirroring the One who takes on our humanity through humility and communing with this Word.

As the writer of Proverbs states, "the fear of the Lord is the beginning of wisdom" (Prov 9:10). Wisdom begins with fear, awe, reverence, or knowing you are not God in humility. Augustine's entire theology pivots around this truth: to be human is to be creaturely. To be creaturely is to relate to One on the other side of the equation—the Creator. Beginning with the greater of the two parties, creatures derive their essence, existence, and fulfillment in the Creator: "You have made us for yourself, and our hearts are restless until they rest in You."[130] Seeking our origin and end goal, the restless heart is dissatisfied in anything less than this goal and our desire for communication points to this communion. Thus, while love is our drive through time, humility is the beginning of this search. Recognizing one is not Creator, but creature is a humble proposition. To be "human" (or the Hebrew term *humus* meaning "from the earth") is to recognize one's creaturely position before the Creator and the rest of creation.[131] But humility does not stop there. Humility and love become the posture, position, and tone by which one grows in virtue through the presence and encounter with the divine Other.

This is the point of Augustine's famous work *De Trinitate*. Augustine here describes two kinds of knowing: *sapientia*, or wisdom pertaining to eternal meaning that involves contemplation, and *scientia*, or knowledge pertaining to the temporal reality inclusive of action and virtue.[132] Augustine finds the image of God broken after the fall and repaired in the

---

[128]   Augustine, *The Trinity* 4.1.4, p. 155.
[129]   Augustine, *The Trinity* 4.1.4, p. 155.
[130]   Augustine, *Confessions* 1.1, p. 3.
[131]   William May, *The Patient's Ordeal* (Indiana University Press, 1991), 133.
[132]   Augustine, *The Trinity* 12.4, p. 337ff.

person of Christ.[133] Throughout the treatise he describes the Son as *sapientia* or wisdom in eternity. Only a divine-human mediator can bridge and harmonize the two disparate forms of knowing, *sapientia* and *scientia*. Lewis Ayres finds the repaired image of God in the person of Christ, with both divine and human natures analogous to our two ways of knowing.[134] Drawing together eternity and time in His person, the Son as Word reveals wisdom. Creatures participate in this wisdom through humility, worship, and love of God.[135] Augustine says,

> This trinity of the mind is not really the image of God because the mind remembers and understands and loves itself, but because it is also able to remember and understand and love him by whom it was made. And when it does this it becomes wise. If it does not do it, then even though it remembers and understands and loves itself, it is foolish. Let it then remember its God to whose image it was made, and understand and love him. *To put in a word, let it worship the uncreated God, by whom it was created with a capacity for him and able to share in him.* In this way it will be wise not with its own light but by sharing in that supreme light, and it will reign in happiness where it reigns eternal. For this is called man's wisdom in such a way that it is also God's. Only then is it true wisdom; if it merely human it is hollow.[136]

God is the supreme wisdom and participation in God by way of humility supplies human wisdom.[137] In this way, humans are not the image of God on their own terms, but because they exist in relationship to the original divine image.[138] Apart from God we become hollow or empty, vacuous images.

---

[133]   Augustine, *The Trinity* 12.4, p. 337ff.

[134]   Augustine, *The Trinity* 13.1–5, pp. 342–66; Lewis Ayres, "The Christological Context of Augustine's *De trinitate* XIII: Toward Relocating Books VIII–XV," *Augustinian Studies* 29, no. 1 (1998): 111–39.

[135]   Augustine, *The Trinity* 14.1–2, pp. 370–72.

[136]   Augustine, *The Trinity* 14.4, p. 384 (emphasis added).

[137]   Augustine, *The Trinity* 14.4, p. 384; see also Autumn Alcott Ridenour, *Sabbath Rest as Vocation: Aging Toward Death* (Bloomsbury T&T Clark, 2018), 113.

[138]   Augustine, *The Trinity* 14.4, p. 384; see also Catherine McDowell's description of the image of God in Gen 1:26–28 in terms of "kin" or kinship, relating to king and cult. Kinship involves our relationship as sons or children of God, while cult relates to kingly authority as divine image / "statuettes" reflecting the presence of God. This contrasts with interpretations that emphasize divine image based on one's capacities or capabilities (Catherine L. McDowell, *The Image of God in the Garden of*

Thus, for Augustine, wisdom is profoundly relational, beyond simply knowing some *thing* or information. Wisdom involves knowing some*one*. The Word or wisdom is beyond comprehension yet also deeply knowable, even personal—"knowable" as both extrinsic object pertaining to the sensory experience and interior subject available through faith in the inner person.[139] Inner and outer, faith is a journey toward eternity in the inner self that seeks God through humility. There is an intimacy and integration in being known inwardly as well as outwardly through this divine–human relationship made manifest through the Word as wisdom.

This is different than the personalization of tech. Crouch critiques the tech empire for promising more that it can deliver through personalized tools and apps that, ironically, deplete us individually and relationally. Tech provides a hyper "personalized, individuated" world through finely honed algorithms and apps.[140] Yet in this "cascade of reflections far more captivating than Narcissus's pool," we are often left lonely and dissatisfied.[141] Promising effortless power, we're often more fragmented and fatigued. Drawing us away from a sense of integrated self with responsibility to our surrounding world causes confusion and deception.

Seeking after wisdom, however, involves the opposite. Seeking to know God, neighbor, and ourselves through humility and the order of love involves knowing our origin and end where communication leads to communion. Rather than pursue a name and image for oneself through domination and instrumental forms of communication that result in Babel, here the image is received, name given, and meaning shared in a community of love. Receiving and acting through contemplation and reflection involves integration and wholeness rather than fragmentation and dispersion. Seeking to be found, wisdom or understanding accompanies knowledge. Meaning interprets information. The extent to which this image reflects its divine imprint and teleological end shared in God and fellow neighbor involves our deeper understanding of creation and our profound interdependence as creatures.

Eden: The Creation of Humankind in Genesis 2:5–3:24 in Light of the mis pi pit pi *and* wpt-r *Rituals of Mesopotamia and Ancient Egypt* [Eisenbrauns, 2015], 117–37).

[139]   Augustine, *The Trinity* 13.6.19–20, pp. 366–69.

[140]   Andy Crouch, *The Life We're Looking For: Reclaiming Relationship in a Technological World* (Convergent, 2022), 10–11.

[141]   Crouch, *Life We're Looking For*, 10–13.

3

A World of Images?

THE PROBLEM WITH LIMITATIONS: TIME AND SPACE

While walking across Harvard Yard in 2002, shortly before the inception of Facebook, I was surprised to hear student voices chanting, "Hey, hey, ho, ho, gravity, it's got to go," alongside, "If Harry Potter can fly, why can't I?"[1] Marching in a circle with picket signs in a benign political demonstration, I watched as undergraduate students chanted through a bullhorn, protesting gravity—magic was in the air. Amused by the group's creativity, I assumed the satire poked fun at student life to offset the stress of final exams late in the semester with the love of a good story. Regardless of the motivation, the desire to outstrip—at least temporarily—those limitations that bind us to the ground suggests our desire for something more. Do we have a restless desire to transcend embodied human limits in time and space? Or some greater desire for social belonging as we lament those limits?

Perhaps Augustine knew this very feeling in his desire to escape the trappings of his own material body through his initial attraction to Manichaean philosophy and its proponents. A philosophy that finds spirit good and matter evil—even if implicitly—is alluring given common frustrations with bodily limits. The promises of Manichaean philosophy allowed Augustine to separate his identity between inner and outer self, or

[1]   I visited Harvard Divinity School in December 2002, which involved walking across the undergraduate campus known as Harvard Yard. While Facebook officially began on February 4, 2004, Mark Zuckerberg and friends began classes at Harvard in 2002.

73

personhood from bodily temptations in the form of vulnerabilities. Separating body from soul, matter from spirit, Augustine finds initial solace through this division much like the disembodied virtual realm that offers temporary reprieve from the demands of material life, distancing self from other through image, avatar, and asynchronous communication.

Augustine also finds this anthropology, dividing soul and body, dissatisfying. Searching for wholeness and integration, Augustine ultimately finds himself through dependence on God that unites part to whole, beauty and harmony, and time with eternity. A Creator behind creation transforms his understanding of nature, including its beauty and wonder, offering meaning for creation and individual agency through imaging God. Dependent on the Creator along with the rest of creation forms a greater understanding of nature and identity, an identity forged through memory, matter (embodiment), and belonging to God as divine image.

FOOL'S GOLD: MANICHAEISM, CONTROL, AND TEMPORARY IMAGES

In *Confessions* 3–4 Augustine turns to Manichaean philosophy, a sect privileging spirit over body and the material realm, to help understand human behavior and his own frustrations with desire and longing. Frustrated by lust, illusive happiness, and success he could never quite grasp in the material world, the early Augustine turns to a Manichaean group for reprieve while also rubbing shoulders with Roman elites. While Augustine anticipates meeting Faustus, a Manichaean teacher, early in the *Confessions*, he finds himself disappointed when the teacher can't answer questions regarding the stars, sun, moon, and science.[2] Appreciating the teacher's initial modesty, Augustine becomes disillusioned with Manichaeism's disconnect from the physical or real world. Separating science from art and nature, eventually leads him to leave the sect.[3] Science and wisdom need not contradict. The two should be connected. Mathematics and science can relate to philosophical meaning. The inadequacy in Faustus's belief that the body and external world are separable from interior life and spiritual reflection propels his next steps on the journey from philosophy to Christian faith.

[2]   Augustine, *Confessions*, trans. Henry Chadwick (Oxford University Press, 1991), 7.12–13, p. 79.
[3]   Augustine, *Confessions* 7.12–13, p. 79.

There are surprising connections between Manichaeism's desire to escape or control bodily limitations and what Andy Crouch describes as the alchemist's desire to "unlock the secrets of nature."[4] By way of the "philosopher's stone," a mythical catalyst that transforms metals to gold, the alchemist looks to control nature and the material world. Like magic, technology often promises illusive control over nature and the world around us.[5] The question is whether we work *with* nature or simply *on* nature, recognizing limits as well as possibility—and to what end we serve.

Technology can offer an alluring power that allows us either to dismiss nature and its possible trappings ("it's simply the body") or control nature through ascetic practices or new capabilities that Crouch describes as "superpowers."[6] Crouch points to the ways in which new superpowers (tech capabilities) offer control while removing our sense of dependence and interaction with nature. They create an illusion of limitless power and possibilities.[7] Ironically, what technology gives, it can also take away.[8] Augustine allows us to see through the surface of technology's allure and recognize the ways digital technology shapes our view of the world, matter, and identity like a form of functional Manichaeism. With digital technologies, embodied matter becomes something to control and time a commodity to harness.[9]

The late bioethicist and Protestant ethicist Allen Verhey acknowledges this as anything but new. With the turn to modern science from the medieval world came a focus on humans and the desire to control nature. Since Francis Bacon, understanding science and medical diagnoses promised new ways of harnessing nature and eliminating disease. Through scientific progress, we were now able to isolate nature, observing its processes

---

[4]   Andy Crouch, *The Life We're Looking For: Reclaiming Relationship in a Technological World* (Convergent, 2022), 64–68.

[5]   Crouch, *Life We're Looking For*, 64–68.

[6]   Crouch, *Life We're Looking For*, 42–47.

[7]   Crouch, *Life We're Looking For*, 42–47.

[8]   See Barth on lordless or chthonic powers in Karl Barth, *The Christian Life: Church Dogmatics IV/4, Lecture Fragments*, trans. Geoffrey W. Bromiley (Eerdmans, 1981); see also Sean McDonough, *Creation and New Creation: Understanding God's Creation Project* (Hendrickson, 2017).

[9]   Digital technologies increasingly hone algorithms to harness our time and attention. See Nir Eyal, *Hooked: How to Form Habit-Forming Products* (Portfolio, 2014), 1–6; Tim Wu, *The Attention Merchants: The Epic Scramble to Get Inside Our Heads* (Vintage Books, 2006).

through the lens of a microscope in the hopes of eradicating certain forms of human vulnerability involving illness.[10] Jeffrey Bishop describes ways in which modern medicine took on a new power through its anatomical view of the human body. Separating persons from their narrative beginning and end allows one to isolate matter under the microscope as if life science were static rather than dynamic.[11] With this new form of science and its specialized focus on parts of the human body came great gains in the realm of discovery, treatment, and even cure. Still these gains also included losses. The modern lens began to skew our ways of viewing nature, the material world, and our philosophical sense of meaning in it.[12] Specialized medicine and emerging medical anthropology viewed the body less like mystery and more like a machine.[13]

Likewise, the invention of photography in 1823 captured live subjects in still time, allowing for observation that promoted distance between subject and object across time and space.[14] In a little over two hundred years, digital images developed into the currency now propelling today's social media giants. As early as 1992, Neil Postman warned that "technology is a branch of moral philosophy, not of science."[15] Decontextualized information spread through telegraphy and photographic imagery brings challenges. Postman questioned the "graphic revolution."[16] Postman says, "The new imagery, with photography at its forefront, did not merely function as a supplement to language, but bid to replace it as our dominant

[10] Robin Gill, *Health Care and Christian Ethics* (Cambridge University Press, 2006), 71–75.

[11] See Jeffrey P. Bishop, *The Anticipatory Corpse* (University of Notre Dame Press, 2011).

[12] See Jacques Ellul, *The Technological Society*, trans. John Wilkinson (Knopf, 1964); Neil Postman, *Technopoly: The Surrender of Culture to Technology* (Vintage Books, 1993).

[13] See Autumn Alcott Ridenour, "'Elderhood' and Sabbath Rest as Vocation: Identity, Purpose, & Belonging," *Journal of Population Ageing* 14, no. 3 (2021): 411–23; Louise Aronson, *Elderhood: Redefining Aging, Transforming Medicine, Reimagining Life* (Bloomsbury, 2019); Tia Powell, *Dementia Reimagined: Building a Life of Joy and Dignity from Beginning to End* (Avery, 2019); Gill, *Health Care and Christian Ethics*.

[14] "Harvard's History of Photography Timeline," Weissman Preservation Center, Harvard University Library, accessed April 6, 2023, https://projects.iq.harvard.edu/photographpreservationprogram/harvards-history-photography-timeline-text-only.

[15] Postman, *Technopoly*, xviii.

[16] Neil Postman, *Amusing Ourselves to Death* (Penguin Books, 1985), 74–79.

means for construing, understanding, and testing reality . . . The new focus on the image undermined traditional definitions of information, of news, and to a large extent, of reality itself."[17]

Time is something we capture *ad nauseam* through image. Sharing fixed images, or contained time through the internet, we're shaped by a world of images on a regular basis. Manichaean in form, images reflect past time or present time (when synchronous) that separate matter and embodiment from spatial, in-person presence. Photographic images copy time and space for later recollection, observation, or consumption. Removed from their original source, these images often lose their narrative meaning.

Calling mass media a "peek-a-boo" culture in which images lose coherence and meaning, Postman questions how television elevates "the interplay of image and instancy to an exquisite and dangerous perfection . . . achiev[ing] the status of 'meta-medium'—an instrument that directs not only our knowledge of the world, but our *ways of knowing* as well."[18] He laments self-contained images without narrative coherence tied to a beginning or end. In a panoply of disparate images, how do we understand meaning or identity without belonging as individuals to communities or as creatures to something greater?

Perhaps it's not surprising that these technological changes also helped shape our philosophical view of nature, meaning, identity, and moral agency. Alan Noble diagnoses modernity's problem as the autonomous self without beginning or end, morphed into a form of "expressive individualism."[19] We must ascribe value to ourselves and nature to give life meaning. Ironically, a world without meaning places a massive burden on individuals to justify themselves—belonging to no one, individualization

[17]   Postman, *Amusing Ourselves to Death*, 74–79.

[18]   Postman, *Amusing Ourselves to Death*, 78–79.

[19]   Alan Noble, *You Are Not Your Own* (IVP, 2021), 70. Expressive individualism pushes beyond Kant's original understanding of autonomy. Kantian autonomy recognizes the individual accountable to moral principles that can be universalized, delineated through the categorical imperative. Expressive individualism, on the other hand, builds on enlightened individualism (where identity is reduced to atomized wills) and Romanticism (highlighting emotion and self-expression). For more on expressive individualism see Robert Bellah et al., *Habits of the Heart: Individualism and Commitment in American Life* (University of California Press, 1985), 47; Charles Taylor, *A Secular Age* (Belknap Press, 2007), 473–5; O. Carter Snead, *What It Means to Be Human: The Case for the Body in Public Bioethics* (Harvard University Press, 2020), 5, 73–86.

ensues.[20] Noble says, "If I am my own and belong to myself, the first and most significant implication is that I am wholly responsible for my life. This is both an exhilarating and terrifying thought."[21] Autonomous individuals must seek ever new ways to innovate and improve themselves, but the standard of perfection is undefined.[22]

When unencumbered in this way, true independence becomes lonely apart from community, belonging, or responsibility. Freedom becomes no freedom. The attempt to craft meaning in a digital milieu generally involves endless attempts at subjective perfection, often received through digital affirmations (emojis) or its alternative, in resignation, a kind of despair that hides through immersive entertainment.[23] Social media and digital technologies encourage both—endless posting for affirmation and endless escape (scrolling) from embodied relationships in time and space. Both approaches mirror Manichaeism as our attempt to compress time or escape embodiment.[24] In an ironic twist, controlling nature exacerbates a sense of powerlessness, causing further dispersion and fragmentation. Instead, Augustinian wisdom describing creaturely dependence yields a different sensibility, one of rest through belonging and integration by imaging God. Imaging and communing with God across time unites us with eternity.

YOU ARE NOT YOUR OWN:
BELONGING AND IDENTITY THROUGH IMAGING GOD

Augustine diagnoses all ancient forms of philosophy as masking fear of death.[25] Manichaeism is one more way to mask this fear through control, separating material from spiritual, body from soul. Yet this philosophy leaves him empty. Reflecting on his restlessness throughout the *Confessions*, Augustine is fragmented.[26] Longing for wholeness, he seeks to be

---

[20]   Shoshana Zuboff, *The Age of Surveillance Capitalism: The Fight for a Human Future at the New Frontier of Power* (Public Affairs, 2019), 31–37.

[21]   Noble, *You Are Not Your Own*, 19.

[22]   I use the term "autonomy" here in the post-Kantian sense akin to expressive individualism. Autonomy as pure freedom to pursue one's own good apart from others or the universal moral law is an illusion. See Noble, *You Are Not Your Own*, 3.

[23]   Noble, *You Are Not Your Own*, 4; see also Taylor, *A Secular Age*, 473–75.

[24]   Noble, *You Are Not Your Own*, 4.

[25]   Robert Dodaro, *Christ and the Just Society in the Thought of St. Augustine* (Cambridge University Press, 2004).

[26]   Stephen J. Duffy, "Anthropology," in *Augustine Through the Ages*, ed. Allan D. Fitzgerald (Eerdmans, 1999), 25; Augustine, *Confessions* 5.14, p. 25; Joseph T.

"collected together and brought to the unity from which we disintegrated into multiplicity."[27] Rather than distinguish soul from body and time from eternity, Augustine yearns for their unity and to understand why they feel in conflict at times.

He turns next to Neoplatonism that offers coherence for understanding his inner and outer conflict observed in the world. With the Platonic philosopher Plotinus, he confirms evil as privation in which good becomes corruptible by turning away from the supreme good.[28] Rather than see matter and spirit in conflict, he comes to see the world—both matter and spirit—lacking its intended good or goal. Yet beyond Neoplatonism, the doctrine of the incarnation or Word made flesh in Jesus Christ serves as the mediator, drawing him to God through humility and his ultimate conversion.[29] Moving from intellectual conviction, what he calls "presumption" to "confession," distinguishes "the way which leads to the home of bliss, not merely as an end to be perceived but as a realm to live in."[30] Christ's incarnation and resurrection will distinguish his convictions from Neoplatonic philosophy.[31] Communion with the God made flesh, both soul and body, brings together the disparate parts of his identity. He ultimately commits his will to God and converts fully to Christianity.[32] Capitulating his will, he finds rest in which "a light of relief," and "the shadows of doubt were dispelled."[33]

The *Confessions* captures his faith journey and the significance of the creation narrative in Genesis for understanding the world and his place in it. Much of Augustine's theology rests on the creation narrative, illuminating our "whence" and our "whither"—for his own life journey and humanity

---

Kelley, ed., *Saint Augustine of Hippo: Selections from Confessions and Other Essential Writings* (SkyLight Paths, 2010), 12–13.

[27]   Augustine, *Confessions* 10.29.40, p. 202.

[28]   Augustine, *Confessions* 7.12.18, p. 124; 7.3.4–5, pp. 113–14.

[29]   Augustine, *Confessions* 7.9.13, p. 121; 7.18.24, p. 128. Reading Neoplatonic writings with St. Ambrose, Augustine finds Christian faith intellectually compelling and later converts upon surrendering his will.

[30]   Augustine, *Confessions* 7.20.26, p. 130.

[31]   Defending what will become the traditional tenets of Nicaea while also anticipating Chalcedon, Augustine holds that Jesus Christ was fully divine and fully human. See Rowan Williams, "Creation," in Fitzgerald, *Augustine Through the Ages*, 251.

[32]   Augustine, *Confessions* 8.12.28–29, pp. 152–53.

[33]   Augustine, *Confessions* 8.12.28–29, p. 153.

at large.[34] In his interpretation of Genesis, Augustine identifies creation *ex nihilo* in which God creates from nothing.[35] This doctrine is significant for distinguishing God from Manichaean dualisms that suggest preexistent matter before creation in which evil, or alternative matter, is equal in power. Instead, Augustine's Neoplatonic influences help distinguish God's transcendence as unchanging and immutable. As Creator, the Trinitarian God exists before time, space, and any change—yet also enters time and space in Jesus Christ. In this way, God is unlike us in his transcendence as wholly other. Yet God is like us in his incarnation that takes up our cause on our behalf.[36] In this way Augustine establishes identity through similarity and difference. We image God in likeness yet remain distinctive.

As wholly Other, God creates the world, including time and space, filling it with his creatures.[37] Relying on a literal and allegorical interpretation of Genesis, Augustine affirms divine order and harmony to the created universe. The progression of the creation story authorizes form and content for each created being that yields species particularity as well as individual particularity. The boundary and limits to each creature in time and space grants them individual identity. The created world is radically dependent on its Creator for life and sustenance. Augustine's allegorical reading of Genesis 1 ends with Sabbath rest as its teleological end.[38]

[34]   Here I borrow the language of "whence" and "whither" from Karl Barth, *Church Dogmatics* III/2, *The Doctrine of Creation*, ed. T. F. Torrance and Geoffrey W. Bromiley (T&T Clark, 2004), sec. 47.4, p. 572. Augustine relays a similar motif in his account of pilgrimage and journey throughout his various works. As Henry Chadwick says, "The last four books [of the *Confessions*] make explicit what is only hinted at in the autobiographical parts, namely that the story of the soul wandering away from God and then in torment and tears finding its way home through conversion is also the story of the entire created order. It is a favourite Neoplatonic theme, but also, as Romans 8 shows, not absent from the New Testament" (Henry Chadwick, introduction to Augustine, *Confessions*, xxiv).

[35]   Williams, "Creation," 251.

[36]   Augustine interprets the Psalms in terms of the *totus Christus*, in which Christ serves as head and the church as body. See Michael Cameron, "*Enarrationes in Psalmos*," in Fitzgerald, *Augustine Through the Ages*, 290–93; Autumn Alcott Ridenour, *Sabbath Rest as Vocation: Aging Toward Death* (Bloomsbury T&T Clark, 2018), 118.

[37]   Ridenour, *Sabbath Rest as Vocation*, 19–27, 46–50.

[38]   Augustine, *On Genesis: A Refutation of the Manichees*, in *On Genesis*, ed. John E. Rotelle, trans. Edmund Hill, The Works of Saint Augustine: A Translation for the 21st Century, part 1, vol. 13 (New City Press, 2002), 1.23.35–25.43, pp. 62–68; Ridenour, *Sabbath Rest as Vocation*, 46–50; Autumn Alcott Ridenour,

Moving toward rest, Augustine locates the teleological intention for each species, including himself: "You made us for yourself, and our hearts are restless until they rest in you."[39]

In this sense, teleological purpose cannot be separate from identity. To be human is to be dependent, including our beginning and end. Radically dependent rather than self-sufficient, identity comes from belonging to God. As Stephen Duffy says, "In this perspective the human person is utterly dependent on God and other humans. Failing to grasp humanity's absolute dependence on God, one cannot understand humanity. Humanity is exocentric."[40] Meaning and fulfillment comes from beyond oneself. Receiving identity from the outside in, changes one's reason for existence and with it, meaning for individual life. Humans and all creation relate to God as transcendent. To be human is to image God. As image bearers, our identity references the source to whom it belongs.

Transcendence remains an important key for establishing identity and belonging for Augustine as well as other wisdom traditions. Yet the goals of social media are generally at odds with the goals of the wisdom traditions.[41] Recognizing the importance of transcendence and nature for discerning wisdom, Jonathan Haidt emphasizes the importance of spending time outdoors to garner a sense of awe and wonder. The wonder of nature helps individuals perceive the self as part of something greater, reflecting one's place in a broader horizon.[42] For Haidt as well as Augustine, recognizing transcendence in nature holds significant meaning for identity.

CREATION AS IMAGE: BEAUTY AND HARMONY IN NATURE

Identity through belonging to God, neighbor, and the world is essential for understanding creation as dependent, harmonious, and beautiful. Augustine describes creation in what later is called the book of nature.[43] Like

---

"Sabbath as Reprioritization," in *Sabbath as Resilience*, ed. Kenneth Barnes and Sara Minard (Wipf and Stock, 2025).

[39]   Augustine, *Confessions* 1.1, p. 3.

[40]   Duffy, "Anthropology," 25.

[41]   Jonathan Haidt, *The Anxious Generation: How the Great Rewiring of Childhood Is Causing an Epidemic of Mental Illness* (Penguin Books, 2024), 207–9, 212–17.

[42]   Haidt, *Anxious Generation*, 212–15.

[43]   Augustine does not coin the phrase "book of nature" but describes creation as "a great book" (Augustine, "Sermon Mai 126.6," in *The Essential Augustine*, ed. Vernon J. Bourke [Hackett, 1974], 123). John Calvin also alludes to nature as a second book of revelation (John Calvin, *Institutes of the Christian Religion*, ed. John T. McNeill [Westminster John Knox, 1960], 1.5.1–2, pp. 51–53).

environmental philosopher Erazim Kohák, Augustine's theology affirms a moral sense of nature—one that challenges the modern technological desire to instrumentalize the world apart from intrinsic purposes by acting on nature apart from inherent goals.[44]

Augustine says, "Some people read books in order to find God. Yet there is a great book, the very appearance of created things. Look above you; look below you! Note it; read it! God, whom you wish to find, never wrote that book with ink. Instead, He set before your eyes the things that He had made. Can you ask for a louder voice than that? Why, heaven and earth cry out to you: 'God made me!'"[45] Recognizing the book of nature alongside Scripture conveys the beauty of divine presence through creation.[46] Building his theology on visible things that point to the invisible from Romans 1, Augustine acknowledges how creation reflects God's goodness, deriving natural law and purpose from above.[47]

Yet understanding Augustine's high regard for creation also comes from his personal encounter with God through prayer.[48] The *Confessions* is an account of his life as a journey returning to God. Engaging in prayerful

[44]   Erazim Kohák concludes his Prolegomenon by saying, "Contrary to Descartes, long before the *cogito* of reflection there is the goodness and the truth of the *sumus*." While there is much overlap between Kohák and Augustine concerning the intrinsic purpose of nature, they depart in Kohák's immanent frame drawing from Husserl that collapses the transcendent in time. Instead, Augustine will maintain transcendence beyond time, future eschatology, and his concept called eternity (Erazim Kohák, *The Embers and the Stars: A Philosophical Inquiry into the Moral Sense of Nature* [University of Chicago Press, 1984], xiii, 18, 218). See also Crouch, *Life We're Looking For*, 64–68. I'm also grateful for coffee with Andy Crouch on March 23, 2023, during which he suggested I read Kohák given my work on creation.

[45]   Augustine, "Sermon Mai 126.6," 123.

[46]   Augustine, "Sermon Mai 126.6," 123. Calvin also conveys divine presence through creation in *Institutes of the Christian Religion* 1.6.1, pp. 69–70. For an excellent contemporary theological look at beauty in creation, see Wesley Vander Lugt, *Beauty Is Oxygen: Finding a Faith That Breathes* (Eerdmans, 2024).

[47]   Augustine, *The City of God*, trans. Henry Bettenson (Penguin Books, 1984), 19.22, p. 1089. While Stoicism influences his understanding of natural law, Scripture shapes his views more concretely based on Genesis in the Old Testament and Paul in the New Testament. See also Frederick Van Fleteren, "Nature," in Fitzgerald, *Augustine Through the Ages*, 586.

[48]   Most—if not all—of his writings passed down through translation and interpretation are from his post-conversion view of the world. In this sense Augustine is not unlike the New Testament, which is written from the post-resurrection view of the apostles and apostolic teaching.

dialogue with God, Augustine looks at creation with a new intoxication, a kind of profound gratitude. It's as if he acknowledges oxygen in his lungs for the first time—when he's been breathing fresh air all along. Augustine now sees himself belonging to the transcendent God behind creation through revelation and communion.

Following his conversion, he now looks at creation through the eyes of awe and wonder. He says, "Even if the creation had either never come into existence or remained formless, nothing could be lacking to the good which you are to yourself. You made it not because you needed it, but from the fullness of your goodness."[49] God creates not from need, but from abundance. Acknowledging the triune work of God in this process, he says,

> When scripture says your Spirit rests on people (Isa 11:2), it means that the Spirit makes them rest on himself. But your incorruptible and immutable will, sufficient to itself and in itself, was "born above" the life which you had made, a life for which to live is not the same as living in perfect happiness, because even while in a fluid state in darkness it had life. It remains for it to be converted to him by whom it was made, more and more to live by the fount of life, to see light in his light (Ps 35:10), and to become perfect, radiant with life, and in complete happiness. Here in an *enigmatic image* (1 Cor 13:12) I discern the Trinity, which you are, my God.[50]

We discern the invisible Creator behind creation. All creation reflects God, both life and light, with opportunity to grow in divine likeness toward "complete happiness."[51]

Throughout his *Confessions*, commentaries on the book of Genesis, *City of God*, and elsewhere, he acknowledges a contingency by which things are made and remade—converted. In this way Augustine establishes a radical dependence by which creation exists alongside new life

[49]   Augustine, *Confessions* 13.4.5, p. 275 (see also n. 4, describing the influence of Plotinus on Augustine's understanding of divine simplicity in which God's being and attributes are inseparable).

[50]   Augustine, *Confessions* 13.5.5–6, pp. 275–76 (emphasis added).

[51]   When I write, "All creatures bear the divine image," I do not intend to reduce the *imago dei* or humans from their unique status in creation described in Gen 1:26–27. Instead, my use of the term "image" draws more from Jonathan Edwards, influenced by Augustine, who describes nature and the created world as "Images and Shadows of Divine Things." The created world bears God's presence and points to the Creator behind creation—the invisible God behind visible reality.

through christological participation or union with Christ.[52] Gerald Bonner says Augustine's understanding of participation follows other patristic authors, including St. Irenaeus, St. Athanasius, Gregory of Nyssa, and Cyril of Alexandria, who were careful to maintain "the absolute ontological distinction between God and creation. Only the Word is the Son of God by nature; the redeemed are children of God by participation"—justified and adopted by grace.[53]

Participation or union with Christ through prayer brings together the fractured sense of self that Augustine feels throughout his life's journey. Confession and communion draw him away from sinful self-alienation and draw him into relationship with the Triune God. When Augustine looks to creation, he turns to the Creator in prayer. Looking to God behind the material world, he writes, "Yet there is a light I love, and a food, and a kind of embrace when I love my God—a light, voice, odor, food, embrace of my inner man, where my soul is floodlit by light which space cannot contain, where there is sound that time cannot seize, where there is a perfume which no breeze disperses, where there is a taste for food no amount of eating can lessen, and where there is a bond of union that no satiety can part. That is what I love when I love my God."[54] He rests in this "bond of union." Encountering divine presence in nature evokes prayerful union with God.

Dialoguing with creation, Augustine asks where its beauty lies. He maintains his attention through a kind of meditation and says,

> And what is the object of my love? I asked the earth it said, "It is not I." I asked all that is in it; they made the same confession (Job 28:12f). I asked the sea, the deep, the living creatures that creep, and they responded: "We are not your God, look beyond us." I asked the breezes which blow and the entire air with its inhabitants said: "Anaximenes was mistaken; I am not your God." I asked heaven, sun, moon, and stars; they said: "Nor are we the God whom you seek." And I said to all these things in my external environment: "Tell me of my God who you are not, tell me something about him." And with

52 Augustine, *Confessions.*

53 Gerald Bonner, "Deification, Divinization," in Fitzgerald, *Augustine Through the Ages*, 265–66. Bonner distinguishes our participation from that of God the Father and God the Son. The Word or Son of God shares in the same nature as God, Father and Spirit. The redeemed children of God are taken up by grace through union with the Son.

54 Augustine, *Confessions* 10.6.9, p. 183.

a great voice they cried out: "He made us" (Ps 99:3). *My question was the attention I gave to them, and their response was their beauty.*[55]

The cry of creation is "He made us." This resonates with Augustine. The point of creation conveys divine presence. Augustine grants creation his attention and focus, receiving its transcendent meaning by reflecting its maker.

Looking to creation in prayer, Augustine communes with the Creator behind the world's beauty. Here he finds integration and wholeness rather than the dispersion and fragmentation endemic not only to the Roman Empire but also to today's digital empire. Union with God uplifts the soul, unlike digital technologies that split our attention, sense of wholeness, and body-soul experience. Spending more time scrolling causes us to feel less human—not more.[56] Even as we are often unaware of wasted time or the negative impact digital tools have on our body, technology depletes our energy rather than refreshing us physically or spiritually.

Augustine's understanding of creation, in contrast, displays what Verhey calls "enchanted nature." Neither subject to idolatry (a kind of pantheism) nor empty of sacred life (a kind of animism), enchanted nature differs from modern tendencies to see nature function as machine.[57] Instead, the narrative of creation found in Genesis describes a "continuing and intimate relationship between God and nature. God is continuously *present* to the creation, involved in its life, and the creation continuously manifests God's power and grace."[58]

Protestant theologian Jonathan Edwards was also captivated by beauty in nature as shadows pointing to their divine source. In his "Heaven is a World of Love" and "Images and Shadows of Divine Things," Edwards describes light and beauty emanating from God. The created world points to its heavenly fulfillment or teleology in union with Christ.[59] The natural

---

[55]   Augustine, *Confessions* 10.6.9, p. 183 (emphasis added).

[56]   Conor Kelly, *The Fullness of Free Time: A Theological Account of Leisure and Recreation in the Moral Life* (Georgetown University Press, 2020), 136.

[57]   Allen Verhey, *Nature and Altering It* (Eerdmans, 2010), 70. Viewing nature as enchanted contrasts Charles Taylor's critique of Protestant interpretations on nature as disenchanted and George Grant's critique that all Protestant theologies lack contemplation. Taylor includes Edwards in a description (taxonomy) of mystics (Taylor, *A Secular Age*, 729–30).

[58]   Verhey, *Nature and Altering It*, 70 (emphasis added).

[59]   Jonathan Edwards, "Images or Shadows of the Divine," in *Selected Writings of Jonathan Edwards*, 2nd ed., ed. Harold P. Simonson (Waveland Press, 2004), 161–65,

world points to its supernatural source. Edwards says, "Thus I believe the grass and other vegetables growing and flourishing, looking green and pleasant as it were, ripening, blossoming, and bearing fruit from the influences of the heavens, the rain and wind and light and heat of the sun, to be on purpose to represent the dependence of our spiritual welfare upon God's gracious influences and the effusions of His holy spirit."[60] Edwards sees not only beauty and harmony in the created world reflecting its Creator, particularly through dependence, but also its redemptive aspect pointing toward its final end.

Edwards's cosmology sees the world much like Augustine, teeming with dependence and grace analogously portrayed through light and the natural world. In fact, Edwards's theology reflects the ambivalent nature of sin and grace this side of the fall through our surrounding world. The rose, which grows with its briars, thorns, and bloom, and the silkworm that wraps us in glorious clothing after its death, point to Christ.[61] Likewise, the daily rising and setting of the sun displays death and resurrection while the hills and mountains point to the celestial heavens and the steep path by which we ascend through challenges and difficulties.[62] Edwards draws together the material and spiritual world as one pointing to divine presence while awaiting its fulfillment.

Edwards also offers a helpful antidote to George Grant's critique of Protestant theology devoid of contemplation or specified ends intrinsic to created nature. Edwards is Thomist in his theology by emphasizing nature's whole rather than emphasizing mechanistic parts that portray instrumental value only.[63] He understands nature as enchanted with meaning rather than Manichaean or nihilistic in ways that belittle the material world or empty its value as seen through the digital empire. Instead, Edwards contemplates the beauty of creation as revelation much like Augustine, while drawing from his contemporary scientific sources—such as Newton—that preserve his own Protestant emphasis on regeneration.

167–68; Jonathan Edwards, "Heaven Is a World of Love," in *The Works of Jonathan Edwards*, vol. 8, *Ethical Writings*, ed. Paul Ramsey (Yale University Press, 1989), 385–6.

[60]   Edwards, "Images or Shadows of the Divine," 161–62.

[61]   Edwards, "Images or Shadows of the Divine," 161–62.

[62]   Edwards, "Images or Shadows of the Divine," 164.

[63]   Michael J. McClymond and Gerald R. McDermott, *The Theology of Jonathan Edwards* (Oxford University Press, 2012), 6; see also Charles Taylor's brief mention of Jonathan Edwards as contemplative alongside other mystics including Teresa of Ávila and Francis of Assisi (Taylor, *A Secular Age*, 729–30).

Edwards recognizes divine simplicity holds the complex world together in coherence. Harold Simonson describes Edwards's analogy of science to theology:

> In short, physics is something more than sequence or mechanism and, by analogy, justification of salvation (effect) is something more than man's faith (cause). Whatever this power is that causes atoms to cohere in sequence is not, said Newtonians, inherent in the atoms. Gravity, they said, is not synonymous with mass or solidity. What the cause of gravity or the coherence of the atoms is, Newton did not or could not say. Edwards, however, pursued the quest to the conclusion that, as gravity inheres in matter, so God inheres in gravity, and, in consequence, God inheres in all things. All things are in God. No matter is merely matter. God gives being and oneness to all substance . . . Man's goodness is not prior but posterior to God's grace. When Edwards declares that God is sovereign, he means just that. In God is coherence.[64]

Acting prior to creation and re-creation, grace brings about the world's coherence. God inheres in all things. The opening to Augustine's *Confessions* says God fills all things yet nothing contains him fully.[65] In other words, the created order exists through dependence or participation in the divine. God's presence is abundant in the natural world, imaging the divine with the story of creation and redemption.

Nature as creation is beautiful in its harmony, order, and form, pointing to something greater than itself. In *The Advantage of Believing* Augustine says,

> Think of the alternation of day and night and the undeviating pattern of the heavenly bodies, the four seasons of the year, the fall and return of the leaves of the trees, the infinite powers of seeds, the beauty of light and colors and sounds and smells, and the variety of tastes. Imagine being able to talk to someone who saw and experienced these things for the first time. That person would be astonished and overwhelmed by the miracles. We, on the other hand, think little of all these things . . . I call a miracle any event that is so

[64]   Harold P. Simonson, introduction to Simonson, *Selected Writings of Jonathan Edwards*, 6–7. This passage alludes to Edwards's description of justification from "Justification by Faith Alone."
[65]   Augustine, *Confessions* 1.2–3, pp. 3–4.

difficult or extraordinary as to be beyond the expectation or power of those it astonishes.[66]

As though putting on a new pair of glasses, Augustine sees creation and its re-creation as miraculous. The created world tells this story when we have eyes to see. The natural world is laden with transcendent meaning, yet we too often miss it when glued to digital devices. Our human tendency treats the familiar as mundane and ordinary. Passing by everyday miracles and breathtaking views, we mediate the world through digital devices that weaken our vision. Augustine draws attention to the extraordinary, perhaps enchanted, ways that creation manifests God's presence through everyday life. His teaching, preaching, and writing call the listener to wake up and respond. Like the psalmist, Augustine affirms all creation sings the praises of its Creator.

Part to Whole

Augustine believes the beauty of nature should be "self-evident to all who are of sound mind."[67] A major theme in classical philosophy involves the significance of parts and how they relate to the whole.[68] For him, the harmonious order of creation is clear. Differing from mechanistic images of nature that treat creation as parts to be used, here nature points to something greater or transcendent. Aristotle's ethics discerns whether, to what degree, and how individual organisms relate to patterns in nature, connecting the particular and universal. Likewise, Plotinus and Neoplatonic philosophy's influence shapes Augustine's understanding of wholeness and simplicity as the highest good. Combined with Scripture, these themes influence his anthropology composed of body and soul as well as his understanding of the divine Trinity.

For Augustine, divine simplicity is essential. The oneness of God not only holds the soul together but also maintains beauty and harmony in nature. Serge Lancel says,

> In the creation the likeness was an image of oneness, which belonged only to God. It was true of things or living beings, where there was

[66]   Augustine, *The Advantage of Believing*, trans. Ray Kearney, in *On Christian Belief*, ed. Boniface Ramsey, The Works of Saint Augustine: A Translation for the 21st Century, part 1, vol. 8 (New City Press, 2005), 16.34, pp. 136–37.

[67]   Augustine, *Confessions* 10.6.10, p. 184.

[68]   Augustine says, "Truth says to me: 'Your God is not earth or heaven or any physical body.' The nature of that kind of being says this. They see it: nature is a physical mass, less in the part than in the whole'" (*Confessions* 10.6.10, p. 184).

oneness in species only by the resemblance of individuals among themselves. The same applied to the soul, which was not one and not happy except insofar as the constant similitude of its actions and virtues conferred on it an appearance of oneness. And that meditation finished with the fleeting gleam of an aesthetic discourse; beauty in nature. Augustine concluded provisionally, lay above all in the harmony and proportion of parts with one another, the expression of their resemblance and relationship with God's creative oneness.[69]

Parts working together as one display creation's interdependence. Through its unity and harmony, nature reflects the Creator's oneness and simplicity.

Three in one, divine simplicity creates a world full of difference. God's creative act involves differentiation, yielding species identity, but also harmony through an ordered hierarchy that holds all things together.[70] Williams discusses the continuity and discontinuity of God with creation. God is like creation in that all created things are in God, derived from his essence. The material world includes intrinsic value apart from instrumental use only, differing from Manichaeism or modern mechanistic views of creation. Yet God is also unlike creation given his being remains fully outside creation, time, and space. In this way creation is neither animistic nor pantheistic ideals that subsume God in nature. Instead, God remains wholly other.[71]

Prayerful encounter with the created world involves recognizing nature as teeming with divine presence, worshipping God in whose image it's made. In this frame of reference, everything is sacred. Creation points to its Creator. Our direct encounter with the world is one of prayerful

[69]   Serge Lancel, *St. Augustine* (SCM, 1999), 176. Iain McGilchrist argues we too easily rely on the left hemisphere of the brain, perceiving the world as mechanistic parts to be acted upon rather than the whole understood through the right hemisphere. Instead, he argues we should align our perception with a more holistic understanding of the brain and world that reinvokes awe and wonder (Iain McGilchrist, *The Matter with Things: Our Brains, Our Delusions, and the Unmaking of the World* [Perspectiva, 2021]).

[70]   Rowan Williams highlights the ways in which Augustine's doctrine of creation offers a substantive interpretation for individual and collective identity, distinguishing its coherence apart from claims of domination or objectification. Williams disagrees with critics challenging Augustine's hierarchical assumptions given the importance in God's difference / unique status for preserving creation. God neither dominates creation nor is subsumed by creation.

[71]   Rowan Williams, "'Good for Nothing'? Augustine on Creation," *Augustinian Studies* 25 (1994): 11.

communion with God and everything that depends on him. Limiting our use of technology in its simulation will remain significant for helping us commune with God through organic life and nature as direct image rather than artificial copy.

Encountering the divine image in creation involves an ordered cosmos rather than chaos. Creation's beauty lies in its interdependence, harmony, and wholeness. Encountering God in creation helps silence the frenetic ways we regularly take in the world through digital technologies, diverting our attention in various directions. We desire order over chaos. Creation's general order points to this good. Williams says, "We can say, then, that creation shares or participates in God by being a coherent system," which Augustine describes as "measure, proportion, and weight."[72]

By *measure*, Augustine means fixed limits or circumscribed boundaries. Boundaries secure identity, setting limits for our good. *Proportion* relates to the intelligible shape of a thing, offering a "fitting response to circumstances," which might include self-regulating physical capacities, such as temperature or moral categories on "feelings and virtue."[73] These limitations hold significant implications for character and growth. We are not freed from embodied limits that technology often masks behind its limitless feeds and continuous stimulation. We need physical rest from technological stimuli that impacts our emotional regulation and capacity for self-control over impulse. We need proportionate rest and sleep. While AI and social media feeds are not technically limitless or infinite given their human creators, they appear limitless given their anytime, anywhere availability. Without boundaries they act more chaotic than ordered—cosmos—in which limits secure significant boundaries important for flourishing.

In terms of *weight*, Augustine refers to the end by which an object wills or loves. We are most defined by our loves and the goals to which they aim. When animated by divine love, we become attuned to our created end that loves God in return and brings joy as well as satisfaction. Attuning to divine love reorients our created end through the activities we share, participating in creation's more integrated whole. By loving God, we encounter the world and its inhabitants through prayer. A prayerful posture opens us to seeing transcendent beauty and purpose in the neighbor, world, and divine

---

[72] Williams cites Wis 11:21 from *On Genesis: A Refutation of the Manichees* 16.26 and *The Literal Meaning of Genesis* 4, in Williams, "'Good for Nothing'?" 12.

[73] Williams, "'Good for Nothing'?" 12.

presence in each object. The world exists in dependent relationship to the divine. Bearing his image, we can encounter divine presence in the neighbor and creation rather than immerse ourselves in its artificial copies.

In this sense, creation involves intrinsic and teleological ends as opposed to meaningless matter in motion prevalent within the modern technological lens.[74] Existence demonstrates some order and beauty through imaging the divine artist. This is not a mere afterthought, but "the direct impact of God on the world . . . the beauty and intelligibility of the world communicates to us the truth that God's action is the kind of action that produces harmonious effects . . . the cause of all harmony and loveliness."[75] For Augustine, to look at the beauty of the world is to see the beauty of God, those invisible attributes made known through the visible world. This does not eliminate the "risk, frustration, and terror" we also experience this side of the fall.[76] But even knowing these risks and frustrations point to the knowledge—or desire—for some order and equilibrium. In fact, all life—biological and moral—seeks what science might call equilibrium and what theology might call rest.

Moreover, Augustine posits that God creates a universe in motion, which draws on Stoic natural law influences by which there are "inbuilt principles that regulate the development of organisms according to predictable patterns (acorns grow into oaks, not daffodils or cows)."[77] Perhaps God's original algorithm, this argument from nature, along with our social arrangements desire peace and order.[78] Matter and spirit draw together properties, whether compound matter by way of chemical bond, or spiritual communion by way of love. The world is meant to be shared. Unity in diversity. The physical world resembles these spiritual realities.[79]

Augustine's premodern cosmology includes the creation of the "heaven of heavens" where the immortal angels participate in the Word or wisdom of God through eternal light.[80] All creation is dependent, even the angels

[74]   Craig M. Gay, *Modern Technology and the Human Future: A Christian Appraisal* (IVP Academic, 2018), 85, 145–47.

[75]   Williams, "'Good for Nothing'?" 13.

[76]   Williams, "'Good for Nothing'?" 14.

[77]   Williams, "'Good for Nothing'?" 14.

[78]   Williams, "'Good for Nothing'?" 14; Augustine, *City of God* 19.

[79]   Calvin even calls "the skillful ordering of the universe" a "sort of *mirror* in which we can contemplate God, who is otherwise invisible" (Calvin, *Institutes of the Christian Religion* 1.5.1, pp. 52–53; emphasis added).

[80]   Augustine, *City of God* 11.10, p. 440.

subsisting on divine light and life. Angels live not on their own resources but by participating in everlasting communion with God.[81] Analogously, we are dependent on God in ways that animate life. Augustine describes two parts to human identity: body and soul. Interpreting Genesis 1–2, he finds God creates matter (body) and breathes life (soul) into humans as the image of God. These parts are similar in their dependence on external sources for breath and life. We are not self-sufficient for life on our own. We are dependent in our need for breath and air.[82]

Reflecting the intended unity and dependence of their parts, Augustine describes humans in terms of "ensouled" bodies. Ensouled bodies are mutable, subject to change, demonstrated through their conditional freedom as depicted in the garden. However, humans (typified through Adam and Eve) eat from the forbidden fruit and forfeit their unified, harmonious existence in the presence of God. Sin is the process by which they become alienated from God and one another. Exiled from the garden, humans now experience separation and even conflict between body and soul, self and other, self and God. Part of what it means to be human after the fall involves experiencing conflict with our Creator, within oneself, and with neighbor. While we are intended for peace, harmony, and order in our created nature, we are born into a world subject to corruption, evil, and sin that works against these good ends. There is no part of creation untouched by this corruption.

This situation has significant implications for the way we encounter disorder, disharmony, conflict, and restlessness in our lives as a result of sin. It's as if we dropped a glass bowl and the pieces shattered. What was once unified is now fractured. Part of what drives Augustine's theology is bringing the shattered pieces together again through the divine–human mediator in Christ that forges a new identity for oneself and relationship with others. The depth of his theology holds significant impact on the ways we understand our relationship to self, neighbor, and creation, including our experience with technology. Belonging to the One who holds together time and eternity, memory and love further secures identity through wholeness and integration. Augustine's focus draws together the pieces of our fragmented self through prayer and communion with God, encountering his image in creation.

[81]   Augustine, *City of God* 12.22, p. 502.
[82]   Augustine, *City of God* 12.22, p. 502; see also Edwards, "Images and Shadows of Divine Things," 162.

Time and Eternity

Perhaps one of Augustine's greatest contributions to Western thought is his description of time and eternity. Predating existentialist philosophers such as Søren Kierkegaard, Jean-Paul Sartre, or Martin Heidegger, Augustine's reflection on identity and our relation to time is prescient. Restless in nature, Augustine questions the role of time for identity in terms of our experience with past, present, and future. To be created is to suffer change and variation. Augustine's interpretation of creation includes a world in motion full of process and development. With the passage of day and night comes the passage of time. Together time and space are cocreated. Rowan Williams says, "For Augustine, the temporal character of the created world is axiomatic: it is a world in motion, a set of processes in which potential is realized."[83] Time measures development and change. Yet without form or substance, we couldn't discuss change. In other words, the two work simultaneously together. With creation comes the passing of day, night, seasons, and change.

John Quinn discusses Augustine's concept of physical time, measuring material objects and psychological time located within memory.[84] Time is experienced in linear fashion as past, present, and future—yet time is perceived by the mind, or memory, in its ability to reflect on the past while projecting into the future. Augustine describes time as measuring duration or the movement of a body from beginning to end.[85] The present moment is always slipping away. Once words slip off the tongue, they cannot be retrieved. The present is constantly slipping into the past while each moment anticipates the future. Yet time is a mysterious experience in which we are existentially aware and nonaware.

We measure time by looking backward and projecting ahead through our own created instruments that measure our experience of this change, most notably through our use of mechanical clocks, calendars, journals, memoirs,

[83] Williams, "Creation," 252. Francis Collins finds Augustine's allegorical interpretation of the creation account involving process helpful in discussions of religion and science as complementary rather than antithetical (Francis Collins, "Science and Faith: Conflict or Complement?" Sermon, Park Street Church, Boston, February 28, 2010, https://www.parkstreet.org/messages/evening-sermon-science -amp-faith-conflict-or-complement/).

[84] John Quinn, "Time," in Fitzgerald, Augustine Through the Ages.

[85] Augustine, Confessions 11.23.30–31.41, pp. 238–45.

newspapers, photography, and even religious ritual.[86] Unfortunately, modern technology often alters our sense of time, making it a commodity to control. Nicholas Carr describes the irony of timekeeping through the evolution of clocks.[87] What began as instruments reminding religious monks to pray progressed to mechanical clocks that drove productivity through industrial capitalism. Differing from prior time-keeping instruments such as sundials that offered a more organic relationship to time or church bells ringing as a divine reminder to pray, new technologies treat time as something to keep, own, or consume.[88] With the aid of digital instruments and increased hyperspeed, we increase efficiency yet demand more output. Operating with the mantra "Time is money," we expect increased productivity.[89] The result is often an "inhuman compression of time" by which the instruments leave us impoverished and wanting.[90] "Time-saving" can often become "time-serving."[91] Faster is not always better.[92]

Unlike the modern technological focus on time in terms of self-gain and productivity, Augustine turns to time for a broader understanding of creation's purpose. While Augustine's understanding of time and eternity takes an inward turn, it does not result in selfishness or self-preoccupation often associated with the modern autonomous lens. Kohák finds his "'inward' vision spans the full range of reality—the presence of God, the sweep of history, the works of humans. If anything, it was the Roman world around him, scorning all inward turn in a feverish preoccupation with the gratification of all its greed."[93] In this way Augustine's relationship to time reflected his reception and openness to God in creation rather than a posture of control and dominance.

---

[86] Religious ritual is distinctive within the items listed. Religious ritual reflects meaning or transcendence, a form of *kairos* time, an appointed time when God works, rather than ordinary *chronos* time, where we inhabit mundane temporality. *Kariotic* moments open us to transcendence, meaning, or gathered time. See Taylor, *A Secular Age*, 54–61.

[87] Nicholas Carr, *The Shallows: What the Internet Is Doing to Our Brains* (W. W. Norton, 2011), 41–44.

[88] Carr, *Shallows*.

[89] Gay, *Modern Technology*, 194–95.

[90] Gay, *Modern Technology*, 195; see also Felicia Wu Song, *Restless Devices: Recovering Personhood, Presence, and Place in the Digital Age* (IVP Academic, 2021), 156.

[91] Gay, *Modern Technology*, 195.

[92] Gay, *Modern Technology*, 195.

[93] Kohák, *Embers and the Stars*, 206.

His focus also distinguished Augustine from his philosophical influences. Contrasting Plato's understanding, Williams says, "You will see how [Augustine] introduces something quite fresh into theological discussion of the image of God in the human subject, which is no longer to be identified with a single feature or cluster of features, but with the orientation of the subject to God, with the radically unfinished character of thinking and wanting."[94] Imaging God is a gift from inception, but also an ongoing activity.

Unfinished in character, the temporal nature of creation involves its inherent development toward a specified goal—whether physical goals or moral goals directed by desire. Moving toward final goals, potential becomes actual. This is visible, or latent, from the smallest organism to the largest, whether seeds that become saplings or embryos that become human. Growth and development cannot short-circuit time. Instead, time is inherent to growth, searching for completion. Williams says, "Creation, then, is the realm in which good or beauty or stability, the condition in which everything is most freely and harmoniously itself in balance with everything else, is being sought and being formed. This is, of course, why there can be no short route to heaven: we must grow into new life, as the *Confessions* constantly reminds us."[95]

Life is growth. We either grow toward or away from our end goal. Just like the flower or tree, we grow toward our desired end or not. As moral creatures, we grow toward or away from loving God. One brings forth fulfillment and the other diminishment. For Augustine, we are made in God's image but grow in his likeness.[96] Growth is twofold—both physical and spiritual, body and soul. Such growth occurs in creation and re-creation. The Incarnate Word who enters time also endures growth and development through his own self-limitation. Jesus Christ's growth through time demonstrates not only participation in the laws of nature he once created, but also humility through his own vulnerability to the ways we problematically subverted the order of these laws through sin.[97] In his divine-human person, Christ not only works within the order of these laws, but also acts on these laws in ways that heal, restore, and transform our nature. As divinely Other, he has the power to create and restore.

---

[94]   Williams, "'Good for Nothing'?" 15.
[95]   Williams, "'Good for Nothing'?" 18.
[96]   Lancel, *St. Augustine*, 76.
[97]   Williams, "'Good for Nothing'?" 18.

In this way Augustine's view of nature is like and unlike the modern lens. Like the modern lens, he acknowledges the power of agency (human or divine) to act on nature, but unlike the modern lens in his teleological vision, nature ends in divine rest and completion. Rather than dominate, Williams says, God creates entirely apart from need—a radically gratuitous act. God's creative act demonstrates radical sharing through gift. As divine Other, God exists in eternal bliss without need for creation. But God chooses to share his nature by way of love.[98] This act of creation distinguishes him from the self-seeking ways we create in time. Instead, God creates without instrumental purposes.[99] Yet God cannot create without reference to himself as our good. In this sense, we are created for God's sake, given his source and fulfillment in all good. Like Irenaeus, the glory of God is the human fully alive. We are most alive when communing with the divine, reflecting his image through dependence, wherein time intersects with eternity.

Perhaps the best analogy for displaying dependence and fulfillment comes from light and life, drawing from the Gospel of John but also characteristic of writings from Augustine to Edwards. Not unlike photosynthesis in the natural world that depends on physical light for life and growth, we are analogously dependent on God's creative and re-creative light to illuminate our identity with life and meaning. Interestingly, light is behind the multiform colors we see. Darkness reflects its absence. Light illuminates and gives meaning to substance whether we try to capture or copy its glow through painting, photography, film, animation, or more recently BRDF, "bidirectional reflectance distribution functions."[100] Giving life to beloved Pixar characters from Woody in *Toy Story* to Merida in *Brave*, BRDF shapes and illuminates its beloved characters.[101] In this way our creative efforts image the divine Creator. Technology at its best images our divine gifts well through creativity with ordered ends.

---

[98]   Williams's provocative title, "'Good for Nothing'?" argues that God creates something radically other than Himself. Are we made simply for nothing? This play on words reflecting how we're made from nothing at creation suggests we are made for something more.

[99]   Williams, "'Good for Nothing'?" 19–22.

[100]   My family and I were exposed to the meaning of BRDF while observing a traveling Pixar exhibition at Boston's Museum of Science during July 2021. See Boston Museum of Science, "The Science Behind Pixar," https://sciencebehindpixar.org/.

[101]   Boston Museum of Science, "Science Behind Pixar."

However, we do not only copy and utilize light to illuminate vision in the physical world, whether artificial or real. Divine illumination also offers shape and meaning to characters formed in God's image. Divine illumination metaphorically offers understanding (moral wisdom), discovery (eureka, whether in science or art), and revelation (spiritual connection). In this case, light reflects the wholeness of eternity, whether at creation where God exercises authority over light (Gen 1) or revelation in which Christ portrays the source of light without need for the sun (John 1; Rev 1).

In contrast to time, which we experience in part and not in whole, Augustine distinguishes eternity thus: "In the eternal, nothing is transient, but the whole is present."[102] He says,

> In the sublimity of an eternity which is always in the present, you are before all things past and transcend all things future . . . Your "years" neither go nor come. Ours come and go so that all may come in succession. All your "years" subsist in simultaneity, because they do not change; those going away are not thrust out by those coming in. But the years which are ours will not all be until all years have ceased to be. Your "years" are "one day" (Ps 89:4; 2 Pet 3:8), and your "day" is not any and every day but Today, because your Today does not yield to a tomorrow, nor did it follow on a yesterday. *Your Today is eternity . . . Yet if the present were always present, it would not pass into the past: it would not be time but eternity.* If then, in order to be time at all, the present is so made that it passes into the past, how can we say that this present also "is"? . . . So indeed we cannot truly say that time exists except in the sense that it tends toward non-existence.[103]

Augustine describes eternity as the antithesis to time and change. It is wholly present. Augustine elevates eternity as simple, whole, unified, unlike our experience of time that involves disintegration. This is a Neoplatonist idea wherein time moves toward nonexistence, a falling away from its origin.[104] Time and change thwart the hope of eternity as meaningless. No wonder we feel anxious.[105]

---

[102]   Augustine, *Confessions* 11.3.13, p. 228.

[103]   Augustine, *Confessions* 11.13.16–14.17, pp. 230–31 (emphasis added).

[104]   Augustine, *Confessions* 11.29.39, p. 244, n. 31.

[105]   Part of the modern critique is its "immanent frame" or "immanent contentment." Charles Taylor notes that when we live with a closed interpretation of reality apart from the transcendent, whether by scientific, social, or technological structures, we find ourselves under pressure. New ideologies (or religions) replace old ones

Not only does the modern philosophical project bracket time from eternity, but technology also copies eternity's breadth through its expansive algorithms and endless digital feeds. While serving as tools that augment our daily life, these tools cunningly capture our time and attention as the "cage that goes everywhere with you."[106] Relying on the theory of behaviorist B. F. Skinner, Taylor asserts that the modern scientific imagination divides time into segments driven by "basic motives," involving "a primitive 'push' with very little emotional understanding, hence minimum meanings, just desire triggered by an object."[107] Shoshana Zuboff calls this "instrumentarian," in which our attention becomes the means for corporations' bottom line.[108] Beholden to the gaze of "Big Data," we're observed and influenced by the algorithms that shape the information available at our fingertips.[109] Splintering our time and attention, we chase objects that consume us on digital media. While they consume us, they exhaust us and reshape us in their image.[110] They wear down our moral fortitude and inner unity, eroding basic virtue while encouraging impulse and vice.[111] The chase for temporal objects wears on us.

Augustine looks to a divine remedy. As Henry Chadwick says, "Temporal successiveness is an experience of disintegration; the ascent to

---

through a continuous process of "destabilization and recomposition" (Taylor, *A Secular Age*, 594–95). See also Blaise Pascal's critique of Montaigne's "immanent contentment." Benjamin Storey and Jenna Silber Storey say, "Indeed, the quest for immanent contentment leaves the restless human heart more anxious than ever, for modernity's very success in remaking the world in man's image allows us to see, with terrifying clarity, that a human life is not the sort of problem a psychological stratagem can solve. In Pascal, the restlessness that is truly modern—the restlessness of the soul that tries and fails to hold itself within the confines of immanence—finds its first and most powerful voice" (Benjamin Storey and Jenna Silber Storey, *Why We Are Restless: On the Modern Quest for Contentment* [Princeton University Press, 2021], 52).

[106] Jaron Lanier, *Ten Arguments for Deleting Your Social Media Accounts Right Now* (Picador, 2018), 5.

[107] Taylor, *A Secular Age*, 595.

[108] Zuboff, *Age of Surveillance Capitalism*, 376ff.; and see fig. 4, pp. 396–97.

[109] Zuboff, *Age of Surveillance Capitalism*, 418.

[110] Zuboff refers to a "blizzard of mirrors" by which we descend with the "like" button on Facebook, "exponentially increasing raw-material supplies" (Zuboff, *Age of Surveillance Capitalism*, 457). Zuboff says, "The more that a user 'liked,' the more that she informed Facebook about the precise shape and composition of her 'hand,' thus allowing the company to continuously tighten the glove and increase the predictive value of her signals."

[111] Max Fisher, *The Chaos Machine: The Inside Story of How Social Media Rewired Our Minds and Our World* (Back Bay, 2023), 96–97.

divine eternity is a recovery of unity."[112] Searching for oneness involves integration—soul and body, part to whole, time and eternity. Augustine's overarching cosmology describes eternity as "gathered time."[113] Augustine says,

> See how my life is a distension in several directions. "Your right hand upheld me" (Ps 17:36; 62:9) in my Lord, the Son of man who is mediator between you the One and us the many, who live in a multiplicity of distractions by many things; so "I might apprehend him in whom also I am *apprehended*" (Phil 3:12–14), and leaving behind the old days I might be *gathered to follow the One*, "forgetting the past" and moving not towards those future things which are transitory but to "the things which are before" me, *not stretched out in distraction* but extended in reach, not by being pulled apart but by *concentration*. So I "pursue the prize of the high calling" where I "may hear the voice of praise" and "*contemplate* your delight" (Ps 25:7; 26:4) which neither comes nor goes.[114]

Augustine describes the way God gathers the pieces of himself through the One mediator, Christ, by whom he is apprehended. He encounters God's "presence" through concentration and focus as opposed to distraction. In this way he demonstrates the role of attentive presence—or prayer—for participation in God. His meditation is not simply self-emptying, but Christ- or Spirit-filling. Contemplating God grants him a sense of presence through union with the divine. Communing with God through prayer in creation draws together time with eternity, imaging God in love. Cultivating presence through imaging the divine unites our temporal actions here with eternity.

Charles Taylor further differentiates Augustine's sense of time from the Neoplatonic tradition that emphasizes eternity as the "really real, full being" outside of time that remains unchanging where "time is a moving image of eternity."[115] Instead, Augustine describes Jesus Christ as the road that unites means to end, displaying eternity's intersection with time.[116] Christian theology elevates the meaning of the body instead of separating it from spiritual reality. Creation, incarnation, and resurrection legitimize

[112] Augustine, *Confessions* 10.29.39, p. 244, n. 31.
[113] Taylor, *A Secular Age*, 595.
[114] Augustine, *Confessions* 11.29.39, pp. 243–44 (emphasis added).
[115] Taylor, *A Secular Age*, 55.
[116] Augustine, *Confessions* 7.27.34, p. 128; Augustine, *On Christian Teaching*, trans. R. P. H. Green (Oxford University Press, 1997), 1.33.37, p. 26.

the material realm and bodily existence. In this, "God enters into the drama of time."[117] Here Christianity departs from Plato in that God enters history and eternity intersects time.

Augustine's "gathered time" involves a kind of simultaneity that Taylor describes as "the gathering together of past into present to project a future. The past, which 'objectively' exists no more, is here in my present; it shapes this moment in which I turn to a future, which objectively is not yet, but which is here *qua* project."[118] Augustine further describes this simultaneity like a musical chord in which all notes sound together though one preceded the other in lived time.

Another example might include good conversation, which involves statements and rejoinder that together make a well-enjoyed whole. As Taylor says:

> Now Augustine holds that God can and does make all time such an instant of action. So all times are present to him, and he holds them in his extended simultaneity. His now contains all time. It is a "*nunc stans.*" So rising to eternity is rising to participate in God's instant. Augustine sees ordinary time as dispersal, distension, losing the unity, being cut off from our past and out of touch with our future. We get lost in our little parcel of time. But we have an irrepressible craving for eternity, and so we strive to go beyond this.[119]

Our temptation, of course, is to elevate our parcel of time, granting it more significance than necessary and so forging a kind of disordered love.[120] Unlike our technological habits that divide our attention, loves, and memory, time in nature and prayerful meditation unite us with the eternal God and the moral sense of nature as a created whole.

Still, the significance of Augustine's description of eternity distinguishes it from Platonic time—an escape to eternity; instead, "God's eternity . . . doesn't abolish time, but gathers it into an instant. This we can only have access to by participating in God's life."[121] Gathering the traces of ourselves, we experience belonging and identity through divine participation and prayer. Openness to God's presence through prayer holds

117 Taylor, *A Secular Age*, 56.
118 Taylor, *A Secular Age*, 56.
119 Taylor, *A Secular Age*, 57.
120 Taylor, *A Secular Age*, 57.
121 Taylor, *A Secular Age*, 57.

significant implications for identity and belonging, which Augustine further describes through memory and love.

Memory, Image, and Love

Augustine considers the depth and intimacy by which the Creator knows him. Herein he finds his identity and sense of belonging. Not only moving outward, but also inward, he comes to know himself relating to God as image. He says, "Indeed, Lord, to your eyes, the abyss of human consciousness is naked (Heb 4:13). What could be hidden with me, even if I were unwilling to confess it to you? I would be hiding you from myself, not myself from you."[122] Plumbing the mysterious depths of his own consciousness, Augustine recognizes God as closer to him than his own thoughts.

In his desire for self-understanding, he describes the role of memory in forging human identity and awareness of God.[123] Recognizing the different capacities of memory, he first describes the ways in which memory recalls images and traces of objects in time and space.[124] Here recollection draws forward images once touched, tasted, smelled, seen, or heard.[125] But beyond recalling the image of objects, we also retain intelligible ideas interpreting meaning and drawing coherence.[126] We also recall emotions experienced through time, deepening our understanding and reflection. Interestingly, Augustine's description of memory sounds like contemporary descriptions of short-term memory and long-term memory.[127] We can reflect on a limited amount of information in the present through working or short-term memory, while long-term memory stores these thoughts drawing them forward during deep reflection, interpretation, and problem-solving.[128]

---

[122]   Augustine, *Confessions* 10.1–2.2, p. 179.

[123]   Turning to memory for identity should not suggest individuals with Alzheimer's disease or dementia lack identity. One way of interpreting Augustinian memory is to recognize God's memory as greater than human memory. God does not forget Augustine or overlook his thoughts even when Augustine hides his thoughts from God. For more in-depth reflection on the importance of divine memory and community recollection see John Swinton, *Dementia: Living in the Memories of God* (Eerdmans, 2012), 195–226.

[124]   Augustine, *Confessions* 10.8.12–14, pp. 185–87.

[125]   Augustine, *Confessions* 10.9.16–10.17, pp. 187–88.

[126]   Augustine, *Confessions*, 188–92; Nello Cipriani, "Memory," trans. Matthew O'Connell, in Fitzgerald, *Augustine Through the Ages*, 553–54.

[127]   Carr, *Shallows*, 120–26.

[128]   Carr, *Shallows*, 120–26.

Through all these modes, Augustine associates memory with thought and identity, which draw him closer toward God:

> Great is the power of memory, an awe-inspiring mystery, my God, a power of profound and infinite multiplicity. And this is mind, this is I myself. What then am I, my God? What is my nature? It is characterized by diversity, by life of many forms, utterly immeasurable. See the broad plains and caves and caverns of my memory. The varieties there cannot be counted, and are, beyond any reckoning, full of innumerable things . . . I run through all these things, I fly here and there, and penetrate their working as far as I can. But I never reach the end. So great is the power of memory, so great is the force of life in a human being whose life is mortal. What then ought I to do, my God? You are my true life. I will transcend even this my power which is called memory. I will rise beyond it to move toward you, sweet light . . . I will pass beyond even that power of mind which is called memory, desiring to reach you by the way through which you can be reached and to be bonded to you by the way in which it is possible to be bonded.[129]

Memory is one of our greatest capacities, drawing coherence across a life through past, present, and future. It is through memory that Augustine encounters objects recalled, the realm of ideas, emotions, God, and his very identity in relation to God. As timebound creatures with a body and soul, memory connects ideas across the lifespan. Reflecting through memory, we enact wisdom in the present moment. Yet as deep as his cavernous memory is, God is beyond memory, filling and holding him together—an identity received by grace. Our memory and identity exist in God's memory.[130]

This holds significant impact on how we conceive technology and its relation to memory. At many levels, digital technologies aid memory,

[129]   Augustine, *Confessions* 10.17.26, p. 194.
[130]   Recognizing God's memory as greater than ours is significant, particularly for individuals experiencing dementia and cognitive challenges to memory. Critiquing Augustine's "spatial" understanding of memory as identity, John Swinton's important work reminds creatures they belong to God and divine memory even when capacities are lost. Remaining in the memory of God and memories shared with our community through time reminds creatures of our primary relational identity when imaging God. Relationality through God's sustenance and action rather than intelligence is primary as *imago dei*, drawing from Ps 139 (Swinton, *Dementia*, 210–22).

copying information and images to later recall in a nanosecond. They are helpful tools that expand our capacities to remember and retain information, allowing us to "set our memories on the shelf" or save them in a digital file folder for later recollection. Yet digital technologies also shape memory. Not only does the sheer volume of information access overwhelm users, but also the speed by which it disrupts consciousness through rapid communication and notifications. How does overwhelming our short-term memory's cognitive load impact our long-term memory and its capacity for deep learning and moral formation?[131] Does increased use of short-term memory encourage impulse and reaction rather than self-control and reflection in their capacity to develop virtue?[132]

Likewise, digital technologies deliver vast opportunities to copy memory through images in the form of photography and film. Digital images are an excellent resource to augment our memory through teaching and recollection. However, too often digital technologies become a primary form of encountering the world. When this is the case we are more heavily influenced by copies of the divine image that commodify creation and human beings, shaping our moral vision in negative ways.

As Carr mentions, wisdom differentiates humans from machines.[133] Machines hold vast amounts of memory and stored data—yet how do they interpret information apart from human actors or algorithms set by human actors?[134] Machines reflect programmed knowledge structures and,

---

[131] Carr, *Shallows*, 123–26. Iain McGilchrist argues we should use our whole brain for perceiving wisdom as opposed to relying on the dominant left hemisphere in its mechanistic division of the world into parts or things. Instead, whole-brain perception, integrating right and left hemispheres, perceives the wisdom of the mind and wisdom of the world we inhabit (McGilchrist, *Matter with Things*).

[132] See Fisher, *Chaos Machine*, 96–97; Justin Barrett and Pamela King, *Thriving with Stone Age Minds: Evolutionary Psychology, Christian Faith, and the Quest for Human Flourishing* (IVP, 2021), 102–10.

[133] Carr, *Shallows*, 216–22.

[134] In a fascinating example, Anthony K. Brandt distinguishes between spontaneous and deliberative knowledge. Spontaneous knowledge reflects computational knowledge associated with algorithms and machine-learning as opposed to deliberative, intentional, or teleological knowledge associated with humans. This is the premise behind Brandt's argument distinguishing between human deliberative knowledge in Beethoven's Ninth Symphony as opposed to an AI-generated Tenth Symphony involving spontaneous knowledge reflecting patterns, sequence, and imitative rhythms (Anthony K. Brandt, "Beethoven's Ninth and A.I.'s Tenth: A Comparison of Human and Computational Creativity," *Journal of Creativity* 33, no. 3 [2023]: 1).

increasingly with generative AI, compound knowledge insight and creative abilities.[135] An ordered way to approach AI tech involves circumscribing boundaries that delineate computational and basic tasks while preserving higher goods involving relationships, learning, embodied activity, and experiences significant to memory and consciousness. While generative AI offers new opportunities to offload cognitive tasks, it also risks eliminating important tasks relevant to working memory that later develops into wisdom.[136] Ongoing questions remain as to whether repetitive tasks can be separated from deeper reflection that draw together purposeful ends without negatively impacting our capacity for wisdom and agency.[137]

Similarly, with generative AI's ability to build complex knowledge structures, we face new questions about how knowledge is sourced, garnered, stored, and synthesized. Will generative AI include "hallucinations" or "knowledge soup" that replace original understanding, including fabrications with wrong information?[138] What happens when knowledge repeatedly builds on copy after copy? Perhaps this is how civilization and cultures transmit knowledge to some degree already. Yet does granting AI tools more access and authority in our workplaces and personal lives also increase its control over us?

As we encounter new digital tools between social media and generative AI, we will face new ethical issues around eyewitness, source theory, and historical records for discernment in individual and collective memory. In this way generative AI might amass vast amounts of knowledge that

---

[135]   Stephen Wolfram, *What Is ChatGPT Doing . . . and Why Does It Work?* (Wolfram Media, 2023), 38–39.

[136]   Matt Beane, "Gen AI Is Coming for Remote Workers First," *Harvard Business Review*, July 22, 2024, https://hbr.org/2024/07/gen-ai-is-coming-for-remote-workers-first.

[137]   Ian Bogost describes how AI lost its spark, reducing new tools from ChatGPT "to the mule worthy burden of mere tasks." While generative AI might help accomplish more basic tasks, he finds humans necessary for verifying information and establishing trust. Yet AI's move into the background also reflects its power. Operating in our everyday world without noticing suggests the technology is here to stay much like the use of other modern conveniences whether dishwashers, refrigerators, or iPhones (Ian Bogost, "AI Has Lost Its Magic," *Atlantic*, April 4, 2024, https://www.theatlantic.com/technology/archive/2024/04/ai-magic-taking-over/677968).

[138]   Given AI's hallucinations, human fact-checking will remain necessary for medical care, invoking a "partnership between humans and AI" or humans and machines through a kind of "symbiotic medicine." See Peter Lee, Carey Goldberg, and Isaac Kohane, *The AI Revolution in Medicine: GPT-4 and Beyond* (Pearson Education, 2023), 15–18.

appear whole, omniscient, or even eternal, but at the expense of its parts. Rather than gather the parts into a whole, this new technology gathers the whole while eliminating its parts—whether copying voice actors, text writers, mathematical equations, or possibly relationships themselves.[139]

Eternity, however, gathers time and divine memory fulfills human identity without eliminating it. Wisdom differs from knowledge in its ability to synthesize and reflect holistically, combining knowledge with experience across time. Augustine's and Carr's understanding of wisdom involve memory and contemplation away from immediate stimuli. Wisdom is an art cultivated and discerned over a lifetime through various stages, including peaks and valleys, gains and failures.

Nature is significant for removing us from the urgency of life's demands to reflect on time as a whole. Opening our eyes to nature reminds us that we're participants in something larger than ourselves. Carr and Turkle cite Thoreau's reverence for nature, encouraging our capacity to contemplate apart from immediate stimuli invoked by the tech world.[140] Even while driving past Walden Pond in Concord, Massachusetts, where Thoreau famously wrote *Walden* away from the urgent demands of Boston city life, my cell phone service often drops, reminding me of technology's frailty and the importance of rest from that way of living.[141] Taking time away in nature helps integrate our sense of belonging to something greater, something transcendent. Away from the restlessness of our digital technologies, the beauty of nature encourages more opportunity for integrating our identity as a whole rather than parts.

In *The Trinity*, Augustine explores the analogous ways the parts relate to the whole as humans image the divine Trinity. In 12.1 he describes the ways in which memory, sense, and reason are connected, much like the

---

[139]   Charlie Warzel, "OpenAI Just Gave Away the Entire Game," *Atlantic*, May 21, 2024, https://www.theatlantic.com/technology/archive/2024/05/openai -scarlett-johansson-sky/678446/.

[140]   Sherry Turkle, *Reclaiming Conversation: The Power of Talk in a Digital Age* (Penguin Books, 2015), 9–11.

[141]   *Black Walden* describes the history of slavery in eighteenth-century Concord, MA, and its segregated aftermath. While Thoreau and transcendentalist philosophers benefitted from a socioeconomic structure that brought leisure, *Black Walden* recognizes the contribution by former slave Brister Freeman, despite challenges in a stratified economic system. See Elise Lemire, *Black Walden* (University of Pennsylvania Press, 2019); Craig Lambert, review of *Black Walden*, by Elise Lemire, *Humanities* 31 no. 5 (2010), https://www.neh.gov/humanities/2010/ septemberoctober/feature/black-walden.

spirit and body, bringing together the eternal and temporal realms.[142] Body and soul, sense and mind work together while acknowledging a rational order.[143] In this way creatures can transcend time through memory, "psychological time," perceiving past, present, and future while living as bodies in physical time.[144] Perceiving past, present, and future as psychological and spiritual beings, we enact moral agency through contemplation and action or prayer and virtue. These are moral capacities developed in real time away from technology and aided through nature. Contemplation and action are pursued through our mind, understanding, and will, which image God through love.[145]

With regard to imaging God Augustine says, "The trinity of the mind is not really the image of God because the mind remembers and understands and loves itself, but because it is also able to remember and understand and love him by whom it was made. And when it does this it becomes wise."[146] Wisdom comes from knowing, remembering, and loving God.[147] Love demonstrates the intention of our heart and mind. Through humility and prayer, the creature before the Creator finds identity through dependence and belonging. This is the beginning of wisdom (Prov 9:10). Foolishness forgets the God by whom and in whose image we are made. In this sense Augustine is consistent throughout his anthropology. Dependence marks creatures, securing identity through belonging as opposed to self-enclosed individualism.

This identity is one that intersects body and soul, time and eternity. God dwells in memory yet remains beyond individual capacity, holding us in divine memory or recognition.[148] This same God "called and cried out loud and shattered my deafness. You were radiant and resplendent, you put to flight my blindness. You were fragrant, and I drew in my breath and now pant after you. I tasted you, and I feel but hunger and thirst for you. You touched me, and I am set on fire to attain the peace which is yours."[149]

[142] Augustine, *The Trinity (De Trinitate)*, ed. John E. Rotelle, trans. Edmund Hill, 2nd ed. (New City Press, 1991), 12.1, pp. 323–24.

[143] Augustine, *The Trinity* 12.1, pp. 323–24.

[144] Quinn, "Time," 833–36.

[145] Augustine also uses the translation/analogy "memory, thought, and will" to describe the Trinity (*The Trinity* 10.4, pp. 300–302).

[146] Augustine, *The Trinity* 14.4, p. 384.

[147] Augustine, *The Trinity* 14.4, p. 384.

[148] Augustine, *Confessions* 10.25.36, pp. 200–201; see also Swinton, *Dementia*, 194–98.

[149] Augustine, *Confessions* 10.27.38, p. 201.

In this passage God is revealed through nature and the tangible senses, uniting time with eternity, matter with spirit, and the external world with internal reflection.

Unlike the modern technological lens that separates nature from spiritual meaning or individuals from external obligation, creation is alive with divine meaning. Enchanted, we live in a world of everyday miracles when we have eternal eyes to see the meaning of each temporal moment. Heaven and nature sing when we align our will with eternal love.[150] Seeking to love God unifies our body and soul with time and eternity through prayer and virtue. Communing with God behind nature reminds us of our creaturely identity and belonging. Building this moral sensibility from nature expands our sense of wholeness and communal responsibility to creation and one another.

In this schema, each temporal moment contains the potential for fullness and divine presence akin to the ways in which light reflects God and illuminates creation. Imaging God is a continuous activity as we grow in likeness on the journey through time. *Exitus reditus*. We come from God and return to him. Belonging to God as divine image brings meaning to individual identity, but also the harmonious beauty and order of creation's whole. Unlike our digital technologies that divide attention, waste time, and draw us away from nature through impulse and immediate stimuli, prayerful contemplation in nature reminds us of the opposite: interdependence and responsibility to one another, encouraging virtue. Rather than prioritize individualization as our primary encounter with the world, we should instead recognize how identity is marked by interdependence, one forged through a divine-human encounter intimately known through face-to-face presence.

---

[150] "Joy to the World," by Issac Watts, 1719.

4
Face to Face

THE POWER OF FACE-TO-FACE PRESENCE

An October 2023 study found differences in neural activity between Zoom interactions and live face-to-face conversations.[1] The study concludes that in-person interactions are superior to Zoom or other online conversations given increased neural activity associated with gaze time, eye-tracking, and pupil dilation, as well as interest involving social cues.[2] The study finds "more coordinated neural activity between the brains of individuals conversing in person," with "reciprocal exchange . . . between the interacting partners."[3] The study confirms that face-to-face interactions increase what most people experience—greater empathy and understanding. Jonathan Haidt describes in-person bonds as "attunement" offering serve and return expression as well as conversation developing our moral and relational muscles. Attunement socially connects us with others, an important skill for adolescents as well as adults.[4]

---

[1]   Bess Connolly, "Zoom Conversations vs In-Person: Brain Activity Tells a Different Tale," *Neuroscience News*, October 26, 2023, https://neurosciencenews.com/zoom-conversations-social-neuroscience-24996/; N. Zhao et al., "Separable Processes for Live 'In-Person' and Live 'Zoom-Like' Faces," in *Imaging Neuroscience* 1 (2023): 1–17, https://doi.org/10.1162/imag_a_00027.
[2]   Connolly, "Zoom Conversations vs. In-Person," 1; Zhao, "Separable Processes for Live 'In-Person' and Live 'Zoom-Like' Faces," 2.
[3]   Connolly, "Zoom Conversations vs. In-Person," 4.
[4]   See Jonathan Haidt, *The Anxious Generation: How the Great Rewiring of Childhood Is Causing an Epidemic of Mental Illness* (Penguin Books, 2024), 55–58.

This is not altogether surprising given the significance of facial recognition for infant and childhood development. As Andy Crouch points out: "Recognition is the first human quest," seeking an "interlocking gaze in those first hours following childbirth."[5] Longing for recognition or "attunement, attachment, and communion,"[6] we instinctually seek to know and be known, love and be loved—like the restlessness driving Augustine's search for belonging.[7] As timebound creatures our journey begins seeking a human face and ends seeking an eternal face.

Yet how do we understand the power of face-to-face interactions on our journey? How do faces connote presence akin to attunement, attachment, and communion? Sherry Turkle finds face-to-face interactions across difference as necessary ingredients for empathy and identity formation.[8] Likewise, philosopher Emmanuel Levinas locates ethics in our face-to-face encounters across difference: seeing the infinite behind the finite other.[9]

---

[5]   Andy Crouch, *The Life We're Looking For: Reclaiming Relationship in a Technological World* (Convergent, 2022), 3; see also Edward Tronick et al., "The Infant's Response to Entrapment Between Contradictory Messages in Face-to-Face Interaction," *Journal of the American Academy of Child Psychiatry* 17, no. 1 (1978): 1–13; Doris Y. Tsao and Margaret S. Livingstone, "Mechanisms of Face Perception," *Annual Review of Neuroscience* 31 (2008): 411–37, cited in Crouch, *Life We're Looking For*, 217.

[6]   Haidt, *Anxious Generation*, 55–58.

[7]   My use of the term "recognition" fundamentally includes a sense of knowing and being known. Using the plain sense of the term, I also acknowledge its philosophical and political categories described as the "politics of recognition" in which identity categories hinge on external recognition in some way—whether through neurological and psychological attachment forged during the infant–adult gaze or as political rights granted through social contract theory. See Charles Taylor, "The Politics of Recognition," in *Multiculturalism: Examining the Politics of Recognition*, ed. Amy Gutmann (Princeton University Press, 1994), 25–73. For my purposes, Charles Mathewes's use of divine recognition in its theological and eschatological weight comes closest to my definition from an Augustinian lens. Describing presence in the eschatological vision given the triune life of perichoresis, Mathewes says, "Both the idea of the last judgment and Paul's promise that one day we will see face to face radically contest our presumption for privacy. (The image of the last judgment when all will stand before the Lord fully revealed, is one moment when this is disquietingly suggested.) Our politics until heaven are but a sad and thin shadow of this divinely charged 'politics of recognition'" (Charles Mathewes, "An Augustinian Look at Empire," *Theology Today* 63, no. 3 [2006]: 305).

[8]   Sherry Turkle, *Reclaiming Conversation: The Power of Talk in a Digital Age* (Penguin Books, 2015), 3.

[9]   Emmanuel Levinas, *Alterity and Transcendence*, trans. Michael B. Smith (Columbia University Press, 1999).

Invoking the deepest questions of recognition and identity, Augustine's theology—like the Scripture to which he turns—addresses the significance of *face* for presence, belonging, and identity through its ancient wisdom.[10] The role of face, both divine and human, is significant for understanding image, identity, and presence through belonging. To explore this further, I consider the significance of face for demonstrating presence in biblical theology, as imaging God in likeness, as imaging Christ through presence, and finally as belonging together through shared communion.

WHAT'S IN A FACE? BIBLICAL EXPRESSIONS OF PRESENCE

We pass by them every day. Scroll or swipe through social media apps full of faces. We open phones and travel through customs in international airports thanks to facial recognition. We glance, greet, smile, cry, blush, gaze, kiss, and express a far range of emotions—or its opposite—hide through still faces.[11] Embodied, we experience all five senses in the facial region, aiding our survival, pleasure, and communication. Here we communicate stories verbally and nonverbally. Particular to each individual, our faces disclose, even controversially at some level, age, gender, race, ethnicity, and certain cultural values with the styling of makeup, piercings, hair, or religious coverings.[12] With these faces, we can observe, dismiss, or behold, seeking to know, understand, and love.

[10] I openly acknowledge the limits of contextual theology in my culturally situated lens by which I approach Augustinian interpretations of Scripture, face, and presence through a Western Protestant Christian perspective. That said, more insight might be discerned through Eastern emphases on face through an honor/shame lens that highlight "name, reputation, status, or face," as well as group belonging. See Jackson Wu and Ryan Jensen, *Seeking God's Face: Practical Reflections on Honor and Shame in Scripture* (Lucid Books, 2022), x–xi, 22–23. Thanks to Alan Tung for discussions about honor/shame culture and its relation to ethics.

[11] In 1975, social science researchers noted six basic emotions across cultures, concluding that anger, fear, disgust, surprise, happiness, and sadness are "universal" across cultures. Researchers later added three more emotions: shame, embarrassment, and pride. However, Batja Mesquita challenges these assumptions and the methods used to study emotion in its supposed "cross-cultural analysis." Mesquita instead argues that emotions can be culturally derived. Challenging the idea that emotions are formed by universal secularists, she contends that emotions are derived "between us" across relationships and cultures (Batja Mesquita, *Between Us: How Culture Creates Emotions* [Horton, 2022], 8–9).

[12] Kevin Vanhoozer notes the controversial understanding of faces in contemporary culture. Do faces represent socially constructed or received identities? He says, "What goes on my face is *makeup*, the rouge of rhetorical construction."

The face cannot be reduced to identity. Yet, the face is generally the entry way by which we encounter and remember one another. Theologian David Ford says, "A face is a distillation of time and memory. Think of the face of someone important to us and it conjures up past events, stories and associations, a world of meaning. It can reach into the future too, with plans, hopes, and fears. Imaginatively, we rehearse our lives and intentions before the faces of those we respect, fear, love . . . What faces do we have habitually in our hearts? Might that be one of the best clues to our identity?"[13]

Augustine would agree. The faces we remember and seek shape us, both human and divine. Whether from good or bad experiences, the degree to which we reflect on their impact forms us in profound ways. English scholar Maurice Hunt says the biblical and Augustinian concept of face influences Western literary works, including Shakespeare, Dostoevsky, Hesse, and C. S. Lewis in *The Divine Face in Four Writers*.[14] In the Judeo-Christian Scriptures, faces are significant. Hunt accounts for the presence and absence of divine faces and the human reception of these accounts.[15] He describes face in the Hebrew and Christian Scriptures: Beginning in the Old Testament, the role of face becomes an important locus for divine presence given that the Hebrew term *panim* translates as "face (356[x]), presence (75[x]), sight (40[x]), countenance (30[x]) and person (20[x]) in the English King James Version with influence in other translations."[16] The term "face" serves as an idiom for presence across Scripture from beginning to end. The creation narrative in Genesis involves God's presence

---

That said, Vanhoozer claims discipleship involves neither artificiality nor arbitrariness, but instead authenticity through received identities (Kevin J. Vanhoozer, *Faith Speaking Understanding: Performing the Drama of Doctrine* [Westminster John Knox, 2014], 115, 138; emphasis added).

[13]   David F. Ford, *Self and Salvation: Being Transformed* (Cambridge University Press, 1999), 18.

[14]   Maurice Hunt, *The Divine Face in Four Writers: Shakespeare, Dostoyevsky, Hesse, and C. S. Lewis* (Bloomsbury, 2016).

[15]   Hunt says, "Both Shakespeare and Dostoyevsky are indirectly indebted to Saint Augustine's argument set forth in on the Trinity that certain passages in the New Testament imply that the figure of Jesus Christ, including his face, constitutes the basis for a Christian's way of knowing—his or her epistemology" (Hunt, *Divine Face in Four Writers*, x).

[16]   These numbers mark translations in the King James Version, though David Ford acknowledges all strands of the Old Testament include *panim* through similar translations (Ford, *Self and Salvation*, 193).

hovering over the surface (face) of the deep; Revelation concludes with a vision of worshipers facing the Lamb (Gen 1:1–3; Rev 22:4).

The face is also important for conveying different ways individuals relate, at times displaying temptation toward sin, at others, empathic reconciliation. God questions Cain about his downcast face before Cain murders his brother Abel and God banishes Cain from his presence (Gen 4:5–6, 14, 16). Jacob wrestles with a mysterious divine figure who leaves him limping, an encounter he describes as seeing the face of God. After agonizing anticipation, Jacob embraces his estranged brother Esau with tears, saying, "I have seen thy face as though I had seen the face of God, and thou wast pleased with me" (Gen 33:10 KJV).[17] Seeing God's face "causes Jacob to see its image in Esau's face."[18] Encountering the divine face becomes a site of transformation (Gen 32:30).[19]

Similarly, when Joseph sees his estranged brothers he turns his face toward them with empathy—even compassion, forgiveness, and reconciliation. Hunt says, "The narrator has devised his story to cause the reader to infer a turning of Joseph's face to his brothers, and to make that synonymous with the expression of the most humane values. Presumably Joseph's brothers saw the same divinity reflected in his face that Jacob saw in Esau's face."[20] Later, when Jacob reunites with his son Joseph, "weeping upon his neck, he says, 'Now let me die, since I have seen thy face, because thou art [yet] alive'" (Gen 46:30).[21] The face is significant in these examples as the site of vulnerability, transformation, and forgiveness between individuals united through love.

In a different example, the guilty son Absalom bows before his father, King David, after experiencing banishment in response to committing murder. Hunt says, "David shows Absalom his face, which causes Absalom out of guilt to hide his face on the ground. But David, forgiving his son, raises him and kisses him on his face."[22] Hunt says these encounters illustrate the proverb "As in water face answereth to face, so the heart of man to man" (Prov 27:19 KJV).[23] The face serves as an "empathic

17 Hunt, *Divine Face in Four Writers*, 8.
18 Hunt, *Divine Face in Four Writers*, 8.
19 Hunt, *Divine Face in Four Writers*, 7.
20 Hunt, *Divine Face in Four Writers*, 8.
21 Hunt, *Divine Face in Four Writers*, 8–9.
22 Hunt, *Divine Face in Four Writers*, 9.
23 Hunt, *Divine Face in Four Writers*, 9.

signifier" that offers value to "seemingly ordinary references to face in the Bible."[24]

Similarly, accounts in the New Testament describe reconciliation, such as the parable of the Prodigal Son, in which the father kisses the younger brother, issuing forgiveness (Luke 15:20, 28). The elders of Ephesus display grief upon realizing they will encounter Paul's face, or presence, for the last time (Acts 20:36–38). But these are more than human encounters involving vulnerability and empathy: Scripture accounts for divine presence through these encounters.

Hidden and revealed, God speaks to Moses face to face and yet passes him by at "a cleft in the rock" (Exod 33:11, 18–23; 34:29–35). Jesus's transfiguration in the Synoptic Gospels complements the prior account of Moses, evoking fear among the disciples. Hunt highlights subtle details in these descriptions: Matthew reports, "His face did shine as the sun, and his raiment was white as the light" (Matt 17:2), while Luke's account says Jesus's "countenance was altered" (Luke 9:29).[25] Encountering divine presence evokes fear among the disciples much like Aaron viewing the face of Moses after his descent from Mount Sinai, resulting in a veil that covers his radiance (Exod 34:29–35).

Describing the face of Christ as the glory of God, Paul proclaims, "We all, with open face beholding in a glass the glory of the Lord, are changed into the same image from glory to glory, even as by the Spirit of the Lord . . . For God, who commanded the light to shine out of darkness, hath shined in our hearts, to give the light of knowledge of the glory of God in the face of Jesus Christ" (2 Cor 3:18; 4:6).[26] Encountering divine presence in the face of Christ ends in transformation. Augustine draws from these passages alongside 1 Corinthians 13, in which "we see through a glass darkly" while longing to see face to face.

The concept of "mirror" or "image" shapes Augustine's thought and the Western tradition. Hunt says, "St. Augustine and certain medieval theologians understood the glass in which we see the glory of the Lord to be within us, and that we perceive with the mind's eye. Since Paul says that God has shined his light into our hearts, this figurative glass was thought to be within the breast. It is in that glass that we see the face of Jesus Christ and have our knowledge of him, for this face radiates the ultimate glory

---

24   Hunt, *Divine Face in Four Writers*, 9.
25   Hunt, *Divine Face in Four Writers*, 6.
26   Hunt, *Divine Face in Four Writers*, 12.

of God."[27] In the figurative glass of the heart, individuals image what they love. As we are made originally in the image of God (Gen 1:27), the presence of Christ is revealed inwardly through our heart. Augustine explores these ideas further through facing God as image and likeness, presence, and communion (1 Cor 13:12).

IMAGING GOD IN LIKENESS

Augustine draws from the creation narrative for understanding individual and human identity. Central to this story is the description of humans made in the image and likeness of God. Lancel says everyone receives the image but can grow in likeness.[28] In other words, the term "image" functions as both noun and verb, status and activity. Everyone is born in the image, but we also have ability to grow in the image over time.

An important starting point for understanding image is to consider the idea of face. Augustine says, "The human face is common to all men. Yet everyone actually has his own."[29] Likening faith to the face by analogy, Augustine describes the universal and particular dimensions of faith—as well as face—that animate the individual within a shared community. For Augustine, self and God / self and other are not mutually exclusive. They are bound to one another through belonging. Philosopher Jean-Luc Marion describes Augustine's approach in *The Self's Place*. As image of the infinite, our finite existence is always referential, attaching to something beyond ourselves.[30] Through confession and praise the self receives an "ego," from without, as gift from God that opens the self to receive another *in* God.[31] Existence is from God and to God while sharing with others in the *imago dei*.

Turning to Augustine's work on the Trinity and Psalms, he invites us into dialogue and praise. From Marion's perspective, Augustine's works might be considered conversation from and to God—a *confessio*—shared

[27] Hunt, *Divine Face in Four Writers*, 12–13.

[28] Serge Lancel, *St. Augustine* (SCM, 1999), 385; Mary T. Clark, "Image Doctrine," in *Augustine Through the Ages*, ed. Allan D. Fitzgerald (Eerdmans, 1999), 441.

[29] Augustine, *The Trinity (De Trinitate)*, ed. John E. Rotelle, trans. Edmund Hill, 2nd ed. (New City Press, 1991), 13.1, p. 346. Esau McCaulley acknowledges the difference in particular believers and transformed faces from every tribe, tongue, and nation (Esau McCaulley, *Reading While Black: African American Biblical Interpretation as an Exercise in Hope* [IVP Academic, 2020], 117).

[30] Jean-Luc Marion, *In the Self's Place: The Approach of St. Augustine*, trans. Jeffrey L. Kosky (Stanford University Press, 2012), 311–12.

[31] Marion, *In the Self's Place*, 42–43, 261, 277–78.

in conversation with the reader. Augustine knew this well as an orator and pastor. Augustine's broad work *The Trinity* culminates near the
end of the volume. He demonstrates human dimensions that image the
Trinity—memory, understanding, and love represent one nature.[32] The
analogy of lover, beloved, and love reflect the three persons.[33] Yet the
image is broken (*The Trinity* book 12) and in need of repair. Jesus Christ
secures this repair (book 13). With book 14, Augustine turns to consider
"The Image Perfected."[34]

Throughout *The Trinity*, as elsewhere, Augustine describes humans in
the image of God. This does not hinge on human capacities but on God's
self-gift. We see through a mirror as an enigma while in time. Recognizing the fragility of his attempt in the first thirteen books describing the
Trinity, Augustine says, "We've been trying to see Him by whom we were
made by means of the image, which we ourselves are, the mirror."[35] Using
the Latin *speculum* or *specula* in the sense of "mirror," a "lookout point,"
he says we are passing from a "blurred image to a clear one."[36] Yet even a
blurred image is still the image of God. Augustine's anthropology draws
from Scripture's analogy.[37] Augustine begins with external analogies or
signs that point to an inward reality. He describes wisdom as seeing and
knowing the Word or Christ.[38] Wisdom is accompanied by action. Virtue

[32] Augustine, *The Trinity* 10.4, p. 300.

[33] Augustine, *The Trinity* 8.5, pp. 255–57.

[34] In this section, Augustine problematically differentiates male and female
as analogous to the inner mind or wisdom on the one hand, and lower knowledge
associated with temporal, material affairs on the other. Here grounding the image
of God in human capacities causes issues particularly through his account of gender difference (Augustine, *The Trinity*, 12.1–2, pp. 322–34). See also Catherine L.
McDowell, *The Image of God in the Garden of Eden: The Creation of Humankind
in Genesis 2:5–3:24 in Light of the* mīs pî pīt pî *and* wpt-r *Rituals of Mesopotamia
and Ancient Egypt* (Eisenbrauns, 2015). The best way to qualify Augustine's position
on women and their capacity for wisdom is to highlight his respect for his own
mother, particularly post-conversion, in which Monica participates with his fellow
philosophers in the *Cassiciacum Dialogues* and represents significant spiritual and
philosophical moments, such as their shared beatific vision at Ostia (Augustine,
Confessions, trans. Henry Chadwick [Oxford University Press, 1991], 9.10.23–24,
pp. 170–71).

[35] Augustine, *The Trinity* 15.3, p. 407.

[36] Augustine, *The Trinity* 15.3, p. 407.

[37] Augustine, *The Trinity* 15.3, pp. 408–9.

[38] Augustine, *The Trinity* 15.3, pp. 410–12.

depends on practical wisdom.[39] Outward actions, or virtue, display inward motives or loves. Images relate to their reference.

Words and gestures also demonstrate outward signs pointing to inner ideas or thoughts—"The Word became flesh" is a similar articulation of the idea (John 1:14). The incarnation communicates God among us in human time and space. The image of God in fullness: fully God and fully human walked among us. The incarnation is the central sign of God in time.[40] At this point consider a reflection in a lake, pool, or mirror. Unlike Narcissus, we are not staring at our own image but rather imaging the one in whom we are made. As creation, we are contingent and dependent on God as image and likeness.[41] We are *images*.

Understanding our identity in terms of image is an important theme with Augustine, mystical theology, and Jonathan Edwards.[42] Edwards expands analogies relating to image drawing from Scripture, such as a seal set in wax, a signet ring on the heart, or signs on one's forehead.[43] As a seal in soft wax or a signet ring on the heart, we signify what we image.[44] Imaging God and growing in likeness involves becoming what we love.[45] We are united with what we most love, growing in its likeness. To image is to reflect outwardly what is loved inwardly. In this sense, humans are made to image or imitate. The question is what or whom we image.[46]

This holds significant implications for digital technologies and today's social media. Digesting countless hours of entertainment and emotional content, we are shaped by the substance we absorb. Just as learning new

---

[39]   Augustine, *The Trinity* 15.3, p. 409.

[40]   Augustine, *The Trinity* 15.3, p. 412.

[41]   Augustine, *The Trinity* 15.3, pp. 408–9.

[42]   Augustine, *The Trinity*, p. 389; see also Kathryn Tanner, *Christ the Key* (Cambridge University Press, 2010), 44; George S. Claghorn, "Introduction to Related Correspondence," in *The Works of Jonathan Edwards*, vol. 8, *Ethical Writings*, ed. Paul Ramsey (Yale University Press, 1989), 633.

[43]   Claghorn, "Introduction to Related Correspondence," 633.

[44]   See Rev 22:4.

[45]   James K. A. Smith, *You Are What You Love* (Brazos, 2016); Gregory of Nyssa, *On the Soul and Resurrection*, cited in Tanner, *Christ the Key*, 45. Interestingly, Jonathan Haidt cites ways in which various religions and spiritualities emphasize the power of thought. For Buddhism and the Stoic Marcus Aurelius, we are what we think. From a sociological lens, religious agency and anthropology include a level of imitation through focused thought, wisdom, or (Augustine's term) love (Haidt, *Anxious Generation*, 216).

[46]   Marion, *In the Self's Place*, 149, 260–61.

languages involves imitation, so does moral formation. Following wise examples, we practice morality in a community of attunement and attachment that directs us toward our final goal. Yet increased amounts of toxic emotions, misinformation, and miscommunication negatively impact individual affect shared through social media outlets. Augustinian wisdom challenges us to see through the digital empire's veneer and seek after our final rest.

Thus the entire anthropological project in Augustine's *Trinity* hangs not on the image of God in human capacities, but in whom we love: "remembering, understanding, and loving *God*."[47] Facing God, we image the divine. Like mystical theology rooted in prayer, whether Augustine, Teresa of Ávila,[48] or Jonathan Edwards, Augustine uses the analogy of light reflecting its source. Sharing in the Supreme Light, we emanate light drawn from its origin. Edwards says, "This light is such as effectually influences the inclination, and changes the nature of the soul. It assimilates the nature to the divine nature, and changes the soul into an image of the same glory that is beheld. 2 Cor 3:18, 'But we all with open face, beholding as in a glass the glory of the Lord, are changed into the same image, from glory to glory, even as by the Spirit of the Lord.'"[49] We reflect what we most spend our time beholding and imaging.

The challenge involves the ongoing journey through time with its temptations and trials given our restless desire to attach to alternative images. Time spent on social media imitates its constant posts and endless reels. Time spent imaging Christ transforms us more in the divine likeness over time. Augustine describes the divine image as "faint," "distorted," or "spoiled" due to sin.[50] Tim Keller, like John Calvin, calls the heart an "idol factory."[51] We experience fragmentation through time given our restlessness apart from the One we're created to image. As formable, malleable creatures (rather than hardwired), our thoughts are "chopping

---

[47]   Augustine, *The Trinity* 14.4, p. 384 (emphasis added).

[48]   Teresa of Ávila, *The Interior Castle, or The Mansions* (TAN Books/Saint Benedict Press, 1997).

[49]   Jonathan Edwards, "A Divine and Supernatural Light," in *Selected Writings of Jonathan Edwards*, 2nd ed., ed. Harold P. Simonson (Waveland Press, 2004), 65.

[50]   Augustine, *The Trinity* 14.2, p. 374.

[51]   Timothy Keller, *Counterfeit Gods: The Empty Promises of Money, Sex, and Power, and the Only Hope That Matters* (Penguin Books, 2009), ix–xxi; John Calvin, *Institutes of the Christian Religion*, ed. John T. McNeill [Westminster John Knox, 1960], 1.11.8–9, pp. 107–10.

and changing motion as we think about now this and now that just as it occurs to us or comes our way."[52] In contrast to fragmented thoughts are true words connected to their source. While we long for wholeness, we often live with scattered thoughts and affections—a disconnect made more challenging through digital distractions.

Through disordered love, we seek lower treasures or created goods apart from the source. Augustine describes this as irrational. It's like going on a treasure hunt only to ignore the treasure once it's found. We want the benefits associated with the treasure but not the treasure itself.[53] Forgetting God involves forgetting oneself.[54] Interpreting Augustine, Marion describes forgetfulness as the original lie. To forget God is to forget to whom we belong. We seek the happy life apart from the giver. Marion says, "Now, it does not consist in not desiring the *vita beata* (happy life), nor even in not wanting what God manifests and gives, but in desiring them and wanting them in such a way that I dispense with God at the very moment when I appropriate what he dispenses to me."[55] We turn from higher to lower goods. In doing so, we turn from God himself.

Citing St. Basil, Kathryn Tanner captures this movement in everyday language: "Like vessels that gain their character from whatever they are made to carry. Earthenware or pure gold, what goes into them for certain purposes establishes what they are; whatever their fundamental constitution as vessels, when full of shit (for example) they can only be shit pots."[56] This idea raises the question as to what we're imaging when consuming countless hours of social media. Imbibing copied images (photos) of the *imago dei* (humans), we are further removed from the source of whom we image. Are we continually looking to lower goods? What we image, reflect, or carry as vessels indicates to whom or what we belong.

Thankfully, creatures are not stuck in a pattern or confined to live as "shit pots." Augustine describes the possibility for change. Renewing the image of God comes from the gift of the incarnation and our willingness

[52]   Augustine, *The Trinity* 15.4, p. 420.
[53]   Augustine, *The Trinity* 14.4, pp. 386–87.
[54]   Augustine, *The Trinity* 14.4, p. 386.
[55]   Marion, *In the Self's Place*, 121.
[56]   Basil the Great, *On the Human Condition*, trans. Nonna Verna Harrison (St. Vladimir's Seminary Press, 2005), 72, cited in Tanner, *Christ the Key*, 45. This translation reminds me of the Greek term *skubalon* from Phil 3:8, where Paul compares religious works to "dung," or "refuse," apart from Christ. Without an eternal reference, human activity and works are mere excrement.

to be reformed in Christ's image. Here Augustine describes the significance of sharing in him through participation or union that results not only in "its being that image, but in being made new and fresh and happy after being old and worn and miserable."[57] For Augustine, this primary transformation comes from our "unveiled face looking at the glory of the Lord in a mirror."[58] Beholding God—face to face—through Scripture and devotion, like Moses or the transfigured Christ through the "mirror" of our hearts, brings about transformative identity and character, drawing us from glory to glory. Our countenance changes when we image the source of our identity and grow in likeness. "Brightfaced," we behold the One to whom we belong.[59] In this way, we don't hide behind masks, but become "holy icons, persons who with 'unveiled faces,' increasingly reflect God's character in all they do."[60]

Beholding Christ refurbishes the image, which Augustine believes will only be complete when face to face with God.[61] He makes an analogy to the ways in which patients experience healing. The first stage involves the baptismal waters with the confession of sin. The second stage involves "curing the debility itself gradually through steady growth in renewal of the image . . . While the outer man decays, the inner man is renewed day by day."[62] Moral development involves realizing our potential as creatures. Whether physically aging or experiencing spiritual growth through sanctification, we are pilgrims on a journey. Augustine believes we grow more in the image by "cleaving to him whose image it is."[63]

We image a God of profound love and self-giving. Recalling Rowan William's description of the Trinitarian God who creates apart from need, this same God enters his own creation through self-limitation in the incarnation, demonstrating the true image of God. Attaching ourselves to this image, cleaving to that nature, fulfills our desire with the unchangeable good residing in the infinite Trinity. Not unlike the miracles

---

57 Augustine, *The Trinity* 14.4, p. 386.
58 Augustine, *The Trinity* 14.5, p. 391. See also 1 Cor 13:12.
59 The term "brightface" is used by C. S. Lewis to describe the face of Psyche, who beholds the divine, an illusion to Moses in the Old Testament and Jesus's transfiguration in the New Testament (C. S. Lewis, *Till We Have Faces: A Myth Retold* [1956; HarperOne, 2017]).
60 Vanhoozer, *Faith Speaking Understanding*, 129.
61 Augustine, *The Trinity* 14.5, p. 389.
62 Augustine, *The Trinity* 14.5, p. 391.
63 Augustine, *The Trinity* 14.4, p. 387.

accounted for in the Gospel of John, we grow in this abundant, unending love. We become like pots brimming with wine at the marriage feast in Cana, springs flowing with living water, or bodies nourished by the bread of life. Through imaging God, our identity is exocentric. We are filled and fulfilled from the outside in. Creaturely, we are most happy and satisfied when beholding the image to whom we belong. Through imaging, our identity takes shape. However, growth over time is not the completed story. Facing our Creator in vulnerability and renewal ends in an ultimate face-to-face encounter.

SEEKING GOD'S FACE FOREVERMORE

Acknowledging where human words fall short, Augustine closes his famous *Trinity* with praise: "So when we do attain to you, there will be an end to these many things which we say and do not attain, and you will remain one, yet all in all, and we shall say one thing praising you in unison, even ourselves being also made one in you."[64] Beholding and attaining Christ through union with him, we will be one in body and spirit, no longer fragmented in thought, word, or deed. Unified in will, desire, and love, our individual identities and relationships with one another will be complete. We will praise God together in full unity. In this heavenly vision we join with the angels who never cease praising God. As fellow citizens, we will see like the angels who even now see, praise, and love the Creator.[65]

Augustine considers the differing ways we might encounter God's face in ultimate union. Seeing fully rather than partially in the eschatological vision, he questions whether we will see with physical eyes or with enlightened spiritual (inner) eyes. He says,

> And so I say that the saints will see God in the body; but whether they will see through the eyes of the body, in the same way as we now see the sun, moon, stars, sea and earth and all things on the earth—that is no easy question. It is, for example, hard to say that the saints will then have bodies of such a kind that they will not be able

[64] Augustine, *The Trinity* 15 (prayer), p. 444.
[65] Augustine, *City of God*, trans. Henry Bettenson (Penguin Books, 1984), 22.29, p. 1082. See also Kevin Vanhoozer quoting 1 Pet 1:12, acknowledging the "things into which angels long to look." Something about revelation, salvation history, and gospel experience through death and resurrection grants the church a front-row seat for eschatological mystery and worship (Vanhoozer, *Faith Speaking Understanding*, 16).

to shut and open their eyes at will; and yet it is more difficult to say that anyone who shuts his eyes there will not see God.[66]

Augustine then makes an analogy to Elisha seeing the servant Gehazi receiving the gifts from Naaman the Syrian without being physically present in 2 Kings 5. Elisha sees with spiritual eyes as a divine gift in time. How much more will worshipers there experience the vision of God through transformed spiritual bodies. Augustine says, "We must conclude then that when perfection has come, when 'the corruptible body no longer weighs down the soul, but when the body, freed from corruption, offers no hindrance to the soul, the saints will certainly need no bodily eyes to see what is there to be seen, since Elisha did not need them to see his servant when he himself was not present."[67]

In this way Augustine likens Elisha's vision to the eyes of our "enlightened" (Eph 1:18), or inner, heart. Whether walking by faith rather than sight (2 Cor 5:7) or through the testimony of Simeon whose eyes "have seen thy salvation" in the Gospel of Luke, the New Testament offers a sense of inner vision that sees or knows God. In the Sermon on the Mount, Jesus says, "Blessed are the pure in heart, for they will see God" (Matt 5:8). Much like our memory and capacity to recollect images, we can spiritually understand and see by faith from within. Edwards calls spiritual sight a kind of sixth sense.[68] Augustine finds continuity between the eschatological heavenly vision and those moments where we see God indirectly through a glass darkly. Just like we are aware of our own body through inward senses, we are aware of spiritual reality through inward senses—even if fragmented through time. However, in the final eschatological vision, we shall see the face of God by the Spirit "without interruption."[69]

Without interruption—Augustine considers another scenario whereby physical and spiritual eyes are linked without disassociation. While he describes Elisha seeing within his heart by miraculous assistance, the saints in that life "will always see him in the spirit."[70] Unlike our experience in time where thoughts are choppy and disrupted and spiritual union

---

[66] Augustine, *City of God* 22.29, p. 1082.
[67] Augustine, *City of God* 22.29, p. 1083.
[68] See Edwards, "Divine and Supernatural Light," 5, 49–65.
[69] Augustine, *City of God* 22.29, p. 1085.
[70] Augustine, *City of God* 22.29, pp. 1085–86.

is fractured by temptations and physical needs, there both spirit and body, immaterial and material natures will be unified:

> Therefore they will be possessed of a very different power, if that immaterial nature is to be seen by their means—that nature which is not confined to any space but is everywhere in its wholeness. For we say that God is in heaven and earth (as he himself says, through his prophet: "I fill heaven and earth"); but that does not mean that we are to say that he has part of himself in heaven and part on earth. He is wholly in heaven, wholly in earth, and that not at different times but simultaneously; and this cannot be true of a material substance. Therefore the power of those eyes will be extraordinary in its potency . . . in the sense of having the ability to see the immaterial.[71]

While God is known indirectly as the invisible reality disclosed through visible things (Rom 1), there God will be seen directly in his governance of the whole universe. Seeing the immaterial, our eyes will see and know God's presence everywhere filling all things: "We shall see wherever we turn our eyes."[72]

Not only will we see God directly, but we will also see God in the neighbor, whereby "the thoughts of our hearts will lie open to mutual observation."[73] No longer separated by distance, misunderstanding, or poor communication—whether the Tower of Babel or those complications exacerbated through technological mediums such as social media—we will instead understand without disruption, false motive, insecurity, malice, or judgment when face to face. There will be endless felicity for those dwelling in the house of God; each part, or individual, will contribute to the whole body in harmony.[74] This shared existence results not in less but more freedom.

Augustine distinguishes between the pre-fall state, in which Adam had the ability not to sin, and the heavenly city of God, where there will be no sin.[75] Unlike our experience in time where we are slaves to sin, there we are free, partaking in Christ.[76] This is a gift from God. Rather than our human nature collapsing into God's nature, instead we will be fully dependent on

---

71 Augustine, *City of God* 22.29, p. 1084.
72 Augustine, *City of God* 22.29, p. 1086.
73 Augustine, *City of God* 22.29, p. 1087.
74 Augustine, *City of God* 22.30, p. 1087.
75 Marianne Djuth, "Will," in Fitzgerald, *Augustine Through the Ages*, 883.
76 Augustine, *City of God* 22.30, p. 1089.

God by way of ongoing communion. United in Christ, we will be united with one another. Augustine says, "In the Heavenly City then, there will be freedom of will. It will be one and the same freedom in all, and indivisible in the separate individuals. It will be freed from all evil and filled with all good, enjoying unfailingly the delight of eternal joys."[77] Citizens in the eschatological heavenly city will share in one freedom and will—fullness of joy. The self will no longer be divided. Divisions among neighbors will cease. Seeing, loving, and praising creatures will be united across differences and particularities, beholding God's presence as one. This vision doesn't deny particularities but holds them together in unity.[78] Yet Augustine doesn't preserve the unified vision for eternity only—he also recognizes unity as a gift for the *totus Christus* or body of Christ in time.

FACE AS PRESENCE

Preaching as Communion

Augustine's *Enarrationes in Psalmos* (*Expositions on the Psalms*), written between approximately 392 and 418 CE, incorporates a figurative reading that emphasizes Christ and the *totus Christus* (body of Christ) at its center.[79] Convinced the whole of Scripture is a drama between Christ and the church, his christological reading serves as a "performative act" in which listeners join with the preacher in worship.[80] This reading holds together the humanity and divinity of Christ where Christ acts as head of the body (*totus Christus*), representing our humanity to God on our behalf. Readers respond as participants, abiding in Christ's body through this divine exchange.[81] Michael Cameron says reading the Psalms with Augustine requires "new eyes," by which "love is a way of seeing."[82] Not only do we see, but we also hear, since the word in liturgy serves as audible sacrament

[77]   Augustine, *City of God* 22.30, p. 1089.
[78]   E.g., the presence of the nations in Rev 7:9–10; and see McCaulley, *Reading While Black*, 117.
[79]   Michael Cameron, "*Enarrationes in Psalmos*," in Fitzgerald, *Augustine Through the Ages*, 290–92. Kevin Vanhoozer describes Christian doctrine as drama. Faith is performative, in which the body of Christ responds to Christ's invitation through the good news (Vanhoozer, *Faith Speaking Understanding*, 95).
[80]   Cameron, "*Enarrationes in Psalmos*," 293.
[81]   Cameron, "*Enarrationes in Psalmos*," 293; Michael Cameron, general introduction to *Essential Expositions of the Psalms*, by Augustine, ed. Michael Cameron (New City Press, 2015), 35.
[82]   Cameron, general introduction to Augustine, *Essential Expositions of the Psalms*, 26.

whereby "you become what you hear."[83] Augustine's sacramental understanding emphasizes outward signs pointing to an inward, spiritual reality. Words preached through the Psalms lead to inner communion with Christ.

For Augustine, preaching was not only informative speech, but a practice in wisdom, a kind of soul therapy.[84] Augustine found communication "a form of indwelling others in the 'bond of love.'"[85] Here he describes a dialogical relation between preacher and parishioner, pastor and the whole body. Quoting Augustine's *Instructing Beginners in the Faith*, Cameron says, "So great is the power of feeling in soul-sympathy, that when listeners are affected by us as we speak, and we are affected by them as they learn, we dwell within each other. In that way listeners sort of 'speak' in us what they hear, and in a sense we 'learn in them what we teach' (12, 17). Outwardly we speak and they listen, but inwardly—through love—they teach and we learn. Only love can reciprocate that way."[86] This reciprocal love comes from shared presence in Christ.

Like David Brooks's description of shared understanding when students learn together in a classroom, the group is transformed.[87] Together they look at the same object in discovery, sharing a revelatory moment. Learning together involves a receptive posture, vulnerable to the object of study and to one another. Perhaps this shared communion reflects Emile Durkheim's "collective effervescence" or "energized communion" directed at their shared vision and affection in unity.[88]

Yet for Augustine, the shared communion comes from shared will and love devoted to God. Christ is both subject and object for listeners in the Spirit. This shared giving and receiving, learning and preaching, images the *perichoretic* relations of the Trinity. Together the Father, Son, and Spirit eternally give and receive in perfect unity. Unified in their diversity,

[83]   Cameron, general introduction to Augustine, *Essential Expositions of the Psalms*, 30–33.

[84]   Paul R. Kolbet, *Augustine and the Cure of Souls: Revising a Classical Ideal* (University of Notre Dame Press, 2010), 73.

[85]   Cameron, general introduction to Augustine, *Essential Expositions of the Psalms*, 35.

[86]   Michael Cameron quotes Augustine, *Instructing Beginners in the Faith* 1.1; 12.17 in Cameron, general introduction to Augustine, *Essential Expositions of the Psalms*, 35.

[87]   David Brooks, *How to Know a Person: The Art of Seeing Others Deeply and Being Deeply Seen* (Random House, 2023), 264. See also the section on shared wisdom in this book, pp. 64–67.

[88]   Haidt, *Anxious Generation*, 203.

they commune in perfection. When Augustine preaches and the body responds in worship, they share a glimpse of this eternal reality in time. Imaging heavenly praise, the body of Christ loves and worships *in medias res.* They share together the mind of Christ.

Expansive Love Through Presence and Likeness

Preaching in this reciprocal love, Augustine embarks on the Psalms. Cameron describes Augustine's approach to the Psalms as a kind of spiritual climbing in prayer, leading the listener to repent from sin and delight in Christ through spiritual medicine and education.[89] The Psalms lead one through prayer, mystery, the spiritual mind to one "gazing upward in love" that ends at the "view from the roof."[90] Augustine's interpretation of the term "face" helps convey a sense of divine presence throughout the Psalms. His translation, "known as the Old Latin version," follows the Septuagint, numbering the Psalms one numeral behind the Hebrew translations (for Pss 9b–147).[91]

Augustine's invocations of face or presence are scattered throughout his homilies on the Psalms. In his "Exposition of Psalm 138" (Ps 139), Augustine reflects on God's knowledge and wisdom "which is too wonderful for me"—beyond reach. Augustine likens the desire for such wisdom to Moses seeking the face of God. Recognizing God's face as majestic in glory, beyond human sight, Augustine likens God's backside to Christ's humanity while he likens the face, or frontside, to Christ's divinity beyond comprehension.[92]

Conceiving the face as analogy rather than literal face, he says, "Inasmuch as he is in the form of God, and thus equal to the Father, he is invisible to human eyes, just as the Father too is invisible. For if not even human wisdom can be perceived with our eyes, can the power and wisdom of God be seen with the eyes of the body? But in the fullness of time our Lord

[89] Cameron, general introduction to Augustine, *Essential Expositions of the Psalms*, 43.

[90] Cameron, general introduction to Augustine, *Essential Expositions of the Psalms*, 44–48.

[91] I follow Augustine's numbering from "the Old Latin version" and place the Hebrew enumeration in parentheses following the passage. The versions catch up at Ps 147. See Cameron, general introduction to Augustine, *Essential Expositions of the Psalms*, 48–49.

[92] Augustine, "Exposition of Psalm 138," in *Expositions of the Psalms, 121–150*, ed. Boniface Ramsey, trans. Maria Boulding, The Works of Saint Augustine: A Translation for the 21st Century, part 3, vol. 20 (New City Press, 2004), 300.

was to assume human flesh and make himself visible even to fleshly eyes, so that our inward minds, so sorely in need of healing, might be cured."[93] Through the incarnation, God becomes flesh to communicate Christ's divine and human natures to us through word, speech, and presence as a particular human face among us. Unlike us, Christ abides in union with the Father through unified will or love on his journey in time. Unlike our fractured word and deed, Christ's word and deed consistently align, and his incarnation takes up our fractured predicament on our behalf.[94]

Likewise, in Augustine's commentary on Psalm 120 (121) he describes the use of the term face as "vision of God" for Christ's divine and human natures. He likens the divine nature to face and human nature to flesh. Passing in front of Moses, God reveals his backside much like Christ becoming human on our behalf.[95] Through the incarnation, God makes his presence known through his human face, though we await the fullness of this encounter in the eschatological vision anticipated by the transfiguration.

Augustine also interprets multiple Psalms in terms of God withdrawing his face from an individual in relation to sin. Regarding Psalm 29 (30:7), Augustine says, "When from time to time you averted your face from me in sin, I became distressed, as the light by which I knew you was withdrawn from me."[96] Through sin, the wisdom and light of God becomes dim. Turning toward creation through disordered love, we turn away from the Creator and away from the source of our belonging and image. Quoting Psalm 43:24 (44:24), he asks, "Why do you turn your face away as though you were not present, as though you had forgotten us?"[97] God turning his face away conveys a sense of relational separation following sin. Yet neither Augustine nor the Psalms leave us without opportunity for healing from the good physician.

---

[93]   Augustine, "Exposition of Psalm 138," 300.

[94]   Rowan Williams, "Augustine and the Psalms," *Interpretation* 58, no. 1 (2004): 17; Autumn Alcott Ridenour, *Sabbath Rest as Vocation: Aging Toward Death* (Bloomsbury T&T Clark, 2018), 120–21.

[95]   Augustine, "Exposition of Psalm 120," in Augustine, *Essential Expositions of the Psalms*, 79.

[96]   Augustine, "Exposition 1 of Psalm 29," in Augustine, *Expositions of the Psalms 1–32*, ed. John E. Rotelle, trans. Maria Boulding, The Works of Saint Augustine: A Translation for the 21st Century, part 3, vol. 15 (New City Press, 2000), 298.

[97]   Augustine, "Exposition of Psalm 43.24–25," in Augustine, *Exposition of the Psalms 33–50*, ed. John E. Rotelle, trans. Maria Boulding, The Works of Saint Augustine: A Translation for the 21st Century, part 3, vol. 16 (New City Press, 2000), 277.

Citing Psalm 33:2 (34), Augustine says, "When you are in trouble, he hears you. But he is a physician, and there is still some diseased tissue in you. You cry out, but he goes on cutting, and he does not stay his hand until he has done all the cutting he knows to be necessary."[98] While he describes the difficulty in our initial confession, like medicine, confession brings about healing—difficult to experience at first, though pain-relieving in the end. He describes this as a work of love.

Many of the Psalms involve confession, repentance, and change. Augustine encourages the listener in this transformative encounter on many occasions. Preaching Psalm 50 (51), he reflects on David's repentance, in which he turns toward his own sin in confession and asks that God turn his face away from the sin.[99] Turning away from sin doesn't mean turning away from the individual entirely (Ps 27:9).[100] Quoting Psalm 68:17 (69:17), he says, "Do not hide your face from your child," connoting humility through confession.[101] God's hidden face encourages the confessor to "kindle prayer into a hotter flame," drawing us closer to God through repentance, confession, and faith.[102] Turning away from pride involves turning toward God in humility and prayer. Turning away from control and dominance involves turning toward God in vulnerability and reception. Through prayer and confession, the individual senses God's face or presence regained.[103]

Next, Augustine offers three beautiful reflections describing the image of God, reflecting his face. Preaching Psalm 4, Augustine describes the light of God's countenance "stamped upon us."[104] He continues,

[98]   Augustine, "Exposition 2 of Psalm 33," in Augustine, *Exposition of the Psalms 33–50*, 39.

[99]   Augustine, "Exposition of Psalm 50," in Augustine, *Exposition of the Psalms 33–50*, 422–23.

[100]   See Augustine, "Exposition 2 of Psalm 26," in Augustine, *Exposition of the Psalms 1–32*, 285.

[101]   Augustine, "Exposition 2 of Psalm 68," in Augustine, *Exposition of the Psalms 51–72*, ed. John E. Rotelle, trans. Maria Boulding, The Works of Saint Augustine: A Translation for the 21st Century, part 3, vol. 17 (New City Press, 2001), 384.

[102]   Augustine, "Exposition of Psalm 87," in Augustine, *Expositions of the Psalms 73–98*, ed. John E. Rotelle, trans. Maria Boulding, The Works of Saint Augustine: A Translation for the 21st Century, part 3, vol. 18 (New City Press, 2002), 270.

[103]   Augustine, "Exposition of Psalm 142," in Augustine, *Expositions of the Psalms 121–150*, 412.

[104]   Augustine, "Exposition of Psalm 4," in Augustine, *Expositions of the Psalms 1–32*, 89.

This light is the complete and true good of humankind; it is seen not with the eyes but with the mind. The psalmist's phrase, stamped upon us, suggests a coin stamped with the king's picture. For the human individual has been made in God's image and likeness, something which each has corrupted by sinning. Therefore true and eternal goodness is ours if we are minted afresh by being born again . . . Just as Caesar demands from you the mark of your likeness, so too does God; and just as money is rendered to Caesar, by the same principle the soul is rendered to God, illuminated and marked by the light of his face.[105]

Stamped and marked like a coin reflecting its king, here the image reflects its Creator.[106] Reflecting this light serves the "complete and true good of humankind" made in God's image. Created and re-created in God's image and likeness, we become marked by the light of his face.

Here Augustine says joy is not sought through chasing false idols outside us but found within the heart where "the light of God's face is stamped. For Christ dwells in the inner person, as the apostle says; and to Christ belongs the capacity to see the truth."[107] For Augustine, Christ speaks "in that inner room where we ought to pray,"[108] Augustine moves inward, a journey through the heart, not for self-enclosure but a fuller sense of agency "in the self's place" by receiving divine presence.[109] Reflecting whom we image and to whom we belong brings fulfillment rather than our diminishment.[110]

[105] Augustine, "Exposition of Psalm 4," 90.

[106] While modern minds might question replacing one empire with another, that of Caesar with that of God, Augustine's transcendent critique points to a servant king rather than dominant ruler. Augustine's order of love argues divine primacy in loving brings life and truth rather than death and deceit accustomed to false gods or sinful rulers. This narrative rejects dominion through human or idolatrous control and instead yields to God in his rightful, just, and original authority.

[107] Augustine, "Exposition of Psalm 4," 90.

[108] Augustine, "Exposition of Psalm 4," 90. Teresa of Ávila's description of the soul as an interior castle sounds like Augustine's description of an inner room (Teresa, Interior Castle).

[109] Marion, In the Self's Place.

[110] See C. S. Lewis, The Great Divorce (Touchstone, 1996). Jonathan Haidt acknowledges that multiple wisdom traditions reflect human elevation when aimed at divinity and diminishment when aimed at something less, such as an anti-divinity or "devil" (Haidt, Anxious Generation, 200).

While Augustine recognizes that the light of God's face shines on the just and unjust, he enjoins us to pray and ask God to illumine his image in us. Likening our imprint to that of a coin, he makes a broader appeal to the *totus Christus*, or body of Christ as a whole. He says,

> Let us recognize ourselves as your image, and hear for ourselves that word in the Song of Songs, "Do you not know yourself, most beautiful of women?" (Song. 1:7). This question is put to the Church: Do you not know yourself? What does it mean? Do you not know that you have been made in the image of God, O precious soul of the Church redeemed by the blood of the stainless Lamb? Consider how valuable you are, reflect on the immense price paid for you. As you say this verse, let us hope as the psalm hopes: may he make his face shine on us, for we carry God's face upon us. Even as the faces of emperors are said to be present, so it is with us, because the sacred countenance of God is truly present in his image.[111]

Speaking to the body as church, he says together "we carry God's face upon us." In this way the whole church reflects God's image, bearing his face or presence. The sacred countenance of God rests on individuals and the corporate body. Recognizing value in the whole body redeemed by Christ, he prays that God's face may shine on us. Encountering divine presence involves being remade in Christ's image.[112]

In a final discussion of face as image, Augustine describes "the unending search for God, powered by love" in Psalm 104 (105). He says, "*Seek his face always*, it continues. What is the Lord's face? Nothing else but the presence of God."[113] Here he acknowledges the face as a signifier for presence. Augustine spends time questioning what it means to seek God's face always. If always, can God ever be found? Reflecting on the three theological virtues of faith, hope, and love, Augustine describes faith as seeing with eternal vision on the journey through time, while hope drives continuous seeking toward the end goal in eternity. Describing hope's final end when God's face is found, he says,

[111] Augustine, "Exposition of Psalm 66," in Augustine, *Expositions of the Psalms 51–72*, 314.
[112] Augustine, "Exposition of Psalm 66," 314.
[113] Augustine, "Exposition of Psalm 104," in Augustine, *Expositions of the Psalms 99–120*, ed. John E. Rotelle, trans. Maria Boulding, The Works of Saint Augustine: A Translation for the 21st Century, part 3, vol. 19 (New City Press, 2004), 185–86 (emphasis original).

May we think, perhaps, that even when we do see him face to face, as he is, we shall still need to search for him, and search unendingly, because he is unendingly lovable? Even now we can say to someone who is present, "I'm not looking for you," meaning, "I do not love you." Conversely, if someone is loved with the choice he is sought even when present, as long as our love is everlasting love, lest he become absent. When we love another, even when we can see that person, we never tire of the presence of the beloved, but want him or her to be present always. This is what the psalm conveys by the words, Seek his face always: let not the finding of the beloved put an end to the love-inspired search; but as love grows, so let the search for one already found become more intense.[114]

In an eloquent passage, Augustine describes the rhythm of "seeking and finding," not unlike the "testimony of the mystics down through the ages."[115] Love involves perpetual seeking and finding. Eternity is a home of unending love—perpetual presence of the beloved rather than absence. There God is "immeasurable" or "unendingly lovable."[116] The eschatological vision suggests not stunted growth but expansive love that is simultaneously dynamic and fulfilling.

What a different formative experience than the digital habit—swipe left or right. Rather than commodify, use, and discard, instead, love involves beholding another subject apart from commodification. The subject exceeds any form of objectification. We are deceived and foolish when we think we can know, like (through notifications), judge, and dismiss. Instead, the fullness of desire seeks continuously to know and love without ceasing not unlike the perpetual motion of love throughout eternity.[117]

Moreover, love involves choice—an ongoing choice. An individual can stand in the physical presence of another without being noticed. Not unlike today's proclivity to ignore our neighbor's presence while attached to screens, Augustine recognizes we can stand in another's presence without

[114] Augustine, "Exposition of Psalm 104," 186.
[115] Maria Boulding, trans. and notes, in Augustine, "Exposition of Psalm 104," 186, n. 13.
[116] Augustine, *Confessions* 10.27.26, p. 194; Augustine, "Exposition of Psalm 104," 186.
[117] Søren Kierkegaard says, "In the same way the life of love is hidden, but its hidden life is in itself motion and has eternity within itself" (Søren Kierkegaard, *Works of Love*, trans. Howard V. Hong and Edna H. Hong [Princeton University Press, 1995], 10).

noticing or caring. Real presence involves intentionality and will. Loving the one with whom we are present involves attentiveness. Love does not end in the presence of the beloved but continually seeks to know the other as subject. Love grows in its depth and intensity. So does its simplicity: times of shared quiet and stillness, the fruit of being known and familiar. Augustine's prophetic voice challenges contemporary understandings of presence as something more than online or physical presence. What distinguishes physical presence from shared presence is attention or intentionality. Presence includes intentionally listening, caring, and serving the beloved through the desire to know and understand.

This is not surprising given Augustine's focus on the will. The weight of our will is our love. For Augustine, the will is the center of choice or desire moving toward its greatest affection. Our loves are greatest when aligned or united to God. Love unites us to God and neighbor: loving God as the end and all temporal objects toward that end.[118] In this sense, all life is sacred and our activities laden with the possibility for eternal love. Practicing presence or willing in love, we image the source to whom we belong.

Transfigurative Presence

Finally, Augustine considers the transfigurative presence of God in his commentaries on 1 John. Citing "We know that when he appears, we shall be like him because we shall see him as he is" (1 John 3:2), he affirms God as unchangeable—unlike us—without decay.[119] We cannot see him as we are, but as we will yet be. To see the eschatological vision in hope, we pray for "holy desire" and transformed nature.[120] Likening human desire to "purses that need stretching," he says, "What you desire, however, you don't yet see. But by desiring you are made large enough, so that, when there comes what you should see, you may be filled."[121] In this passage Augustine says we empty our purses through confession and repentance so that God might fill us more with himself. *Exitus Reditus*—rest in God comes through death and resurrection. This movement involves an emptying and receiving, confession and transformation, repentance and love. Identity is exocentric and deeply spiritual.

---

[118] Djuth, "Will," 884.

[119] Augustine, "Fourth Homily," in Augustine, *Homilies on the First Epistle of John*, ed. Daniel Doyle and Thomas Martin, The Works of Saint Augustine: A Translation for the 21st Century, part 3, vol. 14 (New City Press, 2008), 5, p. 68.

[120] Augustine, "Fourth Homily" 6, p. 69.

[121] Augustine, "Fourth Homily" 5, p. 69.

Rest through belonging to God is an ongoing posture and practice in time. Life is prayer.

Finally, Augustine appeals to the whole church as *totus Christus* to receive this vision through abiding in God:

> This is the sort of thing you should think of if you want to see God: *God is love.* What sort of countenance does love have? What sort of feet does it have? What sort of hands does it have? No one can say. Yet it has feet, for they lead to the Church. It has hands, for they stretch out to the poor person. It has eyes, for that is how he who is needy is understood: Blessed, it says, is he who understands concerning the needy and the poor (Ps 41:1). It has ears, of which the Lord says, He who has ears to hear, let him hear (Luke 8:8). These aren't distinct members occupying space, but he who has charity sees everything all at once with his understanding. Dwell there, and you shall be indwelled. Abide there and you shall be abided in.[122]

Abiding and dwelling, the body of Christ is the locus by which Christ is made present in time through hands, feet, ears, words, and works of mercy. With love we see the incarnational presence of the divine through Christ's body, bearing his image and goodness through love for the poor and needy. Christ loves the world through the *totus Christus,* or church in time. Abiding comes from receiving and dwelling, including those regular formational practices that demonstrate the unity of presence found in embodied community.

FACING THE OTHER THROUGH PRESENCE AND COMMUNION

While most descriptions of face as presence and image come from Augustine's direct reference to figurative terms used in Scripture, whether through his *Exposition of the Psalms* or more systematic analysis of the image of God in *The Trinity,* an indirect reference might be implied through the practice of communion. As Pamela Jackson acknowledges, "Augustine did not leave an extended treatise on the Eucharist," and most descriptions come from a compilation of his sermons and letters.[123] Also, as Augustine's thought predates medieval and Thomistic categories on the Eucharist as real presence, both Protestants and Catholics appeal to varying passages in his works to account for either symbolic use of the term

---

[122] Augustine, "Seventh Homily," in Augustine, *Homilies on the First Epistle of John,* 113.

[123] Pamela Jackson, "Eucharist," in Fitzgerald, *Augustine Through the Ages,* 332.

or real presence.[124] Regardless of one's interpretation or tradition, both branches of Christianity look to Augustine's description of unity within the body and his general sacramental sign language pointing to Christ.[125]

Using symbolic language, Augustine describes the embodied practice and inner mind as it receives Christ's sacrifice reflecting his death and resurrection: "Is the bread of the kingdom of God, but the one who says, *I am the living bread, who have come down from heaven* (John 6:41)? Don't get your gullet ready to eat, but your mind. That precisely is the beauty of this supper. We have believed in Christ, I mean, and so we receive with faith. We know what to think about as we receive; we receive a tiny portion, and in our minds, we take our fill. So, it is not what is seen, but what is believed, that feeds us."[126] The mind and heart is filled while taking communion. Here as elsewhere, Augustine establishes spiritual nourishment available through embodied communion, uniting individuals to Christ by faith and one another in both a metaphorical and mystical sense.

In Sermon 229 the bread and wine become the body and blood of the Word. Whereas the first passage reflects inner or spiritual nourishment, the latter reflects real presence. But in both interpretations, Augustine focuses on union with Christ and his body, stating, "Afterward you came to the water, and you were moistened into dough, and made into one lump. With the application of the heat of the Holy Spirit you were baked, and made into the Lord's loaf of bread."[127] He compares listening parishioners to the dough that composes one loaf of bread. Speaking against division propelled by the Donatist schism, Augustine appeals to the wine consisting of "many grapes, and has now been concentrated into a unity . . . there you are on the table, and there you are in the cup. You are this together with us; we all take this together, all drink together, because we all live together."[128] Likening the body to the elements of bread and wine, he appeals to unity in the body when receiving Christ and living this reality as love toward the neighbor.[129]

---

[124] Jackson, "Eucharist," 332.

[125] Jackson, "Eucharist," 331–33.

[126] Augustine, "Sermon 112," in *Essential Sermons*, by Augustine, ed. Daniel Doyle (New City Press, 2007), 181.

[127] Augustine, "Sermon 229," in Augustine, *Essential Sermons*, 283.

[128] Augustine, "Sermon 229," 284.

[129] Augustine emphasizes communion as sacrifice resulting in praise and works of mercy toward the neighbor in need (Augustine, *City of God* [trans. Bettenson] 10.5–6, pp. 377–79).

Likewise, in a differing reflection on the Eucharist, Augustine describes the physical and spiritual union found in the practice of communion, "The reason these things, brothers and sisters, are called sacraments is that in them one thing is seen, another is to be understood. What can be seen has a bodily appearance, what is to be understood provides spiritual fruit . . . *One bread, one body, we being many are* (1 Cor 10:17). Understand and rejoice. Unity, truth, piety, love. *One bread*; what is this one bread? The one body which we, being many, are."[130] Unified in spirit and body, the practice of communion is an outward expression of the *totus Christus*, body of Christ, receiving spiritual nourishment from Christ, its head, while enduring the journey through time.

Receiving divine presence through preaching and communion, the gathered body experiences shared identity through belonging together.[131] As Kevin Vanhoozer says, "The company of the baptized gather 'in Christ' in order to 'Do this' not only in remembrance but also to *presence* Christ, to display his presence in their midst. The Lord's Supper is a theater of the gospel inasmuch as it communicates this twofold *communio*: union with Christ and communion with one another in Christ."[132]

---

[130]   Augustine, "Sermon 272," in Augustine, *Essential Sermons*, 318.

[131]   While writing of unity through shared identity, I recognize communion, the Lord's Supper, and Eucharist are often sites of division and difference, whether distinctions following Martin Luther's 95 theses and the Protestant Reformation or a number of denominational differences and divisions propelled through the centuries. See Alister McGrath, *Christian Theology: An Introduction*, 5th ed. (Wiley-Blackwell, 2011), 407–20. Furthermore, communion has been a site of racism, dividing congregations over racial or ethnic ties. See J. Todd Billings's discussion on the importance of love and justice propelling communion and a revised Belhar confession associated with South African apartheid congregations. Billings challenges division, saying, "The Spirit's work of reconciliation in the gospel is not the same as reconciliation that can be manipulated or manufactured by society in general. The Eucharist is an eschatological feast celebrated in the present. By the Spirit, the church tastes God's coming kingdom in which many separated peoples 'have been brought near by the blood of Christ. For he is our peace; in his flesh he has made both groups into one and has broken down the dividing wall, that is, the hostility between us' (Eph. 2:13–14). The union and reconciliation that takes place in the one Christ is not a general social policy. It is a Spirit-formed concrete reality that calls peoples who were separated by enmity to live in their true, reconciled identity in Christ" (J. Todd Billings, *Union with Christ: Reframing Theology and Ministry* [Baker Academic, 2011], 102–3).

[132]   Vanhoozer, *Faith Speaking Understanding*, 164–65.

C. S. Lewis describes such unity as membership, critiquing modern individualism and solitude in the mid-twentieth century much like our contemporary focus on autonomy and expressive individualism in a technological age. Avoiding the dual temptation to privilege individualism over and above others, or the temptation to collapse individual thought into the crowd or group think, Lewis finds membership in community central to identity instead. This involves individual and communal participation without reducing one to the other. Each individual plays their specific role in the body, reflecting their received identity through union with Christ as well as responsibility to one another. In unity, the body gathers as a whole without eliminating its parts. Simply put, "we are members of one another."[133]

Theologian David Ford captures the sense of identity and belonging through Eucharist in a way that connects to his overarching theme on face and presence. Building on the work of philosophers Emmanuel Levinas, Paul Ricœur, and Eberhard Jüngel, who emphasize face and dialogical relations in conversation with theology, Ford describes a hospitable self. Ford's term hospitable relates to Augustine's vulnerability or receptiveness before God and other as opposed to the self-enclosed posture of control and domination (*libido dominandi*). The self is transformed through worship, resulting in an "orientation to the face of God and face of other people as primary."[134] Whether worshiping God through the Psalms, Ephesians, or Eucharist, Ford describes the face of Christ and neighbor as the site of transformation.

Ford considers multiple dimensions of face in the Eucharist. He reflects on the ordinariness of the Last Supper and Jesus "incorporating us" into his life.[135] Ford says,

> An essential part of the homeliness is the priority of face to face relationships between those who know each other well. These, together with the ordinary routines and elements, help to give density and universality to the occasion. The specificity of what goes on in this sphere is due to the quality of incorporation that Jesus is realizing. He and the disciples come to the meal with a history of face to face interaction in many situations. It is itself in many ways a repetition

[133] C. S. Lewis, "Membership," in *The Weight of Glory and Other Addresses* (1949; HarperOne, 2001), 158–76.
[134] Ford, *Self and Salvation*, 127.
[135] Ford, *Self and Salvation*, 150.

of other meals together, other occasions for eating, teaching, argument, and surprise developments. All of that accumulation of events in the interpersonal sphere has been incorporating them with Jesus into a distinctive community. What we know of that Jewish milieu confirms the communal, incorporative significance of meals . . . fundamentally standing for togetherness and reconciliation.[136]

Face-to-face interaction is part of daily life shared in community together. Yet the significance of the Last Supper for togetherness and reconciliation, particularly as it points to Jesus's death and resurrection, sets this particular meal apart. Ordinary yet extraordinary, the meal signifies not only Christ's coming sacrifice, but also the community's interpersonal relationships through togetherness, belonging, and reconciliation.

Ford continues describing the central point of the Eucharist as "Facing Jesus Christ" in which he acknowledges the "vagueness" of Christ's face. There is no image or replica of Christ's actual face, despite medieval claims to Veronica's veil.[137] Ford says,

> What is the overall significance of this pervasive theme of the facing of the risen Jesus Christ for the problem of vagueness? His face attracts trust, adoration, love, joy, repentance, attentive listening, and ultimate hope. There is such multifaceted abundance that any notion of precision which requires an overview and appraisal is absurd. Its significance is indicated by the phrase "the glory of God in the face of Christ": this facing is identified with the facing of God. This in turn means that it is a face which relates to every face. Any vagueness is not so much because of abstraction or generality but because of the utter particularity of this face's relating to each face . . . The overwhelming diversity and intensity of these relationships is part of the meaning of transformation "from one degree of glory to another" (2 Cor 3.18).[138]

The vagueness of Christ's face is not an abstraction, but an invitation. Ford acknowledges the diversity of followers Jesus encounters and the generations of followers still encountering the risen Christ over the centuries.

[136] Ford, *Self and Salvation*, 150.
[137] There is no image or replica of Christ's actual face despite medieval legends that Veronica's veil captured the image of Christ's face when wiping the sweat from his brow on the path to Calvary (Golgatha). See Hunt, *Divine Face in Four Writers*, 14–15.
[138] Ford, *Self and Salvation*, 175–76.

Facing us, Christ invites future followers to face the infinite God in our diverse particularity. From our diverse settings, or contexts, we are being transformed from one degree of glory to another.

Each disciple encounters the vagueness of Christ's face as infinite yet personal through the diversity of creatures made in his image—unity in diversity. Ford says, "This too involves abundant particularity, recognizing the face of Christ as reflected in all the faces to which (even when they are not aware of it) he relates."[139] Each face images God yet retains its particularity. Lewis encapsulates this concept by saying, "There is so much of Him that millions and millions of 'little Christs,' *all different*, will still be too few to express Him fully."[140] As diverse creatures, we differ in our particularity while sharing in his image. Vanhoozer calls this "*simul mimesis et authenticos*: simultaneously imitative (i.e., true to Christ) and authentic (i.e., true to oneself)."[141]

Encapsulating the concept of authenticity to Christ and self, Esau McCaulley says, "When we finally meet our savior, we do not come to him as a faceless horde but as transformed believers from every tribe, tongue, and nation. When the Black Christian enters the community of faith, she does not enter a strange land, she is finding her way home."[142] Christ's universality does not erase particularity but lifts it up.

Ford highlights the universal and particular dimensions of these faces without domination or imperial weight.[143] Transfiguration entails not the loss of self but the glorified self. Augustine's beatific vision at Ostia with his mother Monica demonstrates how neither individual loses their particularity but shares divine presence in their particularity:[144] "Rather than lose their identity in the eternal, beatific vision as individuals that are

---

[139] Ford, *Self and Salvation*, 176.

[140] C. S. Lewis, *Mere Christianity*, in *The Complete C. S. Lewis Signature Classics* (HarperOne, 2002), x (emphasis added).

[141] Vanhoozer, *Faith Speaking Understanding*, 138.

[142] McCaulley, *Reading While Black*, 117.

[143] Given his philosophical interlocutors, Ford is sensitive not to import our idolatrous conceptions onto God or the person of Christ. He carefully delineates how Jesus Christ is different than imperial Rome or our own idolatrous concepts given the centrality of Christ's death and humility, and the politics leading toward his death, which includes care for the socially marginalized (Ford, *Self and Salvation*, 183–86).

[144] Augustine, *Confessions* 9.10.23–24, pp. 170–71; James Wetzel, *Augustine: A Guide for the Perplexed* (Continuum, 2010), 41; Ridenour, *Sabbath Rest as Vocation*, 42–43.

'imageless,' instead, they remain recognizable as Augustine and Monica. Their full identities are not erased, but instead, more fully realized through their sharing in the wisdom and goodness of the Eschatological vision."[145] Facing Jesus involves facing God and neighbor as sites to encounter divine presence. As divine and human, he invites us to face both.

Perhaps Dietrich Bonhoeffer best captures the significance of encountering the presence of God within *koinonia*, or Christian fellowship, when he says, "The physical presence of other Christians is a source of incomparable joy and strength to the believer . . . Paul prays night and day . . . exceedingly that we might see your face (1 Thess 3:10). The aged John knows his joy will not be full until he can come to his own people and speak face to face instead of writing with ink (2 John 12)."[146] Bonhoeffer recognizes our embodied reality and the significance of encountering fellow believers at any stage in the Christian walk. His spiritual reflection, *Life Together*, demonstrates the significance of common prayer, worship, and communion for our shared spiritual journey through time. Embodied presence is integral to shared communion in Christ and one another through spiritual disciplines that culminate in Eucharist and *koinonia*.

Koinonia that unifies images of God in Christ through physical, spiritual, and intentional presence stands in contrast to proclamations projected through social media, in which we interact through asynchronous, decontextualized images and tropes. It's not to say that all social media is bad or insignificant. Instead, this is a matter of priority. Prioritizing in-person, face-to-face relationships offers the important ingredients necessary for social attunement, attachment, and communion.[147] Prioritizing face-to-face relations doesn't deny participation in social media or digital technologies, but privileges in-person relations as significant for moral development, agency, and embodied community. Valuing intentional presence in communion elevates the importance of in-person relationships and their role in our moral development across our life span, particularly for adolescents.

[145]   Ridenour, *Sabbath Rest as Vocation*, 42–43.

[146]   Dietrich Bonhoeffer, *Life Together* (Harper & Row Publishers, 1954), 19; see also Reggie Williams for the impact of Abyssinian Baptist Church in Harlem on Bonhoeffer's understanding of Jesus Christ as "vicarious representative action" for the way we embody lived faith commitment through community and action (Reggie L. Williams, *Bonhoeffer's Black Jesus: Harlem Renaissance Theology and an Ethics of Resistance* [Baylor University Press, 2014; 2021], 9–10, 19–22).

[147]   See Haidt on the importance of attunement, attachment, and communion within face-to-face relationships (Haidt, *Anxious Generation*, 55–58).

Likewise, valuing in-person relationships and face-to-face presence holds significant implications for how we relate to generative AI in its capacity to copy divine images on a grand scale. Even if social media portrays what Kate Lucky calls "crueler versions of ourselves . . . at the whims of polarizing algorithms that push them to the extremes," at least a social component remains between two creatures made in God's image.[148] She continues, "We learn something from a scholar, share a meme that makes another user laugh, or see a picture of a friend's baby. We are still interacting with people (though there are bots too). But with ChatGPT, there's no social component. That's the danger. When you're talking to a bot, you're actually alone."[149]

As we long for relationality and dialogue, capabilities now possible through generative AI, the divine image that makes humans distinctive is even more significant. Capable of reciprocity, consciousness, disagreement, and communion across difference, humans made in the image and likeness of God not only share information but together hold open the possibility for real—rather than artificial—empathy, presence, and transformation. Transformation draws people together through intentional communion in shared love.

Citing computer scientist Derek Schuurman, Lucky says, "But the image of God can't be 'explained or mimicked' with a device. It's an ontological status that can be granted only by the Lord, bestowed by the same breath of life that animates dry bones. It's mysterious, not mechanical."[150] Imaging God is a mysterious gift received rather than one of mechanical self-construction. By creating in the divine image, humans can set algorithms and hardwire copies of the image in our material universe. But we cannot generate new life, consciousness, agency, and shared presence *ex nihilo* nor reciprocate the beauty of shared communion across subjective difference. If generative AI risks mimicking these human features, some mysterious difference remains. When facing machines, do we truly encounter the presence of a neighbor capable of communing in the shared image of God? Or are we deceived by our own copies?

Brooks holds a similar concern. There's simply something about human beings that remains different. Brooks explains, "I find myself clinging to

[148] Kate Lucky, "Imago AI: Artificial Intelligence May Not Have a Soul. But It Will Shape Ours," *Christianity Today*, October 2023, https://www.christianitytoday.com/2023/09/artificial-intelligence-robots-soul-formation/.

[149] Lucky, "Imago AI."

[150] Lucky, "Imago AI."

the deepest core of my being—the vast, mostly hidden realm of the mind from which emotions emerge, from which inspiration flows, from which our desires pulse—the subjective part of the human spirit that makes each of us ineluctably who we are."[151] In a deeply Augustinian sense, desire fuels our subjective consciousness through our reflective choices. In synthesizing the disparate parts of ourselves through memory we also move beyond ourselves through sharing together in embodied community.

Intuitive in his findings, Brooks's desire for unique identity, belonging, and connection relates to those scientific studies comparing Zoom interactions with face-to-face conversations. Differences remain between live human interactions and simulated experiences; our brains are more activated during live, in-person conversation. Animated with real life, we share in the sacredness of the divine image. As C. S. Lewis says, "There are no ordinary people. You have never talked to a mere mortal."[152] Considering the significance of live, face-to-face interactions for natural social behaviors, psychiatrist Joy Hirsch concludes, "Online representations of faces, at least with current technology, do not have the same 'privileged access' to social neural circuitry in the brain that is typical of the real thing."[153] There's something unique about human creatures, differing as they do in their shared brain activity. Live, in-person conversation offers presence and connection in a way that differs from artificial simulation.

As Turkle's early volume, *Alone Together*, warns, "We want more from technology and less from each other."[154] Here we might pursue the opposite: wanting more from each other and less from technology. In our desire for control and escape from vulnerability, we are tempted to substitute technology for in-person relationships, but we should resist this temptation in full.[155] Relationships and belonging that help forge identity require hard work, including the possibility of failure and rejection. But such risks are also where attunement, identity, difference, recognition, and reward

[151] David Brooks, "Human Beings Are Soon Going to Be Eclipsed," *New York Times*, July 13, 2023, https://www.nytimes.com/2023/07/13/opinion/ai-chatgpt-consciousness-hofstadter.html, quoted in Lucky, "Imago AI," 50.

[152] C. S. Lewis, "The Weight of Glory," in *Weight of Glory*, 46.

[153] Connolly, "Zoom Conversations vs. In-Person," 5.

[154] Sherry Turkle, *Alone Together* (Basic Books, 2011),

[155] I recognize the significance of and good in some digital simulation through Zoom, FaceTime, Skype, and other platforms for short-term interaction. However, these platforms work best when connected to relationships that exist in real time and space.

are gained. Relationships involve extensive practice through mundane conversation and activities. With tenacity, endurance, and the willingness to see both self and other through differing perspectives, we become vulnerable and moldable as creatures imaging God through communion with one another. Encountering presence through the face of Christ in the neighbor, we are challenged to know and reconcile with God's diverse creation across difference.

Considering the significance of unity found in the early church and its relevance for today, Davi Ribeiro Lin describes the importance of community and face-to-face encounters in a "technologically faceless age."[156] He explains, "After Pentecost, at the center of faith stands not only an individual but a restored community, empowered by the Holy Spirit to become the restored humanity that re-presents Christ to the world . . . stories such as Peter, a Jewish fisherman, sitting at the same table in communion with Cornelius, a Roman centurion, signaled a reconciled and reconciling Spirit-filled community."[157] In this way the encounter with the face of Christ in the other involves unity in diversity—a sense of belonging to one another through embodied communion in the Spirit. It also involves sharing in the abundance of God's gift through worship, feasting, wholeness, play, and joy signified through our common movement toward Sabbath rest.

---

[156] Davi C. Ribeiro Lin, "The Absence of Dialogue in a Technologically Faceless Age: An Augustinian Response of Embrace and Confession," in *Beyond Integral Mission: Fresh Voices from Latin America*, ed. Daniel Clark (Regnum, 2022), 73–84.

[157] Lin, "Absence of Dialogue," 80–81.

5
Sabbath Vision as Belonging

WORKISM AND SOCIAL MEDIA

With the Surgeon General's warning that loneliness is a rising epidemic, several culprits abound: increased time online through work, shopping, video games, social media, and even online religious services following the COVID-19 pandemic.[1] Robert Putnam warned about the benefits derived from "social capital," such as extracurricular religious, community, and volunteer associations, plummeting in the contemporary era.[2] In *The Great Dechurching*, Michael Graham and Jim Davis draw similar insights from sociologists to conclude the main reason forty million Americans stopped attending church in the last twenty-five years—despite abuse scandals and moral corruption—resides with "workism," which involves a slow fade in commitment to religious and community life.[3]

[1]   US Surgeon General, *Our Epidemic of Loneliness and Isolation*, Department of Health and Human Services, 2023, https://www.hhs.gov/sites/default/files/surgeon-general-social-connection-advisory.pdf; Lane Wallace, "Loneliness in Numbers," *Atlantic*, January 5, 2010, https://www.theatlantic.com/national/archive/2010/01/loneliness-in-numbers/32985/; see also Julianne Holt-Lunstad and Carla Perissinotto, "Social Isolation and Loneliness as Medical Issues," *New England Journal of Medicine* 388, no. 3 (2023): 193–95.

[2]   Robert D. Putnam, "Bowling Alone: America's Declining Social Capital," *Journal of Democracy* 6, no. 1 (1995): 65–78; idem, *Bowling Alone: The Collapse and Revival of American Community* (Simon & Schuster, 2000).

[3]   Jake Meador, "The Misunderstood Reason Millions of Americans Stopped Going to Church," *Atlantic*, July 29, 2023, https://www.theatlantic.com/ideas/archive/

Derek Thompson defines workism as "the belief that work is not only necessary to economic production, but also the centerpiece of one's identity and life's purpose; and the belief that any policy to promote human welfare must *always* encourage more work."[4] Workism reflects the slow change from "job" to "career" and later to "calling," devoid of religious implications while equating purpose and self-actualization with work.[5]

Workism mystifies Thompson, given wealthy classes in past generations sought more work to buy time for leisure.[6] Instead, individuals in contemporary elite careers (i.e., tech companies fueling the top ten percent of incomes) work for the sake of more work. Equating career with calling and self-actualization infiltrates work culture expectations across tech and corporate industries. These expectations are compounded by social media. Thompson explains, "The disturbance of social media . . . has amplified the pressure to craft an image of success—for oneself, for one's friends and colleagues, and even for one's parents."[7] Delivering endless streams of content, social media reshapes images of identity, work, and relationships as consumer goods to be instrumentalized, collected, shared, and projected through broadcast.[8] Friendships are one more product to collect and assess through limitless consumption—identity, including work life, is one more goal to broadcast and prove.[9]

2023/07/christian-church-communitiy-participation-drop/674843/; Jim Davis and Michael Graham with Ryan P. Burge, *The Great Dechurching: Who's Leaving, Why Are They Going, and What Will It Take to Bring Them Back?* (Zondervan Reflective, 2023); Derek Thompson, "Workism Is Making Americans Miserable," *Atlantic,* February 24, 2019, https://www.theatlantic.com/ideas/archive/2019/02/religion-workism-making -americans-miserable/583441/.

4   Thompson, "Workism Is Making Americans Miserable."

5   Thompson, "Workism Is Making Americans Miserable." See also Sarah Green Carmichael, "The Research Is Clear: Long Hours Backfire for People and for Companies," *Harvard Business Review,* August 19, 2015, https://hbr.org/2015/08/the -research-is-clear-long-hours-backfire-for-people-and-for-companies.

6   Thompson, "Workism Is Making Americans Miserable."

7   Thompson, "Workism Is Making Americans Miserable."

8   Ian Bogost, "The Age of Social Media Is Ending: It Never Should Have Begun," *Atlantic,* November 10, 2022, https://www.theatlantic.com/technology/ archive/2022/11/twitter-facebook-social-media-decline/672074/.

9   Perhaps the "great resignation" and "quiet quitting" are movements subtly responding to hustle culture exacerbated by social media. See Cal Newport, "The Year in Quiet Quitting," *New Yorker,* December 29, 2022, https://www.newyorker .com/culture/2022-in-review/the-year-in-quiet-quitting; Kim Parker and Juliana Menasce Horowitz, "Majority of Workers Who Quit a Job in 2021 Cite Low Pay,

Promises in new generative AI suggest tech might shoulder more work burdens, leaving more time for leisure and rest. But the transparency of these promises remains unclear, as do past tech marketing pleas. Initial voices within the Industrial Revolution and Digital Age suggested more machines made for more leisure and less work.[10] Yet while automobiles, household appliances, lawn equipment, and computers enable us to accomplish more work at great speed, these advances haven't eliminated the amount of work expected. Instead, the inertia has moved in the opposite direction. Given workism's logic and productivity expectations, we fill extra time with more work or its opposite—forms of leisure that drain through passive digital entertainment as opposed to soul-building forms of leisure attuned to the needs of our body and spirit.

Wrestling with creaturely limits and possibilities, Augustine also understood the restless drive for approval, identity, and belonging through work and public perception in his own political speech writing and desire for praise. Augustine's restlessness opens his vision to life's limits and its teleological fulfillment in Sabbath rest. In his longing for rest, his voice predates a contemporary revival on Sabbath writings and our desire for rest with increased demands in work and digital culture.[11] To reframe our journey through time, I first consider Augustine's teleological vision aimed at eternal Sabbath rest alongside Sabbath theology in Karl Barth; second, describe how Sabbath resistance shapes our understanding of contemporary work, productivity, and the urgency of digital devices through an identity received rather than projected; third, explore the relationship of

---

No Opportunities for Advancement, Feeling Disrespected," Pew Research Center, March 9, 2022, https://www.pewresearch.org/short-reads/2022/03/09/majority-of-workers-who-quit-a-job-in-2021-cite-low-pay-no-opportunities-for-advancement-feeling-disrespected/.

[10]   Craig M. Gay, *Modern Technology and the Human Future: A Christian Appraisal* (IVP Academic, 2018); Andy Crouch, *The Life We're Looking For: Reclaiming Relationship in a Technological World* (Convergent, 2022).

[11]   See Autumn Alcott Ridenour, "Sabbath as Reprioritization," in *Sabbath as Resilience*, ed. Kenneth Barnes and Sara Minard (Wipf and Stock, 2025); Walter Brueggemann, *Sabbath as Resistance: Saying No to the Culture of Now* (Westminster John Knox, 2014); Alan Fadling, *An Unhurried Life: Following Jesus' Rhythms of Work and Rest* (IVP, 2013); John Mark Comer, *The Ruthless Elimination of Hurry* (Waterbrook, 2019); Peter Scazzero, *Emotionally Healthy Spirituality: It's Impossible to Be Spiritually Mature, While Remaining Emotionally Immature* (Zondervan, 2014); Andy Crouch, *The Techwise Family* (Baker Books, 2017), 83–106; and Tish Harrison Warren, *Liturgy of the Ordinary* (IVP, 2016), 141–53.

Sabbath to themes of play and leisure in their importance for being, joy, and communion; and fourth, offer an eschatological Sabbath vision that expands our shared understanding of love, justice, and community.

SABBATH REST AS TELEOLOGICAL VISION AND BELONGING

Augustine's opening line in the *Confessions* describing the restless heart is the most well-known of the work, while far fewer citations acknowledge its closing line: seeking Sabbath rest (as with *City of God*). As commonly referenced, Augustine states, "You have made us for yourself and our heart is restless until it rests in you," establishing a foundational claim regarding human identity received through belonging.[12] Just as his introduction marks the desire for rest through seeking, so does his conclusion mark the fulfillment of rest when found. As creatures our origin and end rests in the Creator.

The close of *Confessions* describes our end goal, involving entrance into the seventh day of Sabbath rest: "The seventh day has no evening and has no ending. You sanctified it to abide everlastingly. After your 'very good' works, which you made while remaining yourself in repose, you 'rested the seventh day' (Gen 2:2–3). This utterance in your book foretells for us that after our works which, because they are your gift to us, are very good, we also may rest in you for the Sabbath of eternal life."[13] Reflecting God's work in creation, we work through time before entering eternal Sabbath rest, the seventh day without evening. Here Augustine likens time and its epochs to the six days of creation, which involve work.

Afterward we enter eternal Sabbath rest, analogous to the seventh day of creation. Augustine continues, "There also you will rest in us just as now you work in us. Your rest will be through us, just as now your works are done through us. But you, Lord, are always working and always at rest. Your seeing is not in time, your movement is not in time, and your rest is not in time. Yet your acting causes us to see things in time, time itself, and the repose which is outside time."[14] Here Augustine recognizes God beyond time, yet God's creative acts impact our life in time, causing us to see objects moving through time, measure time, and thus acknowledge time in its limitation.

Distended through time, our identity longs for wholeness or rest represented through eternity. Augustine's teleology, longing for such wholeness,

[12]   Augustine, *Confessions*, trans. Henry Chadwick (Oxford University Press, 1991), 1.1, p. 3.
[13]   Augustine, *Confessions* 13.37.52, p. 304.
[14]   Augustine, *Confessions* 13.37.52, p. 304.

moves toward eternal Sabbath rest as the fulfillment of time. Like the original creation narrative resulting in Sabbath rest, all creation groans to be set free from corruption, or sin, experienced in fallen time (Gen 3) through its eschatological fulfillment (Rom 8:18–22). In this way Augustine's understanding of history is future directed, seeking rest in eternity. He bookends his *Confessions* by opening with our longing for rest and closing the volume with our entering Sabbath rest.

Likewise, Augustine continues this eschatological theme in the closing of his famous work *City of God*, in which we enter eternal Sabbath rest. He says, "That will truly be the greatest of Sabbaths; a Sabbath that has no evening, the Sabbath that the Lord approved at the beginning of creation, where it says, 'God rested on the seventh day from all his works, which he had been doing; and *God blessed the seventh day* and made it holy, because on that day he rested from all his works . . . We ourselves shall become that seventh day . . . There we shall have leisure to be still, and we shall see that he is God."[15] Paralleling God's rest at the close of creation, Augustine foreshadows how we will enter the eternal seventh day and see God face to face in leisure and rest.

He ascribes this possibility to the work of God. In our human efforts we fall away from God in our determination to be like him on our own terms. However, God graciously shares his nature with us through his works rather than ours. This comes from "participating in him . . . But now restored by him and perfected by his greater grace we shall be still and at leisure for eternity, seeing that he is God, and being filled by him when he will be all in all."[16] On the final day, God will be all in all, filling reality, including our identity and nature. Fulfilled in Christ, "we shall then know perfectly, when we are perfectly at rest, and in stillness see perfectly that he is God."[17] Once face to face, the intimate vision, knowledge, and love of Christ will come to full fruition, shared among believers in the body of Christ.

With Ezekiel, Augustine claims Sabbath serves as a "sign between me and them; so that they might know that I am the Lord, and that I sanctify them (Ezek 20:12)."[18] In this way the practice of weekly Sabbath reflects God's action toward creation. God generously creates from his own nature, a gift received rather than achieved. This is a theme in

---

[15]   Augustine, *The City of God*, trans. Henry Bettenson (New York: Penguin Books, 1984), 22.30, p. 1090.

[16]   · Augustine, *City of God* 22.30, p. 1090.

[17]   Augustine, *City of God* 22.30, p. 1091.

[18]   Augustine, *City of God* 22.30, p. 1090.

Augustine's overarching theology of grace by which God creates, redeems, and restores creation. Creatures receive this gift with humility apart from their own merit. The Sabbath remains a sign of God's gracious posture toward humankind through rest.

Finally, Augustine describes seven ages or epochs within history to demarcate God's creative and redemptive action in time. He utilizes the seven epochs in varying works, including the *City of God* and his commentaries on Genesis. Paralleling the six days of creation followed by the seventh concluding in rest, he describes these epochs as: 1) Adam to the flood; 2) the flood to Abraham; 3) Abraham to David; 4) David to the exile in Babylon; 5) the exile to the coming of Christ; and 6) the coming of Christ to his return.[19] This sixth epoch is the longest as we await Christ's return, enduring an unknown number of generations: "After this present age God will rest, as it were, on the seventh day, and he will cause us, who are the seventh day, to find our rest in him . . . the *seventh* [epoch] will be our Sabbath, whose end will not be an evening, but the Lord's Day, an eighth day, as it were, which is to last forever, a day consecrated by the resurrection of Christ, foreshadowing the eternal rest not only of the spirit but of the body also."[20] We await the full resurrection and restoration of all creation wherein spirit and body will unite in harmony rather than conflict through seeing, loving, and praising its Creator.

Just like Augustine describes the seven epochs of history in the *City of God,* he also accounts for them in *On Genesis: A Refutation of the Manichees* and *The Literal Meaning of Genesis.* In these texts he argues for an allegorical and typological reading of the narrative rather than literal reading only. He also aligns the seven days with the seven stages of life, moving from infancy to old age. Not unlike psychoanalyst Erik Erikson's eight stages of the life cycle, Augustine predates some of the themes in developmental psychology with his analysis of the seven life stages, coinciding with his interpretation of the seven days of creation and seven epochs of history.[21]

These seven stages of life are "infancy, childhood, adolescence, youth (prime), maturity, old age, and rest with 'no evening.'"[22] Augustine describes

---

[19]   Augustine, *City of God* 22.30, p. 1091.

[20]   Augustine, *City of God* 22.30, p. 1091.

[21]   Erik H. Erikson and Joan M. Erickson, *The Life Cycle Completed* (W. W. Norton, 1997).

[22]   Augustine, *On Genesis: A Refutation of the Manichees,* in *On Genesis,* ed. John E. Rotelle, trans. Edmund Hill, The Works of Saint Augustine: A Translation for the 21st Century, part 1, vol. 13 (New City Press, 2002), 1.22.33, pp. 62–68;

the sixth stage as that of old age, likening the age to the coming of Christ: "Now begins the sixth [day] in which the age of the old man (Eph 4:22; Col 3:9) becomes evident . . . In this age, however, as in the old age of a very old man, the new man (Eph 4:24; Col 3:10) is born, who is already living according to the spirit . . . a longing for eternal realities is beginning to show itself."[23] In this way he anticipates what he describes as the sacramental significance of the Sabbath, drawing from Hebrews 4 where an eternal Sabbath remains for the people of God.[24] Foreshadowing this final rest, Augustine's sacramental reading of the Scripture points to the teleological goal whereby we move from creation to new creation. The sixth epoch when Christ comes and the sixth stage of life—old age—transform into new life, anticipating the seventh age of eternal rest that informs our identity and belonging.

Interestingly, Augustine's approach to aging and death as entrance to Sabbath rest contrasts the concern and fear of death prevalent among his philosophical interlocutors advocating honor and empire in Rome. As previously described, Robert Dodaro interprets the *City of God* as a response to *timor mortis*, "fear of death," which Augustine perceived among his philosophical and political peers.[25] While Manichaean and Neoplatonist approaches valued the soul's escape from the body, a more Stoic approach denies emotions by replacing "desire, fear, and joy" with "will, caution, and gladness."[26] Stoic heroism emphasizes invulnerability to emotion through a kind of denial and apathy, not uncommon to social media performances in which individuals "play it cool" through online posts while experiencing emotional ups and downs in response to their peers online. Relationships and recognition equate to performance. While perhaps some posts include a level of transparency, often full transparency is avoided "to save face," not unlike Stoic invulnerability or its opposite risk: drawing negative attention through a kind of twisted narcissism akin to adolescent behavior. Sensationalist by nature, the latter draws attention for the sake of attention or seeks fame for the sake of fame. Augustine found Greek and Roman gods in their claims of heroic virtue to be false

---

Autumn Alcott Ridenour, *Sabbath Rest as Vocation: Aging Toward Death* (Bloomsbury T&T Clark, 2018), 48.

[23] Augustine, *On Genesis: A Refutation of the Manichees* 1.23.39, pp. 64–65.

[24] Ridenour, *Sabbath Rest as Vocation*, 48.

[25] Robert Dodaro, *Christ and the Just Society in the Thought of St. Augustine* (Cambridge University Press, 2004), 32–43.

[26] Augustine, *City of God* 14.9, p. 561; Ridenour, *Sabbath Rest as Vocation*, 38.

fame.[27] Fame is short-lived, whether in ancient Rome or our era of social media shares.

Considering Sabbath from an Augustinian lens, however, reminds creatures not only of their destination but also of their limitations and vulnerabilities that reframe their relationships with God and one another through humility, dependence, and the gift of rest in time. To examine this more deeply, I turn to the theology and practice of Karl Barth's teaching on Sabbath in creation and ethics.

Sabbath Belonging: Identity, Teleology, and Gift

One of the most prolific Protestant theologians of the twentieth century, Karl Barth, possessed a christological drive that permeates his work, informing doctrine from revelation to reconciliation. Like the early church fathers, including Augustine, Barth's christological lens colors his understanding of creation and re-creation. The culmination of creation in Sabbath rest is no exception.

Barth begins his discussion of Sabbath rest describing the seventh day as the completion of creation. God confirms his work in six days, declaring humankind to be very good, and concludes by resting in this additional divine act. God's rest is unlike ours given that recuperation from work is unnecessary. As Creator, God rests in his own nature while celebrating creation as good. Barth says, "Obviously God could not and would not return to an existence without the world and man, since the rest, freedom and joy of this seventh day are described as the completion of His creation of the world and man."[28] God does not retreat from creation but rests in the fullness of this creative gift through himself. In this way he limits himself in choosing creation and demonstrates love through this limit.

Barth describes this limitation further. The fact that God limits his creative activity demonstrates freedom. Limitations accompany the act of creation from the beginning, including time, space, elements, and particular species. Yet despite his infinite nature, God doesn't perpetually create. Barth says, "A world principle without this limit to its creative activity would not be free like God, but would be tied to the infinite motion of its own development and evolution . . . *A being is free only when it can*

---

27   Augustine, *City of God* 5.12, p. 197; John Cavadini, "Pride," in *Augustine Through the Ages*, ed. Allan D. Fitzgerald (Eerdmans, 1999), 680.

28   Karl Barth, *Church Dogmatics* III/1, *The Doctrine of Creation*, ed. T. F. Torrance and Geoffrey W. Bromiley (T&T Clark, 2004), 213.

determine and limit its activity."[29] God is free in his creation and limitation concluding with Sabbath rest. Freedom through limitation is a gift God offers to humans; it also calls into question new understandings of generative AI and its supposed capacity to endlessly create—even beyond its human creators. Herein lies its primary challenge. Should we be in the business of creating without clear limits if the God who creates circumscribes boundaries to his own creation? Does creation without limits exceed the natural boundaries intended for those who image God?

Second, Barth portrays God's freedom through his commitment to love. Building on his prior analogy, he says, "A world principle without this limit to its creative activity would not be loving like God, but would be a being without love, never ceasing, never finding time for any creature, never satisfied with any, always positing other beings in infinite sequence . . . Love has a definite, limited object. Love is a relationship which is itself limited and defined by this object. It is in this way that God loves."[30] God's limit demonstrates his love for creation. He chooses creation in its particularity. Every choice involves limits that create deeper opportunity for loving and knowing, as seen through our closest relationships. God demonstrates the beauty and wisdom of limits in his original choice for creation and species particularity. God creates a cosmos with circumscribed limits and purpose. God rests and enjoys his own work rather than ceaselessly create through restlessness.

In this way God's nature contrasts with human restlessness, our ceaseless working and consumption—whether of objects or relationships through social media, the endless newsfeed, or algorithmic data output—anticipating the hope placed in boundless generative AI. Instead, God treasures the particularity of his own creation with freedom and joy, recognizing goodness in those objects and subjects of his love. All elements of creation, including humans, are created with specific purposes and goals. What goals are associated with generative AI? How is it directed toward specific objects with their purposes made clear through limitation? How does creation without limitation not descend into chaos rather than cosmos?

Creation as cosmos, on the other hand, finds its identity in God's love and limit. Because he creates from love, God deems creation as good and

29   Barth, *Church Dogmatics* III/1, 214 (emphasis added).
30   Barth, *Church Dogmatics* III/1, 214.

worthy of love. Deriving its goodness from God's creative act, the creature "belongs constitutively not only [from] the fact that it is created by God's grace and power, but also the fact that God willed to co-exist with it."[31] By willing to coexist with creation, God anticipates the covenant, incarnation, and union with humanity through his immanence in the world.

The Sabbath is the beginning of God's coexistence with creation in freedom and love: "He has thus united Himself with the world which He created. It completes and crowns all creation that, as the One He Himself was and is and will be, in His rest He associates Himself with it in the fullest possible way . . . and declares Himself as such *to belong to what He has created so entirely different from Himself*."[32] Culminating creation with humanity on the sixth day, God pauses to delight and rejoice in his image. God commits himself by belonging to us, creatures who differ from him while also relating to God in likeness.

Sabbath belongs to creation and is yet another gift: "This is the meaning of the seventh day for God the Creator . . . Not in itself, to be sure, but beyond itself, the creature finds its completion in the fact that God in His own person has given Himself *to belong to it*. Over and over again it will have to seek and find what God intends to undertake and do in *this fellowship*."[33] Creation finds its completion through belonging. Part of our fellowship through belonging involves "seeking and finding" God and our purposes made known through restoration and rest in him (Jer 29:10–14; Matt 7:7–8). As our origin and end, union with the Creator serves as this foundation.

Resting in Sabbath freedom hinges on God's work rather than human work. Sabbath rest precedes human work in the garden. In this way Sabbath is another act of grace which creatures receive: "Sabbath . . . freedom, rest, and joy could be grounded only in those of God and consist only in its response to the invitation to participate in them."[34] As we participate with the Creator to whom we belong, God shares his own rest through the Sabbath. In our belonging to God our identity rests in this gift without the need for performance.[35] Barth's insight holds significant impact for contemporary work and those digital habits that encourage performance for

31   Barth, *Church Dogmatics* III/1, 215.
32   Barth, *Church Dogmatics* III/1, 215 (emphasis added).
33   Barth, *Church Dogmatics* III/1, 216 (emphasis added).
34   Barth, *Church Dogmatics* III/1, 216.
35   Barth, *Church Dogmatics* III/1, 213.

earning reward. Instead, Sabbath rest offers the opposite identity as a gift received rather than achieved through performance.

Finally, Sabbath serves as a sign of future rest free from work. Acknowledging this goal from the beginning, Barth says, "The last day will be a Sabbath day, and man's final time will be a time of rest for him, and indeed of rest in fellowship with the rest of God Himself, of participation in the freedom, rest and joy of His true deity . . . And it is in this—not then in anything he himself can achieve, but in what he receives as a fulfilment of this promise—that he himself and his work will be completed, just as God Himself completed the work of creation, not with another work, but with His rest after all His works."[36] Just like Augustine, Barth describes the movement of history as the movement toward eternal Sabbath rest, fulfilling the promise of ultimate rest beyond this life.

The sign of Sabbath stands at the beginning of creation in its teleological force, directing creatures toward their fulfillment through union with God. Barth concludes, "The object of God's love should become God's creation and therefore belong from the very outset to God. Creatureliness, and therefore creation, is the external basis of the covenant of grace in which the love of God for man moves toward its fulfilment. It is in this teleology that it is presented in the first creation narrative of the Bible."[37] With Augustine, Barth confirms that to be creaturely is to exist in relation to the Creator. Our identity comes from belonging to God by receiving our creaturely givenness rooted and fulfilled in love. This teleological reading helps shape Sabbath practice as reorienting our mundane work and the urgent technological demands around us. Granting eternal vision, Sabbath practice disrupts and reframes the meaning of our work, tech lives, and digital habits.

SABBATH PRACTICE: THE CENTER AND CIRCUMFERENCE OF WORK

Barth moves into the practical discussion of work as it relates to Sabbath rest. In order to discuss rest, he first describes the meaning of work. From the outset he describes Christ and Sabbath as the center, while work serves as the circumference.[38] Under God's providence, work serves the purpose

---

[36] Barth, *Church Dogmatics* III/1, 217.

[37] Barth, *Church Dogmatics* III/1, 217.

[38] Karl Barth, *Church Dogmatics* III/4, *The Doctrine of Creation*, ed. T. F. Torrance and Geoffrey W. Bromiley (T&T Clark, 2004), 516–17.

in caring for our daily bread and material existence.[39] However, work and our technical existence become major problems when they serve as the final goal rather than the means to our material sustenance. Echoing Augustine's concept of disordered love that flips means and ends and challenges the new workism, Barth says, "The work of divine providence does not take place for its own sake but in that teleological connection, so man's work cannot be done for its own sake but only in the teleological connection which it is given by God. If it were to be done for its own sake, this would mean man's being his own end and goal."[40]

When work defaults to existing for its own sake, idolatry reigns and the creature becomes their own god. At this point, work devours the creature since it was not intended to serve as master. To prevent work from devouring creatures, Barth describes the role of Sabbath across his doctrine of creation: "Whether he be farmer, artisan, servant or maid, he is just the man who for six days had to be these things and to perform the corresponding tasks, but whose being and existence are more than all these things and his work . . . that his work cannot devour him but consists of steps towards this goal, is confirmed at the end of each week by the proffered freedom, rest and joy of the workless Sabbath which he is granted."[41] Sabbath offers the limit to work, circumscribing work from its center in Christ. Reflecting on the challenges of the modern world, Barth describes the anxious ways work takes over individuals when it becomes our final goal whether for the sake of profit, competition, or power.[42]

Likewise, Barth considers five criteria constituting good work. The first involves caring for human needs in their universal and particular existence, described as "honest work" with appropriate ends.[43] The second consists in humane work for individuals and groups, preventing isolation through abstraction—not unlike our contemporary isolation made palpable through technology—and exploitation, which he recognizes occurs in problematic ways in both socialist and capitalist contexts.[44] Third, he considers a key motivation for work: earning daily bread. Yet work for

[39] Barth, *Church Dogmatics* III/4, 516–17.
[40] Barth, *Church Dogmatics* III/4, 521.
[41] Barth, *Church Dogmatics* III/1, 213.
[42] Barth, *Church Dogmatics* III/4, 553.
[43] Barth, *Church Dogmatics* III/4, 529–30.
[44] Barth, *Church Dogmatics* III/4, 531–32, 539–44.

material sustenance should also turn our hearts to prayer for spiritual sustenance shared in cooperation with others.[45]

Fourth, he says work should involve reflection with implications for the mechanical trades as well as contemplative vocations belonging to the arts and humanities. He also warns against increased pressure for productive measures in contemplative work, whether scholar, philosopher, poet, or artist.[46] Productivity too often becomes the final goal and changes the nature of particular vocations, whether education, medicine, politics, journalism, or even religion. Too often modern society expects productivity, but reflective, internal work is sufficient if not greater than external work. Here he also notes the vulnerability of individuals with illness or old age given that modern society values them less given its priority on productivity.[47]

Fifth and finally, Barth includes limitation as a criterion for work demonstrated through Sabbath rest. Rest prevents work from devouring its creatures through anxiety, idolatry, and tension. Barth says, "If man's work is to be done aright, relaxation is required. This is true both of outward work and inward. Work under tension is diseased and evil work which resists God and destroys man. It is done under tension, however, when man does not rise above it but is possessed, controlled and impelled by it."[48] This occurs when individuals are controlled by work rather than recognizing its secondary or third importance. As circumference rather than center, work becomes disordered when serving as our primary goal. Barth's concern is more palpable in a tech-driven economy with work available at our fingertips 24/7.

Instead, Sabbath vision and practice is necessary for combating the tyranny of work domination in today's digital empire. Sabbath practice sets an important limit, circumscribing work by offering us freedom. Not only does Sabbath distract us with the beauty and glory of alternative created goods bringing refreshment, but most importantly, Sabbath directs us to worship God.[49] Sabbath welcomes contemplation, opening us to reflection

[45]   Barth, *Church Dogmatics* III/4, 534–37.

[46]   Barth, *Church Dogmatics* III/4, 547.

[47]   Barth, *Church Dogmatics* III/4, 549; see also Ridenour, *Sabbath Rest as Vocation*, 175; Autumn Alcott Ridenour, "'Elderhood' and Sabbath Rest as Vocation: Identity, Purpose, & Belonging," *Journal of Population Ageing* 14, no. 3 (2021): 411–23.

[48]   Barth, *Church Dogmatics* III/4, 552.

[49]   Barth, *Church Dogmatics* III/4, 554–55.

without distraction. However, Sabbath does not end in contemplation of some abstract principle. Rather, true Sabbath opens us to receiving Christ as active subject. To receive the Word involves eternal rest in time. Hearing the Word intersects eternity with time and brings meaning to life. Barth concludes, "For this active receiving is as such man's participation in the rest, the real resting from his work, which is available for the people of God."[50] Real rest comes from our encounter with the God of rest. Rest reframes our work and digital habits by offering resistance, particularly against its evils and idolatries.

SABBATH AS RESISTANCE TO TECHNICAL EMPIRE

Rabbi Abraham Joshua Heschel's classic volume on *The Sabbath* poses an alternative posture of identity and belonging for the Jewish community in response to empire in mid-twentieth-century New York. His approach offers an alternative way of belonging within modern civilization and an alternative understanding of sacred time through the Sabbath's holy day. His prescient work, drawing from Hebrew Scripture, continues to hold significant insights for our contemporary digital empire in terms of alternative identity and belonging as it pertains to sacred time.

Rabbi Heschel's daughter, Susannah Heschel, introduces the volume by recalling Sabbath practices in their home as a child. She claims Sabbath was not a rejection or withdrawal from modernity but a complement to it. Still, she acknowledges her father's political concerns emphasizing freedom and liberty. She quotes him saying, "Inner liberty depends upon being exempt from domination of things as well as from domination of people . . . only very few are not enslaved to things. This is our constant problem—how to live with people and remain free, how to live with things and remain independent."[51] Not unlike Augustine's concern about individual and collective temptations to dominate through empire, Heschel recognizes the ways in which people and things can dominate in modern society. Practicing Sabbath plays an integral role in reframing his understanding of goods, commodities, and persons in their power over others.

Rabbi Heschel continues this theme in the prologue to *Sabbath*, in which he acknowledges the good in work and labor but the harm in love of profit. He says, "There is happiness in the love of labor, there is misery in the love of gain. Many hearts and pitchers are broken at the fountain of

50   Barth, *Church Dogmatics* III/4, 564.
51   Susannah Heschel, introduction to Abraham Joshua Heschel, *The Sabbath* (Farrar, Straus and Giroux, 1951), xiii.

profit. Selling himself into slavery to things, man becomes a utensil that is broken at the fountain."[52] Much like Augustine's description of disordered loves and Barth's description of improper motives in work, Heschel describes how profit becomes idolatry that in turn devours us when treated as the ultimate good. Labor is part of created reality but becomes problematic when profit becomes primary. Instead, Sabbath practice recognizes YHWH's provision for manna and life, celebrating goods to be shared.

In this sense Sabbath frames work rather than work framing the Sabbath. Heschel denies instrumental purposes for Sabbath, namely that its primary focus is to make work more effective. Heschel explains, "The Sabbath is a day for the sake of life. Man is not a beast of burden, and the Sabbath is not for the purpose of enhancing the efficiency of his work. 'Last in creation, first in intention,' the Sabbath is 'the end of the creation of heaven and earth.'"[53] Like Augustine and Barth, Heschel sees the teleological purpose for Sabbath rest as the beginning and end of creation. Because of this, Sabbath is not oriented to work but work to the Sabbath.

A world without Sabbath is a world with a distorted view, separating God from the world.[54] From this perspective, Heschel critiques ways in which Rome "anxiously desired—bread and circus games. But man does not live by bread and circus games alone. Who will teach him how to desire anxiously the spirit of a sacred day?"[55] He does not critique technical civilization as an empire to escape entirely—given his familiarity with exile—but instead recognizes the poverty of empire when pursued as the highest good. Physical bread and circuses, material wealth and entertainment, only last for so long. Heschel recognizes the significance of spiritual sustentation beyond physical needs alone. Like Hitz and Augustine, Heschel affirms that there is greater satisfaction in deeper, spiritual existence than life lived at the surface. Sabbath reminds one of joy in the life to come as well as joy available in life for today.[56]

The problem with technical civilization occurs when the human becomes "dissatisfied with what is available in nature, becomes engaged in a struggle with the forces of nature in order to enhance his safety and to increase his comfort . . . How proud we often are of the multitude of instruments we have succeeded in inventing, of the abundance of

52 Heschel, *The Sabbath*, 3.
53 Heschel, *The Sabbath*, 14.
54 Heschel, *The Sabbath*, 16.
55 Heschel, *The Sabbath*, 18.
56 Heschel, *The Sabbath*, 19.

commodities we have been able to produce . . . in spite of our triumphs, we have fallen victims to the work of our hands; it is as if the forces we had conquered have conquered us."[57] How easily human creation—not unlike Barth's chthonic creation or Ellul's counter creation—conquers us when we treat it as limitless commodities to pursue. In the limitless pursuit of commodities, commodities distort and own their creators.

Heschel offers one more example from the Roman Empire in its geographical expanse and technical arts, including "theaters, amphitheaters, public baths, aqueducts and bridges," along with the Colosseum, Pantheon, and Forum of Trajan as buildings admired "even by the gods."[58] Given its technical advancement, Rome received the "precious epithet . . . the Eternal City. The state became an object of worship, a divinity; and the Emperor embodied its divinity as he embodied its sovereignty."[59] Here Heschel acknowledges false worship.

While Rome claims eternal status, two of its philosophers, Cicero and Seneca, claim that everlasting status involves a noble life recalled through memory. When honor, nobility, and glory for the sake of Rome are touted as the highest goals, "eternal life" might better be called eternal fame, represented through Roman monuments.[60] As Augustine perceived, fame is the reward for empire's virtue.[61] Honor for the sake of Rome or the logic of empire brings notoriety.

Empire still rewards fame as the highest virtue. How easily we turn on digital devices to see images of celebrities filling social media, with fame an ever-increasing pursuit among young people.[62] David Brooks says, "Along with [the] apparent rise in self-esteem, there has been a tremendous increase in the desire for fame. Fame used to rank low as a life's ambition for most people. In a 1976 survey that asked people to list their life goals, fame ranked fifteenth out of sixteen. By 2007, 51 percent of young people

57 Heschel, *The Sabbath*, 27.
58 Heschel, *The Sabbath*, 38.
59 Heschel, *The Sabbath*, 38.
60 Heschel, *The Sabbath*, 39–40.
61 Augustine, *City of God* 5.12, p. 197; Cavadini, "Pride," 680.
62 David Brooks, *The Road to Character* (Random House, 2015), 7, 250–51; see also Kate Ryan, "Welcome to CringeTok, Where Being Insufferable Can Be Lucrative," *New York Times*, June 3, 2023, https://www.nytimes.com/2023/06/03/business/tiktok-cringe-creators-money.html. Finally, I might anecdotally add that conversation with former undergraduate students disclosed the daily influence of celebrities on their thinking through their social media newsfeeds. Imitation is part of social media's allure.

reported that being famous was one of their top personal goals."[63] This has presumably only increased since 2007 with the rise of social media. Digital celebrities, influencers, and online posting changed the landscape of social capital through the ways we relate to one another, blending personal lives and marketing. Our lives are new media to broadcast.

Recognizing the limits of human fame as opposed to divine fame, Heschel quotes Isaiah 40:8, "The grass withereth, the flower fadeth; but the word of our God shall stand for ever."[64] Heschel, seeing through the façade of power, critiques Rome's immanent understanding of fame—not unlike today's passing digital fame. Citing Rabbi Shimon ben Yochai, he says, "These triumphs were shocking, hateful and repulsive. He disparaged the calculating, utilitarian spirit of Roman civilization. He knew that all these splendid edifices and public institutions were not built by the Romans to aid the people but to serve their own nefarious designs: 'All that they made they made for themselves.'"[65] Much like Augustine's own critique of Rome, Heschel's eternal view sees through temporal efforts at short-term fame. Using workers, perhaps through unjust circumstances, Rome built its monuments in vain. Instead, Heschel indicates that our focus should be on spirit as that which fills time rather than on buildings that fill space. Here, spirit fills time with eternity and thus transforms time.[66]

The point of Sabbath, for Heschel, pertains to holiness as the "architecture of time."[67] Heschel's daughter, Susannah, says Sabbath involves a "restfulness that is also a celebration . . . Sabbath holiness fills every corner of the household. Anger is lifted, tensions are gone, and there is a glow on the face."[68] This glow differs from the shine of our digital empire, whether from artificial light or short-term happiness akin to cheer. Its more nefarious face, however, devolves into greed or envy in a chase for fool's gold like Thorin Oakenshield in J. R. R. Tolkien's *The Hobbit*. Rather than chase opportunity, profit, or moments of cheer, Heschel's glow reflects an eternal, divine light received from above. Like Moses's encounter with God on the mountain, transformation, change, and light occur through communion with the divine. Susannah Heschel describes the six days of each

[63] Brooks, *Road to Character*, 7.
[64] Heschel, *The Sabbath*, 40, quoting Isa 40:8 KJV.
[65] Heschel, *The Sabbath*, 39.
[66] Heschel, *The Sabbath*, 39.
[67] Heschel, introduction to Heschel, *The Sabbath*, xiii.
[68] Heschel, introduction to Heschel, *The Sabbath*, xiv.

week as a pilgrimage to Sabbath, ending in a "testimony to God's presence."[69] For Rabbi Heschel, practicing Sabbath involves welcoming God's presence in time, the "presence of an eternal moment."[70]

Heschel further claims that the spirit of Sabbath is like the "spirit on the eve of the Day of Atonement. Everybody would be overcome with an urge to ask forgiveness of each other. We were all seized by inner peace."[71] Practicing Sabbath opens time and space to receive from God, which results in the fruit of divine virtue: forgiveness. An entirely different logic than empire, forgiveness sets the captive free—spiritually, morally, physically, economically. Prioritizing Sabbath invokes an eternal and spiritual lens that reevaluates life's meaning for the remaining six days of the week. While critical of the Roman Empire, Heschel rejects leaving civilization. Instead, Sabbath reframes spiritual goals that impact the remaining six days. Heschel describes this priority thus: "More than an interlude; it is a profound conscious harmony of man and the world, a sympathy for all things and a participation in the spirit that unites what is below and what is above. All that is divine in the world is brought into union with God. This is Sabbath, and the true happiness of the universe."[72] In other words, he reaffirms Sabbath as the teleological goal of creation that offers meaning for the created world in its harmony and unity in God. Sabbath helps reframe our work toward more virtuous goals rather than placing consumer motives as the highest pursuit.

To prioritize Sabbath is to look at time differently. Heschel acknowledges that we think of time as simply a measuring device. Yet we only know our existence through time.[73] Time is bound up with our ever-changing and ever-growing lives. He explains, "Creation is the language of God, Time is His song, and things of space the consonants in the song. To sanctify time is to sing the vowels in union with Him . . . Eternity utters a day."[74] In this way eternity frames time and sanctifies time through the gift of Sabbath. Sabbath resets our identity through belonging to God and the priority of eternity.

Interestingly, Heschel's focus on sanctifying time might reframe today's digital empire in its demands on the attention economy. With the skillful dropping of stimuli catered to individuals through persuasive algorithms,

69   Heschel, introduction to Heschel, *The Sabbath*, xiv.
70   Heschel, *The Sabbath*, 29.
71   Heschel, *The Sabbath*, 31.
72   Heschel, *The Sabbath*, 31–32.
73   Heschel, *The Sabbath*, 96–97.
74   Heschel, *The Sabbath*, 101.

social media and tech users often complain that more screen time passes than they're aware of. Sucked into a seeming time warp, users are surprised to learn their weekly screen time averages. Estimates suggest "Americans spend roughly eleven hours a day with a computer, tablet, phone, or television screen . . . We touch our phones about 2,617 times a day while three in ten adults report being online 'all the time.'"[75] Here Rabbi Heschel's Sabbath practice might help reframe our spiritual and embodied existence by encouraging us to abandon our phones for one twenty-four-hour period a week, which might, in turn, positively impact more spiritually embodied choices throughout the week.[76]

Finally, Heschel locates a connection between Sabbath practice in the third commandment and the tenth commandment, which emphasizes "not coveting" (whether your neighbor's wife, house, oxen, etc.): "We must seek to find a relation between the two 'commandments.' Do not covet anything belonging to thy neighbor; I have given thee something that belongs to Me. What is that something? A day."[77] God shares himself with us from abundance. The divine life extends a whole day in time, reminding us to whom we belong. Sharing rather than hoarding, God offers the gift of a day. In this way Heschel offers a profound insight into how gratitude for divine provision helps guard against the human temptation to covet. A spirit of reception, gratitude, and sharing changes our approach to our surrounding world. Much like Heschel, Old Testament scholar Walter Brueggemann picks up this theme for today's digital and economic culture in his work on resistance.

Sabbath Resistance to Market Ideology in the Digital Empire

Brueggemann offers a prophetic harangue in his contemporary analysis *Sabbath as Resistance: Saying No to the Culture of Now*. Working in the Christian tradition, he draws from Hebrew texts on Sabbath to guard against unhealthy practices in our contemporary, 24/7, multitasking society. While Brueggemann's primary critique is centered on economic practices, particularly in the tradition of Adam Smith's market capitalism, there is much resonance with online multitasking habits—often tied to market practices.

---

[75]   Marcus Mescher, "The Moral Impact of Digital Devices," *Journal of Moral Theology* 9, no. 2 (2020): 65.

[76]   See Andy Crouch's description of a weekly tech Sabbath in Crouch, *Techwise Family*.

[77]   Crouch, *Techwise Family*, 90.

Brueggemann sets the context by acknowledging Adam Smith's market ideology depends "on the generation of needs and desires that will leave us endlessly 'rest-less,' inadequate, unfulfilled, and in pursuit of that which may satiate desire."[78] Fast forward to contemporary market practices in which buying and selling goods is constantly available through internet forums. He says, "Thus requirements concern endless predation so that we are a society of 24/7 multitasking in order to achieve, accomplish, perform, and possess. But the demands of market ideology pertain as much to consumption as they do to production. Thus the system of commodity requires that we want more, have more, own more, use more, eat more, and drink more."[79]

Social media propels this restless desire further given its broadcasting abilities to spread advertisements at a massive level.[80] The advent of social media influencers introduced lifestyle marketing into our everyday lives. While not altogether harmful,[81] the temptation is to promote what Neil Postman calls "not enough" marketing, which suggests the buyer lacks some quality or desirable characteristic apart from purchasing new products.[82] Between emotionally driven headlines and a barrage of advertisements, anxiety runs rampant with increased social media use, particularly for adolescent girls.[83]

[78] Brueggemann, *Sabbath as Resistance*, xii.
[79] Brueggemann, *Sabbath as Resistance*, xii.
[80] Bogost, "Age of Social Media Is Ending."
[81] I qualify the statement that not all "influencing" on social media is harmful. The platform has opened up new opportunities for business, entrepreneurship, social justice movements, and remote work. Yet in its ambivalence I must also recognize the cost it demands on personal lives and the ways it shapes our perceptions as well as interactions with life in the real world. For reflection on how social media influencers changed perceptions of motherhood, projecting idealized motherhood as opposed to the labor/work associated with motherhood, see Sara Peterson, *Momfluenced: Inside the Maddening, Picture Perfect World of Mommy Influencer Culture* (Beacon, 2023).
[82] Neil Postman, *Amusing Ourselves to Death* (Penguin Books, 1985).
[83] Jean M. Twenge, "Have Smartphones Destroyed a Generation?" *Atlantic*, September 2017, https://www.theatlantic.com/magazine/archive/2017/09/has-the-smartphone-destroyed-a-generation/534198/; Ezra Kline, "Why Are Teens in Decline? Here's What the Evidence Says," *New York Times*, May 19, 2023, https://www.nytimes.com/2023/05/19/opinion/ezra-klein-podcast-jean-twenge.html; Matt Richtel, Catherine Pearson, and Michael Levenson, "Surgeon General Warns That Social Media May Harm Children and Adolescents," *New York Times*, May 23, 2023, https://www.nytimes.com/2023/05/23/health/surgeon-general-social-media

While empire takes on new forms, given digital access is anytime and anywhere, the motive for profit maximization is anything but new. Brueggemann turns to the Ten Commandments in Exodus and Deuteronomy to shed wisdom on how the covenant with YHWH illuminates both ancient and contemporary practices. Brueggemann says the fourth commandment on remembering the Sabbath connects the first table of the Decalogue, focused on honoring God, with the second table, relating to neighbor.[84]

For the first commandment, YHWH identifies his name and nature as one who "brooks no rival" leading Israel out of Egypt, out of the land of slavery.[85] YHWH differs from Pharaoh in Egypt, but also the gods of Canaan, Assyria, Babylon, and Persia. Focusing on the gods of Egypt, Pharaoh stands in for all empires that seek "endless production systems."[86] Pharaoh's labor system "endlessly demands more production. What the slaves are to produce is more bricks that are to be used for the building of more 'supply cities' in which Pharaoh can store his endless supply of material wealth in the form of grain (see Exod 1:11). Because the system was designed to produce more and more surplus (see Gen 47:13–26), there is always more need for storage units that in turn generates more need for bricks with which to construct them."[87] Pharaoh's empire involves the negative feedback loop constructing more bricks for more supply cities for more wealth. The accumulation of wealth serves as gift to the gods of Pharaoh.

YHWH God is different. The first commandment distinguishes YHWH from neighboring gods. Unlike imperial productivity, the God of Exodus is one of covenant, faithfulness, mercy, and steadfast love. Brueggemann says, "At the taproot of this divine commitment to *relationship (covenant)* rather than *commodity (bricks)* is the capacity and willingness of this God to rest. The Sabbath rest of God is the acknowledgment that God and God's people in the world are not commodities to be dispatched for endless consumption and so dispatched, as we used to say, as 'hands' in the service of a command economy. Rather they are subjects situated

---

-mental-health.html; Jonathan Haidt, *The Anxious Generation: How the Great Rewiring of Childhood Is Causing an Epidemic of Mental Illness* (Penguin Books, 2024), 143–72.

[84] Brueggemann, *Sabbath as Resistance*, 1. This numbering reflects the Protestant numbering of the Ten Commandments in the tradition of Martin Luther.

[85] Brueggemann, *Sabbath as Resistance*, 2.

[86] Brueggemann, *Sabbath as Resistance*, 3.

[87] Brueggemann, *Sabbath as Resistance*, 3.

in an economy of neighborliness. All of this is implicit in the reality and exhibit of divine rest."[88] YHWH is not an anxious workaholic dependent on endless work.[89]

Building on this idea, the second commandment prohibits worshipping graven images. Unfortunately, Aaron forges a golden calf shortly after Moses receives the Ten Commandments. The calf commodifies God in the image of creation, one controlled through fixed images. Copying the divine through fixed or graven images causes harm. Resisting commodity addiction—whether belonging to Aaron, Pharoah, or common human desire, Brueggemann finds the culmination of creation and exodus resides in Sabbath: "YHWH's a Sabbath-keeping God, which fact ensures that restfulness and not restlessness is at the center of life. YHWH is a Sabbath-giving God and a Sabbath-commanding God."[90] Not only does this help guard against idolatry and consumption, but it also helps guard against "two masters": mammon and endless desire.[91]

Brueggemann also recognizes ways in which the Reformation's emphasis on faith versus works may have negatively turned works into productive measures for performing. Likewise, the Enlightenment's emphasis on individualism encourages securing one's own economic future through individual effort at the expense of the community. Both contribute to our contemporary economic ideology in which advertising functions as a kind of consumeristic liturgy.[92] Social media exacerbates market ideology, commodifying faces and images by pushing the boundaries of moral markets.[93] Rather than succumb to market ideology, which has influenced—if not changed the nature of—sports, education, medicine, politics, journalism, and even religion, Sabbath resistance pushes back against the trend. Sabbath practice and resistance reminds us of the good in *being* rather

---

[88]   Brueggemann, *Sabbath as Resistance*, 6.

[89]   Brueggemann, *Sabbath as Resistance*, 6.

[90]   Brueggemann, *Sabbath as Resistance*, 6.

[91]   Brueggemann, *Sabbath as Resistance*, 10–11.

[92]   Brueggemann, *Sabbath as Resistance*, 13.

[93]   Michael Sandel questions whether changing certain goods and practices from intrinsic to instrumental/monetary exchange fundamentally changes the meaning of the practice. Rather than pursue intrinsic purposes such as sports for the love of play, education for love of learning, justice for love of community, or religion for love of God, practices are tainted by market expansion. Distorting its own goals leads to moral compromise (Michael J. Sandel, *What Money Can't Buy: The Moral Limits of Markets* [Farrar, Straus and Giroux, 2012]).

than *doing*. The good in receiving rather than producing that helps bring about freedom and worship.[94]

Such Sabbath practice also involves resistance to anxiety. By commanding and practicing limits, YHWH demonstrates an end to work as opposed to the digital economy in its limitless social media feed and AI's limitless generativity.[95] YHWH's command includes limits for son, daughter, male and female servant, livestock, and resident alien alike.[96] Brueggemann says, "And as the work stoppage permits a waning of anxiety, so energy is redeployed to the neighborhood. The odd insistence of the God of Sinai is to counter anxious productivity with committed neighborliness. The latter practice does not produce so much; but it creates an environment of security and respect and dignity that redefines the human project."[97] Through limits, YHWH establishes an environment of respect and neighborliness that redefines individuals as ends rather than instruments and communities as ends rather than commodities.

Moreover, limits recognize the connection between love and justice by acknowledging all persons as worthy of protection from instrumental use alone. Every individual—no matter their economic position—is worthy of dignity and participation, evoking an image of a gathered community rather than Egypt's pyramid with the lower class supporting the few at the top.[98] This economic vision includes limits and shared goods based on a theology of trust rather than anxiety, provision rather than fear, and neighborliness rather than competition.[99]

A third aspect of Sabbath resistance addresses multitasking in its relevance to economic ideology and social media habits. Brueggemann offers a fascinating illustration in which "Mr. G," the town grocer, is distracted by the clock through Sunday worship in his desire to quickly resume business. Interestingly, he's on Sabbath time while keenly aware of work time. Mr. G leaves early during the closing hymn each week, and

[94]   Sandel, *What Money Can't Buy*, 19.

[95]   While AI and social media feeds are not technically limitless or infinite given their human creators, they still appear limitless given their anytime, anywhere availability. Without boundaries they act more chaotic than an ordered cosmos in which limits secure significant boundaries important for flourishing. See chapter 3.

[96]   Sandel, *What Money Can't Buy*, 26.

[97]   Sandel, *What Money Can't Buy*, 28.

[98]   Sandel, *What Money Can't Buy*, 28.

[99]   Andy Crouch, *Playing God: Redeeming the Gift of Power* (IVP, 2013), 251–52.

here Brueggemann points to the ways in which we multitask with God and multitask with false worship. He cites warnings from the prophets Isaiah, Hosea, Micah, and Amos regarding how the people worship God with their lips but ignore God with their actions. The people of God loved ritual fasting but perpetuated exploitative economic practices toward the neighbor (Isa 58:1–7).[100] In Amos, wealthy women are compared to the notorious cows of Bashan who indulge in limitless consumerism at the expense of cheap labor (Amos 4:1; 6:4–6).[101] From this perspective, the entire West or North Atlantic region might be indicted for its use of cheap labor for the production and consumption of household goods and clothing. Sabbath should challenge our consumer assumptions and practices. While easier said than done, this more costly option causes us to rethink quality made products rather than quantity, which includes recycling more furniture, clothing, and home goods by resisting our perennial throwaway culture.

Finally, such multitasking reflects a divided heart or what James might call doublemindedness. Religion and theology are not immune from multitasking as churches and nonprofit organizations often utilize technology to expand their reach. At the same time, churches and non-profits might be tempted to produce volume at the expense of quality in their desire for ratings, clicks, and views. When delivering content through journalism and social media, church and non-profit organizations must question the quality and benefit of their content while evaluating their motives for seeking large audiences in mass volume.

This leads to one final point Brueggemann makes linking the fourth commandment with the tenth on coveting. Like Rabbi Heschel, Brueggemann finds the prohibition against coveting one's neighbor's house, oxen, etc. guards against a posture of acquisitiveness. Trusting God through gratitude and Sabbath rest guards against envying the neighbor's status, contributing to a culture of greed. This is particularly important in the environment of social media. Scrolling through endless posts, stories, advertisements, and influencer feeds, we're tempted to covet our neighbor's lifestyle, hobbies, and habits that in turn negatively impact our own self-perception with increased anxiety and depression.

Regularly practicing Sabbath helps guard against covetousness toward the neighbor and greed. Practicing weekly Sabbath resistance might foster

---

[100] Brueggemann, *Sabbath as Resistance*, 63.
[101] Brueggemann, *Sabbath as Resistance*, 64–66.

a different outlook during the remaining six days. The Scripture is full of texts critiquing greed and covetousness throughout the Old and New Testaments. Covetousness is one of the first steps in dishonoring one's neighbor that leads to communal sin and strife. Utilizing the fourth commandment as the hinge command between the first and second tables brings together love for God and neighbor through honoring them both on the Sabbath. Such love and honor are further fulfilled through understanding Sabbath in its relation to leisure and play, as well as communion between God and his people.

SABBATH'S RELATION TO PLAY, LEISURE, JOY, AND COMMUNION

While Augustine specifically discusses Sabbath as the teleological goal of creation, the concept of rest is sometimes more broadly discussed in relation to the role of leisure and play. This holds significant implications not only for Sabbath worship but also understanding rest as leisure and play for body and soul in the challenges posed by a digital culture. Jürgen Moltmann discusses a *Theology of Play* (also translated as a *Theology of Joy*) that challenges a postindustrial culture driven by achievement and productivity. Aware of deep suffering, a theology of play does not ignore historical atrocities, conflict, and war.[102] However, the drive for laughter, joy, and song often subversively resists oppressive structures of evil and injustice even during the most atrocious conflict and wartime circumstances.[103] In terms of focus, Moltmann writes in response to a postwar industrial environment driven by spiritual apathy and industrious workaholism that sets the stage for our contemporary tech practices in the digital age.

Moltmann writes, "Every [person] has a burning desire for happiness and enjoyment."[104] Jubilant laughter unburdens and liberates individuals.[105] After all, laughter is the best medicine. Yet Moltmann finds that laughter and play are considered foolish in a social imaginary shaped by the Industrial Revolution and rationalized labor. Much like the digital revolution, recreation serves a utilitarian perspective. Short-term recreation and vacations exist for the sake of working harder much like today's workism culture. Recreation exists for the sake of work rather than Augustine's

[102] Moltmann's other works focus on suffering, particularly his volume *The Crucified God* (Fortress, 1993); see p. 43, n. 159.
[103] Pointing to counternarratives, such as *Fiddler on the Roof*, Moltmann advocates subversive stories that resist power, empire, and evil principalities.
[104] Jürgen Moltmann, *Theology of Play* (Harper & Row, 1972), 1.
[105] Moltmann, *Theology of Play*, 1.

ideal that work exists for the sake of rest. Flipping the means and ends, postindustrial and technological societies favor recreation and entertainment as short-term relief from the workaday schedule.

This can be significant when noting the history of vacation time. Holidays and vacations were created in large response to the labor movement following the Industrial Revolution.[106] Many corporations currently give more vacation time than is spent given persistent trends in workism.[107] Tech and corporate workers resist taking full vacation time as expectations shift, often piling more work responsibilities on employees for the sake of company expansion and individual promotion that prizes productivity. Thompson quotes Samuel Huntington, "Americans 'work longer hours, have shorter vacations, get less in unemployment, disability, and retirement benefits, and retire later, than people in comparably rich societies.'"[108] Digital practices make work more accessible rather than less with increased expectations for more output.

Moltmann finds utilitarian approaches to leisure persistent throughout history, citing the early Roman Empire's *panem et circenses*, or "bread and games," motto much like Heschel and Augustine before him. He says, "Let us give bread to the people and they'll be satisfied. Let us occasionally take them to the circus and they'll be happy. Since men obviously have a natural inclination toward freedom, freedom can be suppressed but not completely abolished. So every repressive regime must from time to time provide safety valves to release the pent-up pressures of aggression."[109] Moltmann recognizes the way Roman gladiatorial games entertained people and soldiers as analogous to how modern societies organize free time around sporting events. Yet while Roman societies organized public games in a shared space, today's digital empire offers more opportunities for entertainment and diversion on individualistic terms.

[106]   Lydia Dishman, "Americans Have Been Fighting for Paid Vacation for 100 Years," *Fast Company*, August 24, 2018, https://www.fastcompany.com/90220227/the-history-of-how-we-got-paid-vacation-in-the-us.

[107]   Dishman, "Americans Have Been Fighting"; Lauren Hirsch et al., "Why Do Almost Half of Americans Leave Paid Time Off on the Table?" *New York Times*, May 27, 2023, https://www.nytimes.com/2023/05/27/business/dealbook/unused-paid-time-off.html.

[108]   Samuel P. Huntington, *Who Are We? The Challenges to America's National Identity* (Simon & Schuster, 2004), 31, quoted in Thompson, "Workism Is Making Americans Miserable."

[109]   Moltmann, *Theology of Play*, 7.

Rather than drawing large groups together through entertainment, the amount of information and diversion available through the internet appears to be infinite. Whether niche sports, Hulu streaming, or countless YouTube videos, individuals can be lost in moments that splinter our attention away from unified focus and one another. Psychologists cite that loneliness is at an all-time high despite digital connection, resulting in what is now considered a public health crisis.[110] Given recent studies on social media use correlated with an increase in anxiety, depression, and mental fatigue, these forms of entertainment often deplete its users further.[111] More exhausted after endless scrolling or streaming, too much diversion takes away from restful sleep and even work. In a strange way, we are lost to productivity measures through our digital connections—whether adding followers or binge-watching our favorite Netflix season—while also succumbing to productivity measures from corporate algorithms' influence over our time and attention.

Real freedom comes from openness and receptivity to spiritual wholeness in God rather than mastery and domination over time. Like Augustine, Moltmann recognizes the difference between receptivity and freedom through grace as opposed to constraint through control. Too often contemporary leisure and recreation serve as poor forms of mastery and domination.[112] Vacations become to-do lists and leisure becomes bucket lists to be accomplished—later posted on the internet. Moltmann says, "People have lost their capacity for leisure, they no longer know how to do nothing . . . The leisure industry, with good business sense, helps people to find 'something to do' with their leisure."[113] The digital empire only multiplies opportunities for diversion by which we do something—whether watch, scroll, post, or play games. Freedom, however, comes from openness and receptivity and through a sense of wholeness with God and oneself not unlike Sabbath practices aimed at worship and restoration.

Josef Pieper, an original voice on leisure, contrasted the wholeness found in leisure from productivity, saying, "Look at the 'worker' and you

---

[110]   See Holt-Lunstad and Perissinotto, "Social Isolation and Loneliness"; see also Vivek Murthy, "Work and the Loneliness Epidemic," *Harvard Business Review*, September 26, 2017, cited in Crouch, *Life We're Looking For*, 11.

[111]   Jean M. Twenge, *iGen: Why Today's Super-Connected Kids Are Growing Up Less Rebellious, More Tolerant, Less Happy—and Completely Unprepared for Adulthood* (Atria Books, 2017); Kline, "Why Are Teens in Decline?"

[112]   Moltmann, *Theology of Play*, 9.

[113]   Moltmann, *Theology of Play*, 9.

will see that his face is marked by strain and tension, and these are even more pronounced in the case of the 'intellectual worker.' These are the marks of perpetual activity . . . They are the revealing marks of the intellectual sclerosis that comes with not being able to receive or accept, of that hardening of the heart that refuses to suffer anything . . . [falsely believing that] to be passive is always senseless."[114] Like Moltmann's concept of play, leisure for Pieper involves receiving from above a wholeness in being marked by transcendence and ultimately grace. Leisure reminds us we don't have autonomous control because we aren't God.

During his discussion of wholeness, Moltmann considers the role of subversive games and play that challenge the status quo—not unlike Sabbath resistance. From this perspective, even forms of entertainment, such as film, can depict ways of understanding reality that challenge cultural assumptions.[115] Breaking up the monotony of work time, play welcomes a different perspective. Like political satire, play pokes holes through the surface of our operative cultural assumptions. The medieval dances of death depicted in art forms across Europe "served to liberate the people by denuding the privileged classes of their trappings of dignity and their status symbols . . . These are the means the powerless use to shake off their yoke, for in these surprise situations they are escaping the bond of fear which has made their yoke possible"[116]—in this case, fear of death.

Interestingly, the most powerful political mechanism Moltmann finds is fear and worry. Fear of death is a strong motivator for control, work, and distraction. As Augustine recognized in his deconstruction of Rome in the *City of God*, many political and economic societies maintain power through fear and control. The *libido dominandi*, or lust to dominate, plays on this vulnerability manifested in political, philosophical, and economic ideologies across time and space. A theology of play and leisure disrupts existing cultural assumptions and the chthonic powers promising freedom in exchange for our time and attention.

[114] Josef Pieper, *Leisure: The Basis of Culture, with the Philosophical Act* (Ignatius/Pantheon Press, 1952), 30–31.

[115] Moltmann acknowledges ways in which the Protestant Reformation ironically contributed to individualism and productivity despite a theology of grace departing from works-based salvation (Moltmann, *Theology of Play*, 11). See also Max Weber, *The Protestant Ethic and the "Spirit" of Capitalism and Other Writings*, ed. and trans. Peter Baehr and Gordon C. Wells (Penguin Books, 2002).

[116] Moltmann, *Theology of Play*, 14.

Resurrection serves as the ultimate subversive power against death. Moltmann says, "Here already we find ourselves right at the center of the game of theology, the liberating game of faith with God against the evil bonds of fear and the gray pressures of care which death has laid upon us. For resurrection faith means courage to revolt against the 'covenant with death' (Isa 28:15), it means hope for the victory of life which shall swallow up and conquer life-devouring death."[117] In this way Christianity turns the dominant structures of society and chthonic powers of darkness on their head. Resurrection liberates. Death no longer has the final word; resurrection offers the strength of joy and hope.

This is theology as play. Since creation, it was God's good pleasure to share himself with creation as radically different than his own nature. God created not from necessity but from pleasure, as an expression of freedom. In creation there is joy in simple existence. With Barth we can say that the grace of being exists before any merit on the part of creation. Creation, redemption, and resurrection involve such freedom, joy, and play in the gift of being. Likewise, our creative projects include play with directed goals. All games, sports, board games, and video games include rules or limitations. Yet the rules and limitations are the framework by which one plays to win. Metaphorically speaking, games include a moral universe and rules that make space for freedom, risk, and creativity among players.[118] At creation, God includes a moral universe with rules or boundaries that contribute to our freedom and flourishing when kept willingly through love in an Augustinian sense.[119] Love aims at God and the goodness found therein.[120]

New Testament scholar Ben Witherington III builds on this idea: "Play foreshadows the play of the eschaton . . . Play is quite rightly seen as a celebration of life lived to its fullest, its fastest, its highest, its limits. And

[117] Moltmann, *Theology of Play*, 14.
[118] Ben Witherington III, *The Rest of Life: Rest, Play, Eating, Studying, Sex from a Kingdom Perspective* (Eerdmans, 2012), 43–44.
[119] Consider Augustine's account of *libertas*, or freedom, that originates in the ability not to sin (*posse non peccare*; Augustine, *The Augustine Catechism: The Enchiridion on Faith, Hope, and Love*, ed. Boniface Ramsey, trans. Bruce Harbert [New City Press, 2008], 28.104–5, pp. 120–21).
[120] Personifying perhaps Augustine's most famous (and often most misunderstood) line, "Love and do what you will" (Augustine, "Seventh Homily," in Augustine, *Homilies on the First Epistle of John*, ed. Daniel E. Doyle and Thomas Martin, The Works of Saint Augustine: A Translation for the 21st Century, part 3, vol. 14 [New City Press, 2008], 110).

play is something that has some potential to unite us [to others] if done well and wisely. The Olympic vision and spirit of its games reflect this to a small degree . . . games, played well and fairly, fuel a theology of hope for the future. Playing is not a useless activity. It anticipates the joy of the eschaton."[121] In this sense play is a communal activity that brings joy and freedom for its individual players when unified toward a common end. Play is both liberating and social by nature, tapping into the fullness of the human spirit.

Reflecting our freedom for good, Michael Novak's *The Joy of Sports* says, "The first free act of the human is to assign limits within which freedom can be at play. Play is not tied to necessity, except to the necessity of the human spirit to exercise its freedom, to enjoy something that is not practical, or productive, or required for gaining food or shelter."[122] Play or leisure moves us beyond necessities to a fuller life and existence. Perhaps this is why Martha Nussbaum includes play as part of the ten capabilities in her human capabilities approach.[123] Nussbaum considers play integral to human flourishing not unlike a fundamental human right. Jonathan Haidt recognizes play as essential for childhood development.[124] Time off, recreation, and the opportunity for restoration also serve as hallmarks within Catholic Social Teaching and the twentieth century labor movement in its resistance to the demands of the Industrial Revolution across Europe and North America.[125] Play moves us beyond survival and into flourishing from a socio-economic and political reality. Theologically speaking, play personifies freedom, which helps improve not only mental and physical skills, but also "reminds us of our status as child[ren] of God," moving toward the joy of the eschaton.[126]

---

[121] Witherington, *Rest of Life*, 42–43.

[122] Michael Novak, *The Joy of Sports*, quoted in Mark Galli, "A Theology of Play: We Don't Have to Always Be Doing Something Useful," *Christianity Today*, June 21, 2017, https://www.christianitytoday.com/ct/2017/july-august/thou-shalt -have-good-time.html.

[123] Martha C. Nussbaum, *Women and Human Development: The Capabilities Approach* (Cambridge University Press, 2000), 78–81.

[124] See Haidt's argument for a play-based childhood in Haidt, *Anxious Generation*, 49–66.

[125] Pope Leo XIII, *Rerum Novarum* (Encyclical Letter on Capital and Labor), May 15, 1891, https://www.vatican.va/content/leo-xiii/en/encyclicals/documents/ hf_l-xiii_enc_15051891_rerum-novarum.html.

[126] Witherington, *Rest of Life*, 39–43.

The fullness of play involves active participation and rest as opposed to passive recreation akin to distraction. Here the created, embodied presence demonstrates fullness of being and being together—a fullness that rejuvenates body and soul rather than technological amusement that tends to sap energy. Andy Crouch calls this the "muchness" of heart, soul, body, and strength complexes without technological shortcuts offered by machines.[127] Likewise, Conor Kelly differentiates leisure from recreation given leisure's intrinsic value found in "flow" or psychological fulfillment akin to Crouch's "muchness."[128] Leisure and the fullness of play capitalize on our created body and spiritual capacities that channel our strength and love toward shared goods and shared loves.

Common activities, such as rest, sports, play, sex, eating, and studying, are all physical, mental, and spiritual goods when pursued for love of God in kingdom-oriented relationships.[129] Sabbath and play are aspects of human creatureliness that honors God through our creative and redemptive capacities aimed at him. To follow Lewis's critique of pleasure as the highest good, we can say that each of these goods become "lower goods" or Augustinian "disordered loves" when pursued for their own sake apart from God.[130] Instead, through Sabbath worship and rejoicing, we order these goods in ways that restore and replenish rather than fueling us with further restlessness and endless desire.

Play helps us understand our created and teleological end in resurrection not unlike God's work in Sabbath and our human limits. Recognizing our finitude through creation brings freedom, as Moltmann explains: "Infinite responsibility destroys a human being—he is only man and not god."[131] Accepting our limits brings freedom and removes the burden that work hangs entirely on humans. Instead, play along with well-ordered work unites humans with our received identity: "Play as world symbol goes beyond the categories of doing, having, and achieving and leads us into the categories of being, of authentic human existence and demonstrative rejoicing. It emphasizes the creative against the productive and the

---

127   Crouch, *Life We're Looking For*, 35–39, 43–49.
128   Conor Kelly, *The Fullness of Free Time: A Theological Account of Leisure and Recreation in the Moral Life* (Georgetown University Press, 2020), 9.
129   Witherington, *Rest of Life*, ix.
130   C. S. Lewis, "The Weight of Glory," in *The Weight of Glory and Other Addresses* (1949; HarperOne, 2001), 26; idem, *Surprised by Joy: The Shape of My Early Life* (1955; HarperOne, 2017), 205, 209.
131   Moltmann, *Theology of Play*, 23.

aesthetic against the ethical."[132] Both creation and resurrection hang on God's action toward us, a beautiful gift with which we receive and respond with rejoicing. Perhaps it's not surprising that the Levitical law included the Feast of Tabernacles, or the Feast of Booths, involving regular rejoicing for YHWH's provision and care for his people (Lev 23:34, 39–43; Deut 16:13–15). Joy and gratitude are markers of Sabbath worship, rest, and anticipatory play.

Not unlike Augustine's understanding of creation, Moltmann affirms that there is good in giving and receiving from nature and the world around us. Creation is a gift for which we care. Moltmann says, "Man plays with the waves of the ocean and they play with him. He plays with colors, sounds, and words and also becomes their playmate. He speaks and responds, is active and passive, giving and receiving at once. Playing he is neither master nor servant. True not only in games but for the game of life."[133] Active and passive, call and response. In the practice of play, we are neither master nor servant. We find moments of fulfillment that image God in eternity. Here we give and receive by grace through beautiful moments invoking eternity in time.[134]

In an economy of grace we operate by divine rather than human logic.[135] Here identity comes through belonging. In this game, the game of grace, "losers win, the poor are filled, mourners rejoice, and the humbled, exalted."[136] The subversive life of grace is one that ironically fills without achieving but fills through receiving. Freedom ultimately comes from God, our creator and re-creator in Christ. Birth, baptism, and the transfiguration of Jesus points to the ultimate re-creation we might encounter through communion with him.

Sabbath Joy: Transformation and Communion

The height of disruptive play and Sabbath leads to divine presence as the fullness of joy. Here Moltmann moves play more directly toward worship not unlike the goals of Sabbath. He questions why Reformation and modern theology emphasize glory as sovereignty without emphasizing its correlate, beauty. Citing Barth, he claims the beauty of God is the glory of

132 Moltmann, *Theology of Play*, 23–24.
133 Moltmann, *Theology of Play*, 24.
134 See Søren Kierkegaard, *Works of Love*, trans. Howard V. Hong and Edna H. Hong (Princeton University Press, 1995), 10.
135 Moltmann, *Theology of Play*, 24.
136 Moltmann, *Theology of Play*, 24.

God.[137] The beauty of God leads to worship not unlike themes within the work of Jonathan Edwards or C. S. Lewis. Moltmann describes the theophanies of the Old Testament which point to the beauty and presence of God, whether Moses's encounter while hiding in the cleft of a rock or the prophets Isaiah and Jeremiah describing God's presence filling the earth as we see him face to face (Jer 31:34). Face to face, God dwells among us.[138]

In the New Testament, the *doxa* signifies "visible divine brightness" present at the birth and transfiguration of Jesus.[139] Moltmann says, "Since Jesus has been raised into God's future, that future in turn has already come into the present through him. Therefore the 'Lord of glory' (1 Cor 2:8) also stands for the 'God of glory' (Acts 7:2). The brightness of divine glory is reflected in the face of Christ and illuminates the hearts of men through him, just as on the first day of creation the creator 'let light shine out of darkness' (2 Cor 4:6)."[140] This culminating verse portrays the presence and communion of Christ that yields transformation, a key feature of Augustine's theology. The source of creative light that initiates time and space is the same light that re-creates our hearts in the face of Jesus Christ (2 Cor 4:6). The "fulfillment of justification" ends in transfiguration.[141]

Moltmann, like Augustine, appeals to 1 John 3:2 describing when God appears, "we shall be like him." Moltmann says, "[This] does not imply an *apotheosis* of man, where man puts himself into God's place, but it does mean man's ultimate transformation to complete conformity with the visible God by seeing him face to face . . . what is meant here is not just a restoration of man's pure creaturehood but beyond this is a much closer fellowship with God of which we have a foretaste on earth in the fellowship with Christ."[142] Followers of Christ are drawn into close fellowship with him while in time anticipating face-to-face communion. Aesthetics, derived from God's presence and beauty, should drive ethics. Divine beauty leads to worship and rejoicing that motivates our ethical response.[143] Otherwise we promulgate legalism when we separate ethics from worship and love.

---

137 Moltmann, *Theology of Play*, 38.
138 Moltmann, *Theology of Play*, 40.
139 Moltmann, *Theology of Play*, 40.
140 Moltmann, *Theology of Play*, 41.
141 Moltmann, *Theology of Play*, 42.
142 Moltmann, *Theology of Play*, 42–43.
143 Moltmann, *Theology of Play*, 43.

Lewis makes a similar point. Desire for union with beauty and joy should motivate ethics. Obedience without love is legalism. Lewis says we too often follow Kant or the Stoics in our Christian appeal to faith as obedience.[144] Like Augustine, he finds that desire serves as our ultimate motivation. Through worship we long for glory: "And this brings me to the other sense of glory—glory as brightness, splendor, luminosity . . . We do not want merely to see beauty, though, God knows, even that is bounty enough. We want something else which can hardly be put into words—to be united with the beauty we see to pass into it, to receive it into ourselves, to bathe in it, to become part of it."[145] Desiring union with the source of beauty and joy is eternally expansive, where wanting and having are inseparable.[146] Unlike temporal joys that disappear once attained, eternal beauty and joy are unending.

Lewis concludes *Mere Christianity* with a vision of eternal joy. Describing our short-term vision that describes Christianity as a moral framework, he describes a higher vision for communion and fulfillment:

> Though Christianity seems at the first to be all about morality, all about duties and rules and guilt and virtue, yet it leads you on, out of all that, into something beyond. One has a glimpse of a country where they do not talk of those things, except perhaps as a joke. Everyone there is filled full with what we should call goodness as a mirror is filled with light. But they do not call it goodness. They do not call it anything. They are not thinking of it. They are too busy looking at the source from which it comes.[147]

Not unlike Augustine, Lewis anticipates ultimate communion, a fullness or rest found in God. Union with the source of all joy and beauty brings completion: "The whole man is to drink joy from the fountain of joy. As St. Augustine said, the rapture of the saved soul will 'flow over' into the glorified body."[148] While awaiting this final vision where we shall see face to face, unified in body and soul, we see glimpses of eternity in the here and now most palpably reflected through the cross and resurrection.

[144] Lewis, "Weight of Glory," 26.
[145] Lewis, "Weight of Glory," 26.
[146] Lewis, *Surprised by Joy*, 205.
[147] C. S. Lewis, *Mere Christianity*, in *The Complete C. S. Lewis Signature Classics* (HarperOne, 2002), 122–23.
[148] Lewis, "Weight of Glory," 44.

Our worship responds to the God of love and sacrifice. Moltmann describes the exchange by which Christ demonstrates strength in weakness, honor in lowliness, and beauty through death on a cross:

> His glory is not the splendor of otherworldly superior power but the beauty of love which empties itself without losing itself and forgives without giving itself away. If then the glory of God manifests its brightness on this earth in the face of him who was crucified by its laws and powers, it follows that this law and these powers no longer are glorious and need no longer be feared or adored. He who in the world's view has been disgraced by death on the gallows as a common criminal has then been changed into the one who is most highly exalted. The *glory of the crucified God* leads of necessity to a transformation of all values and takes away the glory from those who have proclaimed themselves divine.[149]

Here Moltmann demonstrates the ultimate subversion not only in the incarnation but also through Jesus's death and resurrection. Jesus stands against the powers of this world and the darkness of death. As Lewis says, "The cross comes before the crown."[150]

The power of the resurrection brings justification to the unrighteous, beauty from ugliness, joy from mourning, and hope through faith.[151] The dying and rising, or "the terrible that results in the beautiful," demonstrates the cross as the path to resurrection.[152] The Christian life is one of daily dying and rising, a kind of transfiguration that results in joy. Such rejoicing celebrates a life of worship rather than achievement, reiterating that identity is one received rather than achieved.[153]

---

[149]   Moltmann, *Theology of Play*, 41–42 (emphasis added). In this passage Moltmann draws from his other work, *The Crucified God*. While I agree with his premise that God challenges death and the powers of darkness with the subversive nature of Christ's resurrection, I do not find it necessary to say God the Father suffered on the cross. Instead, I affirm that Jesus Christ, the God-man, was crucified and suffered on our behalf. As James Wetzel says, Augustine recognizes Christ's death not as an illusion but as a real and actual loss. This act grants comfort to those suffering and experiencing loss as true and genuine (James Wetzel, *Augustine: A Guide for the Perplexed* [Continuum, 2010], 41). See also Ridenour, *Sabbath Rest as Vocation*, 42.

[150]   Lewis, "Weight of Glory," 45.

[151]   Moltmann, *Theology of Play*, 42.

[152]   Moltmann, *Theology of Play*, 44.

[153]   Moltmann, *Theology of Play*, 50.

This rest comes from God's own identity as one who rests and works in harmony.[154] Resting in God, we come to recognize our "strivings cease."[155] The response of Sabbath involves trust, surrender, and sharing. Communion draws us into the presence of God. Alan Fadling finds the culture of hurry and rush in our contemporary time prevents us from recognizing the presence of God. Reflecting on 2 Corinthians 3:17–18, he says, "I have found—as you may have—that hurry becomes a veil that obscures the Lord's grandeur and beauty. Then, because my vision of his glory is hazy, my experience of transformation is hindered . . . Instead of seeing the glory of the Lord and being transformed over time by such a vision . . . A veil of hiddenness, fueled by a sense of drivenness, keeps me from beholding the Almighty's face."[156]

Stopping to contemplate and receive through the rhythms of Sabbath and play as children of God directs our attention to the one who offers rest. Sabbath begins and ends with God facing creation in joy and freedom. Disruptive play and Sabbath remind us of our identities received through facing our Creator, encountering his presence in worship, creation, and the world around us. Receiving grace results in the Augustinian reversal in which we use the world to love God rather than loving the world to use God for our own interests.[157] The joy and communion of God is intended to be shared through love and justice, beginning in time while foreshadowing eternity.

Shared Communion, Leisure, and Sabbath

Drawing on the Augustinian and Barthian traditions, Marva Dawn delights in Sabbath as the "climax and focal point" of life.[158] As for many before her, Sabbath rest reflects the teleological goal of creation, invoking God's presence in time with the gift of a day. She describes the holistic rest available in intentionally practicing the Sabbath regularly, thus framing her work week and spiritual life with meaning.[159] Drawing themes from the canon of Scripture, she emphasizes God's "tent" or "tabernacle" among his people (Exod 40:34–38), God's presence or tent dwelling with us at the incarnation

---

[154] Brueggemann, *Sabbath as Resistance*, 87.

[155] Warren, *Liturgy of the Ordinary*, 142.

[156] Fadling, *Unhurried Life*, 186.

[157] Moltmann, *Theology of Play*, 63–66.

[158] Marva J. Dawn, *Keeping the Sabbath Wholly: Ceasing, Resting, Embracing, Feasting* (Eerdmans, 1989), 50.

[159] Dawn, *Keeping the Sabbath Wholly*, 58.

(John 1:14), and God's promise to dwell or tent among his people in the eschatological vision (Rev 7:15).[160] Through practicing Sabbath, the people of God invoke the "very dwelling of his presence" through peace.[161]

Throughout Scripture, the presence of God is meant to be shared. Alongside worship within the faith community, a high priority for Sabbath involves being with the people around us, friends, and loved ones.[162] Rather than the drive for productivity, the point of this day is to share in the relational gifts God bestows on creation. Dawn says, "The point is not necessarily to do anything—perhaps to play, perhaps to share a needed time of gentle affection, but above all simply to be together."[163] This is the opposite of cultural dynamics that involve "doing" for others rather than "being" with others.[164]

Contrasting the tendency to "do" for others rather than "be" with others requires the conversational give and take necessary for individual growth.[165] Being with others more deeply images God through creation, Sabbath, and incarnation; being with others also involves healthier patterns for interpersonal relationships. Samuel Wells says, "In a lot of ways, 'with' is harder than 'for.' You can do 'for' without a conversation, without a real relationship, without a genuine shaping of your life to accommodate and incorporate the other."[166] Sabbath practice requires slowing down, turning off productivity mode, and welcoming God through worship, the wonder of creation, and our relationship with others. The posture behind these practices involves intentional reception of divine grace through Christ in his word and the surrounding community.

In this sense Sabbath practice is deeply tied to fellowship with God and others. The broader church intentionally gathers for Saturday (*Shabbat*) or Sunday (resurrection day) worship.[167] This gift involves embracing the

---

[160] Dawn, *Keeping the Sabbath Wholly*, 64.

[161] Dawn, *Keeping the Sabbath Wholly*, 64.

[162] Dawn, *Keeping the Sabbath Wholly*, 64.

[163] Dawn, *Keeping the Sabbath Wholly*, 21.

[164] See Samuel Wells, "Rethinking Service," *The Cresset* 76, no. 4 (2013): 9–10, cited in Kelly, *Fullness of Free Time*, 66.

[165] Wells, "Rethinking Service," cited in Kelly, *Fullness of Free Time*.

[166] Wells, "Rethinking Service," cited in Kelly, *Fullness of Free Time*, 66.

[167] See Sigve Tonstad and Witherington on the difference between Sabbath (seventh-day worship), drawing from creation in the Hebrew Bible/Old Testament, and the role of Sunday (eighth-day worship), drawing from resurrection in the New Testament, in Witherington, *Rest of Life*, 1–22.

other through both solitude and community.[168] As we see the importance of solitude for friendship in Turkle's *Reclaiming Conversation* or Bonhoeffer's *Life Together*, so we can recognize how solitude and silence mutually enhance our ability to empathize and relate to others from a strong sense of self-understanding or the self laid bare before God.[169] This involves being with one another in vulnerability. Vulnerability involves honesty, humility, and grace. Dawn says, "Solitude and community work together in paradox. Our times of solitude make our times of community deeper because we have learned more about ourselves to offer to the whole. Reciprocally, our times in community rebuild our sense of self through interaction with others and give us food for our personal reflections."[170] Dawn finds these Sabbath practices healing and restorative for our emotional, spiritual, and physical health.

Moreover, Sabbath practice involves deep intentionality. Following the Jewish tradition, the people of God made Sabbath priority across time and space even during exile or persecution. Practicing Sabbath in our modern technological fray seems paltry when compared to grave political oppression. However, given the amount of distraction available at our fingertips and the algorithms set to distract us, intentionality remains paramount.

This distraction relates to what sociologist Emile Durkheim describes as "anomie," or social disintegration prevalent among modern technological societies without a "guiding sense of direction."[171] Often the chaotic dynamic of our contemporary social unrest fills us with overwhelming amounts of information. Individualism runs rampant while desire for solidarity and communion bubbles behind our surface level connections. Dawn describes our longing for deeper bonds: "The choice of God's purposes within the Christian community counteracts the anomie of our society. The grace of God and the continuity of the Church create stability. The Word of God provides authority. The fellowship of God's people offers tight bonds of intimacy. Within these supports, the individual finds order, solidarity, a sense of direction, and hope."[172]

[168] Dawn, *Keeping the Sabbath Wholly*, 74–75.
[169] See Cardinal Robert Sarah, *The Power of Silence: Against the Dictatorship of Noise* (Ignatius, 2016).
[170] Sarah, *Power of Silence*, 73.
[171] Sarah, *Power of Silence*, 112. Haidt also cites Durkheim's description of "anomie" or "normlessness," entailing the loose social bonds prevalent among the virtual world (Haidt, *Anxious Generation*, 194–95).
[172] Dawn, *Keeping the Sabbath Wholly*, 113.

Without direction, community, and hope, distraction moves toward boredom. Norman Wirzba finds this boredom a deep-seated dissatisfaction with life despite the prosperity and wealth surrounding us: "Boredom is not the same as having too much time on our hands. Its root goes much deeper . . . as a failure to find the world and each other compelling and interesting. We find the world boring because we don't see very clearly why it is valuable and good or how and why we practically and beneficially belong to it."[173] Without purpose and belonging that invoke responsibility, we descend into boredom and apathy. This apathy reflects a kind of restlessness tied to the deadly sin known as *acedia* or sloth.

Acedia or sloth contrasts rest. Critiquing modern definitions of *acedia* as idleness or the inability to work, Josef Pieper says idleness is where we ignore human dignity. Pieper explains, "[The idle person] does not want to be as God wants him to be, and that ultimately means that he does not wish to be what he really, fundamentally *is*."[174] *Acedia* involves a kind of spiritual sloth by which individuals ignore the kind of creatures they are and the "divine goodness" that comes from imaging God.[175]

Combating the misconception that idleness or sloth necessarily involves laziness, Pieper finds that *acedia* fuels the kind of restlessness in meaningless work: "work for work's sake," like contemporary "workism."[176] *Acedia* reminds us of Augustine's disordered love, whether profit for profit's sake or communication for communication's sake through an endless supply of information access in our digital empire. Like Augustine's concern that fear of death fueled power in the Roman Empire, fear of death and meaning fuels the aimless busyness prevalent in our tech culture.

False security in the Roman Empire cloaked powerlessness. False security in the digital empire masks fear of meaninglessness. Historically identified as one of the seven capital (or deadly) sins, acedia serves as a source for other sins. Pieper says, "One of the children of *acedia* is despair, which

---

[173] Norman Wirzba, *Living the Sabbath: Discovering the Rhythms of Rest and Delight* (Brazos, 2006), 66.

[174] Pieper, *Leisure*, 44.

[175] Pieper, *Leisure*, 44. See also Christopher D. Jones on Evagrius's description of avarice as "indifference or hatred for what is present, a desire for what is not present, and hatred for the desired objects" (Christopher D. Jones, "The Problem of Acedia in Eastern Orthodox Morality Studies," *Studies in Christian Ethics* 33, no. 3 [2020]: 343); William Mattison III, *Introducing Moral Theology: True Happiness and the Virtues* (Brazos, 2008), 245.

[176] Pieper, *Leisure*, 43.

amounts to saying that despair and the incapacity for leisure are twins."[177] In this sense contemporary tech restlessness and despair are similarly rooted in spiritual sloth, or the denial of our creaturely status with its limits before God.

Acedia is also a sin against the Sabbath. Pieper cites Thomas Aquinas to argue that sloth sins against the Sabbath: "Who would guess, unless he were expressly told so, that Aquinas regarded *acedia* as a sin against the third commandment? He was in fact so far from considering idleness as the opposite of the ethos of work that he simply interprets it as an offense against the commandment in which we are called upon to have 'the peace of mind in God.'"[178] Rather than contrasting with work, acedia contrasts with the wholeness of being, or leisure, before God and others found in Sabbath rest.

Sabbath rest reflects leisure or flow, a kind of psychological fulfillment through focus.[179] Leisure anticipates heavenly rest and finds its final *telos* in union with God.[180] Kelly says, "'*Shabat*' depicts cessation and implies a sense of completion for all creation. Thus, rest becomes an essential component of the proper teleological vision for every creature, amounting to the 'final goal of Creation.'"[181] This final goal points to heavenly rest in the full presence of God and one another. Over against utilitarian values that instrumentalize our time and work for some purpose—generally profit—presence involves the "being with one another" intrinsic to the nature of Sabbath worship in community.

Being together is also hindered through technological distraction, as Kelly explains:

> Just as important, flow cannot tolerate distraction, so it also represents a remedy to one of the major obstacles to authentic human connection in the age of ubiquitous technological connectivity: digital distraction. Specifically, flow counteracts what the psychologist

[177] Pieper, *Leisure*, 45–46.
[178] Pieper, *Leisure*, 45, quoting Aquinas, *Summa Theologica* II-II, 35, 3 ad I; *Quaest. disp. de malo*, II, 3 ad 2. Note also that Roman Catholic theology numbers honoring the Sabbath as the third commandment while Protestant theology numbers honoring the Sabbath as the fourth commandment in the Decalogue. See James F. Keenan, *Moral Wisdom: Lessons and Texts from the Catholic Tradition*, 2nd ed. (Sheed & Ward, 2010), 104.
[179] Kelly, *Fullness of Free Time*, 9–11.
[180] Kelly, *Fullness of Free Time*, 65.
[181] Kelly, *Fullness of Free Time*, 65.

Kenneth Gergen has come to define as the problem of *"absent presence,"* whereby people are physically present together in the same space but mentally absent from one another as they turn their attention to screens of one form or another.[182]

Combating absent presence, leisure involves relational time that welcomes flow. Key to this endeavor is intentional time spent with God and neighbor. Openness to one another through vulnerability and mutual intentionality deepens relationships.

Embodied time together deepens relational bonds, though screen time may supplement existing relationships. Still, embodied presence allows for more spontaneous conversation and engagement with the five senses, enriching our understanding of one another.[183] Presence and mutuality help build communities and "canopies of trust" necessary for human flourishing.[184] These canopies become the backdrop, community, and people present in one's life that help supply the key ingredients of trust and responsibility for individual thriving. Ultimately leisure and Sabbath rest are linked to community and social identity, which empowers and builds stability against the growing challenges of social unrest and workism in our midst.

SABBATH PRACTICE: JUSTICE AND LOVE

The Sabbath commands in the Torah involve physical rest for the whole community with broad social implications. Sabbath is a matter not of individualistic worship but of communal commitment. In fact, rest is a prescription for everyone in the community—from the landowner to the tenant, servant, livestock, and land itself. No creature is exempt from Sabbath rest. The gift involves all creation.

Crouch discusses the Sabbath ladder presented in the Hebrew Bible, building from smaller to larger responsibilities with significance for the broader community. Sabbath responsibilities involve worshiping YHWH with justice toward the neighbor. Sabbath practice places limits on work

[182]   Kelly, *Fullness of Free Time*, 67 (emphasis added).

[183]   See Bess Connolly, "Zoom Conversations vs In-Person: Brain Activity Tells a Different Tale," *Neuroscience News*, October 26, 2023, https://neurosciencenews .com/zoom-conversations-social-neuroscience-24996/; N. Zhao et al., "Separable Processes for Live 'In-Person' and Live 'Zoom-Like' Faces," *Imaging Neuroscience* 1 (2023): 1–17.

[184]   Crouch, *Life We're Looking For*, 163–67, drawing from Peter L. Berger, *The Sacred Canopy: Elements of a Sociological Theory of Religion* (Anchor, 1990).

and productivity, reflecting dependence on YHWH. Not only does Sabbath practice depend on God's provision, it also demonstrates care for the community, land, and livestock's wellbeing. Early community practice involved leaving crops for the sojourner from one's harvest.[185] Like Ruth and Naomi gleaning wheat from their relatives' field, the poor and alien share in the produce. By sharing, the Israelite community demonstrates trust in God's provision for family and community. Each command in the Sabbath ladder reflects trust, as Crouch describes:

> Every day when the workers harvest, they will leave margins; every week, they will observe a sabbath, leaving the crops to grow on their own; every seven years they are enjoined to leave the field alone entirely and live simply on whatever may come up without active cultivation; and every fiftieth year (that is, after seven sevens) they are to celebrate the extraordinary festival of Jubilee, where debts are forgiven, land that has been pledged as security for debts is returned to its original family, and slaves are freed. At each stage of this escalating "sabbath ladder" the powerful are asked to relinquish more of their power and, especially, their privilege—the accumulated fruits of their successful exercise of power. On a daily basis they are to hold back from wringing the last possible ounce of produce from the land, but at intervals of weeks and years and most of all once a lifetime, they are to prodigally withhold the rightful exercise of their power.[186]

While the Sabbath ladder here appears radical in today's market-driven, profit-centered economy, Sabbath practice requires individuals and communities to rethink their relationship to wealth.

Given its tie to creation in which YHWH rests, Sabbath commands in Exodus, Deuteronomy, and Leviticus reflect dependence on the Creator not only for life, but also sustenance. By putting a pause on work once a week and every seven years, the commands reflect trust in the source of all sustenance. Likewise, Sabbath practice includes responsibility to the neighbor and broader creation. Sabbath practice once a week includes all workers from the landowner to servant, livestock, and land. Allowing daily margins for gleaning acknowledges the importance of sustaining a whole community across class and ability. Finally, the vision for Jubilee includes the radical call to relinquish debts, preventing unchecked wealth

---

[185] Crouch, *Playing God*, 247–49.
[186] Crouch, *Playing God*, 249.

accumulation for the few while allowing broad economic opportunity for the many.

Crouch explains, "Through Jubilee . . . Israel would be reminded, and would remind the world, that power was not an achievement but a gift, that prosperity comes not from idolatry or injustice but from gratitude and generosity, that wealth does not have to be hoarded and debts are meant to be forgiven."[187] Jubilee is radical not only for our contemporary digital empire but also for its original setting. Worship avoids both idolatry and injustice; love of God drives us toward justice for the neighbor.

Although Jubilee is commanded by the "clarion call" of Deuteronomy, Isaiah, and other prophets, there is no recording of its practice in the Old Testament.[188] Whether or not Jubilee was ever put into practice, the teaching remains as a foreshadowing of the coming liberator who gives up everything. Crouch says, "But Jubilee was never forgotten. The true God never gave up on his people and the flourishing that his image bearers were meant to bring. When Jesus began his ministry, he found the place in the scroll where Isaiah revived the hope of the Jubilee year and read it aloud (Luke 4). Wherever Jesus went, there were foretastes of Jubilee."[189]

The practice of Sabbath participates in glimpses of Jubilee, honoring God and others through love and justice. Dawn reflects on the importance of Sabbath feasting in communion with God and neighbor. Following the initial Jewish prescription, she emphasizes the role feasting plays on Sabbath. Honoring moments in the biblical past in which God provided double portions of manna for Sabbath, the culmination of feasting involves customary items that remind the community of YHWH's provision.[190] Dawn critiques American culture's overabundant eating without reflection. Instead, she suggests pursuing simplicity and fasting as regular routines in preparation for feasting on Sabbath days. Here she evokes a spiritual discipline that attests to the importance of God's provision, sacrifice, and sharing.

The climax of Christian feasting and sacrifice results in communion or Eucharist, reflecting Christ's sacrifice while anticipating the resurrection. Communion involves receiving and acting and reminds the gathered community of their status before God and the world. Dawn says, "Since in the Lord's Supper we look forward to Christ's coming again and to the

187 Crouch, *Playing God*, 263.
188 Crouch, *Playing God*, 263.
189 Crouch, *Playing God*, 264.
190 Dawn, *Keeping the Sabbath Wholly*, 184.

eternal feasting we will enjoy in his presence, the frequent celebration of the Eucharist (when it is not an empty routine) gives us a foretaste of that Joy."[191] Anticipating the joy to be shared, followers of Christ participate in broader Sabbath feasting by opening their homes and churches to the world through shared meals.[192] These practices involve physical and spiritual presence among neighbors across socioeconomic and ethnic divides by which divine presence and love is shared. In contrast to the digital empire that posts information for consumption, Sabbath feasting entails consuming a common meal together in love.

Finally, Sabbath feasting extends beyond the believing community, as regular fasting and feasting should lead practitioners to care for the poor and neighbor in need. Dawn takes on the issues of poverty, hunger, economic injustice, and peace. Recognizing Christ's own sacrificial provision for our needs along with care for the poor, she challenges Christ followers to extend Sabbath justice and peace for those in need. Just as idolatry and injustice go hand in hand, so too do worship and justice extend to the broader community.

Justice exists for the entire household and socioeconomic sphere within the scope of the biblical Sabbath.[193] In light of Israel's liberation from systemic abuse and exploitation in Egypt, Wirzba says, "the Israelites would have readily seen that Sabbath teaching . . . [was] about the liberation of all to share in the goodness of God. God's grace is not reserved for the select, powerful few. It extends to the whole community of life, even to strangers, animals, and the land itself."[194] No part of creation remains untouched by Sabbath rest.

Practicing the Sabbath year by allowing the land to lie fallow guards against an attitude of fear and distrust, a disposition of anxiety gone awry that seeks power and possessions at the expense of others. Negative anxiety can result in competition, distrust, and misused power—whether economic misuse or digital mistreatment seen through problematic communication patterns that spread rage, emotion, and political lies dubbed as misinformation.[195] Through the use of sensation(alism), economic profit increases with the amount of views and clicks acquired. Sabbath

[191] Dawn, *Keeping the Sabbath Wholly*, 184.
[192] Dawn, *Keeping the Sabbath Wholly*, 184.
[193] Wirzba, *Living the Sabbath*, 39.
[194] Wirzba, *Living the Sabbath*, 39.
[195] Max Fisher, *The Chaos Machine: The Inside Story of How Social Media Rewired Our Minds and Our World* (Back Bay, 2023).

justice might further guard against the spread of unjust misinformation that defames character.

Sabbath justice also challenges the exploitation of data workers who often sign nondisclosure agreements while working for the most powerful tech corporations in the world.[196] In *Code Dependent: Living in the Shadow of AI*, Madhumita Murgia describes the fragmented nature of these individuals—often the world's most marginalized: "disadvantaged youth, women with dependents, minorities, migrants and refugees"[197]—and the work laid upon them. These individuals are often unaware of the clients they serve, how the data they gather is used, or how "their counterparts in other parts of the world are paid for the same job."[198] They have partial and sometimes no knowledge of the products to which they contribute—or of whether these products are considered ethical.

Likewise, Sabbath justice might also guard against exploitation of individuals paid to clean social media sites of language and images of violence and abuse, known as "content moderators."[199] Crouch calls these moderators the "trash collectors of our social media world. They collect the mediated garbage of depraved humanity and dispose of it so the rest of us do not have to see or encounter it . . . often, content moderators only last a few months before they burn out."[200] Murgia describes how content moderators demonstrate symptoms of PTSD, experiencing flashbacks of previously viewed content while cleaning up online sites.[201] "It wasn't just the nature of the content itself that was a problem—it was their working conditions, this reimagining of a human worker as an automaton."[202] Removed from the purpose of their contribution and treated as parts removed from the whole, these workers find their work emptied of meaning.[203] These practices also raise ethical

[196]   Madhumita Murgia, *Code Dependent: Living in the Shadow of AI* (Henry Holt, 2024), 22–24.

[197]   Murgia, *Code Dependent*, 23.

[198]   Murgia, *Code Dependent*, 23–24.

[199]   See Andy Crouch's discussion of digital trash surveillance in Crouch, *Life We're Looking For*, 103.

[200]   Crouch, *Life We're Looking For*, 103.

[201]   Murgia, *Code Dependent*, 208–10.

[202]   Murgia, *Code Dependent*, 209.

[203]   To consider the ethics of work further from a Platonic lens that values workers' and employees' contribution as participants in an industry's purpose, meaning, and holistic vision, see Jeffrey Hanson, *Philosophies of Work in the Platonic Tradition: A History of Labor and Human Flourishing* (Bloomsbury Academic, 2022).

questions around the toxic content they are asked to observe. Instead, Sabbath practice—perhaps challenging these corporate patterns by shutting down social media for 24-hour periods—offers a break from the endless tyranny of information and the onslaught of humanity's vice. It also poses questions about the nature of this work and the importance of just regulations and practices protecting workers' interests regardless of economic status.[204]

Sabbath practice, in its weekly, seventh-, and fiftieth-year celebrations, reminds us in the midst of our work and digital practices of a higher, equalizing authority beyond time and productivity. Wirzba says, "As we cease from our steady toil, we learn the valuable lesson that the whole of creation does not exist exclusively for us and to meet our desires. Creation belongs to God. It is at its best when it fulfills God's intentions for it. We are at our best—we most exhibit the image of God—when our work aids those intentions and when it supports and maintains the generosity of God."[205] Practicing Sabbath in this way enables us to "honor the presence of God in all things and to participate in the ways of life and health."[206] Regular digital fasts and digital sabbaths help reframe the meaning of rest as well as justice in our daily lives.

Regular Sabbath practice should naturally involve advocating for a just workplace that helps develop the whole person through the provision of just benefits for all its workers. Rather than the rhythms of work and rest being separated from faith in a bifurcated reality, Wirzba says they should inform one another: "Given that work is one of the primary means we have for developing and expressing who we are (as well as play, leisure, and worship), [they] must be integrated within faith's journey."[207] In light of this, he proposes that Christians help transform work culture to promote "justice, beauty, and peace."[208] He finds several areas critical for improvement, including work environments, benefits for minimum-wage workers, and the prioritization of quality products rather than "cheap, shoddy, or ugly products" that defile natural resources.[209] These issues are rife for digital markets, from the working conditions for code laborers

---

[204] I will consider questions of justice, principles, and regulations as well as the virtue of justice further in chapter 6.
[205] Wirzba, *Living the Sabbath*, 40.
[206] Wirzba, *Living the Sabbath*, 41.
[207] Wirzba, *Living the Sabbath*, 98.
[208] Wirzba, *Living the Sabbath*, 98.
[209] Wirzba, *Living the Sabbath*, 98.

to the materials composing our electronic devices and their disposal at a massive scale.

In terms of market consumption and digital practices, Wirzba discourages creating "artificial needs and wants in other people, as we do through ubiquitous advertising campaigns . . . turning them into anxious, ungrateful, hapless, even resentful consumers."[210] Seemingly omnipresent, the power of digital advertising persuades users of increased needs and wants. Sabbath practice oriented around justice helps guard against this messaging with reminders of divine provision and the importance of sharing rest.

Change in work and digital habits will not invoke utopia, as Wirzba explains: "Even if Christians were to become committed to the goal of Sabbath joy, it is highly unlikely that anything like the overthrow of a wage-labor system would come about. Our goal, rather, should be to transform particular workplaces and inspire specific workers or working groups to make Sabbath peace and delight their highest priority."[211] Such priorities might include building more collaboration among employers, employees, shareholders, and communities impacted by particular industries. Encouraging them to meet face to face, Wirzba says they might learn each other's aspirations and needs as well as discuss the consequences of their work together.[212] The size and scope of the tech industry provokes further reflection on the importance of principles and regulations for digital corporations in their ethical limits.[213]

Sabbath practices are significant for large- and small-scale corporations and communities. Kelly highlights how Sabbath and leisure involve "everyday solidarity," promoting just economic practices for those "at the resource-poor end of the free time gap."[214] In order to ensure the opportunity for quality free time, he argues for a "living wage floor" as well as structural reforms that include parental leave and vacation time. These benefits are essential for the "temporal poor," aligning not only with biblical Sabbath practices but also with principles of Catholic social teaching: human dignity, the call to family and participation, the dignity of work and the rights of workers, and the preferential option for the poor.[215]

---

[210] Wirzba, *Living the Sabbath*, 98.

[211] Wirzba, *Living the Sabbath*, 98.

[212] Wirzba, *Living the Sabbath*, 98.

[213] Ethical limits, principles, and regulations will be discussed further in chapter 6.

[214] Kelly, *Fullness of Free Time*, 86.

[215] Kelly, *Fullness of Free Time*, 95.

Understanding leisure's connection to solidarity, Kelly draws on arguments from Pope Leo XIII's *Rerum Novarum*, which argues for time off and just labor laws during the Industrial Revolution, in addition to twentieth-century proponents of the living wage.[216] Recognizing digital practices that inform new time constraints for both those on the "time-poverty end" and "resource-rich end," Kelly says a significant amount of time poverty results not only in the hustle to perform multiple jobs but also in "job spill" with the advent of the internet and constant connectivity.[217]

Kelly says, "This form of 'job spill' is an acute problem for those at the resource-rich end of the free time gap because smartphones and other internet-enabled devices have made constant connection—even at home during one's supposedly free time—a part of the employment contract for the most financially secure jobs. A mandatory day off from work would not reverse this trend, because data suggest job spill stems chiefly from unwritten rules, which tend to persist even in the face of legal regulation."[218] Rather than argue for time off on Sundays only, Kelly advocates time off for vacation, holidays, and weekend rest that encourages connection for the good shared across families and faith communities, involving active leisure and worship instead of passive recreation only, such as TV and digital device use.

Finally, Sabbath practices reflect not only just relations with our neighbors but also with creation, offering the land rest. Wirzba makes several suggestions pertaining to consumption, particularly challenging those nations historically impacted by a biblical ethos (North America and Europe) that consume over "60 percent of the world's resources" while making up a "modest 11 percent of the world's population."[219] Encouraging individuals and communities to question their consumption practices—whether food, clothes, water, or daily products—he encourages consumer and corporate pressure for production involving "biomimicry" and "eco-design," which offers more sustainable practices for our natural environment.[220]

In terms of the digital empire, one of the most obvious environmental concerns involves "planned obsolescence" endemic to the design of

---

[216]   Kelly draws from Fr. John Ryan and the National Council of Catholic Women in Kelly, *Fullness of Free Time*, 86–95.

[217]   Kelly, *Fullness of Free Time*, 86–88, 95–97.

[218]   Kelly, *Fullness of Free Time*, 97.

[219]   Wirzba, *Living the Sabbath*, 151.

[220]   Wirzba, *Living the Sabbath*, 153.

digital devices. Over against the design of tech—whether computers, phones, chargers, appliances, or cars—with short lives for profit purposes, designing tech built to last might reduce waste in today's throwaway culture.[221] This could be one of the positive outcomes of generative AI should it be programmed for ecofriendly design and coded with limitations. Not only would this reduce our strain on natural resources, it might also help retrain our sense of time, tempering the urgency and need for instant gratification that shape our relationship to tech objects as well as our relationship to one another.

The tech habits in which we indulge mold us in conscious and subconscious ways that inform how we consume data, information, and the environment, with implications for how we relate to our friends, families, and neighbors in the digital empire. Sabbath reframes our digital habits and attitudes toward modern workism. Reintroducing Sabbath, play, and leisure helps restore freedom through a recognition of our creaturely limits alongside the possibilities found through presence: limits in our creation, limits in our time, limits to work, and limits to our fractured attention. Sabbath and play remind us of intentional presence with God, neighbor, and creation. Such intentional presence includes spiritual practices and virtues in a community seeking to reorder its loves while awaiting the kingdom's fulfillment.

[221] Zygmunt Bauman, *Wasted Lives: Modernity and Its Outcasts* (Polity, 2004), 27.

6

The Digital Empire and
Presence of the Kingdom

On a hot summer evening in Boston, my family and I stumbled upon film night at Fenway, showcasing the 1982 blockbuster *E.T.* on its fortieth anniversary. After dining outside at a downtown restaurant, we entered a post-COVID stadium allowing us to touch the famous Green Monster, view recent World Series trophies, and settle into a night captivated by the imaginary world of Steven Spielberg and music of John Williams. Caught in the swell of the storyline and soundtrack, the crowd cheered together at iconic scenes involving Halloween costumes, elevated bike rides, and the famous connection made between a boy and an extraterrestrial's glowing finger.

Watching the film as an adult years after my initial childhood experience, I was moved by the film's themes, in which the presence of an outside creature—both similar and different—brings together a fractured family and closes the chasm between mystery and scientific control in a concluding scene of unified awe and wonder. Leaving the stadium, I caught the eye of a newly met stranger from the restaurant where we dined prior to the film.

"Wasn't it wonderful?" I asked.

"I cried," she said.

"Me too," I responded.

In two short hours, the fractured fears and stresses from the pandemic were temporarily forgotten through beholding the power of story, recognition across difference, and connection through shared presence.

Like themes across Augustine's own theology and preaching, connection and shared meaning in the face of difference is profound. Recognizing the presence of the other, and particularly the human-divine Other, invokes wonder, revelation, transformation, and unity through its christological center. Yet deconstructing empire by diagnosing its many problems doesn't end in despair. Instead, Augustine tells another story reconstructed around hope and love. But to understand the story's reconstruction, one must understand its fault line in need of repair. In this chapter I explore first the challenges of empire, pride, and dominion prevalent in the city and technology through Jacques Ellul and Augustine; second, its antithesis found in humility through the incarnation; third, the importance of ordered love that unites means and ends; fourth, the place for ethical limits, principles, and regulations *in medias res*; and finally, the importance in cultivating embodied communities of presence and virtue.

THE CHALLENGE OF EMPIRE, PRIDE, AND DOMINION IN THE CITY AND DIGITAL TECHNOLOGIES

Jacques Ellul Interfacing Augustine

Known for the famous line "Two loves have built two cities," Augustine's *City of God* distinguishes two cities commingled in time, contingent upon their primary motivations: love of God or love of self. Writing centuries later, Ellul helps capture this concern through critique and hope. Ellul describes counter-creation—whether cities or technological projects—built on self-security apart from the Creator. Like Augustine's two cities built on love, Ellul's two cities are built around self-protection (Cain) or presence (the Spirit). His origin story begins with Cain taking possession of the world on his own terms, utilizing creation for his own ends. He envies his brother, Abel, assumes control over his life, and subsequently builds a city or civilization on his own terms.[1] The city of Babel, later Babylon, follows in his footsteps, seeking a name for itself: a sign of dominion, empire, and pride.

Much like we see in Revelation and Jeremiah, the city claims "forever it will be sovereign" through its symbolic forms of power loving money,

---

[1]   Jacques Ellul, *The Meaning of the City*, trans. Dennis Pardee (Wipf and Stock, 2003), 3–13.

or "mammon," and its images.[2] Ellul describes the populace as "a people mad over idols," a crowd with inhuman impulses.[3] Pursuing restless activity, they are stuck "knowing that something is missing, but not knowing what. It has a terrible undefined sense of something's being absent, and desperately wants that presence."[4] Restless for presence and purpose, the city seeks security through various means.

Ellul describes the city through the reign of technique or efficiency, in which the end or purpose is subsumed by the means. Describing the totalitarianism of means, Ellul says, "not only are material objects subordinated to technics but man also. The latter is no longer subject; he becomes in his turn the object of the forces he has created. Man no longer seeks to know himself in order that he may acquire self-mastery, but simply in order that he may be used. He is no longer concerned to discover his true 'image,' but to reduce it to the state of 'facsimile.'"[5] He challenges conformity to the technological status quo in its totalizing power over politics and market corruption. Rather than reflect the Creator in whose image we're made, we become "copies" imaging creation, a form of counter-creation or artifice[6] that serves as a weak substitute for end goals and purposes.

C. S. Lewis finds commonalities among technique, magic, and applied science in seeking "to subdue reality to the wishes of men" apart from wisdom, loving power over truth.[7] Lewis rejects the logic of totalizing science: "The regenerate science which I have in mind would not do even to minerals and vegetables what modern science threatens to do to man himself. When it explained, it would not explain away. When it spoke of the parts, it would remember the whole. While studying the *It*, it would not lose what Martin Buber calls the Thou-situation."[8] In observing the world, it would not "kill what it sees."[9] In a critique of subjectivism and nihilism as a reality devoid of purpose, Lewis instead accepts the givenness of nature.

---

[2]   Ellul, *Meaning of the City*, 51–52, 58.

[3]   Ellul, *Meaning of the City*, 127.

[4]   Ellul, *Meaning of the City*, 127.

[5]   Jacques Ellul, *The Presence of the Kingdom*, trans. Olive Wyon (Helmers & Howard, 1989), 62.

[6]   The root term "art" meaning skill or craft relates to artifice, artificial, and artificial intelligence.

[7]   C. S. Lewis, *The Abolition of Man*, in *The Complete C. S. Lewis Signature Classics* (HarperOne, 2002), 728–29.

[8]   Lewis, *Abolition of Man*, 728–29.

[9]   Lewis, *Abolition of Man*, 728–29.

Without purpose we miss the point of nature, communication (or communion), and our meaning as humans.

Lewis describes a world devoid of meaning, "You cannot go on 'seeing through' things forever. The whole point of seeing through something is to see through it. It is good that the window should be transparent, because the street or garden beyond it is opaque. How if you saw through the garden too? It is no use trying to 'see through' first principles. If you see through everything, then everything is transparent. But a wholly transparent world is an invisible world. To 'see through' all things is the same as not to see."[10] Totalizing science/technology sees through nature for our own ends. Nature becomes empty. We miss the point of being human and the joy of communion.

Nihilism, a philosophy without meaning or value, persists in this environment. Jean-Luc Marion diagnoses nihilism in our contemporary empire: "'Nihilism stands at the door,' Nietzsche once warned. No, today it is no longer on the threshold but, for more than a century, has invaded the entire house, to the point of moving in for good. It inhabits us, gnaws at us . . . instead, it is the air we breathe . . . No one calls it by name, it is not seen, it remains faceless, but its symptoms are everywhere."[11] Unnamed and faceless, nihilism pervades everything. Lacking substance, its effects are everywhere. Ironically, a philosophy without values turns to "evaluate" everything.[12]

The "will to power," or desire to evaluate, becomes an unending interpretive circle from which we can't escape; as Marion explains, "This will to power wants nothing but to be intensified . . . For a long time now it has willed nothing to do with beings, the real, the precise, but only its growth. What we today call growth and invoke using this last sacred name no longer concerns the growth of any thing, for neither financial capital, nor economic production, nor military armament, nor technological development is the goal, but only the means."[13] As Ellul, Lewis, and Augustine perceived, means and ends are flipped. Lacking a clear goal that responds to the question "Why?" nihilism "forbids us this question and releases us from it . . . Far from accomplishing the will of man . . . this *causa sui* makes

---

[10]   Lewis, *Abolition of Man*, 730.
[11]   Jean-Luc Marion, "The Utility of Communion," in *A Brief Apology for a Catholic Moment*, trans. Stephen E. Lewis (University of Chicago Press, 2021), 58.
[12]   Marion, "Utility of Communion," 58–62.
[13]   Marion, "Utility of Communion," 61.

him a slave of the worst of masters, himself."[14] Technique rules alongside nihilism without cause or purpose.

Ellul further elaborates on the problem when both church and society at large participate in technique, efficiency, and nihilism without awareness. Concerned about our diminishing reflective capacities as individuals who instead conform to the masses, he says, "A man who spends his days rushing about in his car for hours at a time, at a speed of sixty miles an hour, has the sensation of living on speed, of intense activity and of 'gaining time,' but actually a mental torpor creeps over him. He becomes less and less alive; more and more he is simply an automaton in a machine."[15] Anyone commuting on I-95 around Boston or New York would agree. Many of us hurry along like the White Rabbit in *Alice in Wonderland*, proclaiming, "I'm late! I'm late for a very important date."[16] Felicia Wu Song says we forget why we hurry through time while we image the tools that assist us.[17] The productive expectations in our work lives mirror our own machines.[18]

We begin to image our own creation, a kind of counter-creation, in its mixed motives. AI algorithms reflect mixed motives as they exercise great influence over the way we encounter consumer products, information, one another, and increasingly, the world.[19] Cathy O'Neil's *Weapons of Math Destruction* details what she calls the "dark side of Big Data," in which economic, career, and educational choices are impacted by "the

[14]   Marion, "Utility of Communion," 62.

[15]   Ellul, *Presence of the Kingdom*, 75.

[16]   Felicia Wu Song, *Restless Devices: Recovering Personhood, Presence, and Place in the Digital Age* (IVP Academic, 2021), 151.

[17]   Song, *Restless Devices*.

[18]   Derek Thompson, "Workism Is Making Americans Miserable," *Atlantic*, February 24, 2019, https://www.theatlantic.com/ideas/archive/2019/02/religion-workism -making-americans-miserable/583441/; Jake Meador, "The Misunderstood Reason Millions of Americans Stopped Going to Church," *Atlantic*, July 29, 2023, https://www .theatlantic.com/ideas/archive/2023/07/christian-church-community-participation -drop/674843/.

[19]   Cathy O'Neil, *Weapons of Math Destruction* (Crown, 2016); Clara Angela Brascia, "Paula Gordaliza, Mathematician: 'Algorithms Do Not Work Alone. Whoever Uses Them Should Know What They Are Doing and Why These Decisions Are Being Made,'" *El País*, July 19, 2023, https://english.elpais.com/science-tech/2023-07 -19/paula-gordaliza-mathematician-algorithms-do-not-work-alone-whoever-uses -them-should-know-what-they-are-doing-and-why-these-decisions-are-being -made.html.

algorithmic gods" or statistics programmed by fallible humans.[20] Ellul anticipates the influence of Big Data decades in advance with his critique of mass media, image, and propaganda. Recognizing a sinister influence merging human ingenuity in its best and worst motives, we see how our counter-creation takes on a spiritual force whose inertia impacts—if not controls—many choices made.

Cookies follow us, cultivating "shadow" AI identities that reflect virtual, artificial copies of our real-world selves, partially accurate in quantitative measure yet wholly inaccurate in substance and depth.[21] Observing data collected from her online activities, Madhumita Murgia says, "Through a pattern picked out of my online data, the cookies had created an approximation, a shadow of me that was somehow recognizable."[22] Marketers mine data about our preferences and tastes. We become more machine-like or robotic following prescribed scripts, cookies, or codes while diminished in our human capacities to reflect, contemplate, and make choices. Our choices are increasingly honed, a form of control, while individual freedom is diminished and dehumanized.

Anticipating today's digital empire, Ellul challenges the erosion of wisdom through mass communication. Years before social media, contemporary sensational reporting, and misinformation, Ellul says,

> Our contemporaries only see the presentations that are given them by the press, the radio, propaganda, and publicity. The man of the present day does not believe in his own experiences, in his own judgment, in his own thought: he leaves all that to what he sees in print or hears on the radio. In his eyes, a fact becomes true when he has read an account of it in the paper, and he measures its importance by the size of the headlines! What he himself has seen does not count, if it has not been officially interpreted, if there is not a crowd of people who share his opinion. This statement, which may seem oversimplified, is in reality at the basis of all propaganda. An untrue fact is printed in a newspaper with a circulation of a million: a thousand people know that the fact is false, but nine hundred and ninety-nine thousand believe it to be true. Thus the fact becomes true.[23]

---

[20] O'Neil, *Weapons of Math Destruction*, 2–13.
[21] Madhumita Murgia, *Code Dependent: Living in the Shadow of AI* (Henry Holt, 2024), 2–3.
[22] Murgia, *Code Dependent*, 2–3.
[23] Ellul, *Presence of the Kingdom*, 82–83.

The power of the printed word influences groupthink. Without realizing it, the crowd impacts our understanding. As E. B. White writes in *Charlotte's Web*, "People believe almost anything they see in print."[24]

Groupthink, or the mind of the crowd, occurs when individuals dismiss critical thinking for the sake of approval or group belonging.[25] Augustine highlights this core drive in the *Confessions* as he and his friends steal pears or boast about their sexual exploits. We want to belong. This becomes problematic in *City of God* when political groups seize power. He compares the Roman Empire to armed pirates.[26] In the desire for acceptance or power, the empire spins facts and information for the glory of Rome. Today, "alternative facts" and increased polarization drive contemporary politics, media, and at times, education.[27]

Image-based media devoid of context ricochets over the internet. Without coherence, reporting devolves into "explanatory myths" that "help man avoid the fatigue of thinking for himself."[28] Lacking integrity for information sharing, we become vulnerable to control by commercial interest in the West or state influence in the East. Distraction merged with groupthink makes individuals susceptible to easy answers rather than complex approaches following contemplation and reflection.[29]

At the same time, this critique doesn't deny the importance of group affiliation as part of our identity and belonging. David Brooks reflects on the significance of our ancestors or cultural history contributing to shared identity and how we see the world. Group belonging is helpful for seeing harm and injustice directed at particular groups throughout history. With that said, no individual is one dimensional or reduced to the group only.

[24]   E. B. White, *Charlotte's Web* (HarperCollins, 1952), 89.

[25]   Irving L. Janis, *Victims of Groupthink: A Psychological Study of Foreign-Policy Decisions and Fiascos* (Houghton Mifflin, 1972).

[26]   Augustine, *The City of God*, abridged study edition, trans. William Babcock, notes by Boniface Ramsey, abridgment by Joseph T. Kelley (New City Press, 2018), 71.

[27]   White House correspondent Kellyann Conway first coined the term "alternative facts" representing Press Secretary Sean Spicer in regard to the question of numbers present at the US Presidential Inauguration of Donald Trump in January 2017. See Alexandra Jaffe, "WH Spokesman Gave 'Alternative Facts' on Inauguration Crowd," NBC News, January 22, 2017, https://www.nbcnews.com/storyline/meet-the-press-70-years/wh-spokesman-gave-alternative-facts-inauguration-crowd-n710466.

[28]   Ellul, *Presence of the Kingdom*, 85.

[29]   Ellul, *Presence of the Kingdom*, 85–89.

There is nuance and variety within groups.[30] Viewing the neighbor only through group identity reduces one's humanity to a type, trope, or graven image apart from their individual narrative and dignity as one made in the image of God.[31]

Simplifying complex information and reductionistic tropes that slay our opponent, Ellul anticipates #hashtag long before its advent. Ellul calls reductionistic information "the imperialistic attitude of technics," in which "precision, rapidity, certainty, continuity, and universality" are prized at the expense of contemplation and reflection.[32] Constant connection represents the "absence of communication" that enslaves "intelligence to technical methods" without awareness.[33] Instead, Ellul longs for face-to-face communication that recognizes one another as human beings. His description of imperial tech, anticipating the digital empire, holds much in common with Augustine's concern regarding political empire and the *libido dominandi*.

Augustine: Pride, *Libido Dominandi*, and the Digital Empire

For Augustine, pride is our attempt to replace God as the original sin.[34] His fundamental definition connects to his overarching loves behind the *City of God* and his own *Confessions*—love of self with contempt for God is pride. Augustine finds pride behind multiple institutions and movements through his holistic critique. John Cavadini says pride is "the lust for domination which characterized the Roman Empire; the lust for praise which characterizes the heroic Roman characters; mythological self-exaltation committed by the 'Platonists' and Manichees; and the tendencies of certain kinds of public individuals—both civic and ecclesiastical—to exalt themselves at the expense of service."[35] Pride seeks praise from others and rarely functions as one sin alone. Instead, Augustine, like the medieval church that follows, links pride with a litany of common habits. Later described as the seven deadly sins, they become problematic vices in their

---

[30] See David Brooks, *How to Know a Person: The Art of Seeing Others Deeply and Being Deeply Seen* (Random House, 2023), 235–37.

[31] David W. Gill, "A Fourth Use of the Law? The Decalogue in the Workplace," *Journal of Religion and Business Ethics* 2, no. 2 (2011): article 4, 10–12.

[32] Ellul, *Presence of the Kingdom*, 89–92.

[33] Ellul, *Presence of the Kingdom*, 93.

[34] John Cavadini, "Pride," in *Augustine Through the Ages*, ed. Allan D. Fitzgerald (Eerdmans, 1999), 679; see also Andy Crouch, *Playing God: Redeeming the Gift of Power* (IVP, 2013).

[35] Cavadini, "Pride," 679.

control over us, whether avarice (greed), lust, envy, gluttony, anger, or sloth. Pride stands behind them all.

Cavadini highlights two sins associated with "pride of the world": avarice (greed) and envy. Connecting the "lust of the flesh, the lust of the eyes, and the pride of life" (1 John 2:16) with "the love of money" or "root of all evil," involves pride, greed, and envy.[36] The prideful person compares herself to others (envy) while restlessly seeking more (greed). Today's digital empire compounds all three temptations: Profit drives information sharing, illustrating greed. Praise and recognition motivate social media posting, illustrating pride. Marketing breeds inadequacy and comparison, illustrating envy that produces consumption.

In *The Trinity* Augustine describes pride as delighting in its own power over God's power akin to the *libido dominandi* in *City of God*.[37] Individuals seek power over justice, as Augustine explains: "The soul, loving its own power, slides away from the whole which is common to all into the part which is its own private property . . . but by apostasy of pride which is called the beginning of sin it strives to grab something more than the whole . . . its thrust back into anxiety over a part, and so by being greedy for more, it gets less. That is why greed is called the root of all evils."[38] Seeking part of creation over the whole—whether monetary greed, pleasure, or self-exaltation—individuals use creation for their own purposes rather than the Creator's ordered purpose. Subverting the divine law giver and nature's intended purposes, God's image bearers flip power over justice. Augustine's diagnosis anticipates nihilism. Since original injustice is located in the fall from grace, all "particular injustices actualized in history" reflect this dynamic.[39]

Subverting the "hierarchy of being, with inanimate objects, plants, animals, mortal humans, and immortal angels under God (in that order)," pride utilizes God and the created world for its own ends.[40] Injustice values inanimate objects, or money, over people. Like the power of the ring in *The Hobbit* and *Lord of the Rings*, greed and envy subvert our vision and

---

[36]   Cavadini, "Pride," 680.

[37]   Augustine, *The Trinity (De Trinitate)*, ed. John E. Rotelle, trans. Edmund Hill, 2nd ed. (New City Press, 1991), 12.14, p. 333.

[38]   Augustine contrasts greed with contentment, saying, "By following God's directions and being perfectly governed by his laws it could enjoy the whole universe of creation" (Augustine, *The Trinity* 12.14, p. 333).

[39]   Cavadini, "Pride," 680.

[40]   Cavadini, "Pride," 680.

distort our care ʼfor the world around us.[41] As with Cain taking life and civilization into his own hands, pride becomes its own arbiter of value. In *City of God* book 19 Augustine says, "Thus pride is a perverted imitation of God. For pride hates a fellowship of equality under God and seeks to impose its own dominion on fellow men, in place of God's rule. This means that it hates the just peace of God and loves its own peace of injustice."[42]

Unfortunately, the perpetual self-will, what Augustine calls pride, is self-defeating. Marion says, "We are losing access to the world as it is truly given, to the whole of possible givens, that is to say to things in themselves—or better: to the selves of things. Nihilism extends its *empire* over us, all the more silently and powerfully as it shuts us up in ourselves, closes us in ourselves alone and never shows itself as such. We imagine that we possess the universe, when in fact we ourselves construct our prison, voluntary slaves, willed slaves, slaves of the will to will—and we glorify ourselves by celebrating our autonomy!"[43] Glorifying autonomy in which we reject the givenness of the created world, we become gods enslaved to our own choices and the empire of nihilism.

Peddling nihilism, the digital empire seemingly offers infinite choice while controlling our options. According to Nolen Gertz, this is precisely the danger in what he calls "techno-hypnotic technologies" and their power over us:

> From a Nietzschean perspective, reduced awareness is precisely what we were seeking in the development and use of techno-hypnotic technologies in the first place. Thus our taking for granted that the world presented to us by techno-hypnotic technologies simply is

---

[41] J. R. R. Tolkien, *The Hobbit* (Houghton Mifflin Harcourt, 2012); *The Lord of the Rings* (William Morrow, 2012). Interestingly, Tolkien's use of a magical "ring to rule them all" parallels Plato's description of a ring that offers invisible qualities for its user. In a dialogue with Socrates, Glaucon argues the ring's user would not pursue justice for its own sake but for instrumental reasons as part of a social contract to protect self-interest. Socrates, on the other hand, says the just person would pursue justice as an intrinsic good for its own sake. Virtue, such as justice, makes for a good life (Plato, *Republic*, trans. G. M. A. Grube [Hackett, 1992], 35–37). See also William Mattison III, *Introducing Moral Theology: True Happiness and the Virtues* (Brazos, 2008), 21–25.

[42] Augustine, *City of God*, trans. Henry Bettenson (Penguin Books, 1984), 19.13, pp. 868–69; also quoted in Cavadini, "Pride," 680–81.

[43] Marion, "Utility of Communion," 65–66 (emphasis added).

the world, is the world as it *is*, rather than the world as it has been *shaped to appear to be*, is not a result of our being misled, of our being manipulated into shutting off our skepticism, but rather a result of our desire to shut off our skepticism, to let our guard down, to *relax*.[44]

In our autonomy, we relax and capitulate our choice by outsourcing it to apps, screens, and information technologies to think for us. In this way, we're complicit with the digital empire. According to Nietzsche, this is a dangerous form of self-denial in which we submit our will to others, in this case to for-profit companies.[45]

In this way, the digital empire is not far removed from the Roman Empire in its promise of security in exchange for payment (taxes/attention); personnel (conscripted army/free data); efficient infrastructure (roadways and aqueducts/instant communication with friends); culture (education/information access); and entertainment (theater and gladiatorial games/video games and streaming). So when Cavadini describes the Roman Empire as the "best image of pride" in its lust for domination and idolatrous status as the eternal city, he anticipates our contemporary empire: "Its claim to be the absolute arbiter of value" is a nihilistic empire in digital form.[46]

The drive for success among the Roman heroes, culture, and educational institutions was a desire for praise. In the case of the heroes, individuals pursued virtue for the sake of honor and fame. Augustine sought cultural capitalism through success, valuing group belonging over truth. He explains, "Excellence becomes a matter not of truth but of opinion over convention."[47] Augustine found his own educational ambition rife with pride in his desire for success and acceptance where "the more fraudulent I was, the more likely to be praised."[48] Pride is endemic to a culture that seeks praise and prestige as its end goal, whether fourth-century Rome or the twenty-first-century digital empire.

---

[44]   Nolen Gertz, *Nihilism and Technology* (Rowman & Littlefield International, 2018), 83 (emphasis original).

[45]   See also Jaron Lanier, *Ten Arguments for Deleting Your Social Media Accounts Right Now* (Picador, 2018), 17–21.

[46]   Cavadini, "Pride," 681.

[47]   Cavadini, "Pride," 681.

[48]   Augustine, *Confessions*, trans. Henry Chadwick (Oxford University Press, 1991), 3.5; also quoted in Cavadini, "Pride," 681.

In today's digital and nihilistic empire, the more outrageous and fraudulent a claim, the more it reverberates through social media. The capabilities of AI to distort truth and share at a broad level amplifies the problem even more. Communication becomes twisted when seeking prideful ends. Diminishing the purpose of communication to share truth, solidarity, and communion, individuals and media outlets seek praise or honor through likes, affirmations, and clicks that quickly devolve into confusion at the expense of content. Praise remained a temptation in Augustine's own life following his conversion. Ecclesial work is not immune from the desire for praise. Pride needs a deeper and more meaningful cure—an antidote that comes through humility and presence.

HUMILITY: THE WAY DOWN IS THE WAY UP

Despite our pride and attempts at security apart from the Creator, the same Creator condescends to enter his own creation. God is present at creation, but also "in the midst of it all," redeeming our counter-creative projects, whether cities or technology.[49] Unlike Cain, Ellul says that Christ "wears the mark of wandering," not seeking self-protection or home but accepting the "totality of the human condition."[50] Through the incarnation, God takes on human limitations and endures the fullness of our frail condition.

Throughout his ministry in the Gospels, Jesus displays compassion in his care for the crowd and for individuals. Ellul explains, "He is fulfilling his destiny as the Savior. His compassion is the suffering he experiences for those who suffer. Not only does he suffer with them, he suffers in their stead. Jesus breaks down the partition separating the men of the crowd: he goes into the crowd, bears its misery, its desperation, and its mournful despondency, and makes them his own."[51] He takes on human limitation by belonging to the crowd in humility and suffering.

Ellul says transformation of the crowd occurs with the "presence of awareness."[52] This is the opposite of "techno-hypnotic technologies'" that reduce awareness, numbing us into believing they're neutral tools apart from significant influence over us.[53] Instead, Ellul says, when spiritually aware, the crowd changes from aimless confusion to joyful anticipation,

49   Ellul, *Meaning of the City*, 111.
50   Ellul, *Meaning of the City*, 121–23; Matt 8:20.
51   Ellul, *Meaning of the City*, 128.
52   Ellul, *Meaning of the City*, 129.
53   Gertz, *Nihilism and Technology*, 83.

citing Jesus's own entry into the city of Jerusalem as celebratory.[54] The Gospel narratives demonstrate interfacing individuals within the crowd, whether through miracles of healing, teaching, or physical provision.[55] According to Ellul, Jesus leads individuals not to a better "society on earth" but to himself, "the goal and kingdom of God on earth."[56] When Jesus acts, he unites his service with prayer: "Thy kingdom come, thy will be done, on earth as it is in heaven" (Matt 6:10 RSV).

In this way Jesus inaugurates the presence of a new kingdom, the future eschatological city, through his conformity to God's will and grace. As Kevin Vanhoozer says, "The kingdom of heaven is the place where God's will is joyfully done . . . it's more appropriate to say 'when' is heaven, rather than 'where' is heaven since . . . Through [his] works, Jesus was beginning to bring heaven to earth, the end of time (eschatology) into the middle (history)."[57] Connecting heaven and earth, Jesus demonstrates the fullness of God's communion with humanity in his very person.

Personal and intentional in his teaching and ministry, Jesus encounters individuals as whole persons without fragmentation. His incarnation demonstrates his presence among us through his person and works. Unifying word and deed, he brings about salvation and reveals love in totality. Ellul says, "His incarnation is what sanctifies common things, and therefore the whole nature of things is made common or profane by the incarnation of Christ."[58] Contrasting our fragmentation, Christ's unified mission through his person and work, word and deed, shows a better way to be human. Jesus invites his followers to participate in this kingdom presence.

Preaching and practicing the kingdom involves a radical break from the status quo—whether New Testament believers facing the Roman Empire or contemporary believers facing the digital empire. New Testament scholar Esau McCaulley says the presence of the kingdom challenges

---

[54]   Ellul's interpretation of the "triumphal entry into Jerusalem" derives from the four Gospels in the New Testament (Ellul, *Meaning of the City*, 129–30).

[55]   Ellul, *Meaning of the City*, 129–30; see also Daniel Sulmasy, *The Healer's Calling: A Spirituality for Physicians and Other Healthcare Professionals* (Paulist, 1997).

[56]   Ellul, *Meaning of the City*, 130.

[57]   Kevin Vanhoozer, *Faith Speaking Understanding: Performing the Drama of Doctrine* (Westminster John Knox, 2014), 91–92.

[58]   Ellul, *Presence of the Kingdom*, 139.

worldly "empire's" hold on earthly power.[59] The inbreaking of the kingdom threatens Herod's illusory power protected by the Roman Empire.[60] The presence and practice of the kingdom subversively challenges power structures through the vulnerable birth of a savior who later preaches good news to the sick, marginalized, and weak. The good news of the kingdom challenges power structures with an ethic of love, justice, and peace in the Sermon on the Mount. Following Jesus involves participating in his kingdom vision that defies structures of power and prestige through humility and service. The incarnation and ministry of Jesus demonstrate humility as central.

In this way Christ's incarnation helps transfigure the city and counter-creative projects. Since the Mosaic witness, God has promised transfiguration. He does not abandon humans and their counter-creative projects that construct cities and technologies. Instead, he comes to restore through his own resurrection, presence, and promise of new life. Ellul recognizes Augustine as one of the few theologians who highlights the city as central to the eschatological vision. Drawing from the Old Testament understanding of exile, Augustine emphasizes the role the "two cities" play while commingled in time. Followers of Christ are called to "live quiet lives" of sacrifice and contribute to the common good in humility (1 Thess 4:11–12). But they do this because Jesus Christ unites the means and ends in his person.

ORDERED LOVE: UNITING MEANS TO ENDS IN ELLUL AND AUGUSTINE

Ellul's diagnosis of technique, involving the separation of means from ends, requires a remedy. Like Augustine in *City of God*, book 22, he concludes *The Meaning of the City* with the anticipation of the heavenly city transfigured at the end of time. With Augustine, Ellul finds God's redemptive work at play in our counter-creation—the earthly city—in his willingness to join creation through the incarnation, foil sin and death through the resurrection, and anticipate the coming communion in Christ's presence

[59] See Esau McCaulley, *Reading While Black: African American Biblical Interpretation as an Exercise in Hope* (IVP Academic, 2020), 54–70; see also idem, "A Nation on Fire Needs the Flames of the Spirit," *Christianity Today*, June 2, 2020, https://www.christianitytoday.com/2020/06/george-floyd-protests-racism-nation-on-fire-needs-spirit/.

[60] McCaulley says the advent of Jesus's birth alongside John the Baptist's public witness in the Gospel of Luke threatened Herod's power (McCaulley, *Reading While Black*, 54–55).

for eternity. Anticipating this fulfillment, Christ shines brighter than the sun, illuminating the city (Rev 21:10–11).[61] Ellul describes its completion as follows: "He is everything and everywhere. But at the same time, he is infinitely other than the city. This unity is much more complete than at the time of creation."[62] In this way the heavenly city is the culmination of creation and redemption, as "the place where we shall know by love."[63]

Ellul describes the heavenly city: "The whole vision bursts with light—the stones of the city's foundation, with their brilliant facets, mentioned by Isaiah, the whiteness of the garments, the crystal waters, the glistening gold. Everything casts forth a light coming from God. But this gold is no longer the heavy, proud gold of Babylon—it is light and transparent like crystal. It is lit up by the glory of God, and the Lamb is its flame . . . The dead faces of the men of the city shine suddenly with the beauty of God."[64] Filling them with light, the glory of Christ communes with Christ's people—citizens living together in harmony.

Uniting himself to the city, God transfigures the crowd. Members from the various nations composing the gathered people of God unite with their maker in fulfillment. This vision is not stagnant but dynamic like the river of life flowing from the throne of God and Lamb: "'Wherever the river touches, everything will live.'"[65] Ellul continues, "What a perfect vision of the perpetual current of life flowing from the Trinity to bestow fullness of life wherever it reaches."[66] Eternal life is not fixed but fluid, forever re-created by communion.[67] In this way the Creator also fulfills life through continued participation and dependence on him.

As depicted at the end of the *Chronicles of Narnia*, there is perpetual growth and communion for the life to come. In *The Last Battle* Jewel says, "I have come home at last! This is my real country! I belong here. This is the land I have been looking for all my life, though I never knew it till now. The reason why we loved the old Narnia is that it sometimes looked a little like this."[68] The love of Christ is immeasurable; the grace of Christ inexhaustible. Through these passages, Lewis, along with Ellul and Augustine,

---

[61]   Ellul, *Meaning of the City*, 191.
[62]   Ellul, *Meaning of the City*, 190.
[63]   Ellul, *Meaning of the City*, 207.
[64]   Ellul, *Meaning of the City*, 196.
[65]   Ellul, *Meaning of the City*, 208.
[66]   Ellul, *Meaning of the City*, 208.
[67]   Ellul, *Meaning of the City*, 208.
[68]   C. S. Lewis, *The Last Battle* (HarperTrophy, 1956), 213.

affirms that we are made for growth, though not for its own sake. Tech culture's desire for perpetual expansion and enhancement points to how we are made to grow and change. However, we are made for growth and change through communion—with the one to whom we belong—in our creation and re-creation.

This is different than social media that stops time and captures images of life in motion. Through social media we are tempted to make graven, stagnant images and impressions of others as well as ourselves. In the lack of physical embodied presence, dialogue often ceases while assumption and judgments prevail. The eschatological and incarnational model of Jesus should challenge the way we love and face our neighbors and inspire us to empathy, extending grace for growth and change when we misunderstand one another. Moral agency and relationships in community involve ongoing renewal and communion that is dynamic rather than fixed.

The end has strong implications for the means. Because of Christ's incarnation, ministry, and resurrection, the inbreaking of the eternal kingdom begins in time. God chooses our fallen and creative projects, the city and civilization—along with technology—in its mixed motives, transfiguring self-directed desire into other-driven love through humility and faith. Ellul says, "In him, God adopts man and his works . . . He has chosen to dwell in [the city] . . . Even in resurrection, God does not shatter men's hopes. Rather he fulfills them."[69] With the prayer "Thy kingdom come," material reality is united with the spiritual. In contrast to Manichean, Gnostic, and Neoplatonic philosophies that dismiss the body and material world, Christ makes much of our physical and spiritual reality as embodied creatures that impacts tech habits in the material realm. His ministry and presence are fully embodied and intentional, uniting spirit and matter, will and action.

Christ is the way by which the end and means are joined. His presence brings together in unity the eternal and temporal, the spiritual and material in his person as fully divine and human. Christ's presence holds implications for the Christian pilgrimage through time. Ellul describes, "For Christians there is no disassociation between end and means . . . in the work of God the end and the means are identical. Thus when Jesus Christ is present the Kingdom has 'come upon' us . . . Where Jesus Christ is, there also is this salvation and this Kingdom."[70] For Jesus and his fol-

---

69 Ellul, *Meaning of the City*, 176–77.
70 Ellul, *Presence of the Kingdom*, 64.

lowers, the two spheres, the two cities, are united. No longer focusing on two kingdoms that separate spirit from matter, Christ followers should be Christ's presence within the city or empire, embodied and intentional.

Recognizing the end as fulfilled in Christ illuminates the means used during our journey through time. Ellul says,

> The future of humanity does not depend on mechanical forces. Instead of a progress from the past toward the future it is a movement of the future that explains and informs the present, so that our technical discoveries are never anything more than temporary expedients which need to be put in their right place in the perspective of the Kingdom. But "to put them in their right place" implies that there are secondary aims, limited to these instruments. They are of some use.[71]

In this sense we don't dispense entirely with technology, but we evaluate and use it well, directing our designs toward a good secondary end.[72]

However, the ultimate future goal transforms the present meaning, a process that involves a different standard than nihilism and subjective interest.[73] Recognizing an order of things in Christ, Ellul sounds like Augustine with his notion of the order of love arranging our desires toward God. In this context, goals aimed at natural and beneficial goods might be pursued. However, he warns against objectifying the order of love apart from the Spirit's work, erring on ideology. Ellul emphasizes the importance of presence through communion with the Spirit, a people demonstrating justice, peace, and holiness.[74] In this way communion manifests the presence of Christ through the virtues and fruit of the Spirit. This impacts not only the city but also technology by circumscribing counter-creation in relation to kingdom virtues, whereby the end informs the present.

---

[71]   Ellul, *Presence of the Kingdom*, 72.

[72]   Through secondary aims, technology brings forward significant goods for living in our timebound world with purpose. Here nature might be instrumental at times, but not instrumental only. Nature merits protections in its intrinsic value as sacred while involving use when contributing to the overall good life, but these secondary goods remain subject to ongoing evaluation. For this reason we should prioritize other areas of our lives, spending less time on social media and more time in embodied, ensouled community.

[73]   Ellul, *Presence of the Kingdom*, 73.

[74]   Ellul, *Presence of the Kingdom*, 66–67, 74.

Here Ellul reflects Augustine's famous order of love detailed in terms of *uti et frui*, "use and enjoy," in *On Christian Teaching*.[75] In this order only one thing is to be enjoyed: the Holy Trinity, since only the Trinity can exist for its own sake. Something transcendent must hold the temporal order in check. All other things are to be used or loved toward this end. As the final *telos*, or goal, the highest or transcendent end grants meaning and limits to creation as well as our creative projects. When directed toward an eternal goal, our creative projects aim at helping others and we create products that benefit consumers, rather than producing self-enclosed goals typically driven by greed or profit alone. Loving eternal ends is connected to how we seek the good of our neighbor in time.

As creatures made in the image and likeness of God, we reflect the divine through our creative capacities aimed at loving the neighbor.[76] How might imaging God impact our creative tech design for good? MIT professor Rosalind Picard, designer of emotional intelligence for wearable tech, along with scientists in the MIT Media Lab create technologies with specific human needs in mind, whether for medical or environmental concerns.[77] Picard's research positively impacts caregiver response to epilepsy by way of the smartwatch *Embrace*, along with digital sensors that detect increased stress levels for individuals with autism.[78] As the forerunner in affective computing, Picard's research has helped advance digital

---

[75]   Augustine, *On Christian Teaching*, trans. R. P. H. Green (Oxford University Press, 1997), 1.4, p. 10; 1.18, p. 16; 1.32–33, p. 25.

[76]   See Dorothy Sayers for how we reflect the divine Trinity in our creative capacities. Flow ensues when we use our creative capacities that image the Creator (Dorothy Sayers, *Letters to a Diminished Church* [W Publishing Group, 2004], 11).

[77]   I'm grateful for the opportunity to participate in the Jeffersonian Dinners hosted by MIT's Octet Collaborative exploring technology and ethics in November 2023 and March 2024, as well as two mini-retreats in June 2024 and January 2025. Through these events I've been privileged to meet various MIT faculty members designing technology aimed at significant health pursuits in ways that might benefit the common good. Still, new technologies also open the possibility for nefarious use by bad actors despite the good intentions of tech designers. Picard and fellow faculty members are pursuing questions around ethics and virtue to aid tech design and its output.

[78]   Rosalind W. Picard, "Future Affective Technology for Autism and Emotion Communication," *Philosophical Transactions for the Royal Society B* 364 (2009): 3574–84; idem, "An AI Smartwatch That Detects Seizures," TED Talk, November 2018, https://www.ted.com/talks/rosalind_picard_an_ai_smartwatch_that_detects _seizures; Andy Crouch, *The Life We're Looking For: Reclaiming Relationship in a Technological World* (Convergent, 2022), 80–81.

tools for interpreting emotions.[79] Recognizing challenges while communicating and interpreting emotions in all human relations, her specific research design for individuals with autism or their community members involves measuring emotional stress not yet visible. Her research helps monitor stress levels signaled through the autonomous nervous system (ANS) and electrodermal activity (EDA) before stress erupts in a "meltdown," causing discomfort, panic, or external frustration.[80] Underlying these stressful moments is the desire to communicate and be understood. Monitoring these levels helps autistic individuals and caregivers pursue calming self-regulatory techniques in overstimulating social settings.[81] In this way Picard's wearable tech not only improves quality of life by assisting humans through interactive technologies that aid self-control in the case of autism, but also saves lives as *Embrace* helps to connect embodied, life-saving caregivers with patients facing epileptic seizures in crisis.

Designing tech with human needs in mind reflects embodied neighbor love and solidarity, a care for the common good. Picard's design for wearable tech products in health science helps restore individual agency through self-regulation while connecting patients to caregivers and loved ones in moments of need. This demonstrates a kind of ordered love that enhances communication and relationships with one's surrounding world. When Picard learned her device needed tweaking given feedback disclosed from autistic patients who still felt unseen and misunderstood, she adjusted her research and project goals to better align with patient perception and patient needs.[82] Loving one's neighbor orders the goals and designs behind these forms of medical AI that seek to improve the health and wellbeing of others.

In line with Ellul's vision, this places technology firmly in the place of secondary, instrumental goods in their ability to aid medicine, mental health, communication, education, connection, and friendship without replacing these higher goods. In this sense technology and our digital devices remain creative tools for proper use, but diligently require our ongoing, critical circumscription. Limited in scope, digital devices aid

---

[79] Rosalind W. Picard, *Affective Computing* (MIT Press, 2000).

[80] Picard, "Future Affective Technology," 3574–75.

[81] Picard, "Future Affective Technology"; idem, "AI Smartwatch That Detects Seizures"; see also idem, *Affective Computing*; and Crouch, *Life We're Looking For*, 80–81.

[82] Conversation and dialogue with Rosalind W. Picard, MIT Octet Collaborative Retreat, MIT Endicott House, Boston, January 4, 2025.

human life while requiring accountability for both their producers and consumers. Without virtuous ends they problematically take too much from us in terms of time and influence, whether through unethical design exploiting human vulnerability or ignorance on the part of the user.[83] At its worst, tech design lacks beneficial ends or privileges wealth over human interest. Displacing final ends with instrumental ends leads to nihilism.

Marion, who warns against the dangers of nihilism in its self-enclosed desire for more without reference or standard, points to another logic. He proposes the paradox of the gospel in its surprising juxtaposition to the self-enclosed prison of autonomy and nihilism.[84] Marion says,

> In order to will in a way other than by willing to the power (squared, by the will to will), it is necessary to will something *other* than what my will to power wills. To will another will that is neither my own nor one possessed by me means to will a will that does not come from me, because it comes before me and from elsewhere. In other words, this means to will the will of the Father, the one who precedes me and comes to me from elsewhere. The act that truly characterizes Jesus in himself, as the anointed Holy One of God, as the Christ, consists wholly and uniquely in this displacement of the will, which breaks the circle of the repetition of the same, of perseverance in the affirmation of self alone (of the self alone). He wills what is neither self nor his own; he wills what doesn't continue as the same. Willing the will of another, who precedes me and from whom I proceed, opens the only path that exempts me from remaining in myself, and that dispenses me from annihilating every other thing in one of my evaluations; it breaks the sphere of totality by totalization of values . . . He alone tears himself from nihilism who, in imitating Christ, succeeds in not willing his own will (to will), in order to will elsewhere and from elsewhere.[85]

---

[83]   Shoshana Zuboff argues many digital technologies exploit vulnerability through human resources involving data mining (Shoshana Zuboff, *The Age of Surveillance Capitalism: The Fight for a Human Future at the New Frontier of Power* [Public Affairs, 2019], xv). See also whistleblower Francis Haugen's argument that Facebook knowingly continued practices harmful to the mental health of adolescent girls (Ryan Mac and Cecilia Kang, "Whistle-Blower Says Facebook Chooses Profits over Safety," *New York Times*, October 3, 2021, https://www.nytimes.com/2021/10/03/technology/whistle-blower-facebook-frances-haugen.html).

[84]   Marion, "Utility of Communion," 65.

[85]   Marion, "Utility of Communion," 63–64.

Breaking the cycle of self-enclosure derived from repeated self-willing, Christ shows a higher way by willing with the Father from whom he proceeds. Showing a higher way, Christ loves with the perfect order of love. His will aligns with the Father, re-forming creation and disclosing Christ as the true image of God.[86]

Marion acknowledges that willing another's will goes against the natural desire for self-preservation.[87] Instead, Christ shows a different way in that he loses himself by invoking the presence of God "in the self's place."[88] Rather than yield to social media's algorithms and for-profit corporations who may not have our best interests in mind, true surrender involves deep trust in the One who created and knows us intimately while demonstrating this love through sacrifice.[89]

Recapitulating the self-will to God is more beautiful perhaps when considering the doctrine of creation, in which God unnecessarily wills another reality different than himself for no other purpose than love. Created in the image of God, we extend that divine love across difference. Williams says,

> Thus creation is "good for nothing": its *point* is not to serve a divine need. Our difficulty with the idea is (depressingly) the difficulty of imagining a need-free love, and it is a difficulty felt as much by ancients as by moderns. The early Christian claim that God creates out of nothing presupposed the possibility and reality of a love not based on kinship or similarity, since it presupposed a God willing to make real something wholly other than the divine life and to endow it with beauty, rationality, and liberty. As Clement of Alexandria put it, this is a love that goes beyond the natural claims of koinonia. Now koinonia, community of kind—perhaps "solidarity" . . . is in the Christian vocabulary not the ground but the effect of love, of a free reaching-out to what is and remains ineradicably strange and other.[90]

---

[86]   See 2 Cor 4–6.

[87]   Marion, "Utility of Communion," 64.

[88]   Jean-Luc Marion, *In the Self's Place: The Approach of St. Augustine*, trans. Jeffrey L. Kosky (Stanford University Press, 2012).

[89]   Drawing on Heb 9:23–28, we can affirm that Christ offers a one-time sacrifice and the perpetual loving call through the gift of time. Time involves patient waiting for human response.

[90]   Rowan Williams, "'Good for Nothing'? Augustine on Creation," *Augustinian Studies* 25 (1994): 19–20.

God wills us into existence without need through *creatio ex nihilo*. As bearers of his image we are intimately known, crossing the chasm of divine–human difference with shared meaning and belonging.

What beauty in the creature's response who lovingly offers their will in return. More than a concern for mystics, seeking the presence of God in Christ involves humility and imitation for all disciples. Seeking the way of Christ above herself, St. Teresa of Ávila prays that God might "dilate her heart," much like Augustine's prayer to "expand the purses of his heart that Christ may enter in."[91]

In *Knowing God*, J. I. Packer opens with a prayer from Charles Spurgeon, saying, "A contemplation of the Divinity . . . is a subject so vast, that all our thoughts are lost in its immensity; so deep, that our pride is drowned in its infinity . . . No subject of contemplation will tend to humble the mind, than thoughts of God . . . And whilst *humbling and expanding*, this subject is eminently *consolatory*."[92] Turning the affections and will toward Christ simultaneously humbles, expands, and consoles desire, transforming it to align with God when dwelling in presence or union with him.

Seeking Christ involves humility, a dying and rising; here Teresa points to Augustinian spirituality: "Saint Augustine tells us how he found the Almighty within his own soul, after having long sought for Him elsewhere. This recollection helps us greatly when God bestows it upon us. But do not fancy you can gain it by thinking of God dwelling within you, or by imagining Him as present in your soul . . . His Majesty only bestows this favor on those who have renounced the world, in desire at least."[93] Following Christ necessitates the displacement of sinful desire, or self-love, with primary love of God. This involves desire for Christ over desire for sin and love for the world. By loving Christ in union with him, we align our creatureliness with the Creator who precedes and fulfills desire.

A reoriented will comes from loving God. Augustine finds the reflection sharpens when relating to the image of God in Christ: "For man's true

---

[91]   Teresa of Ávila, *The Interior Castle, or The Mansions* (TAN Books/Saint Benedict Press, 1997), 53, 60; Augustine, "Fourth Homily," in *Homilies on the First Epistle of John*, ed. Daniel E. Doyle and Thomas Martin, The Works of Saint Augustine: A Translation for the 21st Century, part 3, vol. 14 (New City Press, 2008), 69. See also the opening to Augustine, *Confessions* 1.5.6, pp. 5–6.

[92]   Charles H. Spurgeon, quoted in J. I. Packer, *Knowing God* (IVP, 1973), 17–18 (emphasis added).

[93]   Teresa of Ávila, *Interior Castle*, 64–65.

honor is God's image and likeness in him, but it can only be preserved when facing him from whom its impression is received. And so the less love he has for what is his very own the more closely can he cling to God."[94] Facing Christ, we image the one in whom we are made and remade. Given Augustine's understanding of the fall in which our desire is fractured from its original goal, we now turn inward, seeking self-preservation and self-security as the highest good. As Marion prescribes, the imitation of Christ means willing with the one who precedes our will, escaping the prison of self-enclosure by facing God and neighbor in love.

Divine humility is the only prescription that heals our self-enclosure and "the swelling of our pride."[95] Cavadini continues, "The self-willed humiliation of God is just what we need to unsettle the imagination, reordering our affections (*doc. Chr.* I.16) into a way back to God, rousing us to love something beyond our power to assign use and value, arresting our limited and empty vision on something real, the compassion of God, who was unashamed to put aside the power and prestige of divinity and to entrust himself to human testimony . . . and the hands of sinful men."[96] Christ's example of humility reorders love and restores the image in fullness.

Contemplating Christ's wisdom through union with him, we turn toward Jesus in gratitude, reordering our love "by clinging to the Wisdom" by which the "world was ordered."[97] With the power to mend our fragmented self-alienation focused on temporal desire, Christ demonstrates the way down as the way up, reintegrating our end and means. Cavadini says, "The Lord's death and resurrection 'harmonize' or reintegrate our being as our inner self is crucified to the loves for which we had forsaken God and rises to renewal in the preference of justice over power (*Trin.* 4.6) . . . The Mediator rescues us from the self-alienation and disintegration

---

[94]   Augustine, *The Trinity* 12.3, p. 334. Interestingly, more insight might be drawn from Augustine's term "honor" in this statement. Honor/shame are themes in the Old Testament that track well with Eastern cultures emphasizing family and group belonging. For many cultures, "name, reputation, status, or face," are connected, reflecting collective identity as opposed to Western culture's emphasis on the individual alone for identity. See Jackson Wu and Ryan Jensen, *Seeking God's Face: Practical Reflections on Honor and Shame in Scripture* (Lucid Books, 2022), x–xi, 22–23; see also chapter 4, p. 142, n. 532.

[95]   Cavadini, "Pride," 682; see also Augustine, *The Trinity* 8.7; *On Christian Teaching* 1.13.

[96]   Cavadini, "Pride," 682–83.

[97]   Cavadini, "Pride," 682–83.

which pride always was."[98] Following Christ by way of his death and resurrection, we capitulate our desire rooted in self-love for desire in God,
the end and fulfillment of all love. The presence of Christ's compassion,
humility, and love among us becomes the way forward for presence in the
city of God and our engagement with the technological empire. But before
considering the presence of the kingdom and its possibility for virtue, I
must consider some cautions based on Augustine's own realism given the
ambivalent mixture of sin and grace we inhabit while living *in medias res*.

IN MEDIAS RES: ETHICAL LIMITS, PRINCIPLES, AND REGULATIONS

For Ellul as well as Augustine, the Christian belongs to two cities. In this
world Christians have a responsibility tied to the social and theological needs of the community: "All that he does, he ought to do seriously
because he is bound up with the life of other people."[99] Bound to other
people in a community of shared interests, disciples do not escape this
world. Yet the disciple doesn't belong wholly to this world either. Ellul
recognizes we are citizens belonging to the future kingdom or city of God
in which we are strangers or wanderers on the journey through time (Heb
11:13). This world serves as the tabernacle, a provisional situation by
which God dwells in us as we await our eternal home, where we dwell in
fullness. We live *in medias res*, in the middle of things, what Paul describes
as "the already/not yet" between Christ's resurrection and return.

Here disciples belong to "another city serving another master" while
exercising dual citizenship in the temporal world around them.[100] And yet,

---

98 Cavadini, "Pride," 683.

99 Ellul, *Presence of the Kingdom*, 33.

100 Ellul, *Presence of the Kingdom*, 33. The focus of this volume is on Ellul's
sociological and theological claims around technology, communication, political
theology, eschatology, and community for the *already/not yet*. Some of his writings
include the term "Christian anarchism," acknowledging the reality of sin and power
present within governing structures. He challenges citizens to consider where they
place their ultimate trust. While the term "anarchism" is questionable if it suggests
that all order is eschewed, his prescient focus addressing where trust is placed represents his lived experience as one enduring German occupied France during World
War II and his participation in the French Resistance movement. Given that Ellul's
theology includes order, perhaps he preserves the transcendence of the eternal city
given its anticipatory presence and love in fullness while uplifting personal, face-to-
face communities formed around subsidiarity apart from the dehumanization of
empire. His work is deeply aware of sinful structures in the present reality and the
way technology and power too often divide us. For more on his political realism
and hopeful community in the presence of the Spirit see David W. Gill and David

following the incarnation, believers are called to preserve the world as salt and light by grace, humility, and service—the way of Christ—which is the opposite of defensive or even resentful self-preservation.[101] Anticipating the future kingdom based on the resurrection, Christians participate in the institutions and mediating structures that compose our social, political, and increasingly digital life together. Christian faith is not an escape from this world but commitment and presence within the world, contributing to the common good in both its limits and possibilities.

In this way Ellul draws from Jeremiah 29:4–7, much like Augustine, exhorting the people of God to contribute to the welfare of the city while in Babylonian exile.[102] Time and again, Augustine compares faith as a journey through time, pilgrims along the waters of Babylon, "Ye have heard and know that there are two cities, for the present outwardly mingled together, yet separated in heart, running together through the course of time until the end; one whose end is everlasting peace, and it is called Jerusalem; the other whose joy is peace in this world, and it is called Babylon. The meanings of these names too ye remember, that Jerusalem means 'vision of peace'; Babylon, 'confusion.'"[103] Tied to their final ends, peace marks Jerusalem in its long-term goal while Babylon's shortsighted grasp at the means leads to confusion. For Augustine, the transcendent goal holds temporal goods accountable. Otherwise our created goods become disordered, resulting in confusion.

Lovekin, eds., *Political Illusion and Reality: Engaging the Prophetic Insights of Jacques Ellul* (Pickwick, 2018).

[101]   James Davison Hunter, *To Change the World: The Irony, Tragedy, and Possibility of Christianity in the Late Modern World* (Oxford University Press, 2010), 107–8.

[102]   Kristen Deede Johnson, "The Theologian," in *Uncommon Ground: Living Faithfully in a World of Difference*, ed. Timothy Keller and John Inazu (Nelson Books, 2020), 8. Luke Bretherton argues that "the place of exile is now the place where justice and faithfulness can be pursued and how Jerusalem—i.e., where we were most at home—has become a place of faithlessness, oppression, and corruption . . . Instead of seeing suffering, dislocation, and domination as a reason to despair, the Israelites were invited by Jeremiah to see it as the context where God is most powerfully at work bringing new vision and being present in new ways" (Luke Bretherton, *Christianity and Contemporary Politics: The Conditions and Possibilities of Faithful Witness* [Wiley-Blackwell, 2010], 4, quoted in Michael Lamb, *A Commonwealth of Hope* [Princeton University Press, 2022], 227).

[103]   Augustine, *Enarration in Psalm 86*, in *The Political Writings of St. Augustine*, ed. Henry Paolucci (Regnery Gateway, 1962), 317.

The people of God, longing for final peace, are contributors to the good of the city without escaping responsibility. In seeking the prosperity of the city, the people are called to build houses, marry, and have children (Jer 29:4–7). As they work toward the good end of the city, the people prosper if the city prospers, holding a common interest with the surrounding community.

Augustine's approach to the political order entails strong implications for the technological order. Rather than escape our environment, we are called to love the neighbor in time. Seeking faithful presence among the people, we seek faithfulness while engaging the digital empire. Nonetheless, Augustine is realistic about political theology and life in time. Deeply familiar with sin and the complexity of human motivation, Augustine finds time a mixture of sin and grace, permeating every individual as well as society at large. For this reason, he doesn't hesitate to look skeptically at the motives and power behind empire and its influence over our affections and choices. He was one of the first church fathers to deconstruct cultural and philosophical assumptions.[104] He takes seriously evil, sin, and our human limits. Yet he also reconstructs the final city or kingdom around love, grace, solidarity, and hope. Augustine's theology thus provokes our close consideration of the motives, pitfalls, and virtues associated with our digital technologies and their contemporary hold on our life in both their limits and possibilities.

In this sense Augustinian theology is neither wholly engaged in what might be called technophobia, or fear of tech, even with its deep realism about power and illusory idols as temptations. On the other hand, an Augustinian theology neither aligns with technophiles in their love of technology through rose-colored glasses apart from healthy skepticism and critique. The temporal order is always held accountable to the eternal realm for Augustine. The transcendent holds our creative projects and motives accountable to a higher authority and evaluation rather than to self-enclosed autonomy and nihilism.

It is for this reason that Augustine is considered a realist. Developing a contemporary Augustinian approach to the digital empire involves understanding his political ethics and its relation to the *saeculum*. As mentioned earlier, Augustine finds history to be the drama of sin and grace.

---

[104] Charles Mathewes, *Books That Matter: The City of God* (The Great Courses, The Teaching Company, 2016); Christopher Watkin, *Biblical Critical Theory: How the Bible's Unfolding Story Makes Sense of Modern Life and Culture* (Zondervan Academic, 2022), xix–xx.

An ambivalent mixture of sin and grace composes our journey through time.[105] All individuals and institutions are marked by this reality, and no one is exempt, including government, churches, and private tech companies. All are free yet responsible. Time is the gift by which we are graced to live, yet eternal meaning is the key to flourishing and fulfillment. Moral discernment is essential for navigating freedom and responsibility.

For Augustine, power is a perennial human concern. Given his doctrine of original sin, no one is immune from sin nor immune from delusions of power—even the humblest among us. Augustine writes repeatedly against the *libido dominandi* and the lust to dominate others as early as book 2 of *City of God*, but addresses political limits given the tragic accumulation of group power or the crowd in book 19. Writing on the power of group identity and social sin, Augustine describes his youthful exploits with friends in the *Confessions* and critiques gladiatorial games, but still commits to community by remaining bishop of Hippo during the sack of Rome in 410 in his final months of life.[106]

In this context Augustine alludes to the significance of subsidiarity for political governance. While Augustine recognizes the intrinsic good in social life in that we are made for relationships, he also sees the challenges associated with numerous friends as well as densely populated cities. Realist in outlook, he recognizes the greater chance for sin to accumulate with increased numbers of people, "The larger the city, the more is its forum filled with civil lawsuits and criminal trials, even if that city be at peace, free from the alarms or—what is most frequent—the bloodshed, of sedition and civil war. It is true that cities are at times exempt from those occurrences; they are never free from the danger of them."[107] Even in peacetime, cities and nations are never without danger from war. Prone to power rather than justice, the human condition needs accountability.

While critiqued as pessimistic, Augustine is simply aware of the complex nature of evil and lust for domination in the human heart. This is why subsidiarity, or smaller, local governance, is helpful for understanding the needs of individuals within the community rather than broader, imperialistic rule. Likewise, recognizing the importance of loving the neighbor to bolster justice, Augustine also recognizes our limits by emphasizing the

---

[105] R. A. Markus, *Saeculum: History and Society in the Theology of St. Augustine* (Cambridge University Press, 1970), xi.

[106] Serge Lancel, *St. Augustine* (SCM, 1999), 470–76.

[107] Augustine, *City of God* 19.5 (trans. Bettenson), p. 859.

importance of privileging the neighbor in proximity or nearness to you.[108] In this way Augustine privileges personal over impersonal relations.

In terms of the digital empire, Augustinian theology reflects the vulnerability to dominance and power in mass numbers. Like Ellul's "crowd," the depersonalized ways we communicate through the corporate and digital empire leaves its designers and users vulnerable to objectification and commodification.[109] With contemporary digital devices and social media, we become the commodity.[110] Divorced from context, our purposes, while sometimes stated online, are significantly reduced and removed from embodied location—both time and space. We as users are rendered perpetually subject to observation and judgment. Even the term "users" suggests objectification. Social media participants might be better termed consumers, clients, or even products. When the platforms sell attention through algorithms and marketers purchase advertisements, we become the product.[111] We become shadow selves collected through AI data where we're reduced to consumer profiles.[112] Tech companies extract "human natural resources," turning personal information into market commodities.[113] With social media and emergent AI, we find ourselves in a market economy where everything is for sale, including us.[114]

---

[108]   Augustine, *On Christian Teaching* 1.28, p. 21. I must qualify "proximity" or nearness as an argument from finitude not regarding proximate ethnicity or race. See Jake Meador, "Augustine and the Order of Love: Debunking a Dumb Christian Nationalist Argument," *Mere Orthodoxy*, July 7, 2023, https://mereorthodoxy.com/augustine-and-the-order-of-love.

[109]   Albert Borgmann describes the trouble with "the device paradigm," involving the separation of things from their context or world, nature, and purpose. Machines and devices procure the purpose of things from their context, thus reducing them to commodities. He says, "The employment of technological devices has resulted in an ensemble of commodities . . . the professed goal of the technological enterprise" (Albert Borgmann, *Technology and the Character of Contemporary Life: A Philosophical Inquiry* [University of Chicago Press, 1984], 41–42, 48).

[110]   See Shoshana Zuboff's "instrumentarian" description, in which we become subject to corporate/Big Data's use and commodification (Zuboff, *Age of Surveillance Capitalism*, 376, fig. 4, and 396–97).

[111]   Tim Wu, *The Attention Merchants: The Epic Scramble to Get Inside Our Heads* (Vintage Books, 2016), 84, 207.

[112]   Murgia, *Code Dependent*, 2–3.

[113]   Zuboff, *Age of Surveillance Capitalism*, 98–101, 376, fig. 4, and 396–97.

[114]   Michael Sandel raises the question of moral markets and ethical limits with significant questions for bioethics and economics (Michael J. Sandel, *What Money Can't Buy: The Moral Limits of Markets* [Farrar, Straus and Giroux, 2012]).

Here Augustinian sensibilities in connection with Ellul warn us about crowds or mass numbers in our vulnerability to unjust power dynamics, especially when faceless. Ironically, the accumulated number of facial images reduces their value to commodity. As faceless commodities, digital media dehumanizes its clients into products to be used. Given the penchant for power, Augustine worries over the presence of war and violence—all the more disturbing given digital media's easy platform for bad actors ranging from breaks in cybersecurity, terrorism, to state agents.[115] In his realism, Augustine initiates grounds for just war theory in moral discussion. The significance of this theory reflects his core conviction: Though full justice is unrealizable in time, accountability and moral responsibility persist in our call to prevent greater harm.

Here Augustine's just war theory and its need for moral accountability comes to bear on power gone awry in the digital empire. For Augustine, just war is permissible for the sake of defense only. His rudimentary criteria include just cause, legitimate authority, and just intention.[116] What's at stake for Augustine's just war theory is moral accountability. Despite his conviction that imperfect justice remains in this temporal life full of evil, sin, and mixed motives, he still finds power accountable to just terms. His pessimism does not allow for unchecked or absolute power; to the contrary, our social arrangements, politically and morally, require accountability.

The Goals of the Digital Empire: Generative AI?

This leads to questions about moral responsibility for tech companies, designers, and producers. While generative AI's corporate leadership

[115] Lora Kelley, "Social Media's 'Frictionless Experience' for Terrorists," *Atlantic*, October 19, 2023, https://www.theatlantic.com/newsletters/archive/2023/10/social-media-moderation-extremism-israel-hamas/675706/.

[116] Augustine, *City of God* 19.7 (trans. Bettenson), pp. 861–62; Frederick H. Russell, "War," in Fitzgerald, *Augustine Through the Ages*, 876. Augustine also laments war. Even under just circumstances, one only participates through tears. War and violence are never something to celebrate. Both dehumanize us further from the end of human flourishing. While later commentators from Thomas Aquinas to the Geneva Convention add significant detail to Augustine's original description, including *jus ad bellum* (just grounds before war) and *jus in bello* (just grounds during war), the core concerns raised by Augustine remain. See Thomas Aquinas, *Summa Theologica*, trans. Fathers of the English Dominican Province (Ave Maria, 1948), II-II Q. 40.1–4, pp. 1353–57; François Bugnion, "Just Wars, Wars of Aggression and International Humanitarian Law," *International Review of the Red Cross* 84, no. 847 (2002): 523–46, https://www.icrc.org/sites/default/files/external/doc/en/assets/files/other/irrc-847-2002-bugnion-ang.pdf.

have called for regulations, more work is needed. These recent demands perhaps mask deeper existing problems with social media.[117] It's unclear whether corporate leaders are sincerely seeking limits and accountability through their prearranged political meetings or whether they're possibly delaying immediate regulation through lengthy political and bureaucratic process.[118] Just as unchecked power was unacceptable for political empires in Augustine's day, unchecked power for tech companies is unacceptable in today's digital empire.

These concerns lie behind the work of Tristan Harris and Aza Raskin with the Center for Humane Technology. Harris and Raskin take on these questions in their recent online discussion entitled "The A.I. Dilemma," in step with their Netflix documentary *The Social Dilemma* that dispels bright illusions surrounding technology's power. Distinguishing between what they term "Curation AI" manifested through social media and "Creation AI" prevalent with emergent AI technologies, they raise significant concerns. Harris and Raskin say we have lost the battle with social media as we're too entangled with "the monster" to entirely fix its misalignment.[119] Their hope is to get ahead of new AI technologies before we find ourselves completely entangled.

Three premises drive Harris's and Raskin's work: "1) When you invent new technology, you uncover a new class of responsibilities. 2) If the technology confers power, it starts a race. 3) If you do not coordinate, the race ends in tragedy."[120] What began as the race for engagement with social media and the attention economy is now the race for persuasion and intimacy with "creation AI."[121] A primary concern they share is the exponential growth in new "Generative Large Language Multi-Models," abbreviated as "GLLMM" or "Gollems," which they symbolically connect to the emergent capabilities of inanimate clay in Jewish folklore.[122] The problem with "GLLMMs" is their fast and profound ability to cross-code /

[117]   Matteo Wong, "AI Doomerism Is a Decoy: Big Tech's Warnings About an AI Apocalypse Are Distracting Us from Years of Actual Harms Their Products Have Caused," *Atlantic*, June 2, 2023, https://www.theatlantic.com/technology/archive/2023/06/ai-regulation-sam-altman-bill-gates/674278/.

[118]   Wong, "AI Doomerism Is a Decoy."

[119]   Tristan Harris and Aza Raskin, "The AI Dilemma," presentation at the Center for Humane Technology, San Francisco, March 9, 2023, https://www.youtube.com/watch?v=xoVJKj8lcNQ.

[120]   Harris and Raskin, "AI Dilemma."

[121]   Harris and Raskin, "AI Dilemma."

[122]   Harris and Raskin, "AI Dilemma."

coordinate language across specialized and disparate fields—images, fMRI, DNA, biometrics, robotics, video, sound, and stock market—operating four times faster than researchers originally projected. They candidly conclude: "All door locks in society are now open."[123]

New Atlantis editor Ari Schulman agrees. In "Why This AI Moment May Be the Real Deal," Schulman notes that new AI capabilities separate the current model of AI from past projections.[124] While technologies rely on human creators or "men behind curtains," these new abilities change how digital technologies can grasp the world with "translatable breakthroughs."[125] The "transfer phenomena" with translatable breakthroughs grants AI the power to generate new content with significant ethical questions regarding information authority, accountability, public trust, and the common good. Yet despite these new capacities, Schulman concludes human agents are still behind the machines: "Transformers are not conscious, and so not intelligent in the full sense of the word."[126] Preserving difference across the human–AI interface, he warns against our tendency to err on either "alarmism" or "rosy" embrace while avoiding responsibility.[127] Preserving difference keeps human agents accountable.

It is for this reason we should hold the *human agents* accountable to the goals and means associated with their platforms. Schulman explains that we have to evaluate AI for the seriousness by which it disrupts society and everyday life. He concludes,

> The hyperbole of the Tech Backlash let Big Tech off the hook, locking us into a mindset where the problem was a corrupt implementation of technology rather than corrupt technology full stop. This has been a boon for tech companies, who, instead of facing the existential threat of a public that saw their product as a new form of opioids, got away with a "we'll do better" reach of Standard Oil. It is too early

[123] Harris and Raskin, "AI Dilemma."

[124] Ari Schulman, "Why This AI Moment May Be the Real Deal," *New Atlantis*, Summer 2023, https://www.thenewatlantis.com/publications/why-this-ai-moment-may-be-the-real-deal.

[125] Schulman, "This AI Moment," 6–18. He lists a number of capabilities: "generalization across specialization"; "understanding natural language"; "understanding context"; "responsiveness"; "its flexible, implicit, and general grasp of the world"; "the *way* it gains grasp of world resulting in transformer phenomena or translatable breakthroughs"; and finally, demonstrating "'alien' errors rather than 'nonsense.'"

[126] Schulman, "This AI Moment," 18.

[127] Schulman, "This AI Moment," 18.

to say that the new AI class is an inherently antihuman technological paradigm, as social media has proven itself to be. But it is not too early to suspect that AI will dwarf social media in their power to disrupt modern life. If that is so, we had better learn some new and unfamiliar ways of interrogating this technology, and fast. Whatever these entities are—they're here.[128]

Interrogating these technologies is a moral obligation for our time. Just because we can build new tech doesn't mean we should. Searching for theological and philosophical wisdom causes us to pause and see through the current tech momentum, creative projects, and power structures of our day.

By way of theological analogy, this takes us back to the Tower of Babel. Whereas Haidt's original use of Genesis 11 focuses on communication chaos in which social media leaves us with mass confusion, with emerging generative AI we risk building one singular tower at an exponential rate. Interpreting Haidt's analysis of the Tower of Babel, Russell Moore says, "And yet, the problem with the Tower of Babel was not fragmentation. The problem was unity. The builders were united by their own hubris in building something that would ultimately destroy them. The confusion of the languages and the scattering of people were the work of God."[129] Rather than destroy them, God mercifully scatters the inhabitants. Perhaps scattering is the opportunity to rethink human motives and goals associated with the towers of human ingenuity. Scattering disperses and balances power rather than allowing it to accumulate in a single—or few—corporate entities. An apocalyptic moment offers the opportunity to peer behind the curtain of our own paradoxically creative yet destructive powers.

In this sense, *every* moment is apocalyptic.[130] Apocalyptic moments unveil the power structures in our socioeconomic milieu which dominate our attention. Another term might be "kairotic moments" that illuminate our need for wisdom over and above our own "autonomous" efforts.[131] While distanced from the power of ancient Egypt's pyramids and Sphynx, built on the backsides of the poor and enslaved, the gains and losses of

---

[128] Schulman, "This AI Moment," 19.

[129] Russell Moore, "The American Evangelical Church Is in Crisis. There's Only One Way Out," *Atlantic*, July 25, 2023, https://www.theatlantic.com/ideas/archive/2023/07/christian-evangelical-church-division-politics/674810/.

[130] Ellul, *Presence of the Kingdom*, 23.

[131] Charles Mathewes, "An Augustinian Look at Empire," *Theology Today* 63, no. 3 (2006): 306.

these new technologies are emerging in real time, benefiting the few and harming the many. The name Babel, or Babylon, which we could translate as "confusion" or "empire," seems appropriate. This cautionary tale reminds us of the power in hubris and the importance of humility as well as accountability.

Another cautionary concern involves the transhumanist desire to eliminate suffering, death, aging, and a litany of problems through biotechnology. Behind the transhumanist movement is the assumption that we are evolutionarily progressing. The integration of inanimate technology with organic human life is the next step.[132] One transhumanist, Ray Kurzweil, posits the "singularity thesis," proposing that we upload copies of our consciousness to computer systems as a way to experience immortality.[133] His uncanny work predicts the growth of exponential AI by the year 2045. The singularity thesis suggests mass consciousness uploaded to one mind, invoking questions about power and hubris united around a singular goal—again foreshadowed through the Tower of Babel.

The trouble with the overarching transhumanist appeal is its trust in future AI technologies that might in effect fundamentally change current understandings of human nature into something unrecognizable. Ethicist Gerald McKenny explains that "even Nietzsche would reject this motivation as self-hatred, for it rejects human identity."[134]

[132] Nick Bostrom, "A History of Transhumanist Thought," *Journal of Evolution and Technology* 14, no. 1 (2005): 1–25.

[133] Ray Kurzweil, *The Singularity Is Near: When Humans Transcend Biology* (Penguin Books, 2005). Interestingly, Ray Kurzweil's daughter and *New Yorker* cartoonist, Amy Kurzweil, humanizes many of the motivations behind transhumanist goals. Both her volumes highlight the familial desire to connect with the past and future driven by transcendent values born from suffering as descendants from the Holocaust. Preservation from annihilation often came through documentation for Jewish refugees able to migrate away from the horrors of Nazi Germany and its reach. Documentation is also significant for the transhumanist goals through AI. Interestingly, philosophical and religious terms such as "embodiment," "resurrection," and "immortality" are used in Amy Kurzweil's cartoon work. See Amy Kurzweil, *Flying Couch: A Graphic Memoir* (Catapult, 2016); idem, *Artificial: A Love Story* (Catapult, 2023). Thanks to Zachary Ellis for introducing me to Kurzweil and broadening my perspective on the humanist approach etched in her drawings.

[134] Autumn Alcott Ridenour, *Sabbath Rest as Vocation: Aging Toward Death* (Bloomsbury T&T Clark, 2018), 229; Gerald McKenny, "Transcendence, Technological Enhancement, and Christian Theology," in *Transhumanism and Transcendence: Christian Hope in an Age of Technological Enhancement*, ed. Ronald Cole-Turner (Georgetown University Press, 2011), 186.

Philosopher Shannon Vallor, more confident about technological virtue, agrees. On transhumanism she says, "Consider Nietzsche's warning once more. We hear much from transhumanism about what they
want to free us from: sickness, aging, death; the limitations of our
bodily form; the tyrannies of entropy, space, and time. But do we hear
as clearly what they want to free us for?"[135] Dubbed "post-humanity,"
transhumanism appeals to visions beyond what we might know or will
in our current state.

In aiming for a hopeful future, transhumanists claim to have our
best interest and maximum freedom at heart. Late physician Sherwin
Nuland sows doubt about these intentions. Reflecting on transhumanist Aubrey de Grey's anti-aging movement, Nuland says, "If we are
to be destroyed, I am now convinced that it will not be a neutral or
malevolent force that will do us in, but one that is benevolent in the
extreme, one whose only motivation is to improve us and better our
civilization. If we are ever immolated, it will be by the efforts of well-
meaning scientists who are convinced that they have our best interests
at heart."[136]

While transhumanists display hope through science and technology in
its ability to eliminate suffering through life extension, generative AI and
social media seek the good in information access. Describing OpenAI and
its aim, Ross Anderson says, "They wanted to summon a superintelligence
into the world, an intellect decisively superior to that of any human. And
whereas a big tech company might recklessly rush to get there first, for its
own end, they wanted to do it safely 'to benefit humanity as a whole.'"[137]
OpenAI claims that it will benefit humanity as a whole; the question remains
as to how. In what way? If pursuing this kind of goal, why the urgency?
Computer scientists acknowledge problems with these kinds of statements.
Acknowledging the expansive creative capacities of new AI tools, Gina
Helfrich says, "But the companies who created the tools didn't have a clear

[135] Shannon Vallor, *Technology and the Virtues: A Philosophical Guide to a Future Worth Wanting* (Oxford University Press, 2016), 240.
[136] Sherwin Nuland, "Do You Want to Live Forever? Aubrey de Grey Thinks He Knows How to Defeat Aging. He's Brilliant, but Is He Nuts?" *MIT Technology Review*, February 1, 2005, https://www.technologyreview.com/2005/02/01/231686/do-you-want-to-live-forever/.
[137] Ross Anderson, "Inside the Revolution at OpenAI," *Atlantic*, September 2023, https://www.theatlantic.com/magazine/archive/2023/09/sam-altman-openai-chatgpt-gpt-4/674764/.

vision of what they should be for in the first place."[138] The competitive race suggests another gold rush seeking profit with great risks. Is this a new form of manifest destiny? If so, deeper reflection and wisdom is needed.

Accountability and Regulation

Regulation for existing social media and emerging AI technology is needed, particularly in terms of greater transparency and accountability. The European Union's AI Act leads the way in legal regulation, posing criteria for evaluating risk assessment.[139] From the outset, the European Parliament states its goal behind the EU AI Act is "to make sure that AI systems used in the EU are safe, transparent, traceable, non-discriminatory and environmentally friendly. AI systems should be overseen by people, rather than by automation, to prevent harmful outcomes."[140]

Expanding the EU's ethical sentiment on regulation and accountability requires collective effort across nation states. In "The A.I. Dilemma," Harris and Raskin appeal to collective action beyond private oversight alone. They appeal to ethical precedent in historical moments of accountability such as the creation of the Comprehensive Nuclear Test Ban Treaty, the UN's Universal Declaration of Human Rights, or the Bretton Woods Conference's inauguration of the World Bank and International Monetary Fund.[141] They also cite safety regulations for drug companies and airplane manufacturers in the private sphere.[142] Each of these examples involves cooperation and awareness that human interest—both of individuals and collective groups—are at risk. Moral accountability is necessary when the lust for power threatens broader justice.

Examples from bioethics include ethical guidelines for research on human subjects. Unfortunately, statements such as the Nuremberg Code and the *Belmont Report* were issued after significant moral harm.[143]

[138] Gina Helfrich, quoted in Lisa Weidenfeld, "The Future of AI," *Boston College Magazine*, Summer 2024, https://www.bc.edu/bc-web/sites/bc-magazine/summer-2024-issue/features/the-future-of-ai.html.
[139] European Commission, "AI Act: Shaping Europe's Digital Future," https://digital-strategy.ec.europa.eu/en/policies/regulatory-framework-ai; European Parliament, "EU AI Act: First Regulation on Artificial Intelligence," 2023, https://www.europarl.europa.eu/topics/en/article/20230601STO93804/eu-ai-act-first-regulation-on-artificial-intelligence.
[140] European Commission, "AI Act"; European Parliament, "EU AI Act."
[141] Harris and Raskin, "AI Dilemma."
[142] Harris and Raskin, "AI Dilemma."
[143] "The Nuremberg Code," in *Trials of War Criminals Before the Nuremberg Military Tribunals Under Control Council Law No. 10*, vol. 2 (US Government

Following problematic experiments on human subjects by the medical community in Nazi Germany, the Tuskegee Syphilis Study in Alabama, and the Willowbrook hepatitis study in New York, the United States issued federal regulations for Institutional Review Boards (IRBs) in the 1970s.[144] When human lives and futures are at risk, there is precedent for cooperative ethical discussion and regulation.

Jonathan Haidt and Jean Twenge raise awareness around the use of social media and digital devices and its impact on adolescent development.[145] As bioethicist Paul Ramsey insisted early on in his argument against experimentation on children, unchecked power requires considerations of beneficence and justice for vulnerable populations.[146] Haidt proposes collective action strategies for governments, schools, and parents that merit significant hearing, from legal regulations to practical guidance about age limits and phone-free zones.[147] If society can change safety regulations for tobacco companies and car manufacturers, then tech companies wielding power over youths' mental health shouldn't be exempt either. Perhaps this is another Belmont-type moment where collective action and ethical principles are needed to help regulate and hold accountable social media and tech giants in their increased power over the lives and future interests of their users.

Some claim that AI threats are mere histrionic hyperbole, but it is clear that we're in need of a new technological regulatory agency that functions

Printing Office, 1949), https://history.nih.gov; US Department of Health, Education, and Welfare, *The Belmont Report: Ethical Principles and Guidelines for the Protection of Human Subjects of Research*, April 18, 1979, https://www.hhs.gov/ohrp/regulations-and-policy/belmont-report/read-the-belmont-report/index.html.

144   Associated Press, "Victims of Sinister Medical Procedures Included Residents of Staten Island's Infamous Willowbrook State School," *Silive North Shore*, March 1, 2011, https://www.silive.com/northshore/2011/03/victims_of_sinister_medical_pr.html.

145   Jean M. Twenge, *iGen: Why Today's Super-Connected Kids Are Growing Up Less Rebellious, More Tolerant, Less Happy—and Completely Unprepared for Adulthood* (Atria Books, 2017); Greg Lukianoff and Jonathan Haidt, *The Coddling of the American Mind: How Good Intentions and Bad Ideas Are Setting Up a Generation for Failure* (Penguin Books, 2018), 145–61.

146   Paul Ramsey, "The Enforcement of Morals: Nontherapeutic Research on Children," *Hastings Center Report* 6, no. 4 (1976): 21–30.

147   Jonathan Haidt, *The Anxious Generation: How the Great Rewiring of Childhood Is Causing an Epidemic of Mental Illness* (Penguin Books, 2024), 221–26.

alongside governing powers.[148] Mustafa Suleyman argues we need boundaries to contain AI in *The Coming Wave*.[149] Reflecting the uniqueness of AI's threat to international security and state sovereignty, Suleyman and Ian Bremmer call for tech designers to participate in international regulations, especially given tenuous relations, heightened competition, and emerging conflicts across the globe. They say, "A technoprudential mandate would work similarly [much like global financial institutions], necessitating the creation of institutional mechanisms to address the various aspects of AI that could threaten geopolitical stability. These mechanisms, in turn, would be guided by common principles that are both tailored to AI's unique features and reflect the new technological balance of power that has put tech companies in the driver's seat."[150] Efforts by the G7, EU's AI Act, and United States Congressional hearings in 2023 are significant, though continued international cooperation remains paramount.[151]

Regulation involves common principles that begin with bioethical statements like "First, do no harm."[152] Yet the power of these technologies requires urgent attention rather than deregulation that keeps tech exploitable to private actors and prone to individual harm. Bremmer and Suleyman say new regulations should be agile, inclusive, and impermeable across the design and distribution process.[153] They conclude, "In the last century, policymakers began to build a global governance architecture that, they hoped, would be equal to the tasks of the age. Now, they must build a new governance architecture to contain and harness the most formidable, and potentially defining, force of this era."[154] Given the knowledge, power, and capabilities of new AI, the digital empire necessitates moral and political accountability. At their worst, tech giants appear like "a gang of pirates" using data for their own interest, circumventing justice and love for neighbor or the common good.[155]

---

[148] Ian Bremmer and Mustafa Suleyman, "The AI Power Paradox: Can States Learn to Govern Artificial Intelligence—Before It's Too Late?" *Foreign Affairs* 102, no. 5 (2023): 26–43, https://www.foreignaffairs.com/world/artificial-intelligence -power-paradox.

[149] Mustafa Suleyman and Michael Bhaskar, *The Coming Wave: Technology, Power, and the 21st Century's Greatest Dilemma* (Crown, 2024), 35–50, 225–80.

[150] Bremmer and Suleyman, "AI Power Paradox."

[151] Bremmer and Suleyman, "AI Power Paradox."

[152] Bremmer and Suleyman, "AI Power Paradox."

[153] Bremmer and Suleyman, "AI Power Paradox."

[154] Bremmer and Suleyman, "AI Power Paradox."

[155] Augustine, *City of God* (trans. Babcock), p. 71.

Ethics and accountability require seeing beyond the goods of profit and free-market choice alone. Given our complicity in social and political structures with mixed motives for good and evil, Augustine's understanding of limits and moral accountability is prescient. However, his realistic stance that recognizes minimum thresholds in the form of principles or rules also involves a deeper vision of the good life. It's not simply enough to describe moral harms. We must also identify moral goods that motivate and drive us toward a desirable end, resulting in beauty and fulfillment. Turning to virtue and its end offers such a vision.

THE PRESENCE OF THE KINGDOM

Augustine often receives the caricature of negative realist based on interpretations casting his political vision solely on *City of God* book 19, in which he deconstructs the political realm as lacking true justice this side of heaven. Augustine is no utopian. Yet once he deconstructs the problem in Rome, or the *polis*, he reconstructs the common good around something transcendent and higher that holds our present reality in check. Augustine recenters the earthly city on our common loves. The better the loves, the better the *polis*. Eric Gregory changes the landscape further by claiming the center of Augustine's political theory resides in book 10 on Christology rather than book 19.[156] Gregory's work describes the possibilities—rather than limits alone—for Augustine's political and theological vision based on an incarnational interpretation of *uti et frui*, "use and enjoy." In this way Augustine's vision is embodied simultaneously with material and temporal implications as well as humility.

Gregory interprets Augustine's order of love, "use and enjoy," by separating arguments for neighbor love from Kantian interpretations that suggest use as exploitative. Relying on interpretations that involve sharing love of neighbor in God, a parallel to the intersubjective relations within the triune God, Gregory also draws from the "*una caritas* formula" as the "opposite of every kind of dominating 'use' of others."[157] Loving God and neighbor go hand in hand, as seen through Matthew 25:31–46 and Augustine's own

---

[156]   Eric Gregory, *Politics and the Order of Love: An Augustinian Ethic of Democratic Citizenship* (University of Chicago Press, 2008), 379.

[157]   Gregory draws on insight from William Riordian O'Connor: "The *Uti/Frui* Distinction in Augustine's Ethics," *Augustinian Studies* 14 (1983): 50; and from Raymond Canning, *The Unity of Love for God and Neighbour in St. Augustine* (Augustinian Historical Institute, 1993), 19–31, in Gregory, *Politics and the Order of Love*, 343, 347.

sermons about seeing Christ's presence in the neighbor.[158] Gregory says, "The neighbor is a sacramental presence (a repetition of the first sacrament of the Christ), a real subject of love that still points beyond herself."[159]

Christology connects God's presence with neighbor love, uniting works of love with worship. Gregory says, "Eschatological *eudaimonism* does not trap Christian love up in heaven. It is precisely the end that perpetually calls forth not simply longing but also a new ethical beginning in the 'secular time' of Incarnation."[160] He extends Augustine's neighbor love to a democratic citizenship that is realistic about sin yet does not allow for withdrawal.[161] In fact, Augustine's deep theological sociality motivates him.[162] Gregory resonates with concerns regarding the digital empire when he says, "The future of Augustinian liberalism—and so much more—may turn on whether or not we human beings can learn to desire more than ourselves without killing each other or simply forgetting about the shared goods of political life in pursuit of private perfection, aesthetic delight, entertaining distractions, economic security, and even spiritual freedom."[163] Desiring more than ourselves is the antidote to nihilistic despair.

Desire extends not just in love but also hope. Michael Lamb builds on Gregory's political theology in *A Commonwealth of Hope*. Citing Augustine as a man for our time, he recognizes Augustinian hope stands between presumption and despair or triumphalism and resignation. Searching for a better form of community, Lamb looks toward Augustine's eschatological vision through a form of "participationist ontology" that we partially realize through a better community and objects of hope here and now.[164] Lamb explains, "If acts of public service and sacrifice can be a way to worship God and express rightly ordered love and hope, then this account challenges Augustinian communitarians who imply that worship requires avoiding politics to focus on being the church. Politics can also be a labor of liturgy and love."[165]

[158]   Gregory, *Politics and the Order of Love*, 348.
[159]   Gregory, *Politics and the Order of Love*, 349; see also Conor Kelly, *The Fullness of Free Time: A Theological Account of Leisure and Recreation in the Moral Life* (Georgetown University Press, 2020), 19.
[160]   Gregory, *Politics and the Order of Love*, 363.
[161]   See also Eric Gregory, "Politics," in *The Oxford Handbook of Evangelical Theology*, ed. Gerald R. McDermott (Oxford University Press, 2010), 393–95.
[162]   Gregory, *Politics and the Order of Love*, 362.
[163]   Gregory, *Politics and the Order of Love*, 363.
[164]   Lamb, *Commonwealth of Hope*, xiii, 22.
[165]   Lamb, *Commonwealth of Hope*, 223.

Charles Mathewes agrees: The political realm is the training ground for theological virtues by engaging other citizens in the public arena or commonwealth.[166] Moreover, he finds Augustine's heavenly mindedness involves significant theological and political vision. First, we anticipate being "taken up into the divine life of infinite giving in the perichoresis that is the triune God."[167] Second, he continues that this "involves not solitude or privacy . . . but presence. Both the idea of the last judgment and Paul's promise that one day we will see face to face radically contest our presumption for [political] privacy."[168] Anticipating presence in full communion holds significant implications for today.[169]

The Possibility for Presence Through Formational Communities

The question is how we might manifest the presence of Christ in today's political and digital empire. Sociologist James Davison Hunter describes the importance of theological presence as opposed to political power and dominance fueled by resentment, fear, and threat. Hunter critiques the increased politicization of our shared social life in the twenty-first century: "When politicization is oriented toward furthering the specific interests of the group without an appeal to the common weal, when its means of mobilizing the uncommitted is through fear, and when the pursuit of agendas depends more on the vilification of opponents than on the affirmation of higher ideals, power is stripped to its most elemental forms."[170] Deep political polarization has only increased with help from social media algorithms. Politics too often focuses on group interest or party power over the common good. Hunter critiques the Christian right, Christian left, and Neo-Anabaptists for participating in "ressentiment" that primarily engages a "discourse of negation" and "will to power."[171] Hunter's

---

[166] Charles Mathewes, *Republic of Grace* (Eerdmans, 2010), 32–34.

[167] Mathewes, "Augustinian Look at Empire," 305.

[168] Mathewes, "Augustinian Look at Empire," 305.

[169] Jean-Luc Marion recognizes the eschatological and temporal meaning of communion is significant for understanding both the common good and self-gift (Marion, "Utility of Communion," 66–82).

[170] Hunter, *To Change the World*, 106.

[171] Hunter, *To Change the World*, 175. See also Tish Harrison Warren, interview with Russell Moore, "The State of Evangelical America," *New York Times*, July 30, 2023, https://www.nytimes.com/2023/07/30/opinion/state-of-evangelical-america .html; idem, "My Hope for American Discourse," *New York Times*, August 6, 2023, https://www.nytimes.com/2023/08/06/opinion/saying-goodbye-social-media -prayer.html.

description recognizes Augustine's *libido dominandi* as a perennial temptation. Arguments that reduce enemies to stereotypes through negation deconstruct without building bridges or common ground. Hunter points out the irony in Christian ethics that seek to dominate through power rather than serve through humility.

Instead, Hunter argues for a theology of presence. In a digital empire, physical embodied presence is a helpful antidote to political tropes. When physical embodied presence is lacking, a commitment to nuance and multidimensional understandings of the neighbor are needed to reject reductionistic temptations to demean political opponents. Drawing from the doctrine of incarnation, Hunter recognizes that Jesus Christ does not come as a political zealot, overthrowing Rome for the sake of his religious community. To the contrary: he aims to participate faithfully in his Jewish culture in its occupation by the Roman Empire. This will allow him moments of gentle correction and truth: to simultaneously challenge authority, particularly religious voices but also political leaders such as Pilate when questioning the source of his authority. Christ's example and witness leads not to political revolution but to surrender and death on a criminal's cross. The way of Christ leads by humility and sacrifice while loving his neighbor—the opposite of pride, dominance, and the will to power. As 1 Peter 2:23 says, "When they hurled their insults at him, he did not retaliate; when he suffered, he made no threats. Instead, he entrusted himself to him who judges justly" (NIV). Yet even Christ's willingness to die demonstrates the subversive power of his life and resurrection.

Marion describes the significance of benevolent power when derived from rightful authority. Those with true authority over a subject or field don't have to feel threatened: "Power results from authority, but it does not produce it . . . Authority, unlike power, does not declare itself, does not do violence, does not make a spectacle of itself, and even, if need be, is not seen . . . True authority never can disappear, because it rests on nothing but itself, not even on its own affirmation."[172] Jesus did not exhibit ressentiment even when the law he cherished was misapplied or the people he loved were sick and dying. While he did demonstrate righteous indignation over injustice, particularly by religious leaders, he also showed compassion in humility for the ones who took his life (Luke 23:34).

Christ's humility through the incarnation and crucifixion turns pride on its head. The Creator's presence among creation is a profound

---

[172] Marion, "Utility of Communion," 81.

mystery. Hunter reflects on the significance of the incarnation for our age and says, "[The] incarnation is the only adequate reply to the challenges of dissolution; the erosion of trust between word and world and the problems that attend."[173]

Perhaps the biggest threat the digital empire poses regards trust. Social media algorithms have changed the way we communicate in the arenas of politics, public health, and medicine following COVID-19. An ongoing question will be how to rebuild communities of trust based on the incarnational presence of Christ. Highlighting the unified word and action of Christ's ministry, Hunter continues, "Pursuit, identification, the offer of life through sacrificial love—this is what God's faithful presence means. It is a quality of commitment that is active, not passive; intentional, not accidental; covenantal, not contractual. In the life of Christ we see how it entailed his complete attention. It was whole-hearted, not half-hearted; focused and purposeful . . . His very name, Immanuel, signifies all of this— 'God with us'—in our presence (Matt 1:23)."[174] Unlike our fractured attention and dissonance between word and deed, Christ's presence differs.

Our imitation of Christ grows through embodied community and formation. For Christ followers to participate in the common good beyond their convictional community, they need deep habits and patterns of spiritual encounter with the transcendent that changes and molds them more in Christ's image. Hunter says, "Making disciples or formation, then, requires intentionality and it entails the hard work of teaching, training, and cautioning believers with wisdom in the ways of Christ so that they are fit for any calling and any service to him."[175] Here Christ followers grow in the spiritual disciplines and exhibit the character of Christ in their respective vocations. This involves a thick sense of community in which love drives the individual beyond their ecclesial relations into "the new city commons" where they commit to working with others in a diverse context for the "highest ideals and practices of human flourishing in a pluralistic world."[176] In this way the church enacts *shalom* on behalf of others, coupling love with justice and service—following Christ necessarily involves love of neighbor. And this requires that we cultivate a life of labor and love, work and prayer, send and retreat—over and over again.

---

[173] Hunter, *To Change the World*, 241.
[174] Hunter, *To Change the World*, 243.
[175] Hunter, *To Change the World*, 227.
[176] Hunter, *To Change the World*, 279.

Concerns over rising isolation diagnose the twenty-first century as the "Anti-Social Generation" in which we have moved inward, prioritizing individual, private life while remaining digitally connected to political tribes in terms of group interest.[177] What's missing are civic community relations or the "village," teaching us tolerance and social kindness in a pluralistic world.[178] In the village we rub shoulders with people who differ from our convictions, preferences, and cultural distinctiveness. In the village we reenter public spaces in our communities, schools, and civic commitments. Subsidiarity in our local communities is where we build critical relationships and ways of relating across difference at the atomic level. Cultivating relationships and empathy shapes us to love more broadly than our own ecclesial, preferential, or political interest group. Yet this outward embrace also draws from strong communities of character formation that shape the ways we engage across difference both in person and online.

Emphasizing the significance of embodied habits and community formation, Hunter says:

> As a community and an institution, the church is a plausibility structure and the only one with the resources capable of offering an alternative formation to that offered by popular culture . . . the depth and stability of formation directed to depth and stability of the social and cultural environment in which it takes place. Formation into a vision of human flourishing requires an environment that embodies continuity, historical memory, rituals marking seasons of life, intergenerational interdependence, and most important of all, common worship.[179]

The church—imperfect in its local particularity—is essential even still for the formation of faithful presence and neighbor love in the city, as well as the digital empire. This is considerably important given an epidemic of loneliness and increased isolation inspired by modernization, individualization, and digital device use.[180] The church becomes an alternative

---

[177]   Derek Thompson, "The Anti-Social Century," *Atlantic*, January 8, 2025, https://www.theatlantic.com/magazine/archive/2025/02/american-loneliness-personality-politics/681091/.

[178]   Thompson, "Anti-Social Century."

[179]   Hunter, *To Change the World*, 283.

[180]   Shoshana Zuboff describes two modernities in which we moved from individualism with the Industrial Revolution to individualization with the digital revolution (Zuboff, *Age of Surveillance Capitalism*, 31–37).

culture to absence, confusion, and nihilism. We need each other now more than ever. Finding spiritual resonance and communion with God and one another humbles, uplifts, and propels a life of service, responding to the social needs of our neighbor. Love and virtue begin in the church and extend to neighbors near and distant. In light of this I now turn to Augustine's understanding of the theological virtues and their significance for our life as faithful stewards in this time of digital empire.

VIRTUE AND VICE IN THE DIGITAL EMPIRE

Rooted in the order of love, all virtue, natural or theological, is interconnected. Virtue cannot be separated from Augustine's order of love. George Lavere says, "Virtue is . . . the means by which moral order is established in human actions, directing them to their appropriate final end . . . The distinction between the use of creatures and the enjoyment of God is fundamental to a proper understanding of the concept of virtue."[181] Here as with Ellul, the means relate to its transcendent end. Rather than stratify Augustine's theology as something otherworldly, his transcendent focus liberates the nearsightedness of our moral striving in time. Rather than seek happiness in temporal ends—social status, success, productivity, entertainment, friendship, or other goods promised in the digital empire—Augustine situates all temporal and created gifts in relation to this end. Because of this transcendent goal, we see through digital ends that risk eclipsing important goods for being human.

While Augustine critiques pagan notions of virtue, claiming only true piety, or worship, leads to virtue, his interactions with the Stoic and Neoplatonic philosophical traditions profoundly shape and develop his theology.[182] In what is called the "splendid vices," or pagan virtues belonging to Neoplatonism, he learns about the unchanging and eternal ideas of truth, beauty, and goodness.[183] Yet he also finds these ideals need redirection in relationship to God. Christ's incarnation takes on human flesh. In humility, he became human. Augustine offers a transformational project, moving from deconstruction to reconstruction centered on the incarnational

---

[181] George Lavere, "Virtue," in Fitzgerald, *Augustine Through the Ages*, 871–72; Augustine, *The Morals of the Catholic Church*, in *Basic Writings of St. Augustine*, vol. 1, ed. Whitney J. Oates (Random House, 1948), 15, pp. 331–32.

[182] Lamb, *Commonwealth of Hope*, 230–34; Lavere, "Virtue," 872.

[183] For discussion of "splendid vices" see Jennifer Herdt, *Putting on Virtue: The Legacy of the Splendid Vices* (University of Chicago Press, 2008); Lamb, *Commonwealth of Hope*; and on Platonic influences see Lavere, "Virtue," 872.

and resurrected Christ who demonstrates perfect virtue through humility and love. He incorporates natural virtue into this ordered love. Augustine demonstrates the limits of virtue in its dependence on grace, the opposite of pride.[184]

Arguing against Pelagian or Stoic (heroic) efforts to achieve virtue through the law or honor, Augustine shows instead that virtue is contingent upon grace.[185] Mathewes says, "We try to inhabit these virtues not (as in ancient ethics) by achieving morally heroic character but rather by rendering ourselves more fully vulnerable to the action of God in our lives . . . Insofar as we use the language of virtue we must do so with profound care. And the basic way we should use it is to transform it from a language of achievement to a language of suffering, or being willing to be shaped (not to shape ourselves) by the medicine of a gracious God."[186] In this way Augustinian virtue reverses pride by beginning in vulnerability and humility.

Augustine sees Pelagian and Stoic approaches to life as unrealistic in our inability to control circumstances as a buffered self without emotions.[187] In fact, Augustine critiques Stoic virtue for lacking grief in the face of loss. Control through virtue is apathetic or inhuman.[188] Through dependence on God as Creator and Re-creator, grace brings about transformation and growth, directing our emotions with Christ's compassion and the order of love. Yet growth is a matter not of gloating but of gratitude toward God. Mathewes says, "The church is a hospital of virtue, and the virtues are the medicine provided by God."[189] The church, with its ordinances (sacraments), community, and formation, is integral for sanctification.

The key virtues for Augustine are faith, hope, and love. Each interdependent, they offer moral and theological vision for the wayfarer navigating the digital empire. He states, "For 'we walk by faith, not by sight' [2 Cor 5:7], and faith will falter if the authority of scripture is shaken; and if faith falters, love itself decays. For if someone lapses in his faith, he

---

[184] See James Wetzel, *Augustine and the Limits of Virtue* (Cambridge University Press, 1992).

[185] Mathewes, "Augustinian Look at Empire," 304.

[186] Mathewes, "Augustinian Look at Empire," 304.

[187] Augustine, *City of God* 14.3–9 (trans. Bettenson), pp. 550–66.

[188] Instead, we grieve difficult circumstances and the loss of loved ones as genuine and real loss (Augustine, *City of God* 14.3–9, pp. 550–66). See Ridenour, *Sabbath Rest as Vocation*, 36–40.

[189] Mathewes, "Augustinian Look at Empire," 304.

inevitably lapses in his love as well, since he cannot love what he does not believe to be true."[190] In their interconnectedness, faith, hope, and love ground our identity, motivation, and belonging to God as pilgrims in the digital empire. This vision anticipates its fulfillment in which all will be exposed as we encounter Christ face to face.

Augustine completes his definition of virtue ordered toward God by saying "that temperance is love keeping itself entire and incorrupt for God; fortitude is love bearing everything readily for the sake of God; justice is love serving God only and therefore ruling well all else, as subject to man; prudence is love making a right distinction between what helps it toward God and what might hinder it."[191] Love of God orders neighbor love and natural virtue. Rather than appearing otherworldly only, Jesus Christ fulfills virtue. As Augustine explains, "The Son of God is the virtue of God and the wisdom of God—virtue being understood to refer to action, and wisdom to teaching."[192] Christ draws together wisdom and action, contemplation and virtue, word and deed, prayer and service. He is not simply the end—he is the way. Augustine says, "In fact Christ, who chose to offer himself not only as a possession for those who come to their journey's end but also as a road for those who come to the beginning of the way, chose to become flesh."[193]

Christ's virtue, his incarnation and union with humankind through death and resurrection, secures new identity. Rather than self-reliance, virtue is tied to union with Christ and belonging to him. Augustine says, "Present troubles do not separate us; for we feel their burden less the closer we cling to Him from whom they try to separate us."[194] Union with Christ secures divine presence so that we do not walk alone through present circumstances even through life's challenges and difficulties. The more we recognize the challenges of the digital empire, the more we recognize our spiritual poverty and need for grace.[195] Christ achieves virtue by redirecting the goal, motive, and attitude behind our actions as seen through the Sermon on the Mount—neither harboring anger nor lust toward the neighbor. Christ achieves not only the goal of our salvation but also the virtuous life through his person and work while offering love and presence.

[190] Augustine, *On Christian Teaching* 1.37, p. 28.
[191] Augustine, *Morals of the Catholic Church* 15, p. 332.
[192] Augustine, *Morals of the Catholic Church* 16, p. 332.
[193] Augustine, *On Christian Teaching* 1.33, p. 26.
[194] Augustine, *Morals of the Catholic Church* 11, p. 329.
[195] Lavere, "Virtue," 873.

Though we are tested through daily activities and challenges with others, communion sustains Christian life and practice. As Brother Lawrence says, "Our sanctification depends not on changing our works but on doing for God what we would normally do for ourselves . . . always mistaking the means for the end."[196] In line with Augustine's order of love, Brother Lawrence practices communion by loving God behind mundane tasks. Virtuous actions are tied to motives and the will, loving God and neighbor. An identity grounded in communion does not find these loves competitive but integral. In a participationist or relational ontology, we love God and commune with him through loving the neighbor and created world. Intentional habits established over time result in virtue. Prayerful intention, uniting eternal and temporal vision, requires significant reminder, renewal, and focus. Focus is especially important in a digital empire designed to lure and fracture our attention through algorithmic specialization. Moral vision, virtue, and action is paramount for this moment, fostered by embodied communities of love, particularly the church.

Virtues for the Digital Empire

(1) Wisdom and Prudence

Wisdom is a kind of spiritual vision often tied to faith. Psalm 115 describes idols such as silver and gold, or images not unlike contemporary technology that "have mouths but do not speak; eyes, but do not see. They have ears, but do not hear; noses, but do not smell. They have hands, but do not feel; feet, but do not walk; they make no sound in their throats. Those who make them are like them; so are all who trust in them" (Ps 115:5–8). Spiritually blinded to wisdom, vision is limited and myopic, constrained to the physical world only. Idols, such as digital technologies, muffle our senses and capacity to see, hear, touch, taste, and smell the world—nature and its beauty—alongside presence with the neighbor. Instead, the Hebrew and Christian Scriptures challenge spiritual wisdom or vision to see with the heart, mind, or Spirit. Seeing with the Spirit might open our eyes more to the beauty of our surrounding world and presence of the neighbor.

This is perhaps most poignantly captured by Simeon, whose limited physical vision in old age still sees the "Lord's Christ" when holding the infant Jesus of Nazareth. Taking the infant in his arms, he says, "For my eyes have seen your salvation, which you have prepared in the sight of

---

[196] Brother Lawrence of the Resurrection, *The Practice of the Presence of God*, ed. Conrad De Meester, trans. Salvatore Sciurba (ICS, 1994), 106.

all people" (Luke 2:30–31 NIV). Beholding Christ, Simeon finds completion and rest. Likewise, the Apostle Paul, also known as Saul, encounters a blinding light on the road to Damascus that opens his spiritual eyes while making the physical world dim. Transformed through confrontation with the risen Christ, he now sees and beholds the world differently with spiritual wisdom, love, and action (Acts 9:1–31). Wisdom tied to faith is a way of seeing the world differently through spiritual eyes. Faith becomes sight and connects to hope, love, and a host of other virtues.

As Lavere says, "Not only are the virtues interdependent, but all serve charity each in its particular way."[197] In the Aristotelian tradition, prudence is practical wisdom for connecting universal principles with particular circumstances. For Augustine, wisdom is described as *sapientia*, linking *scientia* or temporal knowledge with eternal wisdom.[198] Christ joins wisdom and knowledge together in perfect harmony. Faith through union with Christ offers access to eternal wisdom. Practical wisdom helps offer discernment, knowing right from wrong in time.

Augustine says, "Prudence is love making a right distinction between what helps it toward God and what might hinder it."[199] This includes how we love the neighbor—even through social media and the digital empire. Part of prudence entails recognizing our moral agency belongs primarily in the real world rather than the virtual world. This is particularly important for adolescents who are undergoing physical, emotional, and spiritual development. It's also important for adults as embodied creatures needing friendships and community in the real world. The recent loneliness epidemic only reveals the significance of incarnational, embodied communities. Here the broader church and religious communities have much to offer a culture captivated by the digital empire. Greater moral vision might open our eyes to love that puts on flesh.

Marcus Mescher says, "[Prudence] helps us to make sound judgments for how we use digital tools and networks. For example, how are the Beatitudes and Jesus's emphasis on humility, mercy, and reconciliation (cf. Matt 5:1–12; Luke 6:20–26) reflected in what I post or provide access to?"[200]

[197] Lavere, "Virtue," 873.

[198] Augustine, *The Trinity* 12.4, pp. 337–38; Ridenour, *Sabbath Rest as Vocation*, 215.

[199] Augustine, *Morals of the Catholic Church* 15, p. 332.

[200] Marcus Mescher, "The Moral Impact of Digital Devices," *Journal of Moral Theology* 9, no. 2 (2020): 84–85.

Sound judgments lead us to respect the neighbor. In this sense, prudence or practical wisdom is deeply tied to truthfulness.

(2) Truthfulness

Prudence and truthfulness help combat the digital challenge of "information overload and deception."[201] Immanuel Kant, one of the greatest influences in modern philosophy, privileges truthfulness in his understanding of morality. Often considered the father of modern autonomy, he still recognizes universal obligations associated with autonomous moral agency. In fact, his categorical imperative urging us to "treat persons as an end and not a means only" involves universal obligations.[202] Distinct from postmodern individualistic or relativistic ethics, autonomy and the categorical imperative require that moral maxims (principles) be universal in appeal as well as application toward a shared kingdom of ends, or common good.[203] One of Kant's primary examples includes lying. Lying cannot be universal—either in justification or application. Without truthfulness, trust and social cohesion erode.

Truthfulness not only reflects practical wisdom but also buoys the conditions for trust. Lies, misinformation, and deception for political gain harm the common good. On the flip side, transparency or truthfulness stripped of context also causes harm. For this reason, Shannon Vallor describes the technosocial virtue of honesty as "an exemplary respect for truth, along with the practical expertise to express that respect appropriately in technosocial contexts . . . merely telling the truth, even reliably so, is never sufficient for the virtue of honesty, which requires that we tell the truth not only to the right people, at the right times and places, and to the right degree, but also knowingly, and for the right reasons."[204] In the Gospels, Jesus is intentional about the timing and place when revealing his identity as Messiah, the Christ (Matt 16:15–17; Mark 14:61–62). Transparency in context is significant. Truthfulness needs wisdom. They are interdependent not only for individuals but also for the common good—in the *polis* and digital empire.

[201] Mescher, "Moral Impact of Digital Devices," 70.
[202] Immanuel Kant, *Groundwork for the Metaphysics of Morals*, trans. Arnulf Zweig, in *Justice: A Reader*, ed. Michael Sandel (Oxford University Press, 2007), 2.32, p. 180.
[203] Kant, *Groundwork for the Metaphysics of Morals* 2.32, p. 180.
[204] Vallor, *Technology and the Virtues*, 122.

Pursuing the virtue of truthfulness might also lead to collective action strategies that place pressure on tech companies who appear to be moving away from accountability on their platforms by removing fact-checking activities and cutting employees.[205] Mark Zuckerberg says we've arrived at a new "cultural tipping point."[206] Yet is this a positive tipping point?[207] Just because populist cultural moments question fact-checking doesn't mean that deception, if not explicit lies, are inconsequential whether through social media or real-world experiences.

Pursuing truthfulness is essential to the life and the future of democratic and public institutions—and a necessary ingredient for the privilege of free speech. An enduring legal analogy challenges the balance of individual and communal rights, responsibilities, and interests when falsely yelling "Fire!" in a crowded theater.[208] Lies and panic have real-world consequences and cause harm. Likewise, lies and panic spread through social media have real-world effects—social, emotional, and even physical implications at times.

Truthfulness is significant whether handling information spread across social media or new forms of generative AI. Information is not value neutral, but morally contextualized among the right people, time, place, degree, and purpose. Authority, expertise, and training matter when handling different kinds of knowledge, whether in medicine, science, national security, or information regarding age appropriate content.

---

[205]   Aimee Pichie, "Meta Is Cutting 5% of Its Workforce, or More Than 3600 Employees," CBS News, January 14, 2025, https://www.cbsnews.com/amp/news/meta-layoffs-5-percent-workforce-cuts-low-performers/.

[206]   Pichie, "Meta Is Cutting 5% of Its Workforce."

[207]   Zuckerberg's use of tipping point implies a more positive interpretation borrowing from Malcolm Gladwell's original publication, *The Tipping Point*, rather than Gladwell's more recent *Revenge of the Tipping Point*, recognizing negative ways social change impacts communities and behaviors—by social engineering and design (Malcolm Gladwell, *The Tipping Point: How Little Things Can Make a Big Difference* [Back Bay, 2000]; *Revenge of the Tipping Point: Overstories, Superspreaders, and the Rise of Social Engineering* [Little, Brown, 2024]).

[208]   Carlton F. W. Larson, "'Shouting "Fire" in a Crowded Theater': The Life and Times of Constitutional Law's Most Enduring Analogy," *William & Mary Bill of Rights Journal* 24, no. 1 (2015): 1–33.

(3) Temperance

Temperance, coupled with prudence and truthfulness, constrains individuals from loving an object too much. For Aristotle, temperance involves setting the mean between extremes. In an Augustinian sense this entails locating the object within the order of love. In terms of technology, this might help users and designers consider a gradation of goods. How might we appropriate technology and digital devices in their respective realm as tools? How might we guard against reacting to digital stimuli through impulse and emotion? Both require seeing a gradation of goods. Profit is helpful, but not at the expense of increased miscommunication and its challenge to democracy.

Haidt reflects on the spread of emotional communication over the last decade as "this kind of twitchy and explosive spread of anger."[209] Describing James Madison's "nightmare" where the public divides into factions, teams, or parties based on "mutual animosity," Haidt says these divisions oppress and "descend into arguments over triviality."[210] Madison's prophetic voice anticipates the political confusion prevalent in today's digital empire. Still, institutions need critical accountability, change, and correction when injustice or challenge prevail. Institutions, like people, need change and growth not only to survive but also to thrive.[211] Institutions need constructive forms of critique beyond deconstructive or nihilistic arguments that often end without a path forward, yielding little room for common ground. Communication is beneficial but not at the expense of some level of peace or common ground. Building genuine embodied relationships in time assists our ability to humanize and empathize with diverse perspectives. Temperance tied to faith reorients our vision and aims at communication in the digital sphere.

(4) Self-Control

Temperance shaped by an Augustinian lens might also be called self-control. Described as a "fruit of the spirit" in Galatians 5:22–23, this fruit, or work of love, is set in contrast to works of the flesh in Gal 5:19–21, including "sexual immorality, impurity, sensuality, idolatry, sorcery,

---

[209]   Jonathan Haidt, "Why the Last 10 Years of American Life Have Been Uniquely Stupid," *Atlantic*, April 11, 2022, https://www.theatlantic.com/magazine/archive/2022/05/social-media-democracy-trust-babel/629369/.

[210]   Haidt, "Last 10 Years."

[211]   See Crouch, *Playing God*, 189–206, 207–20.

enmity, strife, jealousy, fits of anger, rivalries, dissensions, divisions, envy, drunkenness, orgies, and things like these" (ESV). How many works of the flesh or vices do self-identifying religious people participate in through social media? How are tweets and political rhetoric used in harmful ways, challenging democracy, and civil discourse? Works of the flesh include "fits of anger, rivalries, dissensions, divisions, envy," and jealousy, yet online outbursts are often justified in the name of ressentiment or power politics. But the Galatians passage warns believers that "those who do such things will not inherit the kingdom of God" (Gal 5:21).

Rather than baptize power politics as a necessary or miserable evil, Augustinian temperance/self-control requires a different response. Avoiding the temptation to indulge anger and rage encouraged through social media algorithms and sensationalist headlines, believers should instead "put on virtue" so that faithfulness might direct self-control through patience, kindness, goodness, and gentleness.[212] Likewise, the book of James in the New Testament warns believers, "So also the tongue is a small member, yet it boasts of great exploits. How great a forest is set ablaze by such a small fire! And the tongue is a fire. The tongue is placed among our members as a world of iniquity; it stains the whole body, sets on fire the cycle of life, and is itself set on fire by hell" (Jas 3:5–6 NRSV). With our words (tongue) or, in this case, pronouncements through social media and digital communication, we ignite a firestorm of information spread—with the power to dichotomize or demonize others and cause political harm in real time, whether in the United States, Brazil, Myanmar, Russia, China, France, or elsewhere. Words can sow political chaos.

In this sense, temperance helps guard against radicalization and urges us to slow down, listen, and offer the benefit of the doubt. Too quickly we question motives and vilify difference. Mescher warns against the harm in media algorithms feeding echo chambers, "making it harder to understand and appreciate the perspective of others who look, think, and live differently, reinforcing an 'us vs. them' tribalism that threatens solidarity and a shared commitment to the common good."[213] For Augustine, the

212 The phrase "put on virtue" borrows from Jennifer Herdt's work (*Putting on Virtue*) in addition to Col 3:12–13, in which Paul charges the church at Colossae to put on the characteristics of Christ, such as "compassionate hearts, kindness, humility, meekness, and patience, bearing with one another in love" and forgiveness.
213 Mescher, "Moral Impact of Digital Devices," 89; see also Lukianoff and Haidt, *Coddling of the American Mind*, 53–77.

Donatist schism exemplified an "us vs. them tribalism" through its purist approach to baptism and church leadership following various responses to the church's experience of civil persecution. Augustine urges (and often in problematic, coercive ways) that the Donatists theologically overcome their self-righteousness and instead accommodate their fellow church members through a form of forgiveness.[214]

In contemporary terms, "straw man" arguments that stereotype both left and right promote Donatist (purist) communication without nuance.[215] Hunter's 2010 observation on resentment across the religious and political spectrum—including progressive, conservative, and Anabaptist ideals—is only exacerbated through algorithmic information spread. Ethicist Dennis Hollinger highlights ways in which committed Christians should be concerned about a host of contemporary issues on both sides of the political aisle.[216] One political party doesn't encompass the common good. To elevate a single platform is to dance with idolatry. Seeking the mean between the extremes, temperance must be fortified by humility, faithfulness, and wisdom. Temperance and self-control are tied to neighbor love in willing the common good for self and other.

[214] Maureen A. Tilley, "The Anti-Donatist Works," in Fitzgerald, *Augustine Through the Ages*, 34–39. Admittedly, the Donatist schism is challenging to fully understand given our historical distance and interpretations that hinge on remaining documents such as letters from St. Augustine and Optatus. R. A. Markus notes that differences in the schism pertained to distinctions in North African regional ecclesiology, following Cyprian, versus a more universal, European ecclesiology belonging to the Roman Catholic Church. That said, the movement involved "terrorist bands of *Circumcelliones* on the Donatist side" and "forcible repression on the official side." (R. A. Markus, "Donatus, Donatism," in Fitzgerald, *Augustine Through the Ages*, 285). Charles Mathewes notes Augustine's complex approach that initially tried to accommodate the Donatists within the church and argue that the Roman Catholic Church could also be "authentically native." While Augustine found coercion theologically problematic, he turned to imperial authorities (coercion) for "civic" reasons, which Mathewes notes is not without its dangers by "instrumentalizing institutional religion" and "collaborating with another" (Mathewes, "Augustinian Look at Empire," 296–97).

[215] Adam Kotsko, "Moralism Is Ruining Cultural Criticism," *Atlantic*, July 26, 2023, https://www.theatlantic.com/ideas/archive/2023/07/oppenheimer-movie-moralizing-reviews-social-media/674823/.

[216] Dennis P. Hollinger, *Creation and Christian Ethics: Understanding God's Designs for Humanity and the World* (Baker Academic, 2024).

(5) Hope

Hope is the realistic theological virtue for the wayfarer in time, including today's digital culture and temptation to despair. Negative headlines, quick judgments, and critical assessment are not helpful from either side and encourage despair and retrenchment rather than empathy, kindness, and compromise for the common good. Hope is tied to faith as it presses toward the final goal that remains unseen. Anticipating the final beatific vision in which we behold Christ and his people face to face, hope is fueled by desire. Mathewes says, "Collectively faith, hope, and love constitute a whole way of life, a way of living in time, of living as longing beings, in the *distension animi*, the 'distension of the soul' that is our lot, and in a culture that would like us to forget history altogether."[217] In forgetting history we too conveniently forget our complicity in structures of injustice and the digital empire's role in stratifying global society politically and economically. Hope propels us to see a better way forward in the future with impact for the here and now.

James F. Keenan distinguishes hope from optimism, saying, "Christian hope is deeply realistic because it is rooted in the cross. As such, Christian hope never lets us dream of imaginary worlds: Christian hope rejects utopianism and any other pipe dream. Christian hope is, rather, the virtue for a very real journey."[218] Hope in this sense is directed toward the future but operative within time. Rooted in the cross, it anticipates resurrection. Hope is realistic about our pain and suffering while recognizing the story does not conclude in despair. Through such realism, hope guards against presumption.[219] Hope protects us from concluding life is fatalistic, absurd, or apocalyptically doomed with no avenue for redemption. Even when facing the worst aspects of the digital empire, whether communication breakdown and political chaos spread through social media or concerns about emergent AI, hope guards against despair. On the flip side, hope also guards against the presumption through our arrogance and pride that the digital empire—along with its conveniences—is not shaping us with malformed desire. When facing the digital empire, hope shows a better way to be human and questions the status quo in our current social reality.

[217] Mathewes, "Augustinian Look at Empire," 304.
[218] James F. Keenan, *Moral Wisdom: Lessons and Texts from the Catholic Tradition*, 2nd ed. (Sheed and Ward, 2004), 162.
[219] Aquinas, *Summa Theologica* II-II Q. 20–21, pp. 1253–59; Lamb, *Commonwealth of Hope*, 227.

(6) Fortitude

For this reason, hope shapes our desire and directs us toward the final goal, moving us through time. Hope—along with faith and love—grounds courage or fortitude. Whereas temperance helps us not love objects too much, fortitude helps us bear the "loss of temporal goods" without despair.[220] Hope with faith shapes fortitude or endurance. Endurance enables us to face the pain of life's challenges in our ability to see Christ as the end, means, and consolation through those circumstances. In the digital empire, fortitude enables the courage to see life differently and voice challenges to the dominant reductionistic political tropes on social media. Hope, fortitude, and endurance are deeply tied to patience. With patience we reorient our vision, guarding against hopeless frustration, anger, and impulse. The fruit of the spirit involving love, joy, peace, patience, kindness, goodness, faithfulness, gentleness, and self-control depends on eternal vision (Gal 5:22–23 ESV).

(7) Patience

Patience is the nature of YHWH in the Hebrew Scriptures as "merciful and gracious, slow to anger, and abounding in steadfast love and faithfulness" (Exod 34:6). Likewise, the people of God are called to demonstrate patience in relation to him. The wisdom literature of Proverbs and Ecclesiastes includes many exhortations regarding patience. Ecclesiastes 7:8–9 says, "Better is the end of a thing than its beginning; the patient in spirit are better than the proud in spirit. Do not be quick to anger, for anger lodges in the bosom of fools" (NRSV). Likewise, Proverbs 15:18 says, "A hot-tempered man stirs up strife, but he who is slow to anger quiets contention" (ESV) and Proverbs 16:32, "Whoever is slow to anger is better than the mighty, and he who rules his spirit than he who takes a city" (ESV). These are powerful words, reminding us of the significance of patience in its ability to guard communication across social media as well as the spread of anger and miscommunication concerning broader political discourse.

A canonical survey of the concept of patience is lengthy. Multiple passages in the New Testament exhort patience, including Ephesians 4:2–3: "Be completely humble and gentle; be patient, bearing with one another in love. Make every effort to keep the unity of the Spirit through the bond of peace" (NIV). From this passage and others, we see that patience is

---

[220] Augustine, *Morals of the Catholic Church* 22, p. 339.

essential for maintaining unity in relationships, whether in the home, church, or broader common good through the *polis*, or city.

The virtue of patience does not deny the role of righteous anger toward injustice. In the Gospel narratives, Jesus Christ demonstrates righteous anger toward those exploiting sacrifice and spiritual worship for economic gain (Matt 21:12–13; Mark 11:15–19; Luke 19:45–48; John 2:13–16). But anger is to be evaluated closely in light of the passages on patience. Medieval theology recognizes anger as a deadly sin given the temptation to live in anger. Often fueled by our own self-justification or self-perception, we live with partial perspective. We fail to consider the whole circumstance, which requires empathically entering another's perspective. Understanding or at least entertaining a differing perspective requires patience and reflection. According to Nicholas Carr, the internet stimulates short-term memory and adrenaline fostering impulse as opposed to whole regions of our brain (long-term memory) more inclined to deep thinking and contemplation.[221] Too easily we respond on social media with impulse rather than patience.[222]

Time spent in nature, reading a book, or dialoguing with another face to face encourages empathy and slow, relaxed thinking. With the rapid communication of social media and our digitally connected lives, we need these deeper contemplative and meditative practices that build relationships, reflection, and the common good. We need to live in communities of conversation across difference, facing God and neighbor in ways that shape us for our good. Patience grows stronger through practice and matures relationships through, not despite, difference.[223]

(8) Love

Such hope, fortitude, and patience are tied to love. Love is the pinnacle virtue for Augustine. Love unites us with Christ and moves us through time. With faith and hope, love attaches us to God and neighbor in appropriate and ordered ways. As Gregory says, Augustinian love includes possibility and limits that prevent us from ignoring the neighbor or subsuming the

---

[221] Nicholas Carr, *The Shallows: What the Internet Is Doing to Our Brains* (W. W. Norton, 2011), 113–25, 212–13, 219–20.

[222] See Max Fisher, *The Chaos Machine: The Inside Story of How Social Media Rewired Our Minds and Our World* (Back Bay, 2023), 96–97.

[223] See Matthew D. Kim, "How to Disagree in Love," *Christianity Today*, October 2023, https://www.christianitytoday.com/2023/09/handle-toxic-friendships-empathy-unity-conflict/.

neighbor in our own selfish projects.[224] Love is tied to justice, which he likens to the divine and human natures of Christ.[225] Scripture continually holds justice together with love. The Ten Commandments describe responsibilities we owe God and neighbor. Jesus summarizes the whole law in terms of love toward God and neighbor. Love does not exclude but promotes and fulfills justice. Whereas we fall short in fulfilling justice, Jesus Christ, the God-man, pays our debt through his death and resurrection.[226] He extends justice through mercy and challenges us to live by reflecting love, mercy, and justice.

Love with justice also entails seeing and listening to the neighbor in their particularity. This involves receptivity with confrontation.[227] Confrontation without receptivity results in harm while receptivity alone risks stunting growth.[228] Instead, love receives the other with a spirit of hospitality while aiming at another's good. This is the space where transformation occurs. In the context of unconditional love, Brooks says, "wise people help you come up with a different way of looking at yourself, your past, and the world around you."[229]

This is precisely how the Gospel narratives display Jesus interacting with individuals, whether the woman at the well, the woman caught in adultery, Zacchaeus, or Mary's sister Martha. He lovingly challenges each individual with compassion. In every case Jesus pauses to see them, while challenging them to become more. Refusing to leave them in their former patterns of sin, dissatisfaction, or social marginalization, he confronts them with love and the possibility for change, lifting them up. Such love is empowering and transformative.

Receptivity and confrontation are important spiritual practices for "life together" in formational communities today.[230] Receiving and confronting Christ through the Scriptures and communion offers the possibility for reflection, change, and transformation. Hebrews 4:12–13 says, "For the

[224] Gregory, *Politics and the Order of Love*.
[225] Gregory, *Politics and the Order of Love*, 175–96.
[226] Col 2:13–14. I do not articulate an entire atonement theory here. However, for more insight on interpretations of atonement from Augustine's theology see Ridenour, *Sabbath Rest as Vocation*, 123–33.
[227] Brooks, *How to Know a Person*, 259; see also Henri J. M. Nouwen, *Reaching Out: The Three Movements of the Spiritual Life* (Image Books, 1966), 99, cited in Brooks, *How to Know a Person*.
[228] Brooks, *How to Know a Person*, 259.
[229] Brooks, *How to Know a Person*, 250.
[230] Dietrich Bonhoeffer, *Life Together* (Harper & Row Publishers, 1954), 27–28.

word of God is living and active, sharper than any double-edged sword, it penetrates even to dividing soul and spirit, joints and marrow; it judges the thoughts and attitudes of the heart. Nothing in all creation is hidden from God's sight. Everything is uncovered and laid bare before the eyes of him to whom we must give account" (NIV). As we encounter Christ through Scripture, we look in a mirror, as Augustine describes. We come to the Scripture to be transformed—a posture willing to receive confrontation through the loving gaze of Christ. In the face of Christ, through Word and community, we are exposed, transformed, and uplifted through the fullness of love. Receptivity and confrontation cause us to face the neighbor with love in humility, leading to justice.

(9) Justice

Justice in the digital empire bears significant weight. Dividing virtual reality from the real world, individuals on social media perform moral behaviors and communication not permitted in the real world. Online behaviors can offer the mask of anonymity, eluding certain forms of moral responsibility.[231] In Plato's *Republic*, Glaucon and Socrates dialogue about whether justice or power brings happiness. Glaucon argues that power found through discovering a magical ring offering invisibility would change moral behavior. If anonymous, Glacon believes individuals would wield their own interest at the expense of the common good.[232] Ironically, social media and digital communication offer the cloak of anonymity through online comments and malicious hacking. Does social media not foster a sense of power through anonymity that erases moral obligation and responsibility to the greater good?

At the same time, online words and behaviors impact the real world in new ways. False information spread on social media induces harm. Fact-checking is significant for preventing the spread of lies and for raising public consciousness through virtue. Justice includes honesty even when truthfulness is uncomfortable across party lines. The importance of not bearing false witness against one's neighbor persists as trust erodes in the absence of a commitment to truth. Justice also demands respect

---

[231]   See Irina Raicu, "To Read—or Not to Read—the Comments: An Ethics Case Study," Markkula Center for Applied Ethics, Santa Clara University, March 1, 2014, https://www.scu.edu/ethics/focus-areas/internet-ethics/resources/to-read--or-not-to-read--the-comments/.

[232]   See Plato, *Republic*, 35–37; see also Mattison, *Introducing Moral Theology*, 21–25.

for human dignity—all creatures made in the image and likeness of God. Brooks compares respect to air: necessary to live, it remains unnoticed unless missing.[233]

Justice guards against bias or privileging in-groups at the expense of difference, which leads to treating others in dehumanizing ways. Justice recognizes that social sin and structural sin develop over time. Augustine reflects on the ways in which group sin snowballs and subtly changes our perspective, desiring security apart from Christ. The kingdom of God, a reality exemplified in Mary's song, lifts up the lowly, hungry, and poor.[234] Justice elevates the marginalized and oppressed by combating racial injustice against minorities, online pornography targeting youth, conspiracy theories that ricochet across social media, or misinformation targeting Myanmar's Rohingya Muslims that ends in genocide.[235]

Justice also protects against identity theft and copyright violations perpetrated by the digital empire, setting up new forms of AI in safe and humane ways.[236] Deepfakes should be regulated if not illegal.[237] Jurisprudence around copyright laws, defamation, and fact-checking should shape our political discourse and digital practices. Current anonymity and communication without accountability breeds problems. While freedom of speech is a high value and should be preserved for liberal democracies, at the same time, communication without accountability is irresponsible.[238] Balancing freedom of speech with responsibility is paramount for public trust and the common good. Information shared across the internet has

[233] David Brooks, "The Essential Skills for Being Human," *New York Times*, October 19, 2023, https://www.nytimes.com/2023/10/19/opinion/social-skills-connection.html; idem, *How Know a Person*, 116.

[234] Luke 1:46–56; McCaulley, *Reading While Black*, 84–90.

[235] See McCaulley, *Reading While Black*; Haidt, *Anxious Generation*, 185–89; Stephanie Pappas, "Conspiracy Theories Can Be Undermined with These Strategies, New Analysis Shows," *Scientific American*, April 5, 2023, https://www.scientificamerican.com/article/how-can-you-fight-conspiracy-theories/; Human Rights Watch, "Myanmar: No Justice, No Freedom for Ronigya 5 Years On," August 24, 2022, https://www.hrw.org/news/2022/08/24/myanmar-no-justice-no-freedom-rohingya-5-years.

[236] Charlie Warzel, "OpenAI Just Gave Away the Entire Game," *Atlantic*, May 21, 2024, https://www.theatlantic.com/technology/archive/2024/05/openai-scarlett-johansson-sky/678446/.

[237] Ian Sample, "What Are Deepfakes and How Can You Spot Them?" *Guardian*, January 13, 2020, https://www.theguardian.com/technology/2020/jan/13/what-are-deepfakes-and-how-can-you-spot-them.

[238] Bremmer and Suleyman, "AI Power Paradox."

moral and societal consequences. Justice avoids vilifying our neighbor through tropes and character assassination. Disagreement will occur, but reasoned arguments are needed. Public discourse should avoid vicious language that harms the neighbor and society at large.

Cultivating virtue is the best path for preserving individual freedoms. But compounded vices and harmful practices require more regulation. In order to preserve the freedoms we cherish in democratic societies, we need more virtue, not less. We cultivate virtue best in small, formational communities. Growing in virtue through interpersonal relationships, neighborhoods, and civic relations helps foster more virtue in the broader digital space.[239]

Justice also protects those negatively impacted by new forms of AI. In *Code Dependent*, Murgia tracks how contemporary AI, designed around questionable algorithms, practices "data colonialism," targeting marginalized groups based on race, geography, and gender with problematic policing, pornographic deepfakes, identity theft, and labor exploitation.[240] She calls for collective action against Big Tech and increased regulation. Participating in justice moves us beyond our own sphere to care for others through policies that protect minority groups and data workers.

Justice also recognizes growing pressures on adolescents and the challenges social media poses to mental, emotional, social, and academic health. Individuals and groups who cultivate justice might also participate in Haidt's suggestions for collective action through "voluntary coordination" that pursues "social norms and moralization," "technological solutions," and "laws and rules" that protect minors.[241] Such collective action protects adolescents and other vulnerable groups against harm while balancing reasonable personal freedoms. Haidt's collective action strategies echo Ramsey's clarion call to protect the interest of children against medical or, in this case, economic experimentation when it contradicts their best interests.[242] Likewise, pursuing strategic goals, policies, rules, and best practices for government, schools, and

---

[239] See David Brooks, "How America Got Mean," *Atlantic*, September 2023, https://www.theatlantic.com/magazine/archive/2023/09/us-culture-moral-education -formation/674765/.

[240] Murgia, *Code Dependent*, 71.

[241] See Haidt's fourth unit on collective action strategies in Haidt, *Anxious Generation*, 223–26.

[242] Haidt, *Anxious Generation*, 232–39; Ramsey, "Enforcement of Morals."

personal households helps to build communal bonds and healthier opportunities for children to flourish.[243]

(10) Mercy and Forgiveness

Justice is also tied to mercy, forgiveness, and ultimately redemption. Whether in the case of Joseph facing his brothers after grave offense or Christ's prayer for forgiveness of his executioners on the cross, Scripture attests that mercy extends the possibility for forgiveness. As the "doctor of grace," Augustine cannot understand his identity and belonging apart from mercy and forgiveness. Forgiveness and the opportunity for reconciliation draws us into peace with God, ourselves, and one another. The aim of justice ends in peace.[244] Forgiveness does not overlook the claims of justice, whether historical or biblical. Instead, reconciliation through the cross entails justice.[245] The kingdom and presence of God is one of *shalom* that remakes relations formerly wrought with conflict and misunderstanding. The city ends in harmony and peace for our material and digital creations.

Unfortunately, mercy and forgiveness are challenging concepts for social media and internet platforms that never forget. YHWH promises to forget sins as far as east from west (Ps 103:12). YHWH blots out the sins of Israel through covenant love (Isa 38:17; 43:25). The teachings of Jesus remind us to forgive not seven times, but seventy times seven (Matt 18:21–22). Yet forgiveness in the divine economy is costly; the cross of Jesus is the pinnacle symbol of this cost. Justice fulfills love while extending mercy. Still, supporting forgiveness includes guarding against cheap demands for forgiveness that dismiss personal or institutional harm.[246] Cheap responses are dissatisfying.[247] Humility and repentance are required

---

[243] See his discussion in Haidt, *Anxious Generation*, 227–95, as well as his Substack, After Babel, at https://www.afterbabel.com/.

[244] Augustine, *City of God* 19 (trans. Bettenson).

[245] See McCaulley, *Reading While Black*, 72–95.

[246] See Jacob and Rachel Denhollander, "Justice: The Foundation of a Christian Approach to Abuse" (paper presented at the 70th Annual Meeting of the Evangelical Theological Society, Denver, November 13, 2018), https://www.fathommag.com/stories/justice-the-foundation-of-a-christian-approach-to-abuse, cited in Timothy Keller, *Forgive: Why Should I and How Can I?* (Penguin Books, 2022), 99.

[247] Depending on the level of offense, forgiveness should be pursued wisely, graciously, and justly. Healthy forgiveness leading to reconciliation involves truth, justice, and time. See Nicholas Rowe and Sheila Wise Rowe, *Healing Leadership Trauma* (IVP, 2024), 118–43. I am also grateful for conversations with Karen E.

for the transformation that leads to reconciliation. Reconciled relationships require time and work toward restoration.

The difficulty in communication across digital platforms involves the flat and reductionistic ways media outlets portray the neighbor as "other" rather than as fellow bearers of God's image. Being quick to judge enlivens the "chaos machine."[248] Instead, disciples should be "quick to listen, slow to speak, and slow to become angry" (Jas 1:19 NIV). Information is shared at lightning speed in decontextualized ways across communities and sows confusion, doubt, and harm. Habits of hastily delivered content are irresponsible. Yet we live in a culture of impulse, instant gratification, and quick judgments, propelling a culture of vindictiveness rather than grace.[249] An empathic, gracious approach to life involves deep listening and reflection. The contemplative, intentional life requires slowing down. Spiritual disciplines take time in formative community. Silence and contemplation are significant for cultivating self-reflection and openness to God as well as neighbor.[250]

Once an ascetic practice for mystics and those devoted to religious life, cultivating the habit of silence is profoundly important for listening to God through the Spirit. Silence is a sort of fasting from words, offering space for deep reflection on God as well as our own behavior, motivations, and sinful attitudes.[251] Silence makes way for communion through listening. Solitude and silence are essential ingredients for relating to others and cultivating empathy.[252] Likewise, reading diverse

---

Mason, Professor of Counseling and Psychology at Gordon-Conwell Theological Seminary, on this topic. For further resources on truth and forgiveness see Ken Sande, *Peacemaker: A Biblical Guide to Resolving Personal Conflict* (Baker, 1997), 190; Miroslav Volf, *Exclusion and Embrace: A Theological Exploration of Identity, Otherness, and Reconciliation* (Abingdon, 1996), 29; E. L. Worthington Jr. et al., "Forgiving Usually Takes Time: A Lesson Learned by Studying Interventions to Promote Forgiveness," *Journal of Psychology and Theology* 28, no. 1 (2000): 3–20.

[248] Fisher, *Chaos Machine*.

[249] See Alan Jacobs on vindictiveness, cited in Keller, *Forgive*, 33.

[250] See Cardinal Robert Sarah, *The Power of Silence: Against the Dictatorship of Noise* (Ignatius, 2017).

[251] Sarah, *Power of Silence*. Felicia Wu Song discusses helpful practical ways for cultivating silence and sacred spaces she calls "Walden zones" as well as "Commitments to Ordered Digital Life" (Song, *Restless Devices*, 186–88, 205).

[252] Sherry Turkle, *Reclaiming Conversation: The Power of Talk in a Digital Age* (Penguin Books, 2015); Bonhoeffer, *Life Together*; Marva J. Dawn, *Keeping the Sabbath Wholly: Ceasing, Resting, Embracing, Feasting* (Eerdmans, 1989).

materials and encountering diverse perspectives grant us empathy. Seeking wisdom through difference helps us evaluate information and delivery through social media with discernment.[253] A life of virtue aims to cultivate reflection and engagement with the digital empire through wisdom, accountability, and mercy.

(11) Presence

Finally, living faithfully and intentionally through love requires presence. Presence is the posture of love embodied in time: intentional nearness, concern, and care for the other. Hunter describes the importance of the church's faithful presence through humility and incarnational witness in its cultural and political posture.[254] In this way the church cultivates important virtues through spiritual formation, offering alternative plausibility structures for a world often confused in the digital matrix.[255] Similarly, Anabaptist theologian James McClendon describes presence as a virtue cultivated in faithful, embodied communities of practice.[256] The doctrine of the incarnation—the Word become flesh—as well as Pauline references to the church as body of Christ reiterate the importance of embodied communities.[257] Embodiment is fundamental for encountering the risen Christ through word, sacrament, and community, particularly when practicing the two central ordinances—baptism and communion.

Paul acknowledges the reality of spiritual presence even in the context of bodily absence (1 Cor 5:3).[258] The letter emphasizes the beauty found in the fellowship of embodied presence but also recognizes we are sometimes, if not often, distant in time and space. While embodied togetherness is better, spiritual presence and solidarity are significant. In this way digital communication—like letter writing for Paul—still contributes to community. The distance of digital communication is acceptable, but such interactions are best when tied to embodied relationships in real time and space.[259] Likewise, prioritizing real world relationships over virtual

[253] O'Neil, *Weapons of Math Destruction*. On the role of reading and literature for developing empathy see Brooks, "Essential Skills for Being Human."

[254] Hunter, *To Change the World*, 283.

[255] Hunter, *To Change the World*, 283.

[256] James William McClendon Jr., *Systematic Theology*, vol. 1, *Ethics* (Abingdon, 2001), 77.

[257] McClendon, *Ethics*, 115–16.

[258] McClendon, *Ethics*, 116.

[259] This is also my interpretation of lexical ordering for prioritizing real-world relationships over virtual relationships in their capacity to morally shape us.

relationships is significant for moral formation. The beginning and end of time implies united presence between body and soul—Christ and the church. Loving both the neighbor and church through time is a way of encountering divine presence among God's image bearers.

In the face of injustice and suffering, McClendon describes the importance of embodiment for worship, hope, and solidarity.[260] Embodied presence draws community together through shared narrative, song, and hope.[261] Such empathic, embodied presence informs Bonhoeffer's communal approach for *Life Together* and his emphasis on the importance of sharing burdens across the body of Christ in which discipleship is costly.[262] Spending time in Harlem's Abyssinian Baptist Church shaped Bonhoeffer's ethic around "vicarious representative action," or co-suffering. This ethic led him to return to Nazi Germany, facing injustice with resistance.[263]

We learn from embodied worship. Physical presence cultivates solidarity with the suffering neighbor and draws us into empathic "strong ties" rather than "weak ties" associated with digital communities.[264] Strong ties evoke love in action. McClendon defines the virtue of presence as "the quality of being there and for the other."[265] "Being there" recognizes the difference between physical presence and absence as well as emotional presence and absence. Both physical and emotional presence are necessary to draw us into the life of the other's needs, interests, and concerns.

Presence involves an intentional posture and key relational ingredients including attention, accompaniment, and the art of conversation.[266] The moral life entails "the everyday acts of encounter. It is the simple capacity

Prioritizing long-term relationships and fidelity as opposed to low commitment ties that we join and quit with ease reflects faithfulness and steadfastness inherent to religious practice. See also Haidt, *Anxious Generation*, 9–10.

[260] McClendon, *Ethics*, 88, 116–17.

[261] McClendon, *Ethics*; John W. Doberstein, introduction to Bonhoeffer, *Life Together*, 7–13; Reggie L. Williams, *Bonhoeffer's Black Jesus: Harlem Renaissance Theology and an Ethics of Resistance* (Baylor University Press, 2014; 2021), 9–22.

[262] McClendon, *Ethics*; Doberstein, introduction to Bonhoeffer, *Life Together*; Williams, *Bonhoeffer's Black Jesus*.

[263] Williams, *Bonhoeffer's Black Jesus*, 9–10, 19–22.

[264] Turkle, *Reclaiming Conversation*, 297.

[265] McClendon, *Ethics*, 116.

[266] Brooks, "Essential Skills for Being Human"; Brooks, *How to Know a Person*.

to make another person feel seen and understood—that hard but essential skill that makes a person a treasured co-worker, citizen, lover, spouse, and friend."[267] Presence shaped by empathy sees the neighbor as *imago dei*, known and beloved by God. Loving the other, we see the face of God.

Experiencing a gnawing sense of absence while desiring divine presence, Augustine says, "We are made for you and our hearts are restless until they rest in you."[268] We are made for belonging through relationship—resting in the presence of God. Our created identity resides in belonging to our Creator and Re-creator. Belonging shapes identity through union with divine love. The arc of belonging through grace involves God's presence with his people from beginning to end, individually and communally.

Presence is provided in the garden, promised in the covenants, and proven in the exodus—along with the incarnation, resurrection, and gift of Pentecost where, in direct contrast to the Tower of Babel, a gathered people are unified through the Holy Spirit. Gifted with the Spirit and divine presence, the gathered people communicate through many languages across difference (Acts 2:1–47). Here the presence of God is embodied in a new temple and the diverse people of God. In worshiping God together they are unified. Individuals offer their bodies as living sacrifices that manifest God's presence (Rom 12:1–2). Whenever and wherever the fruit of the Spirit is manifest, we usher in the kingdom, participating in a new, inaugurated reality while awaiting its fulfillment.

For Augustine (as well as Ellul) the end and means are united. Loving God through loving the neighbor is the way we manifest the presence of the kingdom in time.[269] Loving the neighbor and the common good includes the way we engage social media and digital practices. As it reshapes our vision, faith manifest through love should profoundly impact our digital habits—as users, designers, and deployers of new technologies. As human creation, technology awaits its full redemption. But we can begin that process by practicing the role of presence and love such that tech serves human interest rather than the other way around. Presence accompanied by humility, justice, and forgiveness is stronger than our temptation for domination and power—if we have the eyes to see and courage to love.

---

[267] Brooks, *How to Know a Person*, 271.
[268] Augustine, *Confessions* 1.1, p. 3.
[269] See also Tarcisius J. Van Bavel, "Love," in Fitzgerald, *Augustine Through the Ages*, 512.

Conclusion
Till We Have Faces

In his last novel, *Till We Have Faces*, C. S. Lewis plays on the Greek myth of Cupid and Psyche.[1] Changing the setting and meaning behind the characters, the story focuses on two sisters, Psyche and Orual, and their difference in posture and vulnerability. While multiple religious themes infuse Lewis's rewriting of the story, his motif capitalizes on the role of face, whether bare, veiled, or transformed, and is significant for how we think about what it means to image God, as well as our multiple efforts—technological, political, and psychological—to mask our vulnerabilities and identities.

Laced with deeply Augustinian themes, the myth—pointing to what Lewis calls the "true myth"—takes place in the ancient and barbaric land of Glome where two royal half-sisters grow according to their loves.[2] Lewis describes one sister, Psyche, as barefaced and beautiful, portraying innocence, faith, and love, while the other, Orual, veiled and ugly, portrays worldliness, power, and a form of rational skepticism. Commentators recognize elements of Lewis's own faith journey in the skeptical Orual.[3] While complex in its thematic breadth and devoid of one singular straightforward reading, we can highlight a few points of the novel that relate to Augustinian ideas and the digital empire.

[1]   C. S. Lewis, *Till We Have Faces: A Myth Retold* (1956; HarperOne, 2017).
[2]   Maurice Hunt, *The Divine Face in Four Writers: Shakespeare, Dostoyevsky, Hesse, and C. S. Lewis* (Bloomsbury, 2016), 117.
[3]   Hunt, *Divine Face in Four Writers*, 118.

Psyche, displaying youthful innocence and kindness within the royal family, becomes a symbolic icon for the people of Glome. Yet jealousy and envy ensue, and the crowd turns on her through a barbaric form of sacrificial death. She is found later in the mountains, alive and transfigured, while waiting for Cupid, her divine husband, with joy and affection.

Meanwhile, Orual, a rationalist skeptic like her Greek (Stoic) tutor, the Fox, loves her younger sister Psyche, but with an increasingly possessive and disordered love. After locating the "brightfaced" (transfigured) Psyche on the mountain and learning about her marriage to the god Cupid, she is enraged with a form of disordered love—envy—that cannot bear the idea of sharing Psyche with another. Orual critiques Psyche's marriage and demands she demonstrate loyalty to her through a form of manipulative threat involving self-harm. Psyche concedes, violating her own conscience by foregoing loyalty to the god's wishes. Much like Adam and Eve in the fall from the garden of Eden, both are exiled to a path fraught with challenge and suffering. The novel is largely a story of their remaining journeys, and particularly Orual as the novel's narrator and focus.

One of the key themes throughout the novel involves the role of faces, how they hide our deeper motives and loves or reveal them to the world around us—even ourselves. Orual returns from the mountain wearing a veil over what her father once called an "ugly" face. Hunt considers a variety of commentators' interpretations, concluding that the veil may hide her sense of "shame and guilt over coercing Psyche" or point to "her need for control."[4] Or perhaps "the veil symbolizes Orual's 'inner exile,' . . . 'the physical manifestation of her unwillingness to face the truth.'"[5] One or all these interpretations might be the case.

Hunt discusses the role of face, its hiddenness and disclosure, in terms of power and vulnerability: "Lewis thus emphasizes the powerful advantage over others that the hidden face can give one, whether a man or woman or a god. What it also does, however, and what Orual does not realize, is that obscuring the face isolates its bearer from humankind. Lewis will make the full view of human faces the condition for the giving and receiving of love, for the prompting of moral responsibility for the welfare of others, and for the best realization of one's humanity."[6] Vulnerability, empathy, and responsibility involve the fullness of giving and receiving love when face to face.

[4]   Hunt, *Divine Face in Four Writers*, 130.
[5]   Hunt, *Divine Face in Four Writers*, 130–31.
[6]   Hunt, *Divine Face in Four Writers*, 131.

Throughout the volume Lewis portrays a woman who gains increased political power, eventually becoming Queen of Glome—all while wearing a veil. The veil aids her power over others, beginning with her barbaric father, Trom, and eventually other political leaders whom she defeats. Yet the veil also grants her power over individuals she cares for—overworking them to exhaustion as a kind of devouring love. Near the end of her successful political career, Orual embarks on a journey where she overhears a religious rendition of her personal story—the famous myth of Psyche, Orual, and their commonly overlooked sister, Redival.

Enraged at what she believes to be a misinterpretation and determined to set the record straight, Orual begins writing the story of her life (the novel) and her accusations against the gods. Yet her accusations lead to new revelations about herself as she finally encounters the perspective of others, of those individuals close to her, whom she has completely misunderstood and misjudged from behind her own veil. She is now unveiled and being "unmade" as she encounters difference through the faces and perspectives of those around her, and ultimately the difference that comes from encountering the divine.[7]

Barefaced near the end of part 1 of the novel, Orual finds her sharp, rational accusations and words fall short. She is exposed before the gods and her closest community through a dreamlike haze. Her tome, filled with accusations, dissolves into nothingness, a mere shard to which the gods respond with "no answer."[8] Confused and frustrated, she encounters a legal court surrounded by her closest companions with her life broadcast before her, revealing her once-hidden motives in new ways. Encountering her sister Psyche once more as goddess through a beatific vision, Orual falls to her face in a kind of repentance. She confesses that she never loved Psyche with selflessness, but only with her own interest in mind.[9] As she undergoes a new form of self-recognition through confession and transformation, Orual thinks she's arrived at joy, the fullness of being, but then recognizes this is only a preparation.[10]

As the sunlight grows brighter and the god (formerly known as "the God of the Mountain") approaches with "new terror, joy" and "overpowering sweetness," she is "pierced and unmade."[11] Shortly after recognizing

---

[7]   Lewis, *Till We Have Faces*, 350.
[8]   Lewis, *Till We Have Faces*, 284.
[9]   Lewis, *Till We Have Faces*, 347–49.
[10] Lewis, *Till We Have Faces*, 349.
[11] Lewis, *Till We Have Faces*, 350.

Psyche as "a thousand times more her very self than she had been before the Offering [sacrifice]," Orual says,

> I was being unmade. I was no one. But that's little to say; rather, Psyche herself was, in a manner, no one. I loved her as I would once have thought it impossible to love, would have died any death for her. And yet, it was not, not now, she that really counted. Or if she counted (and oh, gloriously she did) *it was for another's sake.* The earth and stars and sun, all that was or will be, *existed for his sake.* And he was coming. The most dreadful, the most beautiful, the only dread and beauty there is, was coming.[12]

Facing the "dread and beauty" of exposure to the god she once avoided, she looks down to see her reflection in the water appear like Psyche's yet different: "both beautiful (if that mattered now) beyond all imagining, yet not exactly the same."[13] As Orual confronts the end, the means are transformed. Loving for another's (God's) sake orders and transforms all other loves. Hunt concludes that no one encounters the gods "until we have faces." We must be transfigured in love. Confrontation and receptivity. This requires deep and abiding trust that the transformation is for our good—in the full image of God.

Orual is transfigured and changed through imaging God while aided by her companions on the journey. Orual concludes, "I ended my first book with the words 'No answer.' I know now, Lord, why you utter no answer. You are yourself the answer. Before your face questions die away."[14] Orual confesses that her words fall short, not unlike Augustine. In concluding *The Trinity*, Augustine confesses that all human words fall short, praying that whatever is of God might be preserved while whatever is of him might be discarded—in the face of the one who creates and re-creates us.[15]

Awaiting the final vision, Augustine looks to the communion found through complete "divine recognition."[16] Face to face in the presence of the divine, exposed through ultimate vulnerability, we might be transformed through death and resurrection—not only in the future but also through

---

[12]   Lewis, *Till We Have Faces*, 350 (emphasis added).

[13]   Lewis, *Till We Have Faces*, 350.

[14]   Lewis, *Till We Have Faces*, 351.

[15]   Augustine, *The Trinity (De Trinitate)*, ed. John E. Rotelle, trans. Edmund Hill, 2nd ed. (New City Press, 1991), 15 (prayer), p. 444.

[16]   Charles Mathewes, "An Augustinian Look at Empire," *Theology Today* 63, no. 3 (2006): 305.

moments in time. In the presence of God and other we receive identity through belonging and communion—where we finally see, understand, and love.[17] It is one thing to be known and another to be loved. But the greatest of all is to be known and loved. We who are exposed through our weaknesses, fears, and sin on the journey through time are renewed by eternal love. More than a rote prayer rooted in instrumental desire for control, repentance through humility is an ongoing posture of a heart yielded to God in rest.

And yet, while here in exile—*in medias res*—we are tempted to hide, our lives complicated with the defenses and pursuits of political and technological empire. Seeking identity, purpose, and belonging in temporary, material goods—inept in their ability to satisfy—we grow restless. Hiding behind contemporary forms of technology and commodity exchange, we project identity into digital space while seeking recognition through group or social belonging. This pursuit is neither entirely bad nor devoid of meaning, but an Augustinian lens questions the fulfillment purported to be found through the digital empire and demands an accounting for the costs to humanity that our devotion to the empire incurs.

Made in the image of God, we are challenged to consider a greater moral vision and richer existence in embodied communities, not only for the future but also for the here and now. We belong to more than ourselves. We are called to membership. The body of Christ is unified across ecclesial and denominational differences. Similar and different, Christ's members are joined to one another through the God who became other on our behalf. Greater than any empire—political or digital—Christ exposes our illusions of gaining identity or security through mammon, power, false images, or success. We are then exposed for who we really are, through honesty and love. The digital empire is simply one more mask we wear, hiding our fears behind social branding and pronouncements as individuals consumed by the crowd. But as we are drawn into the presence of the One who releases us from performance and productivity, we receive identity through belonging in vulnerability and love. In likeness, we commune with the one we were made to image (Gen 1:26–27; 2 Cor 4:6).

An Augustinian interface with our culture of digital tools awakens us to our current tech reality and its impact on our intellectual, moral, and social development (see chapter 1). Attached to misguided forms of love,

---

[17]   Augustine, *City of God*, trans. Henry Bettenson (Penguin Books, 1984), 22.29–30, pp. 1085–86, 1090–91.

we are tempted to brand ourselves through performance with great cost to our attention, mental health, and relationships. An Augustinian lens exposes our lust for domination (*libido dominandi*) and desire to control through fear and anxiety as disordered attachment. The development of the digital empire masks our desire for meaning through consumption and commodification and flips the means for the end. As Ellul and Augustine suggest, this only results in false forms of power and control.

Communication chaos and confusion ensue. We build illusive communion through decontextualized information and seek knowledge without wisdom (see chapter 2). We desire entertainment and spectacle or knowledge for its own sake and are tempted to disorder our loves. Seeking temporary pleasures leads us to instrumentalize God for the sake of "enjoying" this world. As we imbibe misinformation and propaganda, we descend into groupthink that dehumanizes the neighbor and exchanges the end for means. Instead, the love of God for his own sake reorders knowledge with wisdom. Once awakened beyond ourselves and our myopic vision, we encounter the divine. Preaching not only persuasive words but *the Word* draws individuals to the source of wisdom, the image of God in Christ. Through healing proclamation, wisdom brings wholeness rather than fragmentation and grants identity through belonging. Such belonging reflects our interdependent nature.

Interdependence is found not only between persons but also across the whole of creation in its belonging to God as the "book of nature." We creatures are inscribed with natural limits through time and space that bring identity for our good. But we unfortunately try to use nature for our own instrumental gain, defying its intrinsic meaning and worth (see chapter 3). We crave magic, alchemy, a kind of fool's gold. We desperately try to control nature. Instead, our technologies and counter-creations control us. The digital empire offers benefits at great cost. Trying to escape our limitations (like the followers of Manichaeism) renders us more bound. An Augustinian lens reminds us that we belong not to ourselves but to God. Through beauty in harmony, part to whole, time and eternity, we are made to rest in the One who holds all things together. God suffuses the disparate parts of ourselves together in wholeness. God is greater than our memory, and we receive identity through imaging him in communion and love.

As *imago dei*, we behold the presence of God in the face of others (see chapter 4). Through seeking to know and love we expose our weaknesses and encounter empathy in the face of the neighbor. We are created to image or imitate and so we become who or what we most love. The better the love, the brighter the image. The lesser the love, the duller the image. In the company of Augustine we seek ultimate communion, the final eschatological encounter in which we will see face to face. That hope shapes our teleological vision not only for the future but also for the here and now.

Facing God through time, we are drawn into his presence through the face of Christ. As we are shaped in the humanity and divinity of Christ (as seen through Augustine's preaching of the Psalms) we are transformed by divine presence. Our knowing and loving never cease in our desire for God. As we long for God through shared communion we intentionally seek the presence of God through the gift of neighbor and creation. Through participation in ordinary life and community we are shaped in vulnerability and empathy apart from the performative masks we inhabit in the digital empire. Face to face we disclose our vulnerability and desire for transformation through humility, repentance, and communion.

Presence in the face of difference—between God, self, and neighbor—is best experienced through the placing of constraints on the ambitions of empire. Honoring Sabbath as a divine gift that sets limits on creation brings meaning through an identity received (see chapter 5). In contrast to the drive for ceaseless activity, Augustine reminds us that we're made for ultimate Sabbath rest, while Barth reminds us that God's self-limitation at creation is his willingness to commune with us as gift. Christ and the Sabbath serve as the center and circumference of work along with our technological pursuits.

Rabbi Abraham Joshua Heschel advocates resistance to technological civilization by the practice of Sabbath. The center of eternity's presence in time is found through worship. Unlike Pharaoh and the gods of Babylon, who demand ceaseless productivity, YHWH, the God of Israel, calls his people to cease work. In the cessation of work God's people are called to trust his provision, reminding them that their power and work is never theirs to own or keep. Instead, their produce and power are gifts to share.

In this sense Sabbath relates to play, leisure, joy, and communion. We are made for communion with God, and so Sabbath leisure is more than commodified entertainment—it is rest and spontaneous play in the freedom of our Creator and his creation. As we are transformed through eschatological vision, the beauty of Christ frees us from our performative selves to receive identity from him. In contrast to the dictates of digital empire, we become fully who we are through belonging rather than through proving ourselves by way of mindless work and performative friendship. To make these truths central, the body of Christ is called to practice regular Sabbath habits whereby we cherish the gift of embodied communities in pursuit of justice and love. The patterns of Sabbath help us resist the digital empire and its tyrannous hold on our attention through reprioritization.

Finally, through the implementation of Sabbath practice and intentional presence in the face of neighbor we awaken to the pervasive influences that come from living in the digital empire and our regular temptation for pride and dominion in the city, church, and digital space (see chapter 6). The antidote to our pride and desire for control in the digital empire comes through humility in the presence of the kingdom. The way down is the way up. Following the way of Christ, we are changed through humility and repentance. We find ourselves through losing ourselves. We find rest in belonging and belonging in rest. Exchanging our will for another's breaks through autonomy's self-enclosure and nihilism's self-defeating project. Recognizing that we belong to God and the other we are drawn into communion as a gift to be shared in time and eternity. Christ serves as the ultimate exemplar by his demonstration of humility through the incarnation and his presence with us. In Christ the means are united with the end.

The vision of Christ shows us a new way, seeing through injustice and our half-baked technological projects. We need accountability for our journey through time. A commonwealth redefined by love seeks justice-oriented tech practices for self, community, and other. By recognizing the limits to our own creation and technological ambitions, an Augustinian lens accepts the good in regulation, just habits, and boundaries for our economic and technological desires *in medias res*.

Yet it's simply not enough to issue rules and limits. We should aim for a moral vision captivated by beauty and love. Seeking the presence of the kingdom in time involves teleological union with Christ and moral vision for the here and now. As we enact virtue while eschewing vice, our moral courage is built through humility, prudence, truthfulness, temperance, self-control, hope, fortitude, patience, love, justice, forgiveness, mercy, and intentional presence. The practice of virtue overpowers the desire for control as a hallmark of the digital empire. Grace-filled virtue is essential for envisioning the kingdom until faith becomes sight and at last heaven and earth, time and eternity, are one.

As we await the culmination of this vision, that moment when we are transfigured face to face, "we, who with unveiled faces all reflect the Lord's glory, are being transformed into his likeness with ever-increasing glory which comes from the Lord, who is the Spirit . . . For God, who said, 'Let light shine out of darkness,' made his light shine in our hearts to give us the light of the knowledge of the glory of God in the face of Christ" (2 Cor 3:18; 4:6 NIV).

Epilogue

The Love of God

The love of God is greater far
than tongue or pen can ever tell;
it goes beyond the highest star,
and reaches to the lowest hell.
The guilty pair, bowed down with care,
God gave His Son to win;
His erring child He reconciled,
and pardoned from his sin.

(Refrain)
Oh, love of God, how rich and pure!
How measureless and strong!
It shall forevermore endure—
the saints' and angels' song.

When hoary time shall pass away,
and earthly thrones and kingdoms fall,
when men who here refuse to pray,
on rocks and hills and mountains call,
God's love so sure, shall still endure,
all measureless and strong;
redeeming grace to Adam's race—
the saints' and angels' song.

Could we with ink the ocean fill,
and were the skies of parchment made,
were every stalk on earth a quill,
and every man a scribe by trade;
to write the love of God above
would drain the ocean dry;
nor could the scroll contain the whole,
though stretched from sky to sky.

Frederick M. Lehman, 1917

Bibliography

Alter, Adam. *Drunk Tank Pink: And Other Unexpected Forces That Shape How We Think, Feel, and Behave*. Penguin Books, 2013.

Alter, Adam. *Irresistible: The Rise of Addictive Technology and the Business of Keeping Us Hooked*. Penguin Books, 2017.

Anderson, Ross. "Inside the Revolution at OpenAI." *Atlantic*, September 2023. https://www.theatlantic.com/magazine/archive/2023/09/sam-altman-openai-chatgpt-gpt-4/674764/.

Aquinas, Thomas. *Summa Theologica*. Translated by Fathers of the English Dominican Province. Ave Maria, 1948.

Aronson, Louise. *Elderhood: Redefining Aging, Transforming Medicine, Reimagining Life*. Bloomsbury, 2019.

Augustine. *The Advantage of Believing*. Translated by Ray Kearney. In *On Christian Belief*, edited by Boniface Ramsey. The Works of Saint Augustine: A Translation for the 21st Century, part 1, vol. 8. New City Press, 2005.

Augustine. *The Augustine Catechism: The Enchiridion on Faith, Hope, and Love*. Edited by Boniface Ramsey. Translated by Bruce Harbert. New City Press, 1999; 2008.

Augustine. *The City of God*. Translated by Henry Bettenson. Penguin Books, 1984.

Augustine. *The City of God*. Abridged study edition. Translated by William Babcock. Notes by Boniface Ramsey. Abridgment by Joseph T. Kelley. New City Press, 2018.

Augustine. *Confessions*. Translated by Henry Chadwick. Oxford University Press, 1991.

Augustine. *Enarration in Psalm 86*. In *The Political Writings of St. Augustine*, edited by Henry Paolucci. Regnery Gateway, 1962.

Augustine. *The Essential Augustine.* Edited and translated by Vernon J. Bourke. Hackett, 1974.

Augustine. *Essential Expositions of the Psalms.* Edited by Michael Cameron. New City Press, 2015.

Augustine. *Essential Sermons.* Edited by Daniel Doyle. The Works of Saint Augustine: A Translation for the 21st Century. New City Press, 2007.

Augustine. *Expositions of the Psalms 1–32.* Edited by John E. Rotelle. Translated by Maria Boulding. The Works of Saint Augustine: A Translation for the 21st Century, part 3, vol. 15. New City Press, 2000.

Augustine. *Expositions of the Psalms 33–50.* Edited by John E. Rotelle. Translated by Maria Boulding. The Works of Saint Augustine: A Translation for the 21st Century, part 3, vol. 16. New City Press, 2000.

Augustine. *Expositions of the Psalms 51–72.* Edited by John E. Rotelle. Translated by Maria Boulding. The Works of Saint Augustine: A Translation for the 21st Century, part 3, vol. 17. New City Press, 2001.

Augustine. *Expositions of the Psalms 73–98.* Edited by John E. Rotelle. Translated by Maria Boulding. The Works of Saint Augustine: A Translation for the 21st Century, part 3, vol. 18. New City Press, 2002.

Augustine. *Expositions of the Psalms 99–120.* Edited by John E. Rotelle. Translated by Maria Boulding. The Works of Saint Augustine: A Translation for the 21st Century, part 3, vol. 19. New City Press, 2004.

Augustine. *Expositions of the Psalms 121–150.* Edited by Boniface Ramsey. Translated by Maria Boulding. The Works of Saint Augustine: A Translation for the 21st Century, part 3, vol. 20. New City Press, 2004.

Augustine. *Homilies on the First Epistle of John.* Edited by Daniel E. Doyle and Thomas Martin. The Works of Saint Augustine: A Translation for the 21st Century, part 3, vol. 14. New City Press, 2008.

Augustine. *Instructing Beginners in the Faith.* In *Morality and Christian Asceticism.* Edited by Boniface Ramsey. Translated by Raymond Canning. The Works of Saint Augustine: A Translation for the 21st Century, part 1, vol. 10. New City Press, 2023.

Augustine. *The Literal Meaning of Genesis.* In *On Genesis,* edited by John E. Rotelle, translated by Edmund Hill. The Works of Saint Augustine: A Translation for the 21st Century, part 1, vol. 13. New City Press, 2002.

Augustine. *The Morals of the Catholic Church.* In *Basic Writings of St. Augustine,* vol. 1, edited by Whitney J. Oates. Random House, 1948.

Augustine. *On Christian Teaching.* Translated by R. P. H. Green. Oxford University Press, 1997.

Augustine. *On Genesis: A Refutation of the Manichees.* In *On Genesis,* edited by John E. Rotelle, translated by Edmund Hill. The Works of Saint Augustine: A Translation for the 21st Century 1.13. New City Press, 2002.

Augustine. *The Teacher (De Magistro).* In *Augustine: Earlier Writings,* edited and translated by J. H. S. Burleigh. Westminster John Knox, 2006.

Augustine. *The Trinity (De Trinitate)*. Edited by John E. Rotelle. Translated by Edmund Hill. 2nd ed. New City Press, 1991.

Ayres, Lewis. "The Christological Context of Augustine's *De trinitate* XIII: Toward Relocating Books VIII–XV." *Augustinian Studies* 29, no. 1 (1998): 111–39.

Ayres, Lewis. *Nicaea and Its Legacy*. Oxford University Press, 2004.

Barrett, Justin, and Pamela King. *Thriving with Stone Age Minds: Evolutionary Psychology, Christian Faith, and the Quest for Human Flourishing*. IVP, 2021.

Barth, Karl. *The Christian Life: Church Dogmatics IV/4, Lecture Fragments*. Translated by Geoffrey W. Bromiley. Eerdmans, 1981.

Barth, Karl. *Church Dogmatics III/1–4, The Doctrine of Creation*. Edited by T. F. Torrance and Geoffrey W. Bromiley. T&T Clark, 2004.

Bauman, Zygmunt. *Wasted Lives: Modernity and Its Outcasts*. Polity, 2004.

Beane, Matt. "Gen AI Is Coming for Remote Workers First." *Harvard Business Review*, July 22, 2024. https://hbr.org/2024/07/gen-ai-is-coming-for -remote-workers-first.

Becker, Ernest. *The Denial of Death*. Free Press, 1973.

Bellah, Robert, Richard Madsen, William Sullivan, Ann Swidler, and Steven Tipton. *Habits of the Heart: Individualism and Commitment in American Life*. University of California Press, 1985.

Berger, Peter L. *The Sacred Canopy: Elements of a Sociological Theory of Religion*. Anchor, 1990.

Berry, Wendell. *The Memory of Old Jack*. Counterpoint, 1974.

Billings, J. Todd, *Union with Christ: Reframing Theology and Ministry*. Baker Academic, 2011.

Bishop, Jeffrey P. *The Anticipatory Corpse*. University of Notre Dame Press, 2011.

Bogost, Ian. "The Age of Social Media Is Ending: It Never Should Have Begun." *Atlantic*, November 10, 2022. https://www.theatlantic.com/technology/ archive/2022/11/twitter-facebook-social-media-decline/672074/.

Bogost, Ian. "AI Has Lost Its Magic." *Atlantic*, April 4, 2024. https://www .theatlantic.com/technology/archive/2024/04/ai-magic-taking-over/ 677968.

Bonhoeffer, Dietrich. *Life Together*. Harper & Row Publishers, 1954.

Bonner, Gerald. "Deification, Divinization." In *Augustine Through the Ages*, edited by Allan D. Fitzgerald, 265–66. Eerdmans, 1999.

Borgmann, Albert. *Technology and the Character of Contemporary Life: A Philosophical Inquiry*. University of Chicago Press, 1984.

Bostrom, Nick. "A History of Transhumanist Thought." *Journal of Evolution and Technology* 14, no. 1 (2005): 1–25.

Brandt, Anthony K. "Beethoven's Ninth and A.I.'s Tenth: A Comparison of Human and Computational Creativity." *Journal of Creativity* 33, no. 3 (2023): 1–9.

Bremmer, Ian, and Mustafa Suleyman. "The AI Power Paradox: Can States Learn to Govern Artificial Intelligence—Before It's Too Late?" *Foreign Affairs* 102, no. 5 (2023): 26–43.

Brock, Brian R. *Wondrously Wounded: Theology, Disability, and the Body of Christ*. Baylor University Press, 2020.

Brooks, David. "How America Got Mean." *Atlantic*, August 14, 2023. https://www.theatlantic.com/magazine/archive/2023/09/us-culture-moral-education-formation/674765/.

Brooks, David. *How to Know a Person: The Art of Seeing Others Deeply and Being Deeply Seen*. Random House, 2023.

Brooks, David. *The Road to Character*. Random House, 2015.

Brueggemann, Walter. *Sabbath as Resistance: Saying No to the Culture of Now*. Westminster John Knox, 2014.

Bugnion, François. "Just Wars, Wars of Aggression and International Humanitarian Law." *International Review of the Red Cross* 84, no. 847 (2002): 523–46. https://icrcndresourcecentre.org/wp-content/uploads/2019/08/JUSTWARS.pdf.

Calvin, John. *Institutes of the Christian Religion*. Edited by John T. McNeill. Westminster John Knox, 1960.

Cameron, Michael. "*Enarrationes in Psalmos*." In *Augustine Through the Ages*, edited by Allan D. Fitzgerald. Eerdmans, 1999.

Cameron, Michael. General introduction to *Essential Expositions of the Psalms*, by Augustine, edited by Michael Cameron. New City Press, 2015.

Carr, Nicholas. *The Shallows: What the Internet Is Doing to Our Brains*. W. W. Norton, 2011.

Cavadini, John. "Pride." In *Augustine Through the Ages*, edited by Allan D. Fitzgerald. Eerdmans, 1999.

Cipriani, Nello. "Memory." Translated by Matthew O'Connell. In *Augustine Through the Ages*, edited by Allan D. Fitzgerald. Eerdmans, 1999.

Claghorn, George S. "Introduction to Related Correspondence." In *Ethical Writings*, vol. 8 of *The Works of Jonathan Edwards*, edited by Paul Ramsey. Yale University Press, 1989.

Clark, Mary T. "Image Doctrine." In *Augustine Through the Ages*, edited by Allan D. Fitzgerald. Eerdmans, 1999.

Collins, Francis. "Science and Faith: Conflict or Complement?" Sermon, Park Street Church, Boston, February 28, 2010. https://www.parkstreet.org/messages/evening-sermon-science-amp-faith-conflict-or-complement/.

Comer, John Mark. *The Ruthless Elimination of Hurry*. Waterbrook, 2019.

Crouch, Andy. *The Life We're Looking For: Reclaiming Relationship in a Technological World*. Convergent, 2022.

Crouch, Andy. *Playing God: Redeeming the Gift of Power*. IVP, 2013.

Crouch, Andy. *The Techwise Family*. Baker Books, 2017.

Davis, Jim, and Michael Graham, with Ryan P. Burge. *The Great Dechurching: Who's Leaving, Why Are They Going, and What Will It Take to Bring Them Back?* Zondervan Reflective, 2023.

Dawn, Marva J. *Keeping the Sabbath Wholly: Ceasing, Resting, Embracing, Feasting.* Eerdmans, 1989.

Dindal, Mark, dir. *Chicken Little.* Disney, 2005.

Djuth, Marianne. "Will." In *Augustine Through the Ages*, edited by Allan D. Fitzerald. Eerdmans, 1999.

Doberstein, John W. Introduction to *Life Together*, by Dietrich Bonhoeffer. Harper & Row Publishers, 1954.

Dodaro, Robert. *Christ and the Just Society in the Thought of St. Augustine.* Cambridge University Press, 2004.

Downing, Raymond. *Death and Life in America.* 2nd ed. Cascade, 2021.

Doyle, Daniel E. "Introduction to Augustine's Preaching." In *Essential Sermons*, by Augustine, edited by Daniel E. Doyle. New City Press, 2007.

Duffy, Stephen J. "Anthropology." In *Augustine Through the Ages*, edited by Allan D. Fitzgerald. Eerdmans, 1999.

Dugdale, L. S. *The Lost Art of Dying.* HarperOne, 2020.

Dukas, Paul, dir. "The Sorcerer's Apprentice." In *Fantasia*. Walt Disney Productions, 1940.

Dunnington, Kent. *Addiction and Virtue: Beyond the Models of Disease and Choice.* IVP Academic, 2011.

Edwards, Jonathan. *Ethical Writings.* Vol. 8 of *The Works of Jonathan Edwards*. Edited by Paul Ramsey. Yale University Press, 1989.

Edwards, Jonathan. *Selected Writings of Jonathan Edwards.* 2nd ed. Edited by Harold P. Simonson. Waveland Press, 2004.

Ellul, Jacques. *The Meaning of the City.* Translated by Dennis Pardee. Wipf and Stock, 2003.

Ellul, Jacques. *The Presence of the Kingdom.* Translated by Olive Wyon. Helmers & Howard, 1989.

Ellul, Jacques. *Propaganda: The Formation of Men's Attitudes.* Translated by Konrad Kellen and Jean Lerner. Knopf, 1968.

Ellul, Jacques. *The Technological Society.* Translated by John Wilkinson. Knopf, 1964.

Erikson, Erik H., and Joan M. Erickson. *The Life Cycle Completed.* W. W. Norton, 1997.

European Commission. "AI Act: Shaping Europe's Digital Future." https://digital-strategy.ec.europa.eu/en/policies/regulatory-framework-ai.

European Parliament. "EU AI Act: First Regulation on Artificial Intelligence." 2023. https://www.europarl.europa.eu/topics/en/article/20230601STO93804/eu-ai-act-first-regulation-on-artificial-intelligence.

Evans, G. R. *Augustine on Evil.* Cambridge University Press, 1982.

Eyal, Nir. *Hooked: How to Form Habit-Forming Products.* Portfolio, 2014.

Fadling, Alan. *An Unhurried Life: Following Jesus' Rhythms of Work and Rest.* IVP, 2013.

Fisher, Max. *The Chaos Machine: The Inside Story of How Social Media Rewired Our Minds and Our World.* Back Bay, 2023.

Ford, David F. *Self and Salvation: Being Transformed.* Cambridge University Press, 1999.

Galli, Mark. "A Theology of Play: We Don't Have to Always Be Doing Something Useful." *Christianity Today*, June 21, 2017. https://www.christianitytoday.com/2017/06/thou-shalt-have-good-time/.

Gay, Craig M. *Modern Technology and the Human Future: A Christian Appraisal.* IVP Academic, 2018.

Gertz, Nolen. *Nihilism and Technology.* Rowman & Littlefield International, 2018.

Gill, David W. "A Fourth Use of the Law? The Decalogue in the Workplace." *Journal of Religion and Business Ethics* 2, no. 2 (2011): 1–18.

Gill, David W., and David Lovekin, eds. *Political Illusion and Reality: Engaging the Prophetic Insights of Jacques Ellul.* Pickwick, 2018.

Gill, Robin. *Health Care and Christian Ethics.* Cambridge University Press, 2006.

Gladwell, Malcolm. *Revenge of the Tipping Point: Overstories, Superspreaders, and the Rise of Social Engineering.* Little, Brown, 2024.

Gladwell, Malcolm. *The Tipping Point: How Little Things Can Make a Big Difference.* Back Bay, 2000.

Graham, Billy. *How to Become a Christian.* Good News, 2016.

Graham, Billy. "Technology, Faith, and Human Shortcomings." TED Talk, February 1998. https://www.ted.com/talks/billy_graham_on_technology_and_faith.

Graham, David A. "Trump Isn't Merely Unhinged." *Atlantic*, November 13, 2023. https://www.theatlantic.com/ideas/archive/2023/11/donald-trump-15-most-dangerous-statements/675970/.

Grant, George. "In Defence of North America." In *Technology and Empire*. Anansi Press, 1969; 2018.

Gregory, Eric. "Politics." In *The Oxford Handbook of Evangelical Theology*, edited by Gerald R. McDermott. Oxford University Press, 2010.

Gregory, Eric. *Politics and the Order of Love: An Augustinian Ethic of Democratic Citizenship.* University of Chicago Press, 2008.

Haidt, Jonathan. *The Anxious Generation: How the Great Rewiring of Childhood Is Causing an Epidemic of Mental Illness.* Penguin Books, 2024.

Haidt, Jonathan. "Why the Last 10 Years of American Life Have Been Uniquely Stupid." *Atlantic*, April 11, 2022. https://www.theatlantic.com/magazine/archive/2022/05/social-media-democracy-trust-babel/629369/.

Hanson, Jeffrey. *Philosophies of Work in the Platonic Tradition: A History of Labor and Human Flourishing.* Bloomsbury Academic, 2022.

Harris, Tristan, and Aza Raskin. "The AI Dilemma." Presentation at the Center for Humane Technology, San Francisco, March 9, 2023. https://www.youtube.com/watch?v=xoVJKj8lcNQ.

Heidegger, Martin. "The Question Concerning Technology." In *The Question Concerning Technology and Other Essays*, translated by William Lovitt. Harper & Row, 1977.

Herdt, Jennifer. *Putting on Virtue: The Legacy of the Splendid Vices*. University of Chicago Press, 2008.

Heschel, Abraham Joshua. *The Sabbath*. Farrar, Straus and Giroux, 1951.

Heschel, Susannah. Introduction to *The Sabbath*, by Abraham Joshua Heschel. Farrar, Straus and Giroux, 1951.

Hitz, Zena. *Lost in Thought: The Hidden Pleasures of an Intellectual Life*. Princeton University Press, 2020.

Hollinger, Dennis P. *Creation and Christian Ethics: Understanding God's Designs for Humanity and the World*. Baker Academic, 2024.

Holt-Lunstad, Julianne, and Carla Perissinotto. "Social Isolation and Loneliness as Medical Issues." *New England Journal of Medicine* 388, no. 3 (2023): 193–95.

Horowitch, Rose. "The Elite College Students Who Can't Read Books." *Atlantic*, October 1, 2024. https://www.theatlantic.com/magazine/archive/2024/11/the-elite-college-students-who-cant-read-books/679945/.

Hugo, Victor. *Les Misérables*. Signet Classics, 2013.

Hunt, Maurice. *The Divine Face in Four Writers: Shakespeare, Dostoyevsky, Hesse, and C. S. Lewis*. Bloomsbury, 2016.

Hunter, James Davison. *To Change the World: The Irony, Tragedy, and Possibility of Christianity in the Late Modern World*. Oxford University Press, 2010.

Irenaeus. *Against the Heresies: Books 4 and 5*. Translated and annotated by Scott D. Moringiello and John J. Dillion. Ancient Christian Writers 72. Paulist, 2024.

Jackson, Pamela. "Eucharist." In *Augustine Through the Ages*, edited by Allan D. Fitzgerald. Eerdmans, 1999.

Janis, Irving L. *Victims of Groupthink: A Psychological Study of Foreign-Policy Decisions and Fiascos*. Houghton Mifflin, 1972.

Johnson, Kristen Deede. "The Theologian." In *Uncommon Ground: Living Faithfully in a World of Difference*, edited by Timothy Keller and John Inazu. Nelson Books, 2020.

Jones, Christopher D. "The Problem of Acedia in Eastern Orthodox Morality Studies." *Studies in Christian Ethics* 33, no. 3 (2020): 336–51.

Kant, Immanuel. *Groundwork for the Metaphysics of Morals*. Translated by Arnulf Zweig. In *Justice: A Reader*, edited by Michael J. Sandel. Oxford University Press, 2007.

Kardaras, Nicholas. *Glow Kids: How Screen Addiction Is Hijacking Our Kids—and How to Break the Trance*. St. Martin's Griffin, 2016.

Keenan, James F. *Moral Wisdom: Lessons and Texts from the Catholic Tradition*. 2nd ed. Sheed & Ward, 2004.

Keller, Timothy. *Counterfeit Gods: The Empty Promises of Money, Sex, and Power, and the Only Hope That Matters*. Penguin Books, 2009.

Keller, Timothy. *Forgive: Why Should I and How Can I?* Penguin Books, 2022.

Keller, Timothy. *On Death*. Penguin Books, 2020.

Kelley, Joseph T., ed. *Saint Augustine of Hippo: Selections from Confessions and Other Essential Writings*. Skylight Paths, 2010.

Kelley, Joseph T., et al. "Reading Augustine in a Time of Crisis." Webinar, New City Press, The Augustinian Institute, November 17, 2020. https://www.youtube.com/watch?v=IBtHKUCO_1M.

Kelley, Lora. "The Endless Cycle of Social Media." *Atlantic*, July 7, 2023. https://www.theatlantic.com/newsletters/archive/2023/07/threads-meta-twitter-competitor-mark-zuckerberg/674655/.

Kelley, Lora. "Social Media's 'Frictionless Experience' for Terrorists." *Atlantic*, October 19, 2023. https://www.theatlantic.com/newsletters/archive/2023/10/social-media-moderation-extremism-israel-hamas/675706/.

Kelly, Conor. *The Fullness of Free Time: A Theological Account of Leisure and Recreation in the Moral Life*. Georgetown University Press, 2020.

Kierkegaard, Søren. *Either/Or, Part 1*. Edited by Howard V. Hong and Edna H. Hong. Princeton University Press, 1987.

Kierkegaard, Søren. *Fear and Trembling*. Edited and translated by Howard V. Hong and Edna H. Hong. Princeton University Press, 1983.

Kierkegaard, Søren. *The Sickness unto Death*. Edited and translated by Howard V. Hong and Edna H. Hong. Princeton University Press, 1983.

Kierkegaard, Søren. *Works of Love*. Translated by Howard V. Hong and Edna H. Hong. Princeton University Press, 1995.

Kim, Matthew D. "How to Disagree in Love." *Christianity Today*, October 2023. https://www.christianitytoday.com/2023/09/handle-toxic-friendships-empathy-unity-conflict/.

Kohák, Erazim. *The Embers and the Stars: A Philosophical Inquiry into the Moral Sense of Nature*. University of Chicago Press, 1984.

Kolbet, Paul R. *Augustine and the Cure of Souls: Revising a Classical Ideal*. University of Notre Dame Press, 2010.

Kotsko, Adam. "Moralism Is Ruining Cultural Criticism." *Atlantic*, July 26, 2023. https://www.theatlantic.com/ideas/archive/2023/07/oppenheimer-movie-moralizing-reviews-social-media/674823/.

Kurzweil, Amy. *Artificial: A Love Story*. Catapult, 2023.

Kurzweil, Amy. *Flying Couch: A Graphic Memoir*. Catapult, 2016.

Kurzweil, Ray. *The Singularity Is Near: When Humans Transcend Biology*. Penguin Books, 2005.

LaFrance, Adrienne. "The Coming Humanist Renaissance: We Need a Cultural and Philosophical Movement to Meet the Rise of Artificial Superintelligence." *Atlantic*, June 5, 2023. https://www.theatlantic.com/

magazine/archive/2023/07/generative-ai-human-culture-philosophy/
674165/.

Lamb, Michael. *A Commonwealth of Hope*. Princeton University Press, 2022.

Lambert, Craig. Review of *Black Walden: Slavery and Its Aftermath in Concord, Massachusetts*, by Elise Lemire. *Humanities* 31, no. 5 (2010). https://www
.neh.gov/humanities/2010/septemberoctober/feature/black-walden.

Lancel, Serge. *St. Augustine*. SCM, 2002.

Lanier, Jaron. *Ten Arguments for Deleting Your Social Media Accounts Right Now*. Picador, 2018.

Larson, Carlton F. W. "'Shouting "Fire" in a Crowded Theater': The Life and Times of Constitutional Law's Most Enduring Analogy." *William & Mary Bill of Rights Journal* 24, no. 1 (2015): 1–33.

Lavere, George. "Virtue." In *Augustine Through the Ages*, edited by Allan D. Fitzgerald. Eerdmans, 1999.

Brother Lawrence of the Resurrection. *The Practice of the Presence of God*. Edited by Conrad De Meester. Translated by Salvatore Sciurba. ICS, 1994.

Lee, Graham. *Human Being: Reclaim 12 Vital Skills We're Losing to Technology*. Michael O'Mara, 2023.

Lee, Peter, Carey Goldberg, and Isaac Kohane. *The AI Revolution in Medicine: GPT-4 and Beyond*. Pearson Education, 2023.

Lehman, Frederick M. "The Love of God." 1917. https://hymnary.org/text/the
_love_of_god_is_greater_far.

Lemire, Elise. *Black Walden*. University of Pennsylvania Press, 2019.

Leo XIII. *Rerum Novarum* (Encyclical Letter on Capital and Labor). May 15, 1891. https://www.vatican.va/content/leo-xiii/en/encyclicals/documents/
hf_l-xiii_enc_15051891_rerum-novarum.html.

Lepore, Jill. "Facebook's Broken Vows: How the Company's Pledge to Bring the World Together Wound Up Pulling Us Apart." *New Yorker*, July 26, 2021. https://www.newyorker.com/magazine/2021/08/02/facebooks-broken
-vows.

Levinas, Emmanuel. *Alterity and Transcendence*. Translated by Michael B. Smith. Columbia University Press, 1999.

Lewis, C. S. *The Abolition of Man*. In *The Complete C. S. Lewis Signature Classics*. HarperOne, 2002.

Lewis, C. S. *The Great Divorce*. Touchstone, 1996.

Lewis, C. S. *The Last Battle*. HarperTrophy, 1956.

Lewis, C. S. *Mere Christianity*. In *The Complete C. S. Lewis Signature Classics*. HarperOne, 2002.

Lewis, C. S. *Surprised by Joy: The Shape of My Early Life*. 1955; HarperOne, 2017.

Lewis, C. S. *Till We Have Faces: A Myth Retold*. 1956; HarperOne, 2017.

Lewis, C. S. *The Weight of Glory and Other Addresses*. 1949; HarperOne, 2001.

Lin, Davi C. Ribeiro. "The Absence of Dialogue in a Technologically Faceless Age: An Augustinian Response of Embrace and Confession." In *Beyond*

Integral Mission: Fresh Voices from Latin America, edited by Daniel Clark. Regnum, 2022.

Lucky, Kate. "Imago AI: Artificial Intelligence May Not Have a Soul. But It Will Shape Ours." *Christianity Today*, October 2023. https://www .christianitytoday.com/2023/09/artificial-intelligence-robots-soul -formation/.

Lukianoff, Greg, and Jonathan Haidt. *The Coddling of the American Mind: How Good Intentions and Bad Ideas Are Setting Up a Generation for Failure*. Penguin Books, 2018.

Marion, Jean-Luc. *In the Self's Place: The Approach of St. Augustine*. Translated by Jeffrey L. Kosky. Stanford University Press, 2012.

Marion, Jean-Luc. "The Utility of Communion." In *A Brief Apology for a Catholic Moment*, translated by Stephen E. Lewis. University of Chicago Press, 2021.

Markus, R. A. "Donatus, Donatism." In *Augustine Through the Ages*, edited by Allan D. Fitzgerald. Eerdmans, 1999.

Markus, R. A. *Saeculum: History and Society in the Theology of St. Augustine*. Cambridge University Press, 1970.

Marsden, George M. *Jonathan Edwards: A Life*. Yale University Press, 2003.

Martens, Matthew T. *Reforming Criminal Justice: A Christian Proposal*. Crossway, 2023.

Mathewes, Charles. "An Augustinian Look at Empire." *Theology Today* 63, no. 3 (2006): 292–306.

Mathewes, Charles. *Books That Matter: The City of God*. The Great Courses, The Teaching Company, 2016.

Mathewes, Charles. *Republic of Grace*. Eerdmans, 2010.

Mattison, William, III. *Introducing Moral Theology: True Happiness and the Virtues*. Brazos, 2008.

May, William. *The Patient's Ordeal*. Indiana University Press, 1991.

McCaulley, Esau. "A Nation on Fire Needs the Flames of the Spirit." *Christianity Today*, June 2, 2020. https://www.christianitytoday.com/2020/06/george -floyd-protests-racism-nation-on-fire-needs-spirit/.

McCaulley, Esau. *Reading While Black: African American Biblical Interpretation as an Exercise in Hope*. IVP Academic, 2020.

McClendon, James William, Jr. *Ethics*. Vol. 1 of *Systematic Theology*. Abingdon, 2001.

McClymond, Michael J., and Gerald R. McDermott. *The Theology of Jonathan Edwards*. Oxford University Press, 2012.

McDonough, Sean. *Creation and New Creation: Understanding God's Creation Project*. Hendrickson, 2017.

McDowell, Catherine L. *The Image of God in the Garden of Eden: The Creation of Humankind in Genesis 2:5–3:24 in Light of the* mīs pî pīt pî *and* wpt-r *Rituals of Mesopotamia and Ancient Egypt*. Eisenbrauns, 2015.

McGilchrist, Iain. *The Matter with Things: Our Brains, Our Delusions, and the Unmaking of the World*. Perspectiva, 2021.

McGrath, Alister. *Christian Theology: An Introduction*. 5th ed. Wiley-Blackwell, 2011.

McKenny, Gerald. "Transcendence, Technological Enhancement, and Christian Theology." In *Transhumanism and Transcendence: Christian Hope in an Age of Technological Enhancement*, edited by Ronald Cole-Turner. Georgetown University Press, 2011.

Meador, Jake. "The Misunderstood Reason Millions of Americans Stopped Going to Church." *Atlantic*, July 29, 2023. https://www.theatlantic.com/ideas/archive/2023/07/christian-church-communitiy-participation-drop/674843/.

Mescher, Marcus. "The Moral Impact of Digital Devices." *Journal of Moral Theology* 9, no. 2 (2020): 65–93.

Mesquita, Batja. *Between Us: How Culture Creates Emotions*. Horton, 2022.

Moltmann, Jürgen. *The Crucified God*. Fortress, 1993.

Moltmann, Jürgen. *Theology of Play*. Harper & Row, 1972.

Moore, Russell. "The American Evangelical Church Is in Crisis. There's Only One Way Out." *Atlantic*, July 25, 2023. https://www.theatlantic.com/ideas/archive/2023/07/christian-evangelical-church-division-politics/674810/.

Morozov, Evgeny. *To Save Everything Click Here: The Folly of Technological Solutionism*. PublicAffairs, 2014.

Moyse, Ashley. *The Art of Living for a Technological Age: Toward a Humanizing Performance*. Fortress, 2021.

Murgia, Madhumita. *Code Dependent: Living in the Shadow of AI*. Henry Holt, 2024.

Newport, Cal. "The Year in Quiet Quitting." *New Yorker*, December 29, 2022. https://www.newyorker.com/culture/2022-in-review/the-year-in-quiet-quitting.

Noble, Alan. *You Are Not Your Own*. IVP, 2021.

The Notorious B.I.G. "10 Crack Commandments." On *Life After Death*, released March 25, 1997.

"The Nuremberg Code." In *Trials of War Criminals Before the Nuremberg Military Tribunals Under Control Council Law No. 10*, vol. 2. US Government Printing Office, 1949. https://history.nih.gov.

Nussbaum, Martha C. *Frontiers of Justice: Disability, Nationality, and Species Membership*. Harvard University Press, 2006.

Nussbaum, Martha C. *Women and Human Development: The Capabilities Approach*. Cambridge University Press, 2000.

O'Connor, William Riordian. "The *Uti/Frui* Distinction in Augustine's Ethics." *Augustinian Studies* 14 (1983): 45–62.

Odgers, Candice. "The Panic over Smartphones Doesn't Help Teens." *Atlantic*, May 21, 2024, https://www.theatlantic.com/technology/archive/2024/05/candice-odgers-teens-smartphones/678433/.

O'Donovan, Oliver. *Self, World, and Time*. Vol. 1 of *Ethics as Theology*. Eerdmans, 2013.

O'Neil, Cathy. *Weapons of Math Destruction*. Crown, 2016.

Orlowski, Jeff, dir. *The Social Dilemma*. Exposure Labs, 2020. Netflix.

Packer, J. I. *Knowing God*. IVP, 1973.

Pappas, Stephanie. "Conspiracy Theories Can Be Undermined with These Strategies, New Analysis Shows." *Scientific American*, April 5, 2023. https://www.scientificamerican.com/article/how-can-you-fight-conspiracy-theories/.

Parker, Kim, and Juliana Menasce Horowitz. "Majority of Workers Who Quit a Job in 2021 Cite Low Pay, No Opportunities for Advancement, Feeling Disrespected." Pew Research Center, March 9, 2022. https://www.pewresearch.org/short-reads/2022/03/09/majority-of-workers-who-quit-a-job-in-2021-cite-low-pay-no-opportunities-for-advancement-feeling-disrespected/.

Peterson, Sara. *Momfluenced: Inside the Maddening, Picture Perfect World of Mommy Influencer Culture*. Beacon, 2023.

Picard, Rosalind W. *Affective Computing*. MIT Press, 2000.

Picard, Rosalind W. "An AI Smartwatch That Detects Seizures." TED Talk, November 2018. https://www.ted.com/talks/rosalind_picard_an_ai_smartwatch_that_detects_seizures.

Picard, Rosalind W. "Future Affective Technology for Autism and Emotion Communication." *Philosophical Transactions for the Royal Society B* 364 (2009): 3574–84.

Pieper, Josef. *Leisure: The Basis of Culture, with the Philosophical Act*. Ignatius/Pantheon Press, 1952.

Plato. *Republic*. Translated by G. M. A. Grube. Hackett, 1992.

Postman, Neil. *Amusing Ourselves to Death*. Penguin Books, 1985.

Postman, Neil. *Technopoly: The Surrender of Culture to Technology*. Vintage Books, 1993.

Powell, Tia. *Dementia Reimagined: Building a Life of Joy and Dignity from Beginning to End*. Avery, 2019.

Putnam, Robert D. "Bowling Alone: America's Declining Social Capital." *Journal of Democracy* 6, no. 1 (1995): 65–78.

Putnam, Robert D. *Bowling Alone: The Collapse and Revival of American Community*. Simon & Schuster, 2000.

Quinn, John. "Time." In *Augustine Through the Ages*, edited by Allan D. Fitzgerald. Eerdmans, 1999.

Raicu, Irina. "To Read—or Not to Read—the Comments: An Ethics Case Study." Markkula Center for Applied Ethics, Santa Clara University, March 1, 2014. https://www.scu.edu/ethics/focus-areas/internet-ethics/resources/to-read--or-not-to-read--the-comments/.

Ramsey, Paul. "The Enforcement of Morals: Nontherapeutic Research on Children." *Hastings Center Report* 6, no. 4 (1976): 21–30.

Ridenour, Autumn Alcott. "'Elderhood' and Sabbath Rest as Vocation: Identity, Purpose, & Belonging." *Journal of Population Ageing* 14, no. 3 (2021): 411–23.

Ridenour, Autumn Alcott. "Re-enchanting Nature and Medicine." *Christian Bioethics* 25, no. 3 (2019): 283–98.

Ridenour, Autumn Alcott. "Sabbath as Reprioritization." In *Sabbath as Resilience*, edited by Kenneth Barnes and Sara Minard. Wipf and Stock, 2025.

Ridenour, Autumn Alcott. *Sabbath Rest as Vocation: Aging Toward Death.* Bloomsbury T&T Clark, 2018.

Rosner, Brian. *Known by God: A Biblical Theology of Personal Identity.* Zondervan, 2017.

Rowe, Nicholas, and Sheila Wise Rowe. *Healing Leadership Trauma.* IVP, 2024.

Sande, Ken. *Peacemaker: A Biblical Guide to Resolving Personal Conflict.* Baker, 1997.

Sandel, Michael J. "The Case Against Perfection." *Atlantic*, April 2004. https://www.theatlantic.com/magazine/archive/2004/04/the-case-against-perfection/302927/.

Sandel, Michael J. *What Money Can't Buy: The Moral Limits of Markets.* Farrar, Straus and Giroux, 2012.

Sarah, Cardinal Robert. *The Power of Silence: Against the Dictatorship of Noise.* Ignatius, 2016.

Sayers, Dorothy. *Letters to a Diminished Church.* W Publishing Group, 2004.

Scazzero, Peter. *Emotionally Healthy Spirituality: It's Impossible to Be Spiritually Mature, While Remaining Emotionally Immature.* Zondervan, 2014.

Scherer, Michael, and Ashley Parker. "The Tech Oligarchy Arrives." *Atlantic*, January 20, 2025, https://www.theatlantic.com/politics/archive/2025/01/tech-zuckerberg-trump-inauguration-oligarchy/681381/.

Schulman, Ari. "Why This AI Moment May Be the Real Deal." *New Atlantis*, Summer 2023. https://www.thenewatlantis.com/publications/why-this-ai-moment-may-be-the-real-deal.

Smith, James K. A. *You Are What You Love.* Brazos, 2016.

Snead, O. Carter. *What It Means to Be Human: The Case for the Body in Public Bioethics.* Harvard University Press, 2020.

Song, Felicia Wu. *Restless Devices: Recovering Personhood, Presence, and Place in the Digital Age.* IVP Academic, 2021.

Stevenson, Bryan. *Just Mercy: A Story of Justice and Redemption.* OneWorld, 2015.

Storey, Benjamin, and Jenna Silber Storey. *Why We Are Restless: On the Modern Quest for Contentment*. Princeton University Press, 2021.

Stuntz, William J. *The Collapse of American Criminal Justice*. Belknap Press, 2013.

Suleyman, Mustafa, and Michael Bhaskar. *The Coming Wave: Technology, Power, and the 21st Century's Greatest Dilemma*. Crown, 2024.

Sulmasy, Daniel. *The Healer's Calling: A Spirituality for Physicians and Other Healthcare Professionals*. Paulist, 1997.

Swinton, John. *Dementia: Living in the Memories of God*. Eerdmans, 2012.

Tanner, Kathryn. *Christ the Key*. Cambridge University Press, 2010.

Taylor, Charles. *Cosmic Connections: Poetry in the Age of Disenchantment*. Belknap Press, 2024.

Taylor, Charles. "The Politics of Recognition." In *Multiculturalism: Examining the Politics of Recognition*, edited by Amy Gutmann. Princeton University Press, 1994.

Taylor, Charles. *A Secular Age*. Belknap Press, 2007.

Teresa of Ávila. *The Interior Castle, or The Mansions*. TAN Books/Saint Benedict Press, 1997.

Thompson, Derek. "The Anti-Social Century." *Atlantic*, January 8, 2025. https://www.theatlantic.com/magazine/archive/2025/02/american-loneliness-personality-politics/681091/.

Thompson, Derek. "Workism Is Making Americans Miserable." *Atlantic*, February 24, 2019. https://www.theatlantic.com/ideas/archive/2019/02/religion-workism-making-americans-miserable/583441/.

Tietz, Christiane. *Karl Barth: A Life in Conflict*. Oxford University Press, 2023.

Tilley, Maureen A. "The Anti-Donatist Works." In *Augustine Through the Ages*, edited by Allan D. Fitzgerald. Eerdmans, 1999.

Tolkien, J. R. R. *The Hobbit*. Houghton Mifflin Harcourt, 1937; 2012.

Tolkien, J. R. R. *The Lord of the Rings*. William Morrow, 1954–55; 2012.

Tronick, Edward, Heidelise Als, Lauren Adamson, Susan Wise, and T. Berry Brazelton. "The Infant's Response to Entrapment Between Contradictory Messages in Face-to-Face Interaction." *Journal of the American Academy of Child Psychiatry* 17, no. 1 (1978): 1–13.

Turkle, Sherry. *Alone Together*. Basic Books, 2011.

Turkle, Sherry. *Reclaiming Conversation: The Power of Talk in a Digital Age*. Penguin Books, 2015.

Twenge, Jean M. "Have Smartphones Destroyed a Generation?" *Atlantic*, September 2017. https://www.theatlantic.com/magazine/archive/2017/09/has-the-smartphone-destroyed-a-generation/534198/.

Twenge, Jean M. *iGen: Why Today's Super-Connected Kids Are Growing Up Less Rebellious, More Tolerant, Less Happy—and Completely Unprepared for Adulthood*. Atria Books, 2017.

US Department of Health, Education, and Welfare. *The Belmont Report: Ethical Principles and Guidelines for the Protection of Human Subjects of Research.* April 18, 1979. https://www.hhs.gov/ohrp/regulations-and-policy/belmont -report/read-the-belmont-report/index.html.

US Surgeon General. *Our Epidemic of Loneliness and Isolation.* Department of Health and Human Services, 2023. https://www.hhs.gov/sites/default/files/ surgeon-general-social-connection-advisory.pdf.

Vallor, Shannon. *Technology and the Virtues: A Philosophical Guide to a Future Worth Wanting.* Oxford University Press, 2016.

Van Bavel, Tarcisius J. "Church." In *Augustine Through the Ages,* edited by Allan D. Fitzgerald. Eerdmans, 1999.

Van Bavel, Tarcisius J. "Love." In *Augustine Through the Ages,* edited by Allan D. Fitzgerald. Eerdmans, 1999.

Van Fleteren, Frederick. "Nature." In *Augustine Through the Ages,* edited by Allan D. Fitzgerald. Eerdmans, 1999.

Vander Lugt, Wesley. *Beauty Is Oxygen: Finding a Faith That Breathes.* Eerdmans, 2024.

Vanhoozer, Kevin J. *The Drama of Doctrine: A Canonical Linguistic Approach to Christian Theology.* Westminster John Knox, 2005.

Vanhoozer, Kevin J. *Faith Speaking Understanding: Performing the Drama of Doctrine.* Westminster John Knox, 2014.

Verhey, Allen. *Nature and Altering It.* Eerdmans, 2010.

Volf, Miroslav. *Exclusion and Embrace: A Theological Exploration of Identity, Otherness, and Reconciliation.* Abingdon, 1996.

Wallace, Lane. "Loneliness in Numbers." *Atlantic,* January 5, 2010. https://www .theatlantic.com/national/archive/2010/01/loneliness-in-numbers/32985/.

Warren, Tish Harrison. *Liturgy of the Ordinary.* IVP, 2016.

Warzel, Charlie. "OpenAI Just Gave Away the Entire Game." *Atlantic,* May 21, 2024. https://www.theatlantic.com/technology/archive/2024/05/openai -scarlett-johansson-sky/678446/.

Watkin, Christopher. *Biblical Critical Theory: How the Bible's Unfolding Story Makes Sense of Modern Life and Culture.* Zondervan Academic, 2022.

Weber, Max. *The Protestant Ethic and the "Spirit" of Capitalism and Other Writings.* Edited and translated by Peter Baehr and Gordon C. Wells. Penguin Books, 2002.

Weidenfeld, Lisa. "The Future of AI." *Boston College Magazine,* Summer 2024. https://www.bc.edu/bc-web/sites/bc-magazine/summer-2024-issue/ features/the-future-of-ai.html.

Weissman Preservation Center. "Harvard's History of Photography Timeline." Harvard University Library. https://projects.iq.harvard.edu/ photographpreservationprogram/harvards-history-photography -timeline-text-only.

Wenger, Kenneth. *Is the Algorithm Plotting Against Us? A Layperson's Guide to the Concepts, Math, and Pitfalls of AI*. Working Fires Foundation, 2023.

Wetzel, James. *Augustine: A Guide for the Perplexed*. Continuum, 2010.

Wetzel, James. *Augustine and the Limits of Virtue*. Cambridge University Press, 1992.

White, E. B. *Charlotte's Web*. HarperCollins, 1952.

Williams, Reggie L. *Bonhoeffer's Black Jesus: Harlem Renaissance Theology and an Ethics of Resistance*. Baylor University Press, 2014; 2021.

Williams, Rowan. "Augustine and the Psalms." *Interpretation* 58, no. 1 (2004): 17–27.

Williams, Rowan. "Creation." In *Augustine Through the Ages*, edited by Allan D. Fitzgerald. Eerdmans, 1999.

Williams, Rowan. "'Good for Nothing'? Augustine on Creation." *Augustinian Studies* 25 (1994): 9–24.

Wirzba, Norman. *Living the Sabbath: Discovering the Rhythms of Rest and Delight*. Brazos, 2006.

Witherington, Ben, III. *The Rest of Life: Rest, Play, Eating, Studying, Sex from a Kingdom Perspective*. Eerdmans, 2012.

Wolfram, Stephen. *What Is ChatGPT Doing . . . and Why Does It Work?* Wolfram Media, 2023.

Wong, Matteo. "AI Doomerism Is a Decoy: Big Tech's Warnings About an AI Apocalypse Are Distracting Us from Years of Actual Harms Their Products Have Caused." *Atlantic*, June 2, 2023. https://www.theatlantic.com/technology/archive/2023/06/ai-regulation-sam-altman-bill-gates/674278/.

Worthington, E. L., Jr., T. A. Kurusu, W. Collins, J. W. Berry, J. S. Ripley, and S. N. Baier. "Forgiving Usually Takes Time: A Lesson Learned by Studying Interventions to Promote Forgiveness." *Journal of Psychology and Theology* 28, no. 1 (2000): 3–20.

Wu, Jackson, and Ryan Jensen. *Seeking God's Face: Practical Reflections on Honor and Shame in Scripture*. Lucid Books, 2022.

Wu, Tim. *The Attention Merchants: The Epic Scramble to Get Inside Our Heads*. Vintage Books, 2016.

Zhao, Nan, Xian Zhang, J. Adam Noah, Mark Tiede, and Joy Hirsch. "Separable Processes for Live 'In-Person' and Live 'Zoom-Like' Faces." *Imaging Neuroscience* 1 (2023): 1–17. https://doi.org/10.1162/imag_a_00027.

Zuboff, Shoshana. *The Age of Surveillance Capitalism: The Fight for a Human Future at the New Frontier of Power*. Public Affairs, 2019.

Index of Names

Index of Subjects